Verse by Verse Commentary on

NUMBERS

Enduring Word Commentary Series

By David Guzik

*The grass withers, the flower fades,
but the word of our God stands forever.*
Isaiah 40:8

Commentary on Numbers

Copyright ©2023 by David Guzik

Printed in the United States of America or in the United Kingdom

Print Edition ISBN: 978-1-939466-76-1

Enduring Word

5662 Calle Real #184

Goleta, CA 93117

Electronic Mail: ewm@enduringword.com

Internet Home Page: www.enduringword.com

Scripture references, unless noted, are from the New King James Version of the Bible, copyright ©1979, 1980, 1982, Thomas Nelson, Inc., Publisher.

Contents

Numbers 1 – The Census of Israel

"The Book of Numbers might be called, without any impropriety, 'Moses's Pilgrim's Progress.' It contains a full account of the progress of the pilgrims through the wilderness until they came to the promised land. And, like Bunyan's 'Pilgrim's Progress,' it is not alone a history of any one person or nation, but it is the picture of the life of all God's people." (Charles Spurgeon)

A. The book of Numbers: In the Wilderness.

1. (1) God spoke to Moses in the Wilderness of Sinai.

Now the LORD spoke to Moses in the Wilderness of Sinai, in the tabernacle of meeting, on the first *day* of the second month, in the second year after they had come out of the land of Egypt, saying:

a. **In the second year after they had come out of the land of Egypt**: As recorded in the book of Exodus, God miraculously rescued Israel from their long slavery in Egypt. They came through the Red Sea and saw God provide through the desert wilderness. Israel then came to Mount Sinai where God appeared to them in a spectacular way. At Mount Sinai, Moses went up to meet with God and receive the law. At Mount Sinai, the people of Israel also honored an idolatrous image of a golden calf and were afterward corrected by the LORD.

   i. Camped at Mount Sinai, Israel built a **tabernacle of meeting** as the center of worship and sacrifice. They established a priesthood, receiving God's plan for the priests and the nation at large in Leviticus. At the end of Leviticus, they had been out of Egypt for about a year.

   ii. The main part of the book of Exodus covers about one year, and Leviticus only a month – but the story of the book of Numbers covers more than 38 years.

   iii. "He placed them in circumstances which developed the facts of their inner life, until they knew them for themselves. That is the meaning of the forty years in the wilderness. They were not years in which God had withdrawn Himself from the people and refused to have anything to do with them. Every year was necessary for the teaching of a lesson, and the revealing of a truth." (Morgan)

iv. **On the first day of the second month**: "As the tabernacle was erected upon the first day of the first month, in the second year after their coming out of Egypt, Exodus 40:17; and this muster of the people was made on the first day of the second month, in the same year; it is evident that the transactions related in the preceding book must all have taken place in the space of *one month*, and during the time the Israelites were encamped at Mount Sinai, before they had begun their journey to the promised land." (Clarke)

b. **Now the LORD spoke to Moses**: The book of Numbers approaches it all in God's way. In the wilderness, one may be tempted to launch a hundred different schemes and plans to move forward. But only God's way really works and the book of Numbers tells us about God's way. The idea that **the LORD spoke to Moses** is repeated more than 150 times, and in more than 20 different ways, in Numbers.

i. The wilderness was never meant to be Israel's *destination*. God's intention was to bring them into the Promised Land of Canaan. The wilderness was intended as a temporary place – a place to *move through*, not to *live in*.

ii. "The Hebrew word for *wilderness* (*midbar*) means a place for driving flocks. It is not a completely arid desert, but contains little vegetation and a few trees. The rainfall in such areas is too light, a few inches per year, to support cultivation." (Wenham)

c. **In the Wilderness of Sinai**: The Hebrew title of this book gives us an idea of the theme of Numbers. In Hebrew, this book is titled *In the Wilderness* instead of *Numbers*. The book of Numbers is all about God's people **in the Wilderness** – how they got there, how God dealt with them in the wilderness, and how He brought them out of the wilderness on their way to the Promised Land.

i. "The theme of the book of Numbers is the journey to the Promised Land of Canaan. Its opening ten chapters, covering a mere fifty days, describe how Moses organized Israel for the march from Sinai to the Promised Land." (Wenham)

ii. "The phrase 'Desert of Sinai' locates the census taking in the rugged regions of the Sinai Peninsula. The precise location of the encampment of Israelites near Mount Sinai (Mount Horeb), the mountain of God,

has been debated since at least as early as the fourth century A.D."
(Cole)

d. **After they had come out of the land of Egypt**: The book of Numbers
gives us a big vision: Where is God taking us? What will it take to get there?
What inner qualities must God develop in us and demand in us along the
way? Israel had to be transformed from a people dominated by hundreds of
years of slavery into a people suited for the Promised Land.

i. Promised land people are different from slave people. Israel emerged
from Egypt as a slave people, basically *unsuited* for the Promised Land.
Numbers tells part of the story of how God transformed them into
Promised Land people.

ii. "So the Israelites had been slaves in the land of Goshen; their tasks
were appointed, and their taskmasters compelled their obedience. Their
difficulties had been great, their bondage cruel, but they were free from
the necessity of thought and arrangement. Having escaped from their
taskmaster, they imagined that freedom meant escape from rule. They
had been taught in their year of encampment under the shadow of the
mountain that they had to submit to law, and it was irksome to them,
and they became discontented. This discontent resulted from lack of
perfect confidence in God." (Morgan)

2. (2-3) The command to take a census.

**"Take a census of all the congregation of the children of Israel, by their
families, by their fathers' houses, according to the number of names,
every male individually, from twenty years old and above—all who *are
able to* go to war in Israel. You and Aaron shall number them by their
armies.**

a. **Take a census of all the congregation of the children of Israel**: As
Moses met with the LORD in the tabernacle (verse 1), God commanded
him to **take a census** – but counting only **all who are able to go to war
in Israel**.

i. It was Jethro, the father-in-law of Moses, who suggested that Israel
be organized by their thousands, their hundreds, their fifties, and
their tens (Exodus 18:21). With this organization already in place, the
census would not be difficult.

ii. A month before this, the Israelites were numbered for the sake of
taxation (the money for the tabernacle, Exodus 38:26). Now they were
numbered again for the purpose of organizing and counting an army.

b. **By their families, by their fathers' houses**: God wanted the count made **by their families** because the strength of Israel was determined by looking at the strength of individual families.

c. **From twenty years old and above**: The men for war were counted as those from twenty years old and older, showing that it takes some amount of time and maturity to be able to fight well. It is also interesting that there is no upper age limit declared, though one may be implied.

> i. "One could wish for a Divine conscription, a command laid on every one in youth to be ready at a certain day and hour to take the sword of the Spirit." (Watson)

d. **You and Aaron shall number them by their armies**: This was a military census to see who could fight for Israel in taking the Promised Land. This was the first step towards victory – an *inventory* to understand the resources they had to conquer the Canaan.

> i. Though the Promised Land had been mentioned during the journey out of Egypt to this point, the focus was on getting to Mount Sinai and receiving the law. That was just the beginning; now, the focus turned towards taking the Promised Land and recognizing it would be a *battle*, and they needed to know how many soldiers were available for this battle.

> ii. The taking of this census would have a great effect on the nation. As the count was made, every family knew preparations were being made for war.

e. **By their armies**: The order to count the potential soldiers was not meant to imply that Israel would take the land because of superior forces, or merely because of the bravery of these men. They would receive the Promised Land by the hand of God. Nevertheless, *they still had to fight* and know what they had available to them going into battle.

> i. "The story of the conquest of Canaan is not that of the spoliation of feeble peoples by a stronger, in order to possess a territory. It is that of the purification of a land, in order that there might be planted in it a people from whose history blessing would come to all nations." (Morgan)

> ii. **Shall number them by their armies**: "The term *saba* [**armies**] is generally used in the context of military forces and in the divine appellation *YHWH seba ot*, often translated "Yahweh of hosts" or 'Yahweh of armies.'" (Cole)

> iii. Israel had a literal, physical, fought-in-the-material-world war to fight. As believers, we do not battle against flesh and blood enemies,

but spiritual enemies (Ephesians 6:10-12). We may fail in spiritual battle because we do not take an honest inventory about where we are spiritually. We may overestimate or underestimate our spiritual strength and resources. This census of Israel's soldiers gave them a clear picture of their present strength.

B. Israel takes inventory: The census of Numbers 1.

1. (4-16) The heads of the tribes.

"And with you there shall be a man from every tribe, each one the head of his father's house. "These are the names of the men who shall stand with you: from Reuben, Elizur the son of Shedeur; from Simeon, Shelumiel the son of Zurishaddai; from Judah, Nahshon the son of Amminadab; from Issachar, Nethanel the son of Zuar; from Zebulun, Eliab the son of Helon; from the sons of Joseph: from Ephraim, Elishama the son of Ammihud; from Manasseh, Gamaliel the son of Pedahzur; from Benjamin, Abidan the son of Gideoni; from Dan, Ahiezer the son of Ammishaddai; from Asher, Pagiel the son of Ocran; from Gad, Eliasaph the son of Deuel; from Naphtali, Ahira the son of Enan." These *were* chosen from the congregation, leaders of their fathers' tribes, heads of the divisions in Israel.

a. **A man from every tribe, each one the head of his father's house**: Israel was organized according to the tribes that descended from the original twelve sons of Jacob (who was later renamed *Israel* by God). Each of these twelve tribes designated one man who was **the head of his father's house**, who was to **stand with** Moses and stand for their whole tribe.

i. In a sense, this is a representative form of government; each **head of his father's house** was essentially the "governor" or chieftain of the tribe.

b. **From Reuben...from Simeon**: Twelve tribes are mentioned, but not the tribe of Levi. Yet the number twelve is maintained because from Jacob's son Joseph, two tribes were established (**Ephraim** and **Manasseh**).

i. This was a military census, and the absence of the tribe of Levi among the potential soldiers is important, and will be explained later in the chapter.

ii. **Nahshon**: This was the head of the house of Judah and he is mentioned in the genealogy of Jesus (Matthew 1:4).

c. **These were chosen from the congregation**: It is possible – even likely – that the **head of his father's house** for each tribe was elected (**chosen**) by those in the tribe.

d. **These are the names of the men**: Some take an interest in the names of these **chosen** tribal leaders and the possible meaning of their names (as in Cole and Wenham). In general, the names have a significant and positive spiritual meaning, saying something good about the spiritual life of the Israelite community that left Egypt. These are Hebrew names, believing names, not Egyptian names. Almost all of the names make reference to God (Elohim).

- From the tribe of **Reuben**, **Elizur** – whose name can mean, *(My) God Is a Rock.*

- From the tribe of **Simeon**, **Shelumiel** – whose name can mean, *(My) Peace Is God.*

- From the tribe of **Judah**, **Nahshon** – whose name can mean, *(My) People Are Noble.*

- From the tribe of **Issachar**, **Nethanel** – whose name can mean, *Gift of God.*

- From the tribe of **Zebulun**, **Eliab** – whose name can mean, *(My) God Is Father.*

- From the tribe of **Ephraim**, **Elishama** – whose name can mean, *(My) God Hears.* This man was the grandfather of Joshua (1 Chronicles 7:26-27).

- From the tribe of **Manasseh**, **Gamaliel** – whose name can mean, *Reward of God.*

- From the tribe of **Benjamin**, **Abidan** – whose name can mean, *(My) Father Is Judge.*

- From the tribe of **Dan**, **Ahiezer** – whose name can mean, *(My) Brother Is a Helper.*

- From the tribe of **Asher**, **Pagiel** – whose name can mean, *Met by God.*

- From the tribe of **Gad**, **Eliasaph** – whose name can mean, *(My) God Has Added, Multiplied.*

- From the tribe of **Naphtali**, **Ahira** – whose name can mean, *(My) Brother Is Evil.*

i. "And they are all excellent good names and very significant; hereby is testified to posterity that they forgat not the name of their God when they were in the iron furnace." (Trapp)

2. (17-19) The assembly of the leaders.

Then Moses and Aaron took these men who had been mentioned by name, and they assembled all the congregation together on the first *day* **of the second month; and they recited their ancestry by families, by their fathers' houses, according to the number of names, from twenty years old and above, each one individually. As the** LORD **commanded Moses, so he numbered them in the Wilderness of Sinai.**

a. **They assembled all the congregation together on the first day of the second month**: This great assembly of the tribal leaders happened thirteen months after Israel came out of Egypt.

b. **They recited their ancestry by families**: The leaders of each tribe were responsible for counting the potential soldiers in their tribe. Then, they gathered to make the report to Moses.

i. **They recited their ancestry by families**: The concept of **ancestry** and of **families** was important to the ancient Israelites; they kept genealogical records with care. Spiritually speaking, we can recite our **ancestry**; born again into God's family.

c. **Each one individually**: Every individual was important to God. This wasn't just the assembling of a final number, but a specific mention of each individual.

i. God's guidance to Israel gave attention to both the individual and to the community. Both aspects were important and continue to be important today. Believers take seriously God's concern for both the individual and the community.

ii. "Under the New Covenant there is a distribution of grace to every one, an endowment of each according to his faith with priestly and even kingly powers.... [Yet] The commission each receives is not to be a free-lance in the Divine warfare, but to take his right place in the ranks; and that place he must find." (Watson)

C. The count of the tribes.

1. (20-21) The tribe of Reuben: 46,500 available soldiers.

Now the children of Reuben, Israel's oldest son, their genealogies by their families, by their fathers' house, according to the number of names, every male individually, from twenty years old and above, all who *were able to* **go to war: those who were numbered of the tribe of Reuben** *were* **forty-six thousand five hundred.**

a. **Those who were numbered of the tribe of Reuben were forty-six thousand five hundred**: To many, this seems too large a number, and some people wonder if these numbers are accurate and literal.

i. If one estimates that this count of the men for war represents 70% of the total male population, adds an equal number of females, and then adds another 25% for children, the total population of Israel would be between 2 million and 2.5 million.

ii. "This tremendous number, as well as the sizable figures tendered for each individual tribe, has posed the greatest dilemma for biblical interpreters since the Middle Ages. Many modern commentators summarily dismiss these numbers as hyperbolic or fictitious, while others provide a brief history of interpretation. Numerous suggestions have been proffered for comprehending these unbelievable sums." (Cole)

iii. Cole and Allen mention several different ways these numbers have been understood.

- The census figures are literal and accurate.
- The census figures are literal and accurate but taken from David and Solomon's time and read back into the history of Israel.
- The numbers have been interpreted as forms of gematria – mathematical calculation based on the Hebrew use of letters for numbers in calculations.
- The census figures are misunderstood because the word "thousands" (*elep*) may mean a different number or have a different meaning.
- The census figures are symbolic.
- The census figures are deliberate, purposeful exaggerations.
- The census figures have suffered from textual corruption. The original figures were much lower, but later copiers accidentally or purposefully made them larger. This last idea is not supported by any existing manuscripts.

iv. While mindful of the objections, it is best to trust the simple testimony of the Biblical record. Surely God could provide for such a multitude in the wilderness and occasional discrepancies in the record of these numbers are probably due to scribal errors.

b. **Forty-six thousand five hundred**: These numbers are probably all rounded off to the nearest one hundred (except, for some unknown reason, in the case of the Tribe of Gad).

2. (22-23) The tribe of Simeon: 59,300 available soldiers.

From the children of Simeon, their genealogies by their families, by their fathers' house, of those who were numbered, according to the number of names, every male individually, from twenty years old and above, all who *were able to* **go to war: those who were numbered of the tribe of Simeon** *were* **fifty-nine thousand three hundred.**

3. (24-25) The tribe of Gad: 45,650 available soldiers.

From the children of Gad, their genealogies by their families, by their fathers' house, according to the number of names, from twenty years old and above, all who *were able to* **go to war: those who were numbered of the tribe of Gad** *were* **forty-five thousand six hundred and fifty.**

4. (26-27) The tribe of Judah: 74,600 available soldiers.

From the children of Judah, their genealogies by their families, by their fathers' house, according to the number of names, from twenty years old and above, all who *were able to* **go to war: those who were numbered of the tribe of Judah** *were* **seventy-four thousand six hundred.**

5. (28-29) The tribe of Issachar: 54,400 available soldiers.

From the children of Issachar, their genealogies by their families, by their fathers' house, according to the number of names, from twenty years old and above, all who *were able to* **go to war: those who were numbered of the tribe of Issachar** *were* **fifty-four thousand four hundred.**

6. (30-31) The tribe of Zebulun: 57,400 available soldiers.

From the children of Zebulun, their genealogies by their families, by their fathers' house, according to the number of names, from twenty years old and above, all who *were able to* **go to war: those who were numbered of the tribe of Zebulun** *were* **fifty-seven thousand four hundred.**

7. (32-33) The tribe of Ephraim: 40,500 available soldiers.

From the sons of Joseph, the children of Ephraim, their genealogies by their families, by their fathers' house, according to the number of names, from twenty years old and above, all who *were able to* **go to war: those who were numbered of the tribe of Ephraim** *were* **forty thousand five hundred.**

8. (34-35) The tribe of Manasseh: 32,200 available soldiers.

From the children of Manasseh, their genealogies by their families, by their fathers' house, according to the number of names, from twenty years old and above, all who *were able to* **go to war: those who were**

numbered of the tribe of Manasseh *were* thirty-two thousand two hundred.

9. (36-37) The tribe of Benjamin: 35,400 available soldiers.

From the children of Benjamin, their genealogies by their families, by their fathers' house, according to the number of names, from twenty years old and above, all who *were able to* go to war: those who were numbered of the tribe of Benjamin *were* thirty-five thousand four hundred.

10. (38-39) The tribe of Dan: 62,700 available soldiers.

From the children of Dan, their genealogies by their families, by their fathers' house, according to the number of names, from twenty years old and above, all who *were able to* go to war: those who were numbered of the tribe of Dan *were* sixty-two thousand seven hundred.

11. (40-41) The tribe of Asher: 41,500 available soldiers.

From the children of Asher, their genealogies by their families, by their fathers' house, according to the number of names, from twenty years old and above, all who *were able to* go to war: those who were numbered of the tribe of Asher *were* forty-one thousand five hundred.

12. (42-43) The tribe of Naphtali: 53,400 available soldiers.

From the children of Naphtali, their genealogies by their families, by their fathers' house, according to the number of names, from twenty years old and above, all who *were able to* go to war: those who were numbered of the tribe of Naphtali *were* fifty-three thousand four hundred.

13. (44-46) Summary of the tribes: 603,550 available soldiers in Israel.

These are the ones who were numbered, whom Moses and Aaron numbered, with the leaders of Israel, twelve men, each one representing his father's house. So all who were numbered of the children of Israel, by their fathers' houses, from twenty years old and above, all who *were able to go* to war in Israel—all who were numbered were six hundred and three thousand five hundred and fifty.

a. **All who were able to go to war in Israel—all who were numbered were six hundred and three thousand five hundred and fifty**: This census was repeated 38 years later, at the end of the book of Numbers. The total number of available soldiers in the second census was almost the same – only a loss of some two thousand. But the count of the individual tribes changed significantly, and there is meaning in what happened to each tribe over the critical 38 years.

b. **So all who were numbered of the children of Israel, by their fathers' houses**: In this first census, Manasseh was the smallest tribe and Judah was the largest. There were two tribes in the 30 thousands; three in the 40 thousands; four in the 50 thousands; one in the 60 thousands; and one in the 70 thousands.

c. **All who were numbered were six hundred and three thousand five hundred and fifty**: Based on having 603,550 available soldiers, some estimate the total population of Israel at this time to be between two million and two-and-a-half million people, counting women, children, and others unable to fight.

> i. "What an astonishing increase from *seventy* souls that went down into Egypt, Genesis 46:27, about 215 years before, where latterly they had endured the greatest hardships! But God's promise cannot fail, (Genesis 15:5) and who can resist his will, and bring to naught his counsel?" (Clarke)

> ii. In his commentary, Adam Clarke has an extended section citing Scheuchzer and Reyher, showing how the astounding multiplication of Israel in Egypt was mathematically plausible over four generations.

14. (47-54) The special case of the tribe of Levi.

But the Levites were not numbered among them by their fathers' tribe; for the LORD had spoken to Moses, saying: "Only the tribe of Levi you shall not number, nor take a census of them among the children of Israel; but you shall appoint the Levites over the tabernacle of the Testimony, over all its furnishings, and over all things that belong to it; they shall carry the tabernacle and all its furnishings; they shall attend to it and camp around the tabernacle. And when the tabernacle is to go forward, the Levites shall take it down; and when the tabernacle is to be set up, the Levites shall set it up. The outsider who comes near shall be put to death. The children of Israel shall pitch their tents, everyone by his own camp, everyone by his own standard, according to their armies; but the Levites shall camp around the tabernacle of the Testimony, that there may be no wrath on the congregation of the children of Israel; and the Levites shall keep charge of the tabernacle of the Testimony." Thus the children of Israel did: according to all that the LORD commanded Moses, so they did.

a. **But the Levites were not numbered among them**: Because this was a census of potential soldiers, the tribe of Levi was not counted. They alone among the tribes of Israel did not go to war because they had a special responsibility to God for the priestly duties of Israel.

b. **Only the tribe of Levi you shall not number**: We also must see, that as in the case of Levi, there are some things that can't – or shouldn't – be counted. Israel had to appreciate that some of the most important things can't be counted.

i. Taking inventory is fine; even a necessary first step in organizing for victory and taking hold of God's promises. But it must always be done with the understanding that some of the important factors – as the Levites were in Israel – cannot be counted. No human inventory is totally complete, and God always works mightily through things that cannot be counted.

c. **The children of Israel shall pitch their tents, everyone by his own camp, everyone by his own standard**: As Israel camped around the tabernacle, they were ordered according to the plan God revealed in Numbers 2. The place of each camp was marked by a **standard**, which was probably a flag or a banner.

i. **By his own standard**: "...each person lining up according to the tribal division or flag (*degel*). Rabbi Rashi suggested a colored flag according to the color of stone in the high priest's breastplate (Exodus 28:17–21)." (Cole)

d. **The Levites shall camp around the tabernacle**: In the arrangement of the camp of the tribes of Israel, the Levites were immediately surrounding the tabernacle. Anyone from the other tribes of Israel had to go through the camp of the Levites to get to the tabernacle.

i. **Shall camp around the tabernacle**: "As the living creatures (the ministers) are between the four and twenty elders, the congregation of the faithful, and the throne. (Revelation 4:4)." (Trapp)

e. **Thus the children of Israel did; according to all that the LORD commanded Moses, so they did**: Counting, or taking inventory, is an essential step in organization and moving forward. In preparing to enter the Promised Land Israel had to be *organized*. God is an organized God and moves through organization, even when that organization is not easily seen. Therefore, it was essential that Israel take inventory and count how many men were ready to fight.

i. God counts things. He counts the stars and has a name for each one (Psalm 147:4; Isaiah 40:26). God even counts and knows the number of hairs on the human head (Matthew 10:30).

ii. "He who counts the stars and calls them all by their names, leaves nothing unarranged in his own service." (Spurgeon)

Numbers 2 – The Camp of Israel

A. The tribes of Israel arranged around the tabernacle.

1. (1-2) The command to arrange around the tabernacle.

And the LORD spoke to Moses and Aaron, saying: "Everyone of the children of Israel shall camp by his own standard, beside the emblems of his father's house; they shall camp some distance from the tabernacle of meeting."

a. **Everyone of the children of Israel shall camp by his own standard**: Israel had been on this Exodus journey for more than a year and had assembled in just about any way they had pleased. But now, ready to enter into the Promised Land, they had to take the next step in organization: Ordering themselves.

i. Balaam described the beauty and order of the camp of Israel in Numbers 24:5-6: *How lovely are your tents, O Jacob! Your dwellings, O Israel! Like valleys that stretch out, like gardens by the riverside, like aloes planted by the LORD, like cedars beside the waters.*

ii. "There is a sense in which the orderliness of these early chapters of Numbers is akin to the orderliness of Genesis 1. As God has created the heavens and the earth and all that fills them with order, beauty, purpose, and wonder, so he constitutes his people with order, beauty, purpose, and wonder." (Allen)

iii. "In the War Scroll from the Qumran caves, distinguishable standards were to be carried by each division within the ancestral tribe." (Cole)

b. **They shall camp some distance from the tabernacle of meeting**: At the center of this order was the tabernacle itself. The tribes would arrange themselves in a square to the east, south, west, and north in relation to the tabernacle. Since the tabernacle was symbolically the presence of God with them, this meant all order in Israel began by being centered around God Himself.

19

i. "The Egyptian army under Rameses II (13th century BC) adopted this formation in camp. They camped in a square with the royal tent in the middle. Likewise Israel's king dwelt in the centre of his armies in the tent of meeting." (Wenham)

ii. "The Hebrew word order of v.2 stresses the role of the individual in the context of the community; each one was to know his exact position within the camp. A more literal translation, following the studied order of the Hebrew original, follows: Each by his standard, by the banners of their father's house, the Israelites will encamp; in a circuit some way off from the Tent of Meeting they will encamp. The repetition of the verb 'will encamp' is for stately stress. Here is the meaning of the individual in Israel, and here is the significance of his family." (Allen)

iii. **Some distance**: "Partly out of reverence to God and his worship, and the portion allotted to it, and partly for caution, lest their vicinity to it might tempt them to make too near approaches to it." (Poole)

2. (3-9) The tribes camped to the east of the tabernacle.

"On the east side, toward the rising of the sun, those of the standard of the forces with Judah shall camp according to their armies; and Nahshon the son of Amminadab *shall be* the leader of the children of Judah." And his army was numbered at seventy-four thousand six hundred. "Those who camp next to him *shall be* the tribe of Issachar, and Nethanel the son of Zuar *shall be* the leader of the children of Issachar." And his army was numbered at fifty-four thousand four hundred. Then *comes* the tribe of Zebulun, and Eliab the son of Helon *shall be* the leader of the children of Zebulun." And his army was numbered at fifty-seven thousand four hundred. All who were numbered according to their armies of the forces with Judah, one hundred and eighty-six thousand four hundred; these shall break camp first."

a. **On the east side, toward the rising of the sun**: In the arrangement of the tribes, God started with the **east side**. In our western world, we normally orient things toward the north. In the ancient Near East, things were arranged toward the east, **toward the rising of the sun**.

i. "The placement on the east is very significant in Israel's thought. East is the place of the rising of the sun, the source of hope and sustenance. Westward was the sea. Israel's traditional stance was with its back to the ocean and the descent of the sun." (Allen)

ii. "The front is eastward, and Judah has the post of honour in the van." (Watson)

iii. "Judah encamped foremost. It was fit the lion should lead the way.... This order in their march showed the principality that should continue in this tribe till Shiloh came. Judah herein also was a type of Christ, who is 'the Captain of the Lord's host,' (Joshua 5:14) and 'of our salvation,' (Hebrews 2:10) and goeth before his heavenly armies." (Trapp)

b. **On the east side, toward the rising of the sun, those of the standard of the forces with Judah shall camp according to their armies**: Judah was first, and closest to the tabernacle itself. The tribes of Issachar and Zebulun followed in order after Judah. These tribes would order themselves after **the standard** (the banner or flag) of Judah, which is sometimes considered to bear the image of a *lion*.

i. Different sources cite different emblems or figures on these standards. Keil and Delitzsch admit "Neither the Mosaic law, nor the Old Testament generally, gives us any intimation as to the form or character of the standard," and claim that rabbinical tradition describes the images on each standard. "According to rabbinical tradition, the standard of Judah bore the figure of a lion, that of Reuben the likeness of a man or of a man's head, that of Ephraim the figure of an ox, and that of Dan the figure of an eagle." However, they give no reference to any ancient rabbi, citing only the 16th-century Roman Catholic commentator Jerome de Prado.

ii. Adam Clarke, quoting Johann Jacob Scheuchzer (a Swiss physician and Bible commentator, 1672-1733), says that the "Talmudists" claim the four figures of a lion, a man, a calf, and an eagle for the standards of the four groups of tribes – but Clarke provides no citation.

iii. Louis Ginzberg in his *Legends of the Jews* gives a list without citation: "Judah's standard bore in its upper part the figure of a lion, for its forefather had been characterized by Jacob as 'a lion's whelp'.... Reuben's standard had in its upper part the figure of a man, corresponding to the mandrakes that Reuben, forefather of this tribe, found, for this plant had the form of a manikin.... In the standard of Ephraim was fashioned the form of a fish, for Jacob had blessed the forefather of this tribe by telling him to multiply like a fish.... Dan's standard contained the form of a serpent, for 'Dan shall be a serpent by the way,' was Jacob's blessing for this tribe." Ginzberg also gives a second list (without citation) of a figure or image representing each tribe.

iv. The 1675 Portuguese book *Thesouro de Nobreza* (Thesaurus of Nobility) gives the coats of arms of many noble families both of its time and from history. The first chapter of the book is titled "Weapons of the Tribes of Israel" and it presents an imagined coat of arms for each of the twelve tribes of Israel. Later in the book it pictures imagined coats of arms for Joshua, David, Alexander the Great, Julius Caesar, King Arthur, and many others.

v. "Jewish tradition suggests that the tribal banners corresponded in color to the twelve stones in the breastpiece of the high priest (Exod 28:15–21). Further, this tradition holds that the standard of the triad led by Judah had the figure of a lion, that of Reuben the figure of a man, that of Ephraim the figure of an ox, and that of Dan the figure of an eagle (see the four living creatures described by Ezek 1:10; cf. Rev 4:7). These traditions are late, however, and difficult to substantiate historically, as the Torah does not describe the nature or designs of the banners of Numbers 2." (Allen)

vi. With no reference or citation, Morgan wrote: "On the east – that is, fronting the entrance – the standard-bearing tribe was Judah, with its symbol of a lion of gold on a field of scarlet…. On the west, Ephraim's standard was a black ox on a field of gold…. On the south, Reuben bore the standard on which was a man on a field of gold…. On the north, Dan was the standard-bearing tribe, his symbol being an eagle of gold on a field of blue."

vii. In summary, we don't have firm biblical evidence for what appeared on **the standard** (the banner or flag) of Judah or any of the other tribes, though many figures have been suggested.

Tribe	Keil	Clarke	Th. of Nobility	Ginzberg 1	Ginzberg 2
Reuben	Man	River/Man	Mandrakes	Man	Mandrakes
Simeon		Sword	City		City
Judah	Lion	Lion	Lion	Lion	Lion
Issachar		Donkey	Sun/Moon/Donkey		Sun & Moon
Zebulun		Ship	Ship		Ship
Dan	Eagle	Serpent/Eagle	Serpent	Serpent	Serpent
Naphtali		Stag	Stag		Stag
Gad		Lion	Soldiers		
Asher		Grain	Olive Tree		Olive Tree
Ephraim	Calf	Unicorn	Bull	Fish	Bull
Manasseh		Bull	Unicorn		Unicorn
Benjamin		Wolf	Wolf		Wolf

c. **And Nahshon the son of Amminadab shall be the leader of the children of Judah**: God recognized a specifically called leader (**Nahshon**) for the tribe of Judah, and for each of the tribes following. The order and organization God called Israel to embrace required *leadership*, with leaders both recognized by God and respected by the people.

i. "Without this pattern, apart from this order, the Hebrews would have remained a mob—large, disorganized, unruly, and bound for disaster. With this pattern, and the discipline and devotion it implied, was the opportunity for grand victory." (Allen)

d. **One hundred and eighty-six thousand four hundred**: The total number of available soldiers among the eastward tribes was 186,400.

e. **These shall break camp first**: There was an order to the encampment and for the marching of the tribes. They were to move as an orderly army, not as a random mob.

i. "This whole chapter is very full of interest as revealing the orderliness of the Divine arrangements. This host of God was not a mob, lacking order. It was a disciplined company." (Morgan)

3. (10-16) The tribes camped to the south of the tabernacle.

"On the south side *shall be* the standard of the forces with Reuben according to their armies, and the leader of the children of Reuben *shall be* Elizur the son of Shedeur." And his army was numbered at forty-six thousand five hundred. "Those who camp next to him *shall be* the tribe of Simeon, and the leader of the children of Simeon *shall be* Shelumiel the son of Zurishaddai." And his army was numbered at fifty-nine thousand three hundred. "Then *comes* the tribe of Gad, and the leader of the children of Gad *shall be* Eliasaph the son of Reuel." And his army was numbered at forty-five thousand six hundred and fifty. "All who were numbered according to their armies of the forces with Reuben, one hundred and fifty-one thousand four hundred and fifty; they shall be the second to break camp."

a. **On the south side shall be the standard of the forces with Reuben according to their armies**: On the **south side** of the tabernacle Reuben was the first tribe and set closest to the tabernacle itself. Then the tribes of Simeon and Gad followed in order. The tribes ordered themselves after **the standard** of Reuben, which is sometimes considered to bear the image of a *man*.

b. **One hundred and fifty-one thousand four hundred and fifty**: The total number of available soldiers among the southward tribes was 151,450.

4. (17) The tribe in the middle, with the tabernacle: Levi.

And the tabernacle of meeting shall move out with the camp of the Levites in the middle of the camps; as they camp, so they shall move out, everyone in his place, by their standards.

a. **With the camp of the Levites in the middle of the camps**: The priestly tribe was **in the middle of the camps**, closest to the tabernacle and surrounded by the other tribes.

> i. "There is a sense here of the progressive manifestation of the presence of God in the midst of the people. First he is on the mountain of Sinai; then he comes to the tent without the camp; then he indwells the tent in the midst of the camp. One day he would reveal himself through the Incarnation in the midst of his people (John 1:1–18); and, on a day still to come, there will be the full realization of the presence of the person of God dwelling in the midst of his people in the New Jerusalem (Rev 21:1–4)." (Allen)

b. **So they shall move out, everyone in his place, by their standards**: Apparently, this was not only the way Israel was to make their camp, but also, the way they were to order their march. The taking of Canaan would not be accomplished by a mob but by an organized and orderly group.

5. (18-24) The tribes camped to the west of the tabernacle.

"On the west side *shall be* the standard of the forces with Ephraim according to their armies, and the leader of the children of Ephraim *shall be* Elishama the son of Ammihud." And his army was numbered at forty thousand five hundred. "Next to him *comes* the tribe of Manasseh, and the leader of the children of Manasseh *shall be* Gamaliel the son of Pedahzur." And his army was numbered at thirty-two thousand two hundred. "Then *comes* the tribe of Benjamin, and the leader of the children of Benjamin *shall be* Abidan the son of Gideoni." And his army was numbered at thirty-five thousand four hundred. "All who were numbered according to their armies of the forces with Ephraim, one hundred and eight thousand one hundred; they shall be the third to break camp."

a. **On the west side shall be the standard of the forces with Ephraim according to their armies**: Ephraim was first, and closest to the tabernacle itself on the **west side**. Following the tribe of Ephraim were the tribes of Manasseh and Benjamin. The tribes ordered themselves after **the standard** of Ephraim, which is sometimes considered to bear the image of a *calf.*

b. **One hundred and eight thousand one hundred; they shall be the third to break camp**: The total number of available soldiers among the westward tribes was 108,100.

6. (25-31) The tribes camped to the north of the tabernacle.

"The standard of the forces with Dan *shall be* on the north side according to their armies, and the leader of the children of Dan *shall be* Ahiezer

the son of Ammishaddai." And his army was numbered at sixty-two thousand seven hundred. "Those who camp next to him *shall be* the tribe of Asher, and the leader of the children of Asher *shall be* Pagiel the son of Ocran." And his army was numbered at forty-one thousand five hundred. "Then *comes* the tribe of Naphtali, and the leader of the children of Naphtali *shall be* Ahira the son of Enan." And his army was numbered at fifty-three thousand four hundred. "All who were numbered of the forces with Dan, one hundred and fifty-seven thousand six hundred; they shall break camp last, with their standards."

a. **The standard of the forces with Dan shall be on the north side according to their armies**: Dan was first and closest to the tabernacle itself on the north side. Following the tribe of Dan were the tribes of Asher and Naphtali. The tribes ordered themselves after **the standard** of Dan, which is sometimes considered to bear the image of an *eagle*.

b. **All who were numbered of the forces with Dan, one hundred and fifty-seven thousand six hundred**: The total number of available soldiers among the northward tribes was 157,600.

7. (32-34) Summary: Israel's order around the tabernacle.

These *are* the ones who were numbered of the children of Israel by their fathers' houses. All who were numbered according to their armies of the forces *were* six hundred and three thousand five hundred and fifty. But the Levites were not numbered among the children of Israel, just as the Lord commanded Moses. Thus the children of Israel did according to all that the Lord commanded Moses; so they camped by their standards and so they broke camp, each one by his family, according to their fathers' houses.

a. **These are the ones who were numbered of the children of Israel by their fathers' houses**: The total of 603,550 available soldiers were ordered around the tabernacle. This was the number of men available as soldiers among the tribes of Israel, excluding the tribe of Levi.

b. **So they camped by their standards**: Each tribal group was arranged after the **standards** of the tribes, and they **broke camp** and marched in that same order.

i. "In the marching forth from Mount Sinai, the tribes dutifully and faithfully adhere to these instructions for orderly encampment, assembly and disassembly of the tabernacle, and disembarkment on the journey through the wilderness." (Cole)

ii. "This verse also speaks of significant order—a major accomplishment for a people so numerous, so recently enslaved, and more recently a mob in disarray. The text speaks well of the administrative leadership of Moses, God's reluctant prophet, and of the work done by the twelve worthies who were the leaders of each tribe." (Allen)

B. Observations.

1. God is a God of order; here, before Israel can take the Promised Land, He requires they order themselves also. Not only is it more efficient and useful, but it is also simply more like God – ordered and organized.

a. There is a limit to what we can be and what we can do for the LORD without order and organization. It isn't that order and organization are requirements for progress in the Christian life; they *are* progress in the Christian life, becoming more like the LORD.

b. *Nothing* is accomplished in God's kingdom without order and organization. While it may sometimes *seem* that things progress randomly or chaotically, this is only how it appears to us. Behind the scenes, God always moves with order and organization, though we often cannot perceive it.

2. God orders things according to *His* wisdom, not our wisdom. In the arrangement of the tribes, He did not place the largest tribes closest to the tabernacle (as if bigger is always better); Ephraim, the closest westward tribe, was the third smallest tribe. Nor did the LORD place all the large tribes on the outward perimeter for greatest protection (Benjamin, the second smallest tribe, is on the outer perimeter). God always works with order and organization, but the reasons for God's order and organization may not always make sense to us.

a. Our resistance to God's order and organization is almost always the product of simple selfishness – wanting to do things our own way, instead of the LORD's way. For hundreds of years, the Israelites lived as slaves in Egypt, and slaves don't need to worry much about order and organization. They are told what to do and often have no personal investment in the success of their work. In contrast, free men must be taught the principles of order and organization, and they must submit to these principles.

3. Everything was positioned in relation to the presence of God in the tabernacle. God could have described where the tribe of Judah was in relation to the tribe of Dan, but He did not. The reference point was always God Himself.

a. It is hard to underestimate the trouble people get into in their walk with God because they position and measure themselves in reference to other people instead of God. God is to be our focus, not other people.

4. The tribes of Israel camped around four banners, which are sometimes considered to bear the images of a lion (Judah), a man (Reuben), a calf

(Ephraim), and an eagle (Dan). If the standards did bear these images, we find a remarkable correspondence with the four creatures surrounding the throne of God in Revelation.

a. *The first living creature was like a lion, the second living creature like a calf, the third living creature had a face like a man, and the fourth living creature was like a flying eagle.* (Revelation 4:7)

b. God's order is never arbitrary or just made up on a whim. It is after His heavenly pattern. We must always accept God's order and organization, even when we don't understand it.

Numbers 3 – The Census of the Levites

A. Priests and Levites.

1. (1-4) The priests: The family of Aaron.

Now these *are* the records of Aaron and Moses when the LORD spoke with Moses on Mount Sinai. And these *are* the names of the sons of Aaron: Nadab, the firstborn, and Abihu, Eleazar, and Ithamar. These *are* the names of the sons of Aaron, the anointed priests, whom he consecrated to minister as priests. Nadab and Abihu had died before the LORD when they offered profane fire before the LORD in the Wilderness of Sinai; and they had no children. So Eleazar and Ithamar ministered as priests in the presence of Aaron their father.

a. **Now these are the records of Aaron and Moses**: Now, the census of the tribes of Israel will record the tribe and family of **Aaron and Moses**. This was done as Israel was still at **Mount Sinai**.

i. Adam Clarke noted that Moses did not appoint his sons to leadership in Israel: "Moses passes by his own family, or immediate descendants; he gave no rank or privilege to them during his life, and left nothing to them at his death. They became incorporated with the Levites, from or amongst whom they are never distinguished."

b. **Nadab, the firstborn, and Abihu**: Nadab and Abihu were the two oldest children of Aaron, and the two ranking priests behind him – yet they were struck down by the LORD for offering **profane fire** before the LORD (Leviticus 10:1-7).

i. The death of Nadab and Abihu is referred to at least five times in Leviticus and Numbers. This repetition teaches that God did not want the event forgotten, or the lessons it taught to be neglected.

ii. "Seemingly the most common reports of failure we hear of God's ministers in our own day are of their malfeasance, indolence, greed, lust, and abuse of power. Tragically the lessons of the past are forgotten with frightful ease. The spiritual descendants of Nadab and Abihu continue to occupy the ranks of the 'ministers' of God." (Allen)

c. **Eleazar, and Ithamar**: Therefore, the third and fourth-born sons of Aaron (**Eleazar, and Ithamar**) inherited the priesthood, and passed it down to their sons after them.

d. **The sons of Aaron, the anointed priests, whom he consecrated to minister as priests**: It is important to realize that the priests were only one small family among the Levites. To be a priest and to be a Levite were not the same thing at all. Only those who were descendants of Aaron could be priests.

2. (5-10) The Levites: Their role in relation to Aaron.

And the LORD spoke to Moses, saying: "Bring the tribe of Levi near, and present them before Aaron the priest, that they may serve him. And they shall attend to his needs and the needs of the whole congregation before the tabernacle of meeting, to do the work of the tabernacle. Also they shall attend to all the furnishings of the tabernacle of meeting, and to the needs of the children of Israel, to do the work of the tabernacle. And you shall give the Levites to Aaron and his sons; they *are* given entirely to him from among the children of Israel. So you shall appoint Aaron and his sons, and they shall attend to their priesthood; but the outsider who comes near shall be put to death."

a. **Bring the tribe of Levi near, and present them before Aaron the priest, that they may serve him**: The entire tribe of Levi was given to serve the needs of Aaron and the priests (**they shall attend to his needs**), to serve the needs of the congregation at large (**and the needs of the whole congregation**), and to serve the needs of the tabernacle itself (**attend to all the furnishings of the tabernacle...to do the work of the tabernacle**).

i. These were important aspects of the Levite's service, but they also had at least one other important responsibility: to teach God's word to the people of God. Deuteronomy 24:8 is one passage stating that the priests and the Levites were to teach the people of Israel God's word: *carefully observe and do according to all that the priests, the Levites, shall teach you; just as I commanded them, so you shall be careful to do.*

ii. Levites from the families of Gershon, Kohath, and Merari also served as musicians during the reign of King David (1 Chronicles 6:33-47).

iii. However the Levites served, it was in sacrificial surrender to God. Clarke notes of the phrase **bring the tribe of Levi near**: "*Hakreb* is properly a sacrificial word, and signifies the presenting of a sacrifice or offering to the Lord. As an offering, the tribe of *Levi* was given up entirely to the service of the sanctuary, to be no longer their own, but the Lord's property."

b. **And they shall attend to his needs**: God appointed an order and organization for the Levites and the priests. The Levites were under the direction of Aaron (**that they may serve him.... they are given entirely to him**). Their main mission was to help Aaron and help his work as the priest for Israel.

i. According to Wenham, **attend to his needs** is more literally, "to keep guard." Lexicons explain the verb *somru* as "to keep, watch, guard."

ii. "They had to be permanently on guard, ready to kill any unauthorized person approaching the tent of meeting, its furniture or the altar. The phrase *he shall be put to death* implies a judicial execution, though in this context it is more like a policeman shooting a bank robber." (Wenham) Examples of this kind of "policing" of the sanctuary are found in Exodus 32:25-29 and Numbers 25:7-12.

iii. They were to protect against both enemies (foreign invaders) and "friends" – Israelites not authorized to enter the tabernacle or its courts.

iv. "Whereas Mesopotamian and Egyptian temples had statues of divine emissaries as guardians for their various temples, Israel knew of no such demonic entities in their prophetic religion. There was but one true power in the universe, the God of Israel, and his sanctuary must be protected and secured from the intrusion or defilement by 'the only remaining adversary – man.'" (Cole)

v. "Nothing in the holy things of God was left to chance or improvisation. None of the sacred persons who ministered in his presence was to be unprepared or untaught." (Allen)

c. **To do the work of the tabernacle**: In some ways, being a priest was far more visible and perhaps "glamorous" than being a Levite. But the service of the Levites made the work of the priests possible and was seen by God as having equal value. It was all part of **the work of the tabernacle**.

d. **The outsider who comes near shall be put to death**: This **outsider** could include a Levite who presumed to take the role of a priest. If a Levite grew jealous, and decided he wanted to do the work of a priest, it was strictly forbidden. This sin against God's order and organization was to be severely punished.

i. "Service at the tabernacle may be done only at the express command of God. There is a special poignancy in the words of v.10 as they follow the paragraph reminding us of the deaths of Aaron's sons." (Allen)

ii. In the perspective of the new covenant, God also has an order and an organization. God has appointed offices and roles in the church such as elder, pastor (shepherd), and overseer. There should be an appropriate recognition of such offices and the men who properly fulfill such offices (Hebrews 13:7 and 13:17, Ephesians 4:11-15).

iii. However, in the new covenant every believer is a priest (1 Peter 2:5 and 2:9; Revelation 1:6 and 5:10). While there is structure and order in the new covenant community, all have equal standing before God in Jesus Christ, and equal access to God in Jesus.

3. (11-13) The Levites are a special possession to God.

Then the LORD spoke to Moses, saying: "Now behold, I Myself have taken the Levites from among the children of Israel instead of every firstborn who opens the womb among the children of Israel. Therefore the Levites shall be Mine, because all the firstborn *are* Mine. On the day that I struck all the firstborn in the land of Egypt, I sanctified to Myself all the firstborn in Israel, both man and beast. They shall be Mine: I *am* the LORD."

a. **I Myself have taken the Levites from among the children of Israel instead of every firstborn**: In the law of Moses, God had a special claim to the firstborn of Israel (Exodus 13:1-2 and 13:11-15). As the Exodus passages show, this was true of **both man and beast**. This demonstrated the principle that God has a claim to the first and best of our blessings.

i. Allen notes that the words **instead of** "serve as a clear example of substitution in the Hebrew Scriptures (cf. Gen 22:13: 'a ram…instead of his son'; cf. also Matt 20:28)."

b. **Therefore the Levites shall be Mine, because all the firstborn are Mine**: Levi, the son of Israel and ancestor of the tribe of Israel, was not the firstborn among his brothers. Yet God chose **the Levites** as His own, and regarded them as a replacement for the firstborn of the nation as a whole (**because all the firstborn are Mine**).

B. The census of the tribe of Levi.

1. (14-20) The command to number the tribe of Levi.

Then the LORD spoke to Moses in the Wilderness of Sinai, saying: "Number the children of Levi by their fathers' houses, by their families; you shall number every male from a month old and above." So Moses numbered them according to the word of the LORD, as he was commanded. These were the sons of Levi by their names: Gershon, Kohath, and Merari. And these *are* the names of the sons of Gershon

by their families: Libni and Shimei. And the sons of Kohath by their families: Amram, Izehar, Hebron, and Uzziel. And the sons of Merari by their families: Mahli and Mushi. These *are* the families of the Levites by their fathers' houses.

a. **Number the children of Levi**: Though they were not counted among the available soldiers of Israel (Numbers 1:47-49), the Levites were still to be counted.

b. **Number every male from a month old and above**: For the military census of Numbers 1, Israel counted every male twenty years old and above (Numbers 1:45). The Levites were not counted for military service, so they counted **every male from a month old and above**.

c. **By their fathers' houses**: The tribe of Levi was to be categorized by the families, with the main grouping according to Levi's three sons: **Gershon, Kohath, and Merari**.

2. (21-26) The census and duties of the family of Gershon.

From Gershon *came* the family of the Libnites and the family of the Shimites; these *were* the families of the Gershonites. Those who were numbered, according to the number of all the males from a month old and above; of those who were numbered *there were* seven thousand five hundred. The families of the Gershonites were to camp behind the tabernacle westward. And the leader of the fathers' house of the Gershonites *was* Eliasaph the son of Lael. The duties of the children of Gershon in the tabernacle of meeting *included* the tabernacle, the tent with its covering, the screen for the door of the tabernacle of meeting, the screen for the door of the court, the hangings of the court which *are* around the tabernacle and the altar, and their cords, according to all the work relating to them.

a. **The families of the Gershonites were to camp behind the tabernacle westward**: The Gershonites (7,500 males) were to camp on the west side of (behind) the tabernacle. This was in between the tribe of Ephraim and the tabernacle itself.

b. **The duties of the children of Gershon**: The Gershonites were to take care of the skins that covered the tabernacle itself. **According to all the work relating to them** means the **children of Gershon** were responsible for the disassembly, transport, assembly, and upkeep of the **tent with its covering**, the screens, the **hangings**, and their **cords**.

3. (27-32) The census and duties of the family of Kohath.

From Kohath *came* the family of the Amramites, the family of the Izharites, the family of the Hebronites, and the family of the Uzzielites;

these *were* the families of the Kohathites. According to the number of all the males, from a month old and above, *there were* eight thousand six hundred keeping charge of the sanctuary. The families of the children of Kohath were to camp on the south side of the tabernacle. And the leader of the fathers' house of the families of the Kohathites *was* Elizaphan the son of Uzziel. Their duty *included* the ark, the table, the lampstand, the altars, the utensils of the sanctuary with which they ministered, the screen, and all the work relating to them. And Eleazar the son of Aaron the priest *was to be* chief over the leaders of the Levites, *with* oversight of those who kept charge of the sanctuary.

a. **These were the families of the Kohathites**: The Kohathites (8,600 males) were to camp on the south side of the tabernacle. This was in between the tribe of Reuben and the tabernacle itself.

i. "Some Kohathites under the rebellious leadership of Korah would later challenge the authority of Moses and Aaron over the Israelite community (Numbers 16:1-50)." (Cole)

ii. **The families of the Amramites**: "The term 'Amramites' reminds us of the family of Aaron and Moses. Aaron is an Amramite (see Exodus 6:20). The presence of the family of the Amramites suggests that Amram was not the direct father of Aaron, Miriam, and Moses but an ancestor. Hence, Aaron and Moses were from the family of Kohath, of the tribe of Levi." (Allen)

b. **Their duty included the ark**: The Kohathites were to take care of the furniture of the tabernacle: The ark of the covenant, the **table** of showbread, the **lampstand**, the **altars**, and other tools and furnishings. **All the work relating to them** means they were responsible for the covering, the proper transport, the placement, and the maintenance of these holy articles.

c. **Eleazar the son of Aaron the priest was to be chief over the leaders of the Levites**: All the Levites with duties related to the **charge of the sanctuary** were under the supervision of the priests.

4. (33-37) The census and duties of the family of Merari.

From Merari *came* **the family of the Mahlites and the family of the Mushites; these** *were* **the families of Merari. And those who were numbered, according to the number of all the males from a month old and above,** *were* **six thousand two hundred. The leader of the fathers' house of the families of Merari** *was* **Zuriel the son of Abihail. These** *were* **to camp on the north side of the tabernacle. And the appointed duty of the children of Merari** *included* **the boards of the tabernacle, its bars, its pillars, its sockets, its utensils, all the work relating to them, and the**

pillars of the court all around, with their sockets, their pegs, and their cords.

a. **These were the families of Merari**: The family of Merari (6,200 males) was to camp on the north side of the tabernacle. This was in between the tribe of Dan and the tabernacle itself.

b. **The appointed duty of the children of Merari included the boards of the tabernacle**: The family of Merari was to take care of the structural aspects of the tabernacle including the **pillars**, the **boards**, and so forth. **All the work relating to them** means they were responsible for the disassembly, the transport, the assembly, and the maintenance of these articles that gave a frame, structure, and stability to the tabernacle.

5. (38-39) The camp of the priests.

Moreover those who were to camp before the tabernacle on the east, before the tabernacle of meeting, *were* Moses, Aaron, and his sons, keeping charge of the sanctuary, to meet the needs of the children of Israel; but the outsider who came near was to be put to death. All who were numbered of the Levites, whom Moses and Aaron numbered at the commandment of the LORD, by their families, all the males from a month old and above, *were* twenty-two thousand.

a. **Those who were to camp before the tabernacle on the east**: The family of Aaron, and Moses, were to camp on the **east** side of the tabernacle – closest to the entrance, which was on the east side of the sanctuary.

i. "Moses and Aaron had the most honored location, as we would expect. They guarded the entrance to the Tent of Meeting, and they did so facing the sun. There is a sense in which the opening of the tent best faces the east, for this is the direction of the encampment of the people. Later on Solomon was to build the holy temple in Jerusalem. Its entrance also would face east. The morning sun would shine first on the entrance of the Holy Place, as a symbol of the life-giving light of God that illumines the place of his presence." (Allen)

b. **Moses, Aaron, and his sons, keeping charge of the sanctuary**: God's order and organization extend to certain jobs for certain people to do. The families of the Levites had certain callings that they were to fulfill. There was no one man or family to do everything; God made them dependent on one another to accomplish the work.

c. **To meet the needs of the children of Israel**: The work of the priests and the Levites was for the glory and honor of God. Yet another essential part of their service was to simply **meet the needs of the children of Israel**. Knowing the nature of their work, this was largely focused on their spiritual needs, but certainly included needs beyond the spiritual. To do their work well as priests and Levites, they needed to be servants, and sympathetic to the people and their **needs**.

d. **But the outsider who came near was to be put to death**: The work of the priests and Levites was only to be done by those born into the established families. It was exclusive, and not open to anyone based on their desire or ambition. This old covenant emphasized a sense of exclusion; the new covenant emphasizes inclusion.

e. **Were twenty-two thousand**: The number of males among the Levites totaled 22,000 men.

i. "The total of 22,000 Levites given in verse 39 does not tally with the totals of the individual clans given in verses 22, 28, 34 which come to 22,300. The discrepancy is most easily explained as textual corruption in verse 28. The number of Kohathites may originally have been 8,300. 3 (Hebrew *sls*) could quite easily have been corrupted into 6 (*ss*)." (Wenham)

6. (40-51) The exchange of the firstborn.

Then the LORD said to Moses: "Number all the firstborn males of the children of Israel from a month old and above, and take the number of their names. And you shall take the Levites for Me; I *am* the LORD; instead of all the firstborn among the children of Israel, and the livestock of the Levites instead of all the firstborn among the livestock of the children of Israel." So Moses numbered all the firstborn among the children of Israel, as the LORD commanded him. And all the firstborn males, according to the number of names from a month old and above, of those who were numbered of them, were twenty-two thousand two hundred and seventy-three. Then the LORD spoke to Moses, saying: "Take the Levites instead of all the firstborn among the children of Israel, and the livestock of the Levites instead of their livestock. The Levites shall be Mine: I *am* the LORD. And for the redemption of the two hundred and seventy-three of the firstborn of the children of Israel, who are more than the number of the Levites, you shall take five shekels for each one individually; you shall take *them* in the currency of the shekel of the sanctuary, the shekel of twenty gerahs. And you shall give the money, with which the excess number of them is redeemed, to Aaron and his sons." So Moses took the redemption money from those who were over and above those who were redeemed by the Levites. From the firstborn of the children of Israel he took the money, one thousand three hundred and sixty-five *shekels,* according to the shekel of the sanctuary. And

Moses gave their redemption money to Aaron and his sons, according to the word of the LORD, as the LORD commanded Moses.

a. **Number all the firstborn males of the children of Israel**: In Numbers 3:11-13 God told Moses that the LORD would claim Levites as a substitute for the firstborn males of Israel. As the first and presumably the best of God's blessings, the firstborn belonged to God. A firstborn lamb would be sacrificed to the LORD, but God did not want human sacrifice. He received the Levites instead, and this command to **number all the firstborn males of the children of Israel** was part of that exchange. They were to **take the Levites instead of all the firstborn among the children of Israel**.

> i. There can be a difference between what God lays claim to and what He materially receives. God laid claim to all of Israel, and spiritually they all belonged to Him and His purpose. Materially, God received only the tribe of Levi in the place of all Israel. The same concept is true regarding our material possessions. Everything we have belongs to God; it is all His. Materially speaking, we return to Him a proportion in the place of all that belongs to us.

b. **All the firstborn males, according to the number of names**: However, there were 22,273 firstborn sons in Israel; and there were only 22,000 Levite males (Numbers 3:39). There were more firstborn sons than Levite males. The extra 273 firstborn sons were assigned a value in money (**five shekels for each one individually**), and the money was given to the tabernacle. This amounted to **one thousand three hundred and sixty-five shekels** of what God called **redemption money**.

> i. The number of firstborn sons is low if accounted for all the nation; it would mean that only one in 27 sons were firstborns – an unlikely percentage. It is more probable that the 22,273 firstborn sons were those born in the thirteen months since their departure from Egypt.

> ii. "The price for the redemption of the excess firstborn of the Israelites was five shekels, or about 2.1 ounces of silver per person according to the twenty-gerah sanctuary shekel." (Cole)

> iii. "*Five shekels apiece* was the price to be paid for the redemption of a first-born a month old, Numbers 18:15, 16; but this money, though paid for these 273 persons, was probably paid out of the common stock of all." (Poole)

> iv. The firstborn of Israel were redeemed with a silver shekel, but under the new covenant the believer is redeemed with something far more costly and precious: the blood of Jesus Christ, as a lamb without blemish (1 Peter 1:18-19).

Numbers 4 – Duties of the Priests

"The sense of order and organization already observed in this book comes to its finest point in this chapter." (Allen)

A. The duty of the Kohathites.

1. (1-3) Those fit for service.

Then the LORD spoke to Moses and Aaron, saying: "Take a census of the sons of Kohath from among the children of Levi, by their families, by their fathers' house, from thirty years old and above, even to fifty years old, all who enter the service to do the work in the tabernacle of meeting."

a. **Take a census of the sons of Kohath**: A general count of the men of the family of Kohath was recorded in Numbers 3:27-28. There were found to be 8,600 males among the **sons of Kohath**. This second count was required to see the number of the **sons of Kohath** who were of age to serve in the tabernacle.

i. When the sons of Levi are mentioned in Numbers 3:17, their order is Gershon, Kohath, and Merari – this was presumably their birth order. However, in Numbers 4 Kohath is dealt with before Gershon and is given a (seemingly) more prestigious duty: the transport of the most holy furnishings of the tabernacle.

ii. "The reason for this elevation of the second son over his older brother seems to be based on the sovereign selection of the Lord and the favored work he gives this family in proximity to the holiest things." (Allen)

iii. God elevates the unexpected. In the culture of the Old Testament, an elder son was always favored over a younger son. It is not always so with God. In His unfolding plan, God favored Isaac over Ishmael, Jacob over Esau, Joseph over Reuben, Moses over Aaron, and David over his brothers. God does not *always* go against the culture's expectation of whom to favor by their birth, but He *often* does.

b. **From thirty years old and above, even to fifty years old**: Among the males of the family of Kohath, only those between the ages of **thirty** and **fifty** were allowed to do the **work in the tabernacle of meeting**.

i. In some ways, the years between 30 and 50 were thought to be the "prime" of a man's life (combining both wisdom and physical strength). When it came to the **work in the tabernacle of meeting**, God wanted the best from the family of Kohath.

ii. Numbers 8:24 says that the Levites entered their service at 25 years of age. According to some sources, the years between 25 and 30 were used for training. "The rabbins say that the Levites began to learn to do the service at *twenty-five*, and that having been instructed *five* years, they began the public service at *thirty*." (Clarke)

iii. Adam Clarke thought that this, in principle, pointed to a retirement age for pastors and ministers: "A preacher who devotes his whole time and strength to the service of the Church of God from twenty to fifty or sixty years of age, should be then excused from his *severer labour*, and maintained at the charge of the sanctuary. This would not only be a great comfort to a worn-out servant of God but also of great use to the work of the ministry, which, to be faithfully and effectually performed, requires all the powers of the body and mind of man. *Old faithful ministers* are to be highly respected for their work's sake, and to be supplied with all the necessaries and comforts of life; but how little can they do in the public ministry of the word, however willing to work, when their eye waxes dim and their bodily strength fails!"

2. (4-14) The work of packing the furniture and utensils of the tabernacle.

"This *is* the service of the sons of Kohath in the tabernacle of meeting, *relating to* the most holy things: When the camp prepares to journey, Aaron and his sons shall come, and they shall take down the covering veil and cover the ark of the Testimony with it. Then they shall put on it a covering of badger skins, and spread over *that* a cloth entirely of blue; and they shall insert its poles.

"On the table of showbread they shall spread a blue cloth, and put on it the dishes, the pans, the bowls, and the pitchers for pouring; and the showbread shall be on it. They shall spread over them a scarlet cloth, and cover the same with a covering of badger skins; and they shall insert

its poles. And they shall take a blue cloth and cover the lampstand of the light, with its lamps, its wick-trimmers, its trays, and all its oil vessels, with which they service it. Then they shall put it with all its utensils in a covering of badger skins, and put *it* on a carrying beam.

"Over the golden altar they shall spread a blue cloth, and cover it with a covering of badger skins; and they shall insert its poles. Then they shall take all the utensils of service with which they minister in the sanctuary, put *them* in a blue cloth, cover them with a covering of badger skins, and put *them* on a carrying beam. Also they shall take away the ashes from the altar, and spread a purple cloth over it. They shall put on it all its implements with which they minister there; the firepans, the forks, the shovels, the basins, and all the utensils of the altar; and they shall spread on it a covering of badger skins, and insert its poles.

a. **This is the service of the sons of Kohath**: This section (Numbers 4:4-14) describes what the priests (**Aaron and his sons**) had to do *before* the **sons of Kohath** could do their work.

b. **When the camp prepares to journey**: The **tabernacle of meeting** was a portable temple or house of God. Because Israel journeyed through the wilderness on their way to the land of Canaan, they needed a temple or house of God that could move with them. The **tabernacle of meeting** was a temple in a tent. The various pieces of furniture had to be properly packed for moving.

i. "He who counts the stars and calls them all by their names, leaves nothing unarranged in his own service." (Spurgeon)

c. **They shall take down the covering veil and cover the ark of the Testimony with it**: The **ark** of the covenant was holy, so it could only be covered and prepared for transport by the priests. The priests first covered it with the **veil** that separated the holy place from the most holy place, then they covered the **veil** with **badger skins** and finally with a **cloth entirely of blue**.

i. **They shall insert its poles**: The ark of the covenant was not supposed to be directly touched by human hands. It had rings on the side, through which **poles** were inserted. The ark was carried by these **poles** (Exodus 25:12-14). This method of carrying with rings and poles was also used for the table of showbread (Exodus 25:26-28), the altar of burnt offering (Exodus 27:6-7), and the altar of incense (Exodus 30:4-5).

ii. "All the preparation suggests a rigorous training schedule before actual work would be done by a given priest." (Allen)

d. **The table of showbread**: This, along with its associated utensils (**dishes, pans, bowls, pitchers for pouring**), was covered first with a **scarlet cloth**, then with **a covering of badger skins**.

e. **The lampstand of the light**: This, along with its associated utensils (**lamps, wick-trimmers, trays, oil vessels**), was covered with a **blue cloth**, then with **a covering of badger skins**.

f. **The golden altar**: This (also known as the altar of incense), along with its **utensils of service**, was covered in a **blue cloth**, then with **a covering of badger skins**. The **ashes** from the altar were collected on a **purple cloth**, together with other **implements** associated with the altar of incense, and then covered with **badger skins**.

i. "The Samaritan Pentateuch and the Septuagint add the bronze laver at the conclusion of v. 14 that is missing from the MT [Hebrew text]." (Cole)

3. (15-20) The moving of the furniture and utensils of the tabernacle.

And when Aaron and his sons have finished covering the sanctuary and all the furnishings of the sanctuary, when the camp is set to go, then the sons of Kohath shall come to carry *them;* but they shall not touch any holy thing, lest they die.

"These *are* the things in the tabernacle of meeting which the sons of Kohath are to carry.

"The appointed duty of Eleazar the son of Aaron the priest *is* the oil for the light, the sweet incense, the daily grain offering, the anointing oil, the oversight of all the tabernacle, of all that *is* in it, with the sanctuary and its furnishings."

Then the LORD spoke to Moses and Aaron, saying: "Do not cut off the tribe of the families of the Kohathites from among the Levites; but do this in regard to them, that they may live and not die when they approach the most holy things: Aaron and his sons shall go in and appoint each of them to his service and his task. But they shall not go in to watch while the holy things are being covered, lest they die."

a. **When the camp is set to go, then the sons of Kohath shall come to carry them; but they shall not touch any holy thing, lest they die**: The Kohathites were forbidden to touch any of the tabernacle furniture. Only the priests could prepare the **furnishings of the sanctuary**; the **sons of Kohath** were commanded to **carry** them.

b. **The appointed duty of Eleazar the son of Aaron the priest**: Apparently, these were aspects of the priestly work that were under the supervision of

Eleazar the son of Aaron. Numbers 4:16 is an interesting summary of many of the duties of the priests.

- **The oil for the light**: The priests supplied oil for the lampstands and kept the lamps burning.

- **The sweet incense**: The priests prepared and burned the incense for the altar of incense.

- **The daily grain offering**: The priests brought a daily offering to the altar of burnt offering.

- **The anointing oil**: The priests kept and applied the holy **anointing oil**, used to anoint rulers, priests, and others designated by God.

- **The oversight of all the tabernacle, of all that is in it, with the sanctuary and its furnishings**: The priests were responsible for everything at the tabernacle in general. The tabernacle (the house of God) was not under the authority of the civil leaders of Israel (kings, magistrates, elders). It was supervised by the priests of Israel.

c. **Aaron and his sons shall go in and appoint each of them to his service and his task**: The Kohathites had a permanent place of service before the LORD and for Israel. They were to be specially appointed as individuals (**appoint each of them to his service**) for their work. Even though their work was "only" transporting the furnishings of the tabernacle, it was properly regarded as important, worthy service to God, deserving of a specific appointment.

d. **Lest they die**: The Kohathites were not to even look at the **holy things** as the priests covered them and prepared them for moving. They had a specific role to fulfill in their work for the LORD and were not to go beyond that role. The penalty for going beyond what God had appointed could be death.

B. The duty of the Gershonites.

1. (21-23) Those of the sons of Gershon fit for service.

Then the LORD spoke to Moses, saying: "Also take a census of the sons of Gershon, by their fathers' house, by their families. From thirty years old and above, even to fifty years old, you shall number them, all who enter to perform the service, to do the work in the tabernacle of meeting.

a. **Take a census of the sons of Gershon**: A general count of the men of the family of Gershon was recorded in Numbers 3:21-22. There were found to be 7,500 males among the **sons of Gershon**. This second count was required to see the number of the **sons of Gershon** who were of age to serve the tabernacle.

b. **From thirty years old and above, even to fifty years old**: As with the Kohathites, they were to count only those between the ages of **thirty** and **fifty** who were allowed to do the **work in the tabernacle of meeting**. When it came to the **work in the tabernacle of meeting**, God wanted the best combination of wisdom and strength from the family of Gershon.

i. **All who enter to perform the service**: "The words 'to perform the service' are, as the margin tells us, literally, to 'war the warfare.'" (Maclaren)

ii. The hint of warfare in this phrase in this context is meaningful. The service of these Levites was relatively mundane. They did not perform sacrifices and were not even allowed to *look* at the sacred furnishings of the tabernacle. Yet, their service was described in some sense as warfare. This speaks to a truth that many servants of God have known: when one begins to serve the LORD, His people, and a needy world in the name of Jesus, the warfare begins.

2. (24-28) The duties of the Gershonites.

This *is* the service of the families of the Gershonites, in serving and carrying: They shall carry the curtains of the tabernacle and the tabernacle of meeting *with* its covering, the covering of badger skins that *is* on it, the screen for the door of the tabernacle of meeting, the screen for the door of the gate of the court, the hangings of the court which *are* around the tabernacle and altar, and their cords, all the furnishings for their service and all that is made for these things: so shall they serve.

"Aaron and his sons shall assign all the service of the sons of the Gershonites, all their tasks and all their service. And you shall appoint to them all their tasks as their duty. This *is* the service of the families of the sons of Gershon in the tabernacle of meeting. And their duties *shall be* under the authority of Ithamar the son of Aaron the priest."

a. **This is the service of the families of the Gershonites**: While the Kohathites were responsible for carrying the furnishings of the tabernacle, the Gershonites were responsible for carrying the tabernacle coverings. This included the various **curtains**, **hangings**, **cords**, and **all the furnishings** associated with the "walls" of the tabernacle.

i. **The covering of badger skins**: This is rendered differently in some translations. The Revised Standard Version has "goatskin." The New English Bible has "porpoise-hide." "The Hebrew word rendered 'sea cow' (*tahas*) is similar to the Arabic term for the dolphin; hence, porpoise-hide or hide of sea cows seems correct." (Allen)

b. **Aaron and his sons shall assign all the service of the sons of the Gershonites**: As with the Kohathites, the work of the Gershonites was under the supervision of the priests (**Aaron and his sons**). Here, it was **under the authority of Ithamar**, one of the sons of Aaron.

C. The duty of the family of Merari.

1. (29-30) Those fit for service.

"As for the sons of Merari, you shall number them by their families and by their fathers' house. From thirty years old and above, even to fifty years old, you shall number them, everyone who enters the service to do the work of the tabernacle of meeting.**

a. **As for the sons of Merari, you shall number them**: A general count of the men of the family of Merari was recorded in Numbers 3:33-34. There were found to be 6,200 males among the **sons of Merari**.

b. **Who enters the service to do the work of the tabernacle**: This second count was required to see the number of the **sons of Merari** who were of age to serve the tabernacle – those men from 30 to 50 years old.

i. **To do the work of the tabernacle**: "The work of the ministry is not an idle man's occupation." (Trapp)

2. (31-33) The duties of the family of Merari.

And this *is* what they must carry as all their service for the tabernacle of meeting: the boards of the tabernacle, its bars, its pillars, its sockets, and the pillars around the court with their sockets, pegs, and cords, with all their furnishings and all their service; and you shall assign *to each man* by name the items he must carry. This *is* the service of the families of the sons of Merari, as all their service for the tabernacle of meeting, under the authority of Ithamar the son of Aaron the priest."

a. **This is what they must carry as all their service for the tabernacle of meeting**: Those of the family of Merari were called to pack and transport the **boards**, **pillars**, and associated parts of the frame and structure of the tabernacle. This was difficult and important work. These boards and pillars and other pieces were usually covered with precious metals, and the estimated weight of the tabernacle was some 19,000 pounds (more than 8,600 kilos).

b. **You shall assign to each man by name the items he must carry**: This was a highly organized work with each piece assigned to a specific man, **under the authority of Ithamar the son of Aaron the priest**. The high level of organization shows the importance of the work, leaving none of it up to chance or the mere preference of the workers.

i. **Assign to each man by name**: "Because their items were small and numerous, each Merarite was responsible for one particular item, so that none of them would be lost." (Wenham)

ii. **Sockets, pegs, and cords**: These are humble, everyday things. Yet, "Their work was as important as that of any other family group; for without it the more desirable, prestigious work of the tabernacle could not be done. Hence the Merarites could take an interest even in the placing of a post, a peg, or a rope...because the worship of God could not proceed—nor could the camp move out—unless these people were doing their holy work." (Allen)

D. Summary of the census of the Levites.

1. (34-48) The final count according to the families.

And Moses, Aaron, and the leaders of the congregation numbered the sons of the Kohathites by their families and by their fathers' house, from thirty years old and above, even to fifty years old, everyone who entered the service for work in the tabernacle of meeting; and those who were numbered by their families were two thousand seven hundred and fifty. These *were* the ones who were numbered of the families of the Kohathites, all who might serve in the tabernacle of meeting, whom Moses and Aaron numbered according to the commandment of the LORD by the hand of Moses.

And those who were numbered of the sons of Gershon, by their families and by their fathers' house, from thirty years old and above, even to fifty years old, everyone who entered the service for work in the tabernacle of meeting; those who were numbered by their families, by their fathers' house, were two thousand six hundred and thirty. These *are* the ones who were numbered of the families of the sons of Gershon, of all who might serve in the tabernacle of meeting, whom Moses and Aaron numbered according to the commandment of the LORD.

Those of the families of the sons of Merari who were numbered, by their families, by their fathers' house, from thirty years old and above, even to fifty years old, everyone who entered the service for work in the tabernacle of meeting; those who were numbered by their families were three thousand two hundred. These *are* the ones who were numbered of the families of the sons of Merari, whom Moses and Aaron numbered according to the word of the LORD by the hand of Moses.

All who were numbered of the Levites, whom Moses, Aaron, and the leaders of Israel numbered, by their families and by their fathers' houses, from thirty years old and above, even to fifty years old, everyone who

came to do the work of service and the work of bearing burdens in the tabernacle of meeting; those who were numbered were eight thousand five hundred and eighty.

a. **These were the ones who were numbered of the families of the Kohathites**: Of the family of Kohath, there were 2,750 men between the ages of 30 and 50 who were found fit for the service of the tabernacle.

b. **These are the ones who were numbered of the families of the sons of Gershon**: Of the family of Gershon, there were 2,630 men between the ages of 30 and 50 who were found fit for the service of the tabernacle.

c. **These are the ones who were numbered of the families of the sons of Merari**: Of the family of Merari, there were 3,200 men between the ages of 30 and 50 who were found fit for the service of the tabernacle.

d. **All who were numbered of the Levites**: The total of those available **to do the work of service and the work of bearing burdens in the tabernacle of meeting** from the families of the Kohathites, the sons of Gershon, and the sons of Merari was 8,580.

2. (49) The organization and order of the Levites.

According to the commandment of the LORD they were numbered by the hand of Moses, each according to his service and according to his task; thus were they numbered by him, as the LORD commanded Moses.

a. **According to the commandment of the LORD they were numbered**: This census was commanded by God and had a definite purpose in His plan.

b. **Each according to his service and according to his task**: Each man from these three family divisions eligible to serve had a role to play in doing the work of the tabernacle. No one family could do all the work. God made them dependent on each other to do the work.

i. "It is worthy of note that these Levites, although they were all equally consecrated to God, had not all exactly the same work to perform. God is not the God of all uniformity. There is a wondrous unity of plan and design in all that he does, but there is also an equally marvellous variety." (Spurgeon)

ii. Later, God would explain through the Apostle Paul that the church is to work like a body (1 Corinthians 12:12-31). Like a human body, the church has many parts, looking different, doing different jobs, and meeting different needs. Some parts are more visible, some less, but they are all essential – and all have the same DNA code.

iii. Much trouble is caused in the service of the LORD by those who desire a different calling than they have, or who are jealous of those who have a different calling, or by those who exalt one calling and abase another. Everyone has a place and a job, and all can set themselves to do it.

Numbers 5 – Separating from Sin

A. Separation from the effects of sin.

1. (1-2) The command to separate the ceremonially unclean.

And the LORD spoke to Moses, saying: "Command the children of Israel that they put out of the camp every leper, everyone who has a discharge, and whoever becomes defiled by a corpse.

a. **And the LORD spoke to Moses**: This is repeated three times in this chapter (also in verses 5 and 11), heading each of three sections. Allen noted at least three important implications from this phrase.

- That Moses was truly a prophet of the LORD.

- That the commands God spoke to Moses were not secret revelations; they were meant to be spread throughout the whole community of Israel.

- That these words of God were authoritative commands, not suggestions.

b. **Command the children of Israel that they put out of the camp**: As Israel prepared to march to the Promised Land, they had to separate those considered to be ceremonially unclean. This included the **leper** (Leviticus 13; actually, describing a broad range of skin diseases), those with a **discharge** (Leviticus 15), and those who touched a dead body, except that of a close relative (Leviticus 21:1). What God commanded in Leviticus now had to be done.

i. "Probably this ordinance gave the first idea of a *hospital*, where all those who are afflicted with contagious disorders are put into particular wards, under medical treatment." (Clarke)

ii. **Everyone who has a discharge**: "It seems likely that only the longer-term discharges, that required a sacrifice to be offered when they cleared up, are meant here." (Wenham)

iii. **Whoever becomes defiled by a corpse**: "The ultimate tangible sign of uncleanness in ancient Israel was the corpse. Processes of decay and disease in dead flesh were evident to all. Physical contact with a corpse was a sure mark of uncleanness and quite possibly a source of infection." (Allen)

c. **Put out of the camp**: It wasn't that any of these things made a person, or proved a person to be, a notorious sinner (though that was often wrongly assumed). Rather, it was that leprosy, unclean discharges, and dead bodies were reminders of the effects of sin – from which Israel must separate themselves as they prepared to march towards the Promised Land.

i. We could consider these three sources of uncleanness as an analogy of humanity's sin nature, inherited from Adam. A leper does not choose leprosy, but receives it, so our sin nature is not chosen – but inherited from Adam. We choose individual acts of sin, but our sin nature was received.

ii. At this stage in Israel's progression to the Promised Land, they had been organized and ordered by God – now, they would be challenged to become a community that valued purity. God desired to make Israel a "Promised Land people" – and that meant a purified, holy people.

2. (3-4) The breadth and reason of the command.

You shall put out both male and female; you shall put them outside the camp, that they may not defile their camps in the midst of which I dwell." And the children of Israel did so, and put them outside the camp; as the LORD spoke to Moses, so the children of Israel did.

a. **You shall put out both male and female**: Neither men nor women were to be excluded from this command. Neither sympathy nor perceived superiority could spare someone from the effects of sin in the world and our sinful nature.

i. "This does not, of course, mean they were left behind to perish, but that they were not allowed to march in their proper place with the tribes of their people." (Morgan)

b. **In the midst of which I dwell**: The great reason for this commanded separation was that God lived in the camp of Israel, so there had to be an effort to separate from sin and its effects.

i. "The essential issue in all laws of purity in Israel was not magic or health or superstition; the great reality was the presence of Yahweh in the camp; there can be no uncleanness where he dwells. The last words of v.3 are dramatic in their presentation: 'I am dwelling in their midst.'" (Allen)

ii. God is concerned with far more than our individual acts of sin; He demands that our sin nature be addressed. Only in Jesus can our sin nature – (the old man) be crucified, and the nature of Jesus (the new man) be given to us, making us new creations. God does not have a relationship of love and fellowship with the old man, but He does with the new man.

iii. To be a "Promised Land person" means that the effects of sin and the fall are, in some way, addressed. Promised Land people are not sinlessly perfect; but they are not openly, obviously, walking in the sin nature – as illustrated by those set outside the camp.

iv. The New Jerusalem – the eventual, ultimate dwelling place of God with His people – will have nothing unclean within (Revelation 21:27).

B. Separation from the damage our sin does.

1. (5-7) The command to make restitution.

Then the LORD spoke to Moses, saying, "Speak to the children of Israel: 'When a man or woman commits any sin that men commit in unfaithfulness against the LORD, and that person is guilty, then he shall confess the sin which he has committed. He shall make restitution for his trespass in full, plus one-fifth of it, and give *it* to the one he has wronged.

a. **Commits any sin that men commit in unfaithfulness against the LORD**: This probably is directed against the person who makes a contract with another person and is unfaithful to the contract. Their sin is not only against the other person; they have also sinned **against the LORD**.

b. **And that person is guilty**: The judges of Israel were to make just, righteous judgments regarding the guilt or innocence of the accused, according to the evidence presented. This deals with the person found **guilty**.

c. **Then he shall confess the sin**: The first step in restitution was for the guilty man or woman to admit and agree to their guilt, and to do so before God and the community.

d. **He shall make restitution for his trespass in full**: In addition to the confession of the sin, the guilty man also had to repay what he had defrauded. The just solution was not to put the guilty man in jail but to command that he restore what he had taken.

i. Because restitution is commanded, it indicates a case of sinning against another person (such as with theft, Leviticus 5:14-6:7) or in some cases withholding from God that which belongs to Him.

ii. "The practical importance of this law is obvious. Israel had been drawn up in battle array to march towards the Promised Land. But their unity would be shattered if they were squabbling among themselves and taking God's name in vain. Through restitution and sacrifice, peace with God and harmony within the nation could be restored." (Wenham)

e. **Plus one-fifth of it**: The restitution commanded must include a 20% penalty. The thief had to pay back what they took, *and more.*

i. "For without *restitution*, in every possible case, God will not forgive the iniquity of a man's sin. How can any person in a case of defraud, with his neighbour's property in his possession, expect to receive mercy from the hand of a just and holy God?" (Clarke)

2. (8) How to make restitution when the victim is dead.

But if the man has no relative to whom restitution may be made for the wrong, the restitution for the wrong *must go* to the LORD for the priest, in addition to the ram of the atonement with which atonement is made for him.

a. **If the man has no relative to whom restitution may be made for the wrong**: This assumes that if wrong were done to someone who had died, the guilty party would pay the restitution (what was taken plus 20%) to a **relative** of the deceased who had suffered the wrong.

i. **No relative**: "The term for 'close relative' is *goel*, the protector of the family rights, sometimes translated 'kinsman-redeemer' (e.g., Ruth 4:3)." (Allen)

b. **The restitution for the wrong must go to the LORD**: If a surviving relative could not be found to receive the restitution, then the restitution payment must **go to the LORD**. The payment of restitution was just as important – if not *more* important – for the guilty one paying it as it was for the victim receiving it.

i. Notably, when it went **to the LORD**, it was **for the priest**. The priest received it on behalf of the LORD. "The priest is the Lord's receiver. Tithes are due to the ministers of Christ 'that liveth,' because due to him, and they are in his stead." (Trapp)

c. **In addition to the ram of the atonement**: A ram was part of the guilt offering described in Leviticus 5:14 through 6:7.

3. (9-10) The right of the priests to their portion of an offering.

Every offering of all the holy things of the children of Israel, which they bring to the priest, shall be his. And every man's holy things shall be his; whatever any man gives the priest shall be his.'"

a. **Every offering of all the holy things of the children of Israel, which they bring to the priest, shall be his**: Many of the offerings God commanded of Israel included a portion of meat from the sacrificed animal that belonged to the priest. Often, part of the offering was returned to the one who brought the offering so their family could have a fellowship meal before the LORD; but the priest was to also receive his portion.

b. **Whatever any man gives the priest shall be his**: By God's command, the priest's work for the LORD and for God's people supplied food for his family.

C. Separation from the suspicion of sin: the law of jealousy.

1. (11-14) The situation calling for the law of jealousy.

And the LORD spoke to Moses, saying, "Speak to the children of Israel, and say to them: 'If any man's wife goes astray and behaves unfaithfully toward him, and a man lies with her carnally, and it is hidden from the eyes of her husband, and it is concealed that she has defiled herself, and *there was* no witness against her, nor was she caught—if the spirit of jealousy comes upon him and he becomes jealous of his wife, who has defiled herself—or if the spirit of jealousy comes upon him and he becomes jealous of his wife, although she has not defiled herself;

a. **If any man's wife goes astray and behaves unfaithfully toward him**: This unique passage deals with the problem of a **spirit of jealousy** in a marriage. Part of the foundation for marriage is the expectation that one's spouse will be romantically and sexually faithful, and there is a justified jealousy that comes from this expectation. However, there may also be unfounded jealousy that can damage a marriage. This passage gave Israel a way to deal with a **spirit of jealousy** that may or may not be justified.

i. "This law was given partly to deter wives from adulterous practices, and partly to secure wives against the rage of their hard-hearted husbands, who otherwise might upon mere suspicions destroy them, or at least put them away." (Poole)

b. **If the spirit of jealousy comes upon him and he becomes jealous of his wife**: Sometimes jealousy in a marriage is revealed to be justified; other times it is found to be false. Either way, God gave Israel a way to deal with this **spirit of jealousy**.

i. Sometimes a husband or wife knows by intuition if their spouse has been unfaithful, through interpreting dozens of subtle indications. Yet, this intuition is not infallible – it is sometimes wrong. Accusations of infidelity that can't be "proven" should be rightly resolved, and God gave Israel this unusual procedure to resolve such matters.

ii. This unusual law is evidence that God does not want couples to live in an on-going state of jealousy. The LORD gave a ceremony to resolve jealous feelings in a marriage, by either proving them or disproving them.

iii. This ceremony only dealt with an adulterous wife and not a husband because, for the most part, the law of Moses was "case law." It was not meant to anticipate every potential situation, but to give examples that set precedence for other cases. Though not stated, it is likely that a similar ceremony would be practiced if a wife became suspicious of a husband's adultery.

iv. Allen relates a different type of testing to determine if an accused woman had committed adultery among the Babylonians, found in the Code of Hammurabi: "The presumed unfaithful woman was to undergo the ordeal of trial by death by flinging herself into the sacred Euphrates River. If she were guilty, it was presumed she would drown; if innocent, she would survive the ordeal and would be able to return to her husband with no attachment of guilt." (Allen)

2. (15) The offering to resolve a spirit of jealousy.

Then the man shall bring his wife to the priest. He shall bring the offering required for her, one-tenth of an ephah of barley meal; he shall pour no oil on it and put no frankincense on it, because it *is* a grain offering of jealousy, an offering for remembering, for bringing iniquity to remembrance.

a. **Then the man shall bring his wife to the priest**: This meant that the husband did not have the right to do as he pleased with his wife. He had to **bring his wife to the priest** and have the matter resolved by a higher authority. It was a serious, solemn thing to bring before **the priest**, discouraging groundless or frivolous accusations.

i. This law must be seen considering its alternative in ancient (and sometimes modern) shame and honor cultures. In some such cultures, it would not be unusual for a jealous husband to simply murder his wife in the name of his honor and family honor.

ii. Without doubt, this law saved women who were innocent yet falsely accused because of the wrath of a jealous husband.

b. **He shall bring the offering required for her**: The jealous husband was to bring a certain amount of **barley meal**, and this grain only – not accompanied by any oil or frankincense, things that customarily accompanied a grain offering.

c. **He shall pour no oil on it and put no frankincense on it**: There was to be no oil or frankincense, things added to sweeten a typical grain offering. There is nothing sweet about this **offering for remembering, for bringing iniquity to remembrance**. This offering was bitter, not sweet, because either a wife would be found guilty of adultery, or a husband found guilty of unfounded suspicion.

d. **For bringing iniquity to remembrance**: It wasn't that perhaps the wife committed adultery and didn't "remember" it. The sacrifice was not for the husband or wife to remember, but for the whole community to remember the terrible nature of either adultery or false accusation.

3. (16-28) The ceremony of the offering to fulfill the law of jealousy.

'**And the priest shall bring her near, and set her before the LORD. The priest shall take holy water in an earthen vessel, and take some of the dust that is on the floor of the tabernacle and put *it* into the water. Then the priest shall stand the woman before the LORD, uncover the woman's head, and put the offering for remembering in her hands, which *is* the grain offering of jealousy. And the priest shall have in his hand the bitter water that brings a curse. And the priest shall put her under oath, and say to the woman, "If no man has lain with you, and if you have not gone astray to uncleanness *while* under your husband's *authority*, be free from this bitter water that brings a curse. But if you have gone astray *while* under your husband's *authority*, and if you have defiled yourself and some man other than your husband has lain with you"— then the priest shall put the woman under the oath of the curse, and he shall say to the woman—"the LORD make you a curse and an oath among your people, when the LORD makes your thigh rot and your belly swell; and may this water that causes the curse go into your stomach, and make *your* belly swell and *your* thigh rot."**

Then the woman shall say, "Amen, so be it."

Then the priest shall write these curses in a book, and he shall scrape *them* off into the bitter water. And he shall make the woman drink the bitter water that brings a curse, and the water that brings the curse shall enter her *to become* bitter. Then the priest shall take the grain offering of jealousy from the woman's hand, shall wave the offering before the LORD, and bring it to the altar; and the priest shall take a handful of the offering, as its memorial portion, burn *it* on the altar, and

afterward make the woman drink the water. When he has made her drink the water, then it shall be, if she has defiled herself and behaved unfaithfully toward her husband, that the water that brings a curse will enter her *and become* bitter, and her belly will swell, her thigh will rot, and the woman will become a curse among her people. But if the woman has not defiled herself, and is clean, then she shall be free and may conceive children.

a. **Take some of the dust that is on the floor of the tabernacle and put it into the water**: This water was made bitter from the **dust that is on the floor of the tabernacle**; while the woman held the grain offering in her hand (a reminder of fellowship with God), the priest pronounced an oath over the woman.

i. The idea of the phrase **uncover the woman's head** in verse 18 is to unbind and "let down" her hair. "The unbinding of the woman's hair is another hint that she was viewed as unclean. 'Lepers' had to let their hair hang loose as a mark of their uncleanness." (Wenham)

b. **The priest shall put her under oath, and say to the woman**: In his oath, the priest would solemnly announce that if the woman was innocent of the accusation of adultery, she would **be free from this bitter water that brings a curse**. But if she was in fact guilty of adultery, she would be under the curse.

i. "The terminology that bitter water brings a curse is problematic. The Hebrew phrase could also be translated 'the curse-bringing water of bitterness.' It is not just that the water was bitter tasting but that this water had the potential of bearing with it a bitter curse." (Allen)

ii. The effect of the curse was to make **your thigh** (here, a euphemism for the womb) **rot and your belly swell**.

iii. After the priest said this, the woman had to respond: **Amen, so be it**. She had to agree that if she was innocent, she deserved vindication; but if guilty, she deserved the punishment of the curse. A verdict of "guilty yet excused" was never in mind. Guilty or innocent, adultery was regarded as sin.

c. **The priest shall write these curses in a book, and he shall scrape them off into the bitter water**: After reading the curse, and hearing the woman's agreement, the priest would write the oath on a scroll – and scrape the dried ink **into the bitter water**.

i. The water was made bitter in two ways. First, it contained the dust from the floor of God's holy tabernacle. Second, it contained the ink from the scroll containing God's curse upon the sinner. The combination of seeing the holiness of God *and* the just penalty upon sinners is **bitter**.

ii. "Early Jewish exegesis likened the drink made from the ashes of the golden calf to the draught administered to suspect women." (Wenham)

d. **The priest shall take the grain offering**: After this, the priest offered the grain offering – a picture of fellowship and thanks to God – and the accused woman drank the bitter water.

e. **The water that brings a curse will enter her and become bitter**: Over time, the judgment of God would be evident. If she came down with some type of internal disease, especially affecting her womb, it would be seen as evidence of her guilt. But if she was free from disease, and continued to bear children, it would be seen as vindication.

i. Notably, if the woman was guilty, her punishment was not in the hand of her husband or even the community. Under the law of jealousy, the punishment of the woman was only in the hand of God. If the woman was innocent, it was known to the entire community.

ii. According to Adam Clarke, some Jewish rabbis also said that if the woman was guilty, the same disease would come upon the man that she had committed adultery with; but they also said that even if the wife had been guilty, but her husband had been guilty of adultery also, the bitter water would have no effect on her.

iii. This ceremony could only work with some supernatural element involved; drinking water with dust and ink doesn't normally cause internal disease in only those guilty of adultery. However, the mental stress of knowing your guilt and openly proclaiming the rightness of judgment upon yourself cannot be good for one's health.

iv. At the very least, because this was a public ceremony, it made the entire community aware of the evil of adultery – and the seriousness of trying to hide your sin. The existence of the ceremony itself was an incentive to faithfulness in marriage, and therefore it was good for the entire nation.

v. Surely, both the holiness of God and the perfection of His word testify against us. We should be forced to drink a bitter cup that would destroy us – but Jesus drank it for us.

4. (29-31) Conclusion to the law of jealousy.

This *is* the law of jealousy, when a wife, *while* under her husband's *authority*, goes astray and defiles herself, or when the spirit of jealousy comes upon a man, and he becomes jealous of his wife; then he shall

stand the woman before the LORD, and the priest shall execute all this law upon her. Then the man shall be free from iniquity, but that woman shall bear her guilt.

a. **This is the law of jealousy**: This was a ceremony meant to bring resolution. Either the husband was right or wrong in his jealousy; if his wife had in fact been adulterous, he was right – if she had not been, he was wrong. The issue had to be settled, and this was the way given by God to ancient Israel to settle it.

i. "The very fact of these instructions shows how important it is, in the mind of God, that, in the interest of true national strength, family life should be maintained at its strongest and purest." (Morgan)

b. **The priest shall execute all this law**: The effect of this law was to promote faithfulness in marriage and to set marriages free from the dark cloud of suspicion.

Numbers 6 – The Vow of a Nazirite

A. The vow of a Nazirite.

1. (1-2) The purpose for the vow of a Nazirite.

Then the LORD spoke to Moses, saying, "Speak to the children of Israel, and say to them: 'When either a man or woman consecrates an offering to take the vow of a Nazirite, to separate himself to the LORD,'"

    a. **To separate himself to the LORD**: The vow of the Nazirite was to express one's special desire to draw close to God and to separate oneself from the comforts and pleasures of this world. This vow could be taken by a **man or woman** in Israel.

        i. **Consecrates an offering**: According to Allen and Cole, the Hebrew word here translated **consecrates** has the idea of something exceptional, wonderful, or miraculous.

- This was a special vow, significantly beyond a normal promise or vow.
- This was a comprehensive vow, concerning what one ate, how one looked, and with whom one associated.

        ii. "The English word *Nazirite* transliterates Hebrew *nazir*, meaning "set apart." (Wenham)

        iii. "The word Nazirite is sometimes confused with Nazarene, the word used to describe Jesus in terms of his hometown origin (see Matt 2:23; Mark 14:67; 16:6; Acts 24:5). While these words are based on the same root (*nazar*, 'to vow'), they are distinctive words." (Allen)

    b. **To take the vow of a Nazirite**: There were several remarkable Nazirites in the Bible: Samson (Judges 13:5), John the Baptist (Luke 1:15), and Paul (Acts 18:18). The mother of Samson (Manoah's wife) took the vow of a Nazirite during her pregnancy (Judges 13:4).

i. The things prohibited for the Nazirite took some of the things forbidden for the priests and made the prohibitions stronger. Priests were not allowed to drink while serving as priests (Leviticus 10:9); Nazirites were never allowed to drink. Priests could mourn the death of their closest relatives according to custom (Leviticus 21:1-6), Nazirites could not.

ii. In a significant way, the Nazirite vow gave every Israelite the opportunity to make a priest-like vow and live in a priest-like consecration to God, at least for a time. The priesthood was restrictive. Only men of a certain age from a very particular family could be priests. The consecration of a Nazirite vow was open to all, including women.

iii. "Throughout the biblical period the discipline of Nazirite vows was highly respected. Samson, Samuel and contemporaries of Amos (Amos 2:11f.) took the vow. Josephus mentions that these vows were popular in the first century AD." (Wenham)

iv. Adam Clarke supposes that the vow of a Nazirite was never taken for less than a year. Less than that period would not allow enough hair to grow out to burn on the fire of the altar (as in Numbers 6:18).

v. "There was absolutely nothing monastic in this order. These men did not separate themselves from the ordinary life of their fellows, yet they did maintain an attitude of special separation, the signs of which were arranged for." (Morgan)

2. (3-8) Requirements for fulfilling the vow of a Nazirite.

He shall separate himself from wine and *similar* drink; he shall drink neither vinegar made from wine nor vinegar made from *similar* drink; neither shall he drink any grape juice, nor eat fresh grapes or raisins. All the days of his separation he shall eat nothing that is produced by the grapevine, from seed to skin. All the days of the vow of his separation no razor shall come upon his head; until the days are fulfilled for which he separated himself to the LORD, he shall be holy. *Then* he shall let the locks of the hair of his head grow. All the days that he separates himself to the LORD he shall not go near a dead body. He shall not make himself unclean even for his father or his mother, for his brother or his sister, when they die, because his separation to God *is* on his head. All the days of his separation he shall be holy to the LORD.

a. **He shall separate himself from wine and similar drink**: The Nazirite was forbidden to eat or drink anything from the grape vine (**from seed to skin**). This was a form of self-denial connected with the idea of a special consecration to God. Generally speaking, wine and grape products were thought to be a blessing (Proverbs 3:10), things to be gratefully received from God (Psalms 104:15).

i. **From wine and similar drink** would include all intoxicating drinks – such as beer or distilled spirits. The Nazirite was to keep his distance from everything intoxicating or related to the grapevine.

b. **No razor shall come upon his head**: During the time of a Nazirite vow, the hair was allowed to grow, and then it was cut at the conclusion of the vow. This was a way of outwardly demonstrating to the world that this man or woman was under a special vow.

i. Regarding the hair of a Nazirite, Cole remarks concerning the word *nazir*: "The word is also used of 'untended' vines during the time of the sabbatical year (Leviticus 25:5, 11). Presumably these vines are termed *nazir* because they were not tended or trimmed, just as the Nazirite was not to trim his or her hair during the period of special vow. Thus a *nazir* was a person who was specially consecrated to the Lord and who was marked out as distinct by his or her unusual manner of hairstyle."

ii. Women could take the Nazirite vow, and they did not normally cut their hair in ancient Jewish culture. Their Nazirite vow was probably expressed in not caring for their hair, letting it hang loose and keeping it relatively unkempt.

iii. In the case of Samson, his strength came from his Nazirite vow of consecration and separation to God – so when Delilah cut his hair (the most public, visible example of the vow), his strength was lost.

iv. Samson had broken the vow before – both at drinking parties (Judges 14:10), and by touching a dead carcass (Judges 14:8-9). But until Delilah cut his hair, he had not broken the Nazirite vow in the most obviously public way. This illustrates the principle that there is a sense in which public sins *do* matter more because they bring more disgrace to the name of God and His people.

c. **He shall not go near a dead body**: The third aspect of the Nazirite vow was the strict avoidance of **a dead body**. Dead bodies – even those of a close relative – were not to be approached during the period of a Nazirite vow. Separation from death – the most obvious and terrible consequence of sin – was essential during the period of the vow.

i. **Father...mother...brother...sister**: These words were a serious caution to the potential Nazirite. Even if their **father** or **mother** died during the days of their vow, they could not mourn for them as normal. Even a priest was allowed to care for the dead body of a close relative (Leviticus 21:1-3), but this was not allowed for the Nazirite.

ii. "Jesus alludes to this aspect of the dedication of his disciples when he admonished them to 'Follow me, and let the dead bury their own dead' (Matt 8:21–22)." (Cole)

iii. "Some contend strongly that the Nazarite was a type of our Lord; but neither analogy nor proof can be produced. Our blessed Lord both drank wine and touched the dead, which no Nazarite would do." (Clarke)

d. **All the days of his separation he shall be holy to the LORD**: It is interesting that there were no other moral requirements, such as abstinence from sexual relations in marriage.

i. "There was to be no monastic association of Nazirites, no formal watch kept over their conduct. They mingled with others in ordinary life, and went about their business as at other times. But the unshorn hair distinguished them; they felt that the eye of God as well as the eyes of men were upon them, and walked warily under the sense of their pledge." (Watson)

3. (9-12) Consequences of breaking the vow.

And if anyone dies very suddenly beside him, and he defiles his consecrated head, then he shall shave his head on the day of his cleansing; on the seventh day he shall shave it. Then on the eighth day he shall bring two turtledoves or two young pigeons to the priest, to the door of the tabernacle of meeting; and the priest shall offer one as a sin offering and *the* other as a burnt offering, and make atonement for him, because he sinned in regard to the corpse; and he shall sanctify his head that same day. He shall consecrate to the LORD the days of his separation, and bring a male lamb in its first year as a trespass offering; but the former days shall be lost, because his separation was defiled.

a. **If anyone dies very suddenly beside him**: If one's vow was broken (perhaps by someone dropping dead next to the Nazirite), then the Nazirite's hair was to be shaved off, sacrifice made, and the vow would begin all over again.

b. **But the former days shall be lost, because his separation was defiled**: The sacrifices required for even the accidental breaking of the Nazirite vow were a **sin offering** and a **burnt offering**. God required a sacrifice of atonement, a sacrifice of rededication, and the wiping away of the **former days** of the vow.

i. "The Mishna relates how Queen Helena had almost completed seven years of a Nazirite vow when she was defiled and therefore had to keep it for another seven years." (Wenham)

B. Concluding the vow of a Nazirite.

1. (13-15) Items needed for sacrifice.

Now this *is* the law of the Nazirite: When the days of his separation are fulfilled, he shall be brought to the door of the tabernacle of meeting. And he shall present his offering to the LORD: one male lamb in its first year without blemish as a burnt offering, one ewe lamb in its first year without blemish as a sin offering, one ram without blemish as a peace offering, a basket of unleavened bread, cakes of fine flour mixed with oil, unleavened wafers anointed with oil, and their grain offering with their drink offerings.

a. **He shall be brought to the door of the tabernacle of meeting**: The vow of a Nazirite ended with a public ceremony, with extensive sacrifice: **One male lamb...one ewe lamb...one ram...a basket of unleavened bread... drink offerings**.

i. "The offerings of the Nazirite at the completion of the period of the vow (v.13) were extensive, expensive, and expressive of the spirit of total commitment to Yahweh during this period of special devotion." (Allen)

b. **He shall present his offering to the LORD**: The normal fulfillment of the vow would require the sacrifice of three animals and more. This was an expensive vow to fulfill. The Nazirite vow was not something that could be entered into lightly.

i. When Paul visited Jerusalem, he was invited to pay the expenses of some Christians who had taken a Nazirite vow and were ready to conclude it with this ceremony (Acts 21:23-24).

2. (16-21) The sacrifice offered.

Then the priest shall bring *them* before the LORD and offer his sin offering and his burnt offering; and he shall offer the ram as a sacrifice of peace offering to the LORD, with the basket of unleavened bread; the priest shall also offer its grain offering and its drink offering. Then the Nazirite shall shave his consecrated head *at* the door of the tabernacle of meeting, and shall take the hair from his consecrated head and put *it* on the fire which is under the sacrifice of the peace offering. And the priest shall take the boiled shoulder of the ram, one unleavened cake from the basket, and one unleavened wafer, and put *them* upon the

hands of the Nazirite after he has shaved his consecrated *hair*, and the priest shall wave them as a wave offering before the LORD; they *are* holy for the priest, together with the breast of the wave offering and the thigh of the heave offering. After that the Nazirite may drink wine. "This is the law of the Nazirite who vows to the LORD the offering for his separation, and besides that, whatever else his hand is able to provide; according to the vow which he takes, so he must do according to the law of his separation."

a. **Then the priest shall bring them before the LORD**: In the first part of the ceremony for the conclusion of a Nazirite vow, the priest offered the required animals and the grain offering.

b. **Shall take the hair from his consecrated head and put it on the fire**: After the priest made the sacrifice, the Nazirite's head was shaved, and the hair put in the fire of the altar.

c. **Put them upon the hands of the Nazirite...the priest shall wave them as a wave offering before the LORD**: It may be that they waved these pieces before the LORD together, or perhaps the priest took the pieces back from the Nazirite. Either way, there was the active participation of the Nazirite in this ceremony.

d. **After that the Nazirite may drink wine**: This was the official conclusion of the vow. This was presumably part of a fellowship meal with the portions of meat from the sacrifice allowed to the one who concluded the vow.

C. The priestly blessing.

1. (22-23) The command to bless the people.

And the LORD spoke to Moses, saying: "Speak to Aaron and his sons, saying, 'This is the way you shall bless the children of Israel. Say to them:'"

a. **This is the way you shall bless**: Moses, Aaron, and their spiritual descendants were commanded to **bless** the people of God. They were to do it according to the procedure detailed in the following verses.

i. "The priests were always there pronouncing this blessing at the close of the daily morning service in the temple and later in the synagogues." (Wenham)

ii. It is important that the priestly blessing follows the section on the vow of the Nazirite. Whenever there is some special act to demonstrate consecration or separation to God, we easily think that these specially separated people are the ones – perhaps the only ones – whom God wants to bless or will bless. We need to be reminded that though there is great value in special acts of consecration, we can't think of God's blessing as something that is earned by those special acts. God loves to bless His people, and blesses them far more freely than they usually imagine.

iii. "So Christ did upon his apostles, which was his last action upon earth, (Luke 24:50) and so must all pastors do that would do good on it, pray down a blessing on their people." (Trapp)

b. **Say to them:** The Bible does not present many written prayers that were meant to be repeated. Another example would be what is often called "The Lord's Prayer" in Matthew 6:9-13 (perhaps better titled "The Disciple's Prayer").

i. "Free prayer is most useful, and it will ordinarily consort best with the movements of the free Spirit; but in the case of a benediction, it is well that it was dictated to the man of God. The children of Israel might miss blessing through the ignorance, or forgetfulness, or unbelief of Aaron; and therefore it was not left to him; but he had to learn by heart each word and sentence. In this wise, and in no other, was he to bless the people. I like this; for if God himself puts the very words into the mouth of his priest, then they are God's words." (Spurgeon)

ii. "That this blessing was important in the lives of ancient Israelites is attested in the copy of it found in the excavations of Ketef Hinnom to the southwest of Mount Zion and the Old City of Jerusalem. In digging within the compound of the Scottish St. Andrew's Church on the western slope of the Hinnom Valley in 1979, the expedition led by archaeologist G. Barkai unearthed a late seventh to sixth century B.C. burial complex. Among the remains recovered was a phylactery containing two silver scrolls the size of a small cigarette, upon which were written two versions of the priestly blessing. These had been used as amulets during the lives of the individuals interred there or as burial pendants. The text on the larger one is nearly identical to that of the Masoretic text, and an abbreviated version of the second and third blessings was written on the smaller. As such they attest the authenticity and antiquity of the Priestly Benediction. These texts also contain the oldest attestation to the Tetragrammaton found to date in Jerusalem." (Cole)

2. (24-26) The Aaronic blessing.

"The Lord bless you and keep you;
The Lord make His face shine upon you,
And be gracious to you;

The LORD lift up His countenance upon you,
And give you peace."

a. **The LORD bless you**: This simple desire begins everything. God loves to **bless** His people, and He wants leaders who long for the people to be blessed. This also recognizes that all blessing really comes from God; and without His blessing, nothing really works right.

i. We remember also that God's blessing has always in mind our greatest and highest good. We often expect God's blessing to mean a life of comfort and ease – but that certainly isn't for our greatest and highest good. God knows how we need to be blessed, even if we don't.

ii. We have often settled for *happiness* or *comfort* or *wealth* when God wanted us to be *blessed*. True *blessing* from God is higher than happiness or wealth or comfort.

b. **And keep you**: To be kept by the LORD is blessing indeed. Some are *kept* by their own sin and desire, some are *kept* by idolatry and greed, and others are *kept* by their own bitterness and anger. But to be kept by the LORD ensures life, peace, and success.

c. **The LORD make His face shine upon you**: To have the glorious, pleased face of God shining upon a man is the greatest gift he could have. To know that as God looks upon you, He is well pleased – not because of who you are, or what you have done, but because you are in Jesus Christ – there is no greater source of peace and power in life.

i. We can imagine a father disciplining his son and putting the son out of his presence – and then receiving the son back to see his loving face again. This is how God receives sinners who come to Jesus by faith.

ii. "Why should he fret when God smiles? What matters though all the world should censure, if Jehovah countenances his servant. A look of approval from God creates a deep, delightful calm within the soul." (Spurgeon)

d. **And be gracious to you**: The idea is that God would show tender mercy and care for His people.

e. **The LORD lift up His countenance upon you**: The priest was to pray that God would look upon His people; when He blesses, keeps, shines, and is gracious towards His people. Any look that God directs toward His people is filled with nothing but blessing. His loving attention is on the believer.

i. To **lift up** one's eyes or face means to pay attention, and to look favorably towards. "When God smiles on his people, they can be sure that he will *be gracious* to them, that is, he will deliver them from all their troubles. He will answer their prayers and save them from their enemies." (Wenham)

f. **And give you peace**: The Hebrew word is *shalom*, which is more than the end of aggression. This **peace**, this *shalom* is God's word for wholeness and goodness and total satisfaction in life. This is the abundant life Jesus promised (John 10:10).

g. **The LORD...the LORD...the LORD**: The repetition of LORD three times does not prove the Trinity, but it illustrates it.

- *God the Father* blesses and keeps His children.
- *God the Son* makes God's face to shine on us and brings us grace.
- *God the Holy Spirit* communicates God's attention to us, and gives us peace.

    i. "The thrice-mentioned YHWH, which grammatically need not be repeated, and the final resounding "I will [surely] bless you," serve to heighten the emphasis that the God of Israel is the source of all grace, blessing, hope, and peace." (Cole)

    ii. "I will not say that this teaches the doctrine of the Trinity; but I must say that, believing the doctrine of the Trinity, I understand the passage all the better. The shadow of the Triune God is on the sacred benediction in the name thrice repeated." (Spurgeon)

h. **You...you...you...you...you...you**: It is repeated six times for emphasis – God wants to bless **you**. We often feel as if God really wants to bless someone *else*. He wants to bless *us*.

    i. "So long as you are resting upon Christ—Jesus, the great High Priest, speaks from the eternal glory, and he says, 'The Lord bless thee.' 'Oh! but I do not deserve it.' Just so; but 'the Lord Bless thee.' 'I am so unworthy, I am so backsliding.' Yes, but the Lord Jesus Christ knows all, covers all. We will read it, then: 'The Lord Bless *thee—thee,* and keep *thee:* the Lord make his face to shine upon *thee,* and be gracious unto *thee:* the Lord lift up his countenance upon *thee,* and give *thee* peace.' Oh! have you got that wrought into your very hearts?" (Spurgeon)

    ii. As God bestows His blessing on us, we must receive it by faith. We must be like Jacob – who would not let go of God until God blessed him.

    iii. "The prayer is cast in poetic form and is probably one of the oldest poems in Scripture." (Wenham)

3. (27) The fruit of the blessing.

So they shall put My name on the children of Israel, and I will bless them.

a. **So they shall put My name on the children of Israel**: To be blessed by God is to have His **name on** you – to be identified with who He is and all His nature. This was a great gift, to have God's name upon them.

i. Aaron was commanded to pronounce this blessing over the people of Israel – not over the other nations. Though God blesses all mankind, there is a definite and strong sense in which He has blessing *only* for His people. We have to join ourselves to Him to gain that blessing.

b. **And I will bless them**: God *promised* to bless according to these words. This makes these words appropriate for pastors to pronounce over their congregations. More importantly, every believer should remember that we have a High Priest in heaven – Jesus Christ – who lives forever to pray for us and to bless us.

i. "When God saith, 'I will,' all the devils in hell cannot turn aside the blessing, and all the ages of eternity cannot change the King's word." (Spurgeon)

ii. "The Lord has blessed his people, and he would have them know it. He has blessed them with all spiritual blessings in heavenly places in Christ Jesus, and it is his wish that they should experience the fullness of this blessedness. Are any of the Lord's people without a sense of this blessing? It is not the will of God that you should continue in this low condition." (Spurgeon)

Numbers 7 – The Gifts of the Twelve Tribes

A. The giving of the first gifts.

1. (1-3) Six carts and twelve oxen offered at the conclusion of the building of the tabernacle.

Now it came to pass, when Moses had finished setting up the tabernacle, that he anointed it and consecrated it and all its furnishings, and the altar and all its utensils; so he anointed them and consecrated them. Then the leaders of Israel, the heads of their fathers' houses, who *were* the leaders of the tribes and over those who were numbered, made an offering. And they brought their offering before the Lord, six covered carts and twelve oxen, a cart for *every* two of the leaders, and for each one an ox; and they presented them before the tabernacle.

a. **When Moses had finished setting up the tabernacle**: The material in Exodus, Leviticus, and Numbers regarding Israel in the wilderness is presented more according to theme than according to strict chronology. The tribal donations to the tabernacle took place after Exodus 40, and during the period of the priest's ordination described in Leviticus 8 and 9. These 12 days began when the tabernacle was completed.

i. "The transactions mentioned in this chapter took place on the *second day* of the *second month* of the *second year* after their departure from Egypt; and the proper place of this account is immediately after the *tenth* chapter of *Leviticus*." (Clarke)

b. **And they brought their offering before the Lord**: The leaders of each tribe bring a total of six carts (**a cart for every two of the leaders**) and twelve oxen (**each one an ox**), given to transport the tabernacle through the wilderness.

c. **Six covered carts and twelve oxen**: At this time, such carts were a great luxury – and no doubt, a significant offering from the tribes.

i. "The Hebrew word for 'cart' (*agalah*) is modified by the noun *sab* ('litter'), used only here and in Isaiah 66:20. This phrase has traditionally been understood to describe a covered wagon, though the precise meaning of the wording is debated. Covered wagons would certainly be appropriate for transporting the sacred items." (Allen)

2. (4-9) The distribution of the carts and oxen.

Then the LORD spoke to Moses, saying, "Accept *these* from them, that they may be used in doing the work of the tabernacle of meeting; and you shall give them to the Levites, *to* every man according to his service." So Moses took the carts and the oxen, and gave them to the Levites. Two carts and four oxen he gave to the sons of Gershon, according to their service; and four carts and eight oxen he gave to the sons of Merari, according to their service, under the authority of Ithamar the son of Aaron the priest. But to the sons of Kohath he gave none, because theirs *was* the service of the holy things, *which* they carried on their shoulders.

a. **Two carts and four oxen he gave to the sons of Gershon**: The family of Gershon received two carts with their four oxen; they had the responsibility of transporting the fabrics of the tabernacle (Numbers 4:25-26).

b. **Four carts and eight oxen he gave to the sons of Merari**: The family of Merari received four carts with their eight oxen; they had the job of transporting the boards and pillars of the tabernacle (Numbers 4:31-32).

i. "Double the number of what the Gershonites had, because their carriage was heavier; God proportions the burden to the back." (Trapp)

c. **But to the sons of Kohath he gave none**: The family of Kohath received no carts and no oxen; they were to carry the holy furniture of the tabernacle (Numbers 4:15) and were to carry all things on their shoulders – so, to remove any temptation to disobey, Moses gave them no carts.

B. The second giving of gifts.

1. (10-11) Twelve leaders of the twelve tribes to bring dedication gifts to the tabernacle, one on each day for twelve days.

Now the leaders offered the dedication *offering* for the altar when it was anointed; so the leaders offered their offering before the altar. For the LORD said to Moses, "They shall offer their offering, one leader each day, for the dedication of the altar."

a. **The leaders offered the dedication offering**: What follows are identical descriptions of each tribe offering specific items for the use of the tabernacle. They each offered a silver platter and a silver bowl (each holding a grain offering), and a gold pan holding incense. Along with these they were also to present one bull, ram, and a lamb as a burnt offering; a goat as a sin offering; along with two oxen and five rams, goats, and lambs as a peace offering.

> i. "*Peace-offerings* are more numerous, because the princes and priests, and some of the people, did make a feast before the Lord out of them, and celebrated it with great rejoicing." (Poole)

b. **For the altar when it was anointed**: This puts the presentation of the tribal gifts at the same time when the priests were consecrated in Leviticus 8-9.

> i. "The altar was the focal point of daily worship, and it was therefore appropriate that when it was dedicated a representative from every tribe should offer all the regular sacrifices. It set a precedent and demonstrated that the worship was for every tribe and supported by every tribe." (Wenham)

c. **One leader each day**: These identical offerings were offered over twelve days, with one day set aside for one of the tribes. To us, this may seem like meaningless repetition in this longest of all the chapters in Numbers. Nevertheless, God had several important reasons for this.

- To show that each tribe pledged their allegiance to Yahweh; that they each supported the work of the tabernacle, the priesthood, and the system of sacrifice commanded by God and carried out by the priests.

- To show the importance of each individual tribe, giving each tribe its own day of celebration and attention. These tribes were all related, but different – and each of them was important to God and should be regarded as important among Israel as a whole. Each tribe would receive attention, like each graduate at a commencement ceremony.

- To show the importance of each individual gift, giving full attention to every tribe's gift. Every gift mattered.

- To show that God wanted to be approached with some degree of organization and order. The tribes came in a specific order, the same order that they were organized in for their march through the wilderness.

- To show that at God's altar, every tribe came as an equal. No tribe was better than the others at the altar for atonement, dedication to God, and fellowship with the LORD.

> i. "While all the story might have been told in a very few sentences, it is set forth with elaborate attention to detail. Every man is named and every gift is recorded. Thus, while the whole reveals unity of purpose

and of equality of giving, in the divine recognition there is a remarkable attention to individual devotion." (Morgan)

ii. The repetition of these offerings over twelve days gave a sense of ritual and ceremony to the participation of the tribes at the tabernacle. Ceremony and ritual have some place among the people of God. Different parts of the broader Christian family may debate the degree of emphasis on the role of ceremony and ritual, but it is undeniable that there is *some* place for ritual and ceremony in the gatherings of God's people.

2. (12-88) The giving of the dedication offerings over twelve days.

And the one who offered his offering on the first day *was* Nahshon the son of Amminadab, from the tribe of Judah. His offering *was* one silver platter, the weight of which *was* one hundred and thirty *shekels*, and one silver bowl of seventy shekels, according to the shekel of the sanctuary, both of them full of fine flour mixed with oil as a grain offering; one gold pan of ten *shekels*, full of incense; one young bull, one ram, and one male lamb in its first year, as a burnt offering; one kid of the goats as a sin offering; and for the sacrifice of peace offerings: two oxen, five rams, five male goats, and five male lambs in their first year. This *was* the offering of Nahshon the son of Amminadab.

On the second day Nethanel the son of Zuar, leader of Issachar, presented *an offering*. For his offering he offered one silver platter, the weight of which *was* one hundred and thirty *shekels*, and one silver bowl of seventy shekels, according to the shekel of the sanctuary, both of them full of fine flour mixed with oil as a grain offering; one gold pan of ten *shekels*, full of incense; one young bull, one ram, and one male lamb in its first year, as a burnt offering; one kid of the goats as a sin offering; and as the sacrifice of peace offerings: two oxen, five rams, five male goats, and five male lambs in their first year. This *was* the offering of Nethanel the son of Zuar.

On the third day Eliab the son of Helon, leader of the children of Zebulun, *presented an offering*. His offering *was* one silver platter, the weight of which *was* one hundred and thirty *shekels*, and one silver bowl of seventy shekels, according to the shekel of the sanctuary, both of them full of fine flour mixed with oil as a grain offering; one gold pan of ten *shekels*, full of incense; one young bull, one ram, and one male lamb in its first year, as a burnt offering; one kid of the goats as a sin offering; and for the sacrifice of peace offerings: two oxen, five rams, five male goats, and five male lambs in their first year. This *was* the offering of Eliab the son of Helon.

On the fourth day Elizur the son of Shedeur, leader of the children of Reuben, *presented an offering*. His offering *was* one silver platter, the weight of which *was* one hundred and thirty *shekels,* and one silver bowl of seventy shekels, according to the shekel of the sanctuary, both of them full of fine flour mixed with oil as a grain offering; one gold pan of ten *shekels,* full of incense; one young bull, one ram, and one male lamb in its first year, as a burnt offering; one kid of the goats as a sin offering; and as the sacrifice of peace offerings: two oxen, five rams, five male goats, and five male lambs in their first year. This *was* the offering of Elizur the son of Shedeur.

On the fifth day Shelumiel the son of Zurishaddai, leader of the children of Simeon, *presented an offering*. His offering *was* one silver platter, the weight of which *was* one hundred and thirty *shekels,* and one silver bowl of seventy shekels, according to the shekel of the sanctuary, both of them full of fine flour mixed with oil as a grain offering; one gold pan of ten *shekels,* full of incense; one young bull, one ram, and one male lamb in its first year, as a burnt offering; one kid of the goats as a sin offering; and as the sacrifice of peace offerings: two oxen, five rams, five male goats, and five male lambs in their first year. This *was* the offering of Shelumiel the son of Zurishaddai.

On the sixth day Eliasaph the son of Deuel, leader of the children of Gad, *presented an offering*. His offering *was* one silver platter, the weight of which *was* one hundred and thirty *shekels,* and one silver bowl of seventy shekels, according to the shekel of the sanctuary, both of them full of fine flour mixed with oil as a grain offering; one gold pan of ten *shekels,* full of incense; one young bull, one ram, and one male lamb in its first year, as a burnt offering; one kid of the goats as a sin offering; and as the sacrifice of peace offerings: two oxen, five rams, five male goats, and five male lambs in their first year. This *was* the offering of Eliasaph the son of Deuel.

On the seventh day Elishama the son of Ammihud, leader of the children of Ephraim, *presented an offering*. His offering *was* one silver platter, the weight of which *was* one hundred and thirty *shekels,* and one silver bowl of seventy shekels, according to the shekel of the sanctuary, both of them full of fine flour mixed with oil as a grain offering; one gold pan of ten *shekels,* full of incense; one young bull, one ram, and one male lamb in its first year, as a burnt offering; one kid of the goats as a sin offering; and as the sacrifice of peace offerings: two oxen, five rams, five male goats, and five male lambs in their first year. This *was* the offering of Elishama the son of Ammihud.

On the eighth day Gamaliel the son of Pedahzur, leader of the children of Manasseh, *presented an offering.* His offering *was* one silver platter, the weight of which *was* one hundred and thirty *shekels,* and one silver bowl of seventy shekels, according to the shekel of the sanctuary, both of them full of fine flour mixed with oil as a grain offering; one gold pan of ten *shekels,* full of incense; one young bull, one ram, and one male lamb in its first year, as a burnt offering; one kid of the goats as a sin offering; and as the sacrifice of peace offerings: two oxen, five rams, five male goats, and five male lambs in their first year. This *was* the offering of Gamaliel the son of Pedahzur.

On the ninth day Abidan the son of Gideoni, leader of the children of Benjamin, *presented an offering.* His offering *was* one silver platter, the weight of which *was* one hundred and thirty *shekels,* and one silver bowl of seventy shekels, according to the shekel of the sanctuary, both of them full of fine flour mixed with oil as a grain offering; one gold pan of ten *shekels,* full of incense; one young bull, one ram, and one male lamb in its first year, as a burnt offering; one kid of the goats as a sin offering; and as the sacrifice of peace offerings: two oxen, five rams, five male goats, and five male lambs in their first year. This *was* the offering of Abidan the son of Gideoni.

On the tenth day Ahiezer the son of Ammishaddai, leader of the children of Dan, *presented an offering.* His offering *was* one silver platter, the weight of which *was* one hundred and thirty *shekels,* and one silver bowl of seventy shekels, according to the shekel of the sanctuary, both of them full of fine flour mixed with oil as a grain offering; one gold pan of ten *shekels,* full of incense; one young bull, one ram, and one male lamb in its first year, as a burnt offering; one kid of the goats as a sin offering; and as the sacrifice of peace offerings: two oxen, five rams, five male goats, and five male lambs in their first year. This *was* the offering of Ahiezer the son of Ammishaddai.

On the eleventh day Pagiel the son of Ocran, leader of the children of Asher, *presented an offering.* His offering *was* one silver platter, the weight of which *was* one hundred and thirty *shekels,* and one silver bowl of seventy shekels, according to the shekel of the sanctuary, both of them full of fine flour mixed with oil as a grain offering; one gold pan of ten *shekels,* full of incense; one young bull, one ram, and one male lamb in its first year, as a burnt offering; one kid of the goats as a sin offering; and as the sacrifice of peace offerings: two oxen, five rams, five male goats, and five male lambs in their first year. This *was* the offering of Pagiel the son of Ocran.

On the twelfth day Ahira the son of Enan, leader of the children of Naphtali, *presented an offering.* His offering *was* one silver platter, the weight of which *was* one hundred and thirty *shekels,* and one silver bowl of seventy shekels, according to the shekel of the sanctuary, both of them full of fine flour mixed with oil as a grain offering; one gold pan of ten *shekels,* full of incense; one young bull, one ram, and one male lamb in its first year, as a burnt offering; one kid of the goats as a sin offering; and as the sacrifice of peace offerings: two oxen, five rams, five male goats, and five male lambs in their first year. This *was* the offering of Ahira the son of Enan.

This *was* the dedication *offering* for the altar from the leaders of Israel, when it was anointed: twelve silver platters, twelve silver bowls, and twelve gold pans. Each silver platter *weighed* one hundred and thirty *shekels* and each bowl seventy *shekels.* All the silver of the vessels *weighed* two thousand four hundred *shekels,* according to the shekel of the sanctuary. The twelve gold pans full of incense *weighed* ten *shekels* apiece, according to the shekel of the sanctuary; all the gold of the pans *weighed* one hundred and twenty *shekels.* All the oxen for the burnt offering *were* twelve young bulls, the rams twelve, the male lambs in their first year twelve, with their grain offering, and the kids of the goats as a sin offering twelve. And all the oxen for the sacrifice of peace offerings were twenty-four bulls, the rams sixty, the male goats sixty, and the lambs in their first year sixty. This *was* the dedication *offering* for the altar after it was anointed.

a. **His offering was one silver platter**: Each leader brought a silver platter and a silver bowl, each full of fine flour mixed with oil as a grain offering; a gold pan with incense, a bull, a ram, a male lamb, a young goat, two oxen, five rams, five adult goats, and five more lambs.

i. Each silver plate weighed about three pounds, each silver bowl about two pounds, and a gold shovel about four ounces. "The term *shekel* was used throughout the Levant and Mesopotamia as a standard weight measure, generally ranging from ten to thirteen grams." (Cole)

ii. Clearly, they were *generous* in their giving. God must show Promised Land people how to be givers – one of the best measures of one who has moved from a slave mind-set to a Promised Land mind-set. The slave by nature is a taker because he is often unsure of provision. People suited to God's Promised Land are generous because they trust in a God who has promised to meet all their needs.

b. **His offering was one silver platter**: Each tribal leader brought exactly the same offering over the twelve days.

i. Clearly, they were *humble* in their giving. By requiring the same gift from every tribe, God made sure that no tribe or tribal leader glorified himself through his giving. We must resist the tendency to give with the motive of being seen by others. People suited to God's Promised Land care about God's glory, not their own.

ii. "In each case the giving was equal, thus precluding the possibility of any spirit of rivalry and realizing unity of purpose." (Morgan)

c. **This was the dedication offering for the altar from the leaders of Israel**: Each offering was recorded in the same way – seemingly, "wasting" space in the Scriptures. God's purpose was to draw attention to each tribe's offering, though they were all the same.

i. Godly giving is always noticed by God, even if it is the same or less than many other gifts. God sees and "records" every gift given in a right heart, even if it is only worth two mites (Mark 12:42-44). God notices every gift given in honor and obedience to Him.

3. (89) Moses meets with God and hears His voice.

Now when Moses went into the tabernacle of meeting to speak with Him, he heard the voice of One speaking to him from above the mercy seat that *was* on the ark of the Testimony, from between the two cherubim; thus He spoke to him.

a. **Moses went into the tabernacle of meeting**: People suited to God's Promised Land need leadership, and they need leaders who hear from God and know His voice.

b. **He heard the voice of One speaking to him**: We rarely read in the Bible of exactly how God spoke to Moses. Here, at the tabernacle, we see that it was in an audible voice, not merely an impression in the mind.

i. "This is perhaps the one instance in which we have a clear statement that in communing with God, Moses did actually hear a voice. The communications which he received were more than subjective impressions; they were objective expressions." (Morgan)

ii. "There is no form or visible manifestation, no angel or being in human likeness, representing God. It is only a Voice that is heard." (Watson)

iii. "Though Moses saw no similitude, but *only heard a voice*, yet he had the fullest proof of the *presence* as well as of the *being* of the Almighty. In this way God chose to manifest himself during that dispensation, till the fulness of the time came, in which the WORD *was made flesh, and* DWELT AMONG US." (Clarke)

Numbers 8 – Lighting of the Lamps, the Levites Cleansed for Service

A. The lighting of the lamps.

1. (1-3) Lamps are placed on the lampstand.

And the Lord spoke to Moses, saying: "Speak to Aaron, and say to him, 'When you arrange the lamps, the seven lamps shall give light in front of the lampstand.'" And Aaron did so; he arranged the lamps to face toward the front of the lampstand, as the Lord commanded Moses.

a. **When you arrange the lamps**: The lampstand was described and made in Exodus 25:31-40, but the lampstand by itself could give no light. It had to have lamps placed upon it that made the light. The purpose of the lampstand was not to make light but to make the light more visible.

i. The lamps burned a specially made olive oil and needed to be continually filled with oil to provide constant light. "A *candlestick* or *lamp* without *oil* is of no use; *oil* not burning is of no use. So a *Church* or *society of religious people* without the *influence* of the *Holy Ghost* are dead while they have a name to live." (Clarke)

ii. Revelation 1:20 presents lampstands as a picture of the church, the new covenant community of God's people. By this illustration, we see the principle that the church itself does not light the world, but it does provide a "platform" for the light of Jesus to be seen.

b. **He arranged the lamps to face toward the front of the lampstand**: The light from the lampstand in the tabernacle was focused to bring the most illumination to the rest of the tent, especially for the table of showbread in front of the lampstand, and the altar of incense to the left of the lampstand.

i. "In this way there would always be *light* on the *bread*; the twin symbols of life would work together to speak of the life-giving mercies of the Lord, whose attention is ever on his people." (Allen)

ii. "Upon that table the light from the golden lampstand ever fell. Thus were typified the great principles of the life of fellowship with God, which have their fulfillment for us in Christ. We have a table of communion, but it is well to remember that upon it the light is ever shining. We only have right to that table as we dwell in that light." (Morgan)

2. (4) Description of the lampstand.

Now this workmanship of the lampstand *was* hammered gold; from its shaft to its flowers it *was* hammered work. According to the pattern which the LORD had shown Moses, so he made the lampstand.

a. **The lampstand was hammered gold**: The lampstand was **hammered** out of pure gold, with no specific dimensions given, but after the pattern of a modern-day menorah. It had one middle shaft with three branches coming out of each side, for a total of seven places for lamps.

i. Many items in the tabernacle were made of wood and covered with gold, such as the ark of the covenant, the altar of incense, and the table of showbread. The lampstand was different, made out of solid gold.

ii. "Not hollow, but solid and massive gold, beaten out of one piece, and not of several pieces joined or soldered together." (Poole)

iii. **Hammered gold**: John Trapp commented on the King James Version translation, *beaten gold*: "To show that ministers must beat their brains to beat out the sense of the Scriptures, as the fowl beats the shell, to get out the fish, with great vehemency."

b. **According to the pattern which the LORD had shown Moses**: This is another statement of the important idea that the tabernacle and its furnishings were built **according** to a **pattern** – the **pattern** revealed to Moses when he met with the LORD on Mount Sinai (Exodus 25:9, 25:40, 26:30).

B. Cleansing and dedication of the Levites.

1. (5-7) Cleansing and sprinkling.

Then the LORD spoke to Moses, saying: "Take the Levites from among the children of Israel and cleanse them *ceremonially*. Thus you shall do to them to cleanse them: Sprinkle water of purification on them, and let them shave all their body, and let them wash their clothes, and *so* make themselves clean.

a. **Take the Levites from among the children of Israel and cleanse them ceremonially**: The record of the dedication of the priests is in Leviticus 8-9. This is the record of the dedication of the Levites. The Levites did not offer sacrifices for atonement, dedication, or fellowship with God (as the priests did), but their service to God was nevertheless valued and important. *Their work of practical service also required dedication and consecration to the* LORD.

i. "The Levites are helpers to the priests, and the language describing their consecration is somewhat distinct from that of the priests. The priests were made holy, the Levites clean; the priests were anointed and washed, the Levites sprinkled; the priests were given new garments, the Levites washed theirs; blood was applied to the priests, it was waved over the Levites." (Allen)

b. **Sprinkle water of purification on them**: This ceremonial cleansing pictured a cleansing of sin and was also part of the priestly consecration (Exodus 29:4). The **water of purification** was the water mixed with the ashes of the red heifer (Numbers 19:1-9).

i. This cleansing with water is also part of the new covenant as described in Ezekiel 36:25: *Then I will sprinkle clean water on you and you shall be clean.*

c. **Let them shave all their body**: The shaving of the Levites as part of their consecration was mainly a symbol of their purification (as the bodies of cleansed lepers were shaved, Leviticus 14:9) and consecration (as Nazirite heads were shaved at the end of their vow, Numbers 6:9, 18). Yet the Levites were also given to God from Israel as their "firstborn" – God received the tribe of Levi instead of each individual firstborn boy from Israel. Newborn babies are relatively free from hair, and this also corresponds with the shaving of the Levites in their dedication to God.

i. "Since Semitic men were characterized generally in the ancient world by wearing beards and by ample bodily hair, shaving these men's bodies must have been regarded as a remarkable act of devotion to God." (Allen)

2. (8-15) The dedication of the Levites through sacrifice.

Then let them take a young bull with its grain offering of fine flour mixed with oil, and you shall take another young bull as a sin offering. And you shall bring the Levites before the tabernacle of meeting, and you shall gather together the whole congregation of the children of Israel. So you shall bring the Levites before the LORD, and the children of Israel shall lay their hands on the Levites; and Aaron shall offer the

Levites before the LORD, *like* a wave offering from the children of Israel, that they may perform the work of the LORD. Then the Levites shall lay their hands on the heads of the young bulls, and you shall offer one as a sin offering and the other as a burnt offering to the LORD, to make atonement for the Levites.

"And you shall stand the Levites before Aaron and his sons, and then offer them *like* a wave offering to the LORD. Thus you shall separate the Levites from among the children of Israel, and the Levites shall be Mine. After that the Levites shall go in to service the tabernacle of meeting. So you shall cleanse them and offer them, *like* a wave offering.

a. **Then let them take a young bull with its grain offering**: As a bull was sacrificed, representatives from **the whole congregation** of Israel laid their hands on the Levites, to bless them and pray for their dedication before the LORD. It would be clear to both the Levites and the nation that the Levites were servants of both the LORD and the nation.

b. **Like a wave offering from the children of Israel**: A normal **wave offering** presented something to God (such as a portion of meat or bread) with a motion that communicated the idea "This is Yours, LORD." In this consecration of the Levites, the **children of Israel** came before God and essentially said, "These Levites belong to You, LORD."

i. "In the case of the Levites, we may suspect that Aaron and his sons would place hands on their shoulders and then cause them to move from side to side in a symbolic way to represent the fact that they were a living sacrifice presented before the Lord and that they now belonged to the priests to assist them in their work of service in the tabernacle." (Allen)

3. (16-19) The Levites are regarded as Israel's firstborn given to God.

For they *are* wholly given to Me from among the children of Israel; I have taken them for Myself instead of all who open the womb, the firstborn of all the children of Israel. For all the firstborn among the children of Israel *are* Mine, *both* man and beast; on the day that I struck all the firstborn in the land of Egypt I sanctified them to Myself. I have taken the Levites instead of all the firstborn of the children of Israel. And I have given the Levites as a gift to Aaron and his sons from among the children of Israel, to do the work for the children of Israel in the tabernacle of meeting, and to make atonement for the children of Israel, that there be no plague among the children of Israel when the children of Israel come near the sanctuary."

a. **I have taken them for Myself instead of all who open the womb, the firstborn of all the children of Israel**: This theme was previously stated in Numbers 3:40-51. God's "possession" of the tribe of Levi was an expression of His lordship over all of Israel.

> i. "The Levites belonged to the Lord in exchange for his deliverance of the firstborn sons of Israel at the time of the tenth plague." (Allen)

> ii. "The Levites thereby *make atonement* (Hebrew *kipper*) *for the people of Israel* (19), that is pay the ransom price (*koper*). However, the Old Testament never countenances human sacrifice; so the Levites in their turn lay their hands on two bulls to make atonement for them." (Wenham)

b. **I have given the Levites as a gift to Aaron and his sons**: The Levites were not only set apart for God's glory. They were also set apart for the help and benefit of the priests (**Aaron and his sons**).

> i. **That there be no plague**: "This is added as a reason why God appointed them to serve in or about the tabernacle, that they might watch and guard it, and not suffer any of the people to come near it, or meddle with holy things, which if they did, it would certainly bring a plague upon them." (Poole)

4. (20-22) Doing what God had commanded for the cleansing, dedication, and work of the Levites.

Thus Moses and Aaron and all the congregation of the children of Israel did to the Levites; according to all that the LORD commanded Moses concerning the Levites, so the children of Israel did to them. And the Levites purified themselves and washed their clothes; then Aaron presented them, *like* a wave offering before the LORD, and Aaron made atonement for them to cleanse them. After that the Levites went in to do their work in the tabernacle of meeting before Aaron and his sons; as the LORD commanded Moses concerning the Levites, so they did to them.

a. **According to all that the LORD commanded**: This was simple, wonderful obedience. God told Moses and the children of Israel to perform these dedication rituals for the Levites and they did them, just as God **commanded**.

> i. "The implicit obedience of Moses and the people of Israel to the commands of God in the areas of ritual and regimen leave us quite unprepared for their complaints against his loving character and their outrageous breaches of faith in the rebellions that begin in the narrative of chapter 11." (Allen)

b. **After that the Levites went in to do their work**: After the dedication ceremony at the tabernacle, the real work of the Levites had to begin. The work of the Levites was not focused on ceremonies (though these ceremonies had their place).

5. (23-26) The time of service for Levites.

Then the LORD spoke to Moses, saying, "This *is* what *pertains* to the Levites: From twenty-five years old and above one may enter to perform service in the work of the tabernacle of meeting; and at the age of fifty years they must cease performing this work, and shall work no more. They may minister with their brethren in the tabernacle of meeting, to attend to needs, but they *themselves* shall do no work. Thus you shall do to the Levites regarding their duties."

a. **From twenty-five years old and above**: A Levite's time of active service was to begin at age thirty and last until fifty according to Numbers 4:3, 4:23, and 4:30. Yet their formal training began at age twenty-five, with a five-year apprenticeship.

b. **At the age of fifty years they must cease performing this work**: Since much of the work of the Levites involved hard, physical labor, it was from this work that **they must cease** when they turned fifty, allowing the younger men to bear the burden. There were other things that they could continue to do after fifty (**minister with their brethren in the tabernacle**).

i. "They would no longer dismantle and transport the tabernacle and its furnishing, but they could continue to serve as guards, insuring the sanctity of the holy place." (Cole)

ii. "His mercy precluded a man doing the work that was demanded when he might be past his physical prime. There were to be no elderly, doddering Levites stumbling about in the precincts of the Holy Place, carrying poles too heavy for them to carry or doing things they were no longer able to do." (Allen)

iii. The words **perform** (for entering service in verse 24) and **performing** (for leaving service in verse 25) are military words, used to describe warfare. Coming into service – even practical service among God's people – can be a battle and leaving service can also be a battle.

c. **Thus you shall do to the Levites regarding their duties**: Moses, the children, of Israel, and the Levites all did as God directed them. The Levites showed the qualities of the kind of people ready to inherit the Promised Land: those who are cleansed, dedicated, and doing the work.

Numbers 9 – Keeping the Passover; the Cloud by Day and Fire by Night

A. Keeping the Passover.

1. (1-5) The first Passover in the wilderness.

Now the LORD spoke to Moses in the Wilderness of Sinai, in the first month of the second year after they had come out of the land of Egypt, saying: "Let the children of Israel keep the Passover at its appointed time. On the fourteenth day of this month, at twilight, you shall keep it at its appointed time. According to all its rites and ceremonies you shall keep it." So Moses told the children of Israel that they should keep the Passover. And they kept the Passover on the fourteenth day of the first month, at twilight, in the Wilderness of Sinai; according to all that the LORD commanded Moses, so the children of Israel did.

a. **Let the children of Israel keep the Passover at its appointed time**: Israel celebrated the first Passover as they left Egypt (Exodus 12). Now, one year later (**the first month of the second year**), God commanded Israel to **keep the Passover** a second time.

i. It was not a surprise for Israel to hear that Passover must be kept every year. When Passover was first instituted, God told Israel they were to keep it *throughout their generations* (Exodus 12:14).

ii. The tabernacle was finished on the first day of the first month of the second year (Exodus 40:2, 17). On this day the cloud of glory covered the tabernacle (Numbers 9:15-23). About this time the tribal leaders brought their gifts (Numbers 7) and the priests were consecrated (Leviticus 8).

iii. "The long stay at the base of Mount Sinai was not a time of inactivity or indolence. It was a time of great activity in celebration of the goodness and mercy of the Lord and in preparation for what was expected to have been the soon triumphal march into the land of Canaan." (Allen)

b. **According to all its rites and ceremonies you shall keep it**: Passover reminded Israel of when God "passed over" His people when Egypt's firstborn were judged in the last plague upon Egypt.

i. The blood of the lamb, applied to the door posts of the home, was seen by the angel of God's judgment – and seeing the blood, the angel "passed over" and spared the home covered by the blood of a lamb. Passover was kept as a continual reminder of this occasion of judgment passed over, and of the deliverance from slavery that followed.

ii. "Exactly how the regulations in Exodus 12 were carried out is not stated: possibly the blood was smeared on the tents instead of on the lintels and doorposts." (Wenham)

iii. Jesus fulfilled the Passover sacrifice by His death on the cross (1 Corinthians 5:7). The covering of His blood causes the judgment of God to "pass over" His people. We are commanded to continually remember our occasion of being spared judgment and the deliverance that followed, by remembering Jesus' work on the cross through the Lord's Supper.

c. **So the children of Israel did**: Israel was properly obedient to God. We don't find any significant disobedience against God or distrust of Him on Israel's part in the first 10 chapters of Numbers, while they camped at Mount Sinai. This makes their distrust of God and rebellion against Him even more shocking and without excuse from Numbers 11 on.

2. (6-14) The case of the unclean men: Should they keep Passover?

Now there were *certain* men who were defiled by a human corpse, so that they could not keep the Passover on that day; and they came before Moses and Aaron that day. And those men said to him, "We *became* defiled by a human corpse. Why are we kept from presenting the offering of the LORD at its appointed time among the children of Israel?"

And Moses said to them, "Stand still, that I may hear what the LORD will command concerning you."

Then the LORD spoke to Moses, saying, "Speak to the children of Israel, saying: 'If anyone of you or your posterity is unclean because of a corpse, or *is* far away on a journey, he may still keep the LORD's Passover. On the fourteenth day of the second month, at twilight, they may keep it. They shall eat it with unleavened bread and bitter herbs. They shall leave none of it until morning, nor break one of its bones. According to

all the ordinances of the Passover they shall keep it. But the man who *is* clean and is not on a journey, and ceases to keep the Passover, that same person shall be cut off from among his people, because he did not bring the offering of the LORD at its appointed time; that man shall bear his sin.

'And if a stranger dwells among you, and would keep the LORD's Passover, he must do so according to the rite of the Passover and according to its ceremony; you shall have one ordinance, both for the stranger and the native of the land.'"

a. **There were certain men who were defiled by a human corpse, so that they could not keep the Passover**: This was an attempt to resolve two principles. The first principle was that every Israelite must be included in Passover. The second principle was that no one in a state of ritual uncleanness could take part in the normal religious life of the community.

i. These outward, external symbols of uncleanness were important and could not be ignored. These outward signs of uncleanness reminded Israel of their inward uncleanness. "The concept of ritual impurity is so foreign to modern thinking as to be nearly unintelligible to most readers.... The best way to think of the notion of 'uncleanness' is as a teaching device to remind the people of Israel of the holiness of God." (Allen)

ii. "It is probable that the defilement mentioned here was occasioned by assisting at the burial of some person—a work both of necessity and mercy." (Clarke)

iii. These **certain men** were probably not the only ones in Israel who had defiled themselves right before Passover. These men *wanted* to keep the Passover and were bold enough to ask Moses (and to ask God through Moses) for an exception to the previous command (as Leviticus 7:20 and 22:3).

b. **Stand still, that I may hear what the LORD will command**: Moses needed God's wisdom to resolve these principles. It wasn't good to exclude people from keeping Passover. It also wasn't good to disrespect God's holiness by allowing the ceremonially unclean to participate. To this point, God had not spoken on this issue, and therefore Moses needed to seek God about it.

c. **He may still keep the LORD's Passover**: God told Moses that those unclean at Passover (and those **far away on a journey**) could still keep the feast, but they must do it one month later (**on the fourteenth day of the**

second month). This solution made keeping the Passover possible, yet it respected God's holiness and the principles of ritual purity.

i. God made provision for the unclean to remember God's spared judgment and deliverance. The unclean were among those who most needed to remember what God did for His people through Passover.

ii. "Historically, the application of this second month alternative Passover occurred during the reign of Hezekiah (2 Chronicles 30:1–27)." (Cole)

d. **But the man who is clean and is not on a journey**: However, those among Israel who were clean and not traveling *must* keep Passover or be **cut off from among his people**. The punishment for not keeping Passover was severe: **That man shall bear his sin**, instead of having their sin borne by the Passover lamb.

i. "Thus, both participation in the passover when unclean and abstention for no good reason are equally dangerous." (Wenham)

ii. In the same way, we *must* partake of Jesus, or we will bear our own sin. Jesus said: *Most assuredly, I say to you, unless you eat the flesh of the Son of Man and drink His blood, you have no life in you.... He who eats My flesh and drinks My blood abides in Me, and I in him.* (John 6:53, 56)

e. **And if a stranger dwells among you**: Additionally, it didn't matter what bloodline or ethnic group the person came from. Even the **stranger** among Israel could and must keep the Passover, or they would be cut off. A Jew with the purest bloodlines would be cut off if they neglected Passover, and a Gentile **stranger** would be accepted if they kept God's Passover.

i. However, the Gentile visitor had to come under the law of the God of Israel. Exodus 12:48 required that those from outside Israel could keep Passover if they were first circumcised.

ii. "The inclusion of the alien in covenantal legislation such as this reminds us of God's great grace and also of his determined purpose to reach out through his people to all peoples." (Allen)

f. **He must do so according to the rite of the Passover and according to its ceremony**: The "second Passover" had to be kept according to the same **rite** and **ceremony** as the normal feast. The meal and the ritual had to be the same.

i. "Rabbi Gamaliel, the teacher of Saul…is quoted as saying that if anyone does not eat the lamb, the unleavened bread, and the bitter herbs, he has not kept the Passover. He built his words on v.11." (Allen)

ii. This command suggested three points to Charles Spurgeon:

- Spiritually speaking, we are to feed upon Jesus Christ.
- We are to feed upon the whole of Christ: all His person, all His offices, all His teaching, all His warnings, all His commands, all His work.
- We receive Christ in community, in union with others.

B. The cloud and the fire guide Israel.

1. (15) The presence of God with Israel is displayed by the cloud and fire.

Now on the day that the tabernacle was raised up, the cloud covered the tabernacle, the tent of the Testimony; from evening until morning it was above the tabernacle like the appearance of fire.

a. **Now on the day that the tabernacle was raised up**: When the tabernacle was originally built (**raised up**), God blessed it by showing His presence in the form of the cloud by day and the fire by night (Exodus 40:34-38).

b. **The cloud covered the tabernacle**: This **cloud** of God's *Shekinah* glory was evident at different times in Israel's history. For example, when Solomon built the temple, the cloud of glory filled the temple (1 Kings 8:10-11). When Israel had completely turned away from God, and before the temple was destroyed by conquering Babylonians, the cloud of glory departed (Ezekiel 10:3-4, 18-19).

c. **From evening until morning it was above the tabernacle like the appearance of fire**: These signs were more than the visible assurance of God's presence. The cloud by day and the fire by night were also helps and comforts to Israel. The **fire** at night was a comfort to Israel amid a dark wilderness, and the **cloud** by day was a shade from the hot wilderness sun.

i. This idea of God's presence as a protective shade is repeated in other places.

- *For You have been a strength to the poor, a strength to the needy in his distress, a refuge from the storm, a shade from the heat* (Isaiah 25:4).
- *The LORD is your keeper; the LORD is your shade at your right hand. The sun shall not strike you by day* (Psalm 121:5-6).

2. (16-23) Guidance by the cloud by day and the fire by night.

So it was always: the cloud covered it *by day*, and the appearance of fire by night. Whenever the cloud was taken up from above the tabernacle, after that the children of Israel would journey; and in the place where the cloud settled, there the children of Israel would pitch their tents.

At the command of the LORD the children of Israel would journey, and at the command of the LORD they would camp; as long as the cloud stayed above the tabernacle they remained encamped. Even when the cloud continued long, many days above the tabernacle, the children of Israel kept the charge of the LORD and did not journey. So it was, when the cloud was above the tabernacle a few days: according to the command of the LORD they would remain encamped, and according to the command of the LORD they would journey. So it was, when the cloud remained only from evening until morning: when the cloud was taken up in the morning, then they would journey; whether by day or by night, whenever the cloud was taken up, they would journey. *Whether it was* two days, a month, or a year that the cloud remained above the tabernacle, the children of Israel would remain encamped and not journey; but when it was taken up, they would journey. At the command of the LORD they remained encamped, and at the command of the LORD they journeyed; they kept the charge of the LORD, at the command of the LORD by the hand of Moses.

a. **So it was always**: Though Israel had been organized and ordered by God; cleansed, set apart, and blessed; generous in giving, and walking according to their priesthood, they still had to be guided by God each step of the way to make it to the Promised Land of Canaan. God did not do all those previous things to make them able to march towards the Promised Land *without* Him, but to make every step in constant dependence on Him.

i. **Always**: "The text suggests the permanent abiding of the cloud over the camp in the words 'this is how it continued to be.' The Hebrew word *tamid* has the sense of 'continually,' 'incessantly.'" (Allen)

b. **Whenever the cloud was taken up from above the tabernacle, after that the children of Israel would journey**: When the **cloud** moved, Israel moved; when the **cloud** stayed, Israel stayed. They only went where the presence of God led them, and they only stayed where the presence of God stayed.

i. "These were symbols one would not, could not ignore. They were awesome and eerie, unnatural and unexpected, comforting and protective. To relieve the heat of the desert sun, there was a cloud by day. To reverse the cold darkness of the desert night, there was the comforting fire overhead." (Allen)

ii. "The New Testament also uses cloud imagery to describe the presence of God. Our Lord was overshadowed by the cloud at his transfiguration, and disappeared into a cloud at his ascension (Luke 9:34; Acts 1:9)." (Wenham)

iii. In a similar way, believers must be led by the presence of God. Colossians 3:15 says, *let the peace of God rule in your hearts*. This means to let the presence of God's peace be an umpire or a judge in our hearts and lives.

c. **Whether it was two days, a month, or a year**: The movement of the cloud was unpredictable. God would not allow Israel to be led by routine or tradition. They had to see and respond to the presence of God.

i. "The thrice-repeated refrain sums it up, 'At the command of the LORD they encamped, and at the command of the LORD they set out' (20, 23; cf. 18). The cloud hovering over the tabernacle provided the perfect means of divine guidance: the people had to respond with perfect obedience." (Wenham)

ii. "No responsibility rested on the people save that of obedience. They were not called on to consider the time or direction of their march, but it was equally true they were not permitted to object or delay. All of which served to keep the fact of the sovereign authority of Jehovah perpetually before them." (Morgan)

iii. "GOD chose to keep this people so dependent upon himself, and so submissive to the decisions of his own will, that he would not even give them regular times of marching or resting; they were to do both when and where God saw best." (Clarke)

iv. "We need to hold the present with a slack hand, so as to be ready to fold our tents and take to the road, if God will. We must not reckon on continuance, nor strike our roots so deep that it needs a hurricane to remove us." (Maclaren)

Numbers 10 – Two Silver Trumpets, the Departure from Sinai

A. Two silver trumpets.

1. (1-2) Two silver trumpets.

And the LORD spoke to Moses, saying: "Make two silver trumpets for yourself; you shall make them of hammered work; you shall use them for calling the congregation and for directing the movement of the camps.

a. **Make two silver trumpets**: The two silver trumpets were used to direct the movement of the camps for marching and for battle, and to gather the nation together for an assembly.

   i. These **silver trumpets** are distinct from the trumpets made from a ram's horn, the *shofar* that was used to announce the Day of Atonement (Leviticus 25:9) and at Jericho (Joshua 6:4).

   ii. "I suspect that considerable time would have been necessary for Moses (and/or his artisans) to make these trumpets of hammered silver.... God may have instructed Moses to have these trumpets fashioned months before the people actually set out on their triumphant march." (Allen)

   iii. "The trumpets are described by Josephus and pictured on the arch of Titus in Rome. They were straight pipes, a little less than 18 in. (45cm) long with a flared opening at the end." (Wenham)

   iv. "These instruments were about two feet long with very narrow tubes, and when blown in certain patterns, they emitted a bright and piercing sound that would communicate clearly to the people the desired intent." (Cole)

b. **You shall use them for calling the congregation and for directing the movement of the camps**: The trumpets were helpful *tools* for the journey to the Promised Land. Without them it would be difficult to assemble the nation and march towards Canaan.

i. Before we can obey God, we must first give Him our attention. The trumpets were used to get the attention of the people of Israel.

2. (3-10) The system of blowing trumpets.

When they blow both of them, all the congregation shall gather before you at the door of the tabernacle of meeting. But if they blow *only* one, then the leaders, the heads of the divisions of Israel, shall gather to you. When you sound the advance, the camps that lie on the east side shall then begin their journey. When you sound the advance the second time, then the camps that lie on the south side shall begin their journey; they shall sound the call for them to begin their journeys. And when the assembly is to be gathered together, you shall blow, but not sound the advance. The sons of Aaron, the priests, shall blow the trumpets; and these shall be to you as an ordinance forever throughout your generations.

"When you go to war in your land against the enemy who oppresses you, then you shall sound an alarm with the trumpets, and you will be remembered before the LORD your God, and you will be saved from your enemies. Also in the day of your gladness, in your appointed feasts, and at the beginning of your months, you shall blow the trumpets over your burnt offerings and over the sacrifices of your peace offerings; and they shall be a memorial for you before your God: I *am* the LORD your God."

a. **When they blow both of them, all the congregation shall gather**: Distinctive sounds were made to indicate gathering for assembly, marching, or warfare. Israel heard the trumpet and gathered as directed.

i. "If we follow Jewish tradition, long blasts…were used to assemble the people to Moses, to the tent of meeting and for worship. Short staccato blasts…were used in battle and to order the camps to move off." (Wenham)

b. **Whether it was two days, a month, or a year**: God also promised to hear the trumpet of Israel in warfare, and to act on behalf of the nation. In a sense, God heard the trumpet and responded to His people in their need.

c. **Also in the day of your gladness**: Trumpets were also a way of celebrating the gathering of God's people and the presence of the LORD with them.

i. God will use the sound of a trumpet to gather His people for the ultimate assembling together – the catching away of the church, to meet the Lord in the air (1 Thessalonians 4:16-18).

d. **They shall be a memorial for you before your God**: In many ways, the nature and use of these sliver trumpets illustrate the nature and practice of preaching.

- There was value in a variety of trumpets and tones (*make two silver trumpets*, Numbers 10:2).

- The trumpet requires effort in making the sound (the nature of sounding a trumpet).

- The sound should be made clear (*use them for calling the congregation*, 10:2).

- The sound should be loud enough to be heard (*use them for calling the congregation and for directing the movement of the camps*, 10:2).

- If the sound continued too long, it became mere noise.

- The trumpets could not make many different notes (*make two silver trumpets*, 10:2) presumably without valves or slides to change the tone.

- The sound gathers the people of God (*use them for calling the congregation*, 10:2).

- The sound leads the people of God forward (*for directing the movement of the camps*, 10:2).

- The trumpets were to get the attention of the people (*you shall use them for calling the congregation*, 10:2).

- The people were to respond to the sound of the trumpets (**When they blow both of them, all the congregation shall gather before you**).

- The trumpets were to instruct and guide the people (**When you sound the advance**).

- The trumpets sometimes called just to the leaders (**if they blow only one, then the leaders, the heads of the divisions of Israel, shall gather to you**).

- The sound tells the people of glad news (**Also in the day of your gladness, in your appointed feasts**).

- The sound leads the people of God into battle (**then you shall sound an alarm with the trumpets**).

- The trumpet was to sound an alarm (**then you shall sound an alarm with the trumpets**).

- The sound comes from an instrument shaped by hammering, hard impact (*you shall make them of hammered work*, 10:2).

- The sound is also heard by God Himself (**you will be remembered before the L**ORD **your God, and you will be saved from your enemies**).

- The sound was made by someone called, cleansed, sanctified and anointed (**The sons of Aaron, the priests, shall blow the trumpets**).

- The sound had a special significance to the people of God (**they shall be a memorial for you before your God: I am the L**ORD **your God**).

- The sound proclaimed the work of atoning sacrifice (**you shall blow the trumpets over your burnt offerings**).

- The sound celebrated peace with God and a right relationship with Him (**and over the sacrifices of your peace offerings**).

- The trumpets only worked effectively with the evidence of God's presence (the trumpets told them to start marching, but the pillar of cloud or pillar of fire showed them where to go).

B. Departure for the Promised Land.

1. (11-13) The march to Canaan begins.

Now it came to pass on the twentieth *day* **of the second month, in the second year, that the cloud was taken up from above the tabernacle of the Testimony. And the children of Israel set out from the Wilderness of Sinai on their journeys; then the cloud settled down in the Wilderness of Paran. So they started out for the first time according to the command of the L**ORD **by the hand of Moses.**

a. **The cloud was taken up from above the tabernacle**: As the cloud began to move, one might imagine the huge sense of excitement that flowed through the people. This marked the start of their departure from Mount Sinai and their journey to Canaan, the land promised to their forefathers and to them.

i. Israel was now on their way to the Promised Land. Previously, their journey had been *from* Egypt and slavery; now they **set out from the Wilderness of Sinai** and were on their way *to* Canaan and liberty.

ii. **The cloud settled down in the Wilderness of Paran**: After this initial departure from Sinai, they were positioned to continue into Canaan. "The Desert of Paran is a large plateau in the northeastern Sinai, south of what later would be called the Negev of Judah, and west of the Arabah. This forms the southernmost portion of the Promised Land, the presumed staging area for the assault on the land itself." (Allen)

iii. "Stops were made at Kibroth-hattaavah and Hazeroth before they finally reached the wilderness of Paran (11:35; 12:16). This is the largest and most barren of the wildernesses traversed by the Israelites, covering much of the Northern Sinai peninsula." (Wenham)

b. **So they started out for the first time according to the command of the LORD by the hand of Moses**: This was the **first time** Israel marched as an organized, prepared *nation*. They were not the same group that escaped Egypt as a mob.

i. They had been fully prepared to walk as people suited to God's Promised Land, and the preparation work was focused on this exact point: bringing them to Canaan.

- They had become ordered and organized (Numbers 1-4).
- They had become cleansed and purified (Numbers 5).
- They had become set apart and blessed (Numbers 6).
- They had learned how to give and how to function as priests (Numbers 3 and 7-8).
- They were made to remember judgment spared and deliverance brought (Numbers 9).
- They had God's presence as a guide and the tools needed to lead the people (Numbers 9 and 10).

ii. "Israel, on the move from the Desert of Sinai (v.12), was on a journey that in a few weeks could lead them into the conquest of the land of Canaan. This was a day not to be forgotten.... At last the Israelites were on their way to Canaan!" (Allen)

iii. One would be tempted to think that after such extensive preparation – a virtual transformation from slave people to Promised Land people – the actual entrance into Canaan would be easy. This was *not* the case. The preparation was exactly that – preparation. Ahead of them were the greatest challenges, challenges that could only be met by faith. To use an example, a soldier might think basic training finishes something – but it doesn't. It only prepares for a greater challenge, the actual battle itself.

2. (14-28) Description of the order of march.

The standard of the camp of the children of Judah set out first according to their armies; over their army was Nahshon the son of Amminadab. Over the army of the tribe of the children of Issachar *was* **Nethanel the son of Zuar. And over the army of the tribe of the children of Zebulun** *was* **Eliab the son of Helon. Then the tabernacle was taken down; and the sons of Gershon and the sons of Merari set out, carrying the tabernacle. And the standard of the camp of Reuben set out according to their armies; over their army** *was* **Elizur the son of Shedeur. Over the army of the tribe of the children of Simeon** *was* **Shelumiel the son of Zurishaddai. And over the army of the tribe of the children of Gad** *was* **Eliasaph the son of Deuel. Then the Kohathites set out, carrying the holy things. (The tabernacle would be prepared for their arrival.) And the standard of the camp of the children of Ephraim set out according to their armies; over their army** *was* **Elishama the son of Ammihud. Over the army of the tribe of the children of Manasseh** *was* **Gamaliel the son of Pedahzur. And over the army of the tribe of the children of Benjamin** *was* **Abidan the son of Gideoni. Then the standard of the camp of the children of Dan (the rear guard of all the camps) set out according to their armies; over their army** *was* **Ahiezer the son of Ammishaddai. Over the army of the tribe of the children of Asher** *was* **Pagiel the son of Ocran. And over the army of the tribe of the children of Naphtali** *was* **Ahira the son of Enan. Thus** *was* **the order of march of the children of Israel, according to their armies, when they began their journey.**

a. **The standard of the camp of the children of Judah set out first**: They marched according to the order God had commanded earlier in the book. This means that they took God's word seriously and followed it exactly – just as those who will receive God's promises should.

b. **Then the tabernacle was taken down**: After it was first built at the foot of Mount Sinai, this was the first time the **tabernacle** was taken apart and transported. Everything was done as God commanded, with each family of Levites taking their appointed role.

c. **When they began their journey**: This was only the beginning. There were many more challenges of faith ahead for Israel. Up to this point – the beginning of their journey – the record in Numbers shows consistent obedience. We are unprepared for the later disobedience and rebellion of Israel, and for the bitter truth that all those stately men mentioned in these verses would die in the wilderness among a generation of unbelief, unwilling to trust God's promise to enter Canaan.

3. (29-32) Moses appeals to his brother-in-law to stay with Israel.

Now Moses said to Hobab the son of Reuel the Midianite, Moses' father-in-law, "We are setting out for the place of which the LORD said, 'I will give it to you.' Come with us, and we will treat you well; for the LORD has promised good things to Israel." And he said to him, "I will not go, but I will depart to my own land and to my relatives." So Moses said, "Please do not leave, inasmuch as you know how we are to camp in the wilderness, and you can be our eyes. And it shall be, if you go with us; indeed it shall be; that whatever good the Lord will do to us, the same we will do to you."

a. **Come with us, and we will treat you well**: Moses was a wise enough leader to know his limitations, and to know that he needed help. Moses knew God's help often comes through men like his brother-in-law Hobab.

i. Though Israel was guided by God, there was still help needed by man – men like Hobab. God plans it this way, often arranging His help to come, at least in part, through people He has ordained to help us.

ii. They didn't need Hobab to tell them where to go; the pillar of cloud and fire did that. Hobab's knowledge and experience were helpful in finding water, potential food, fuel, and other things in the places where the LORD directed them to march and camp.

iii. **Come with us, and we will treat you well**: "It is a question which every body of Christians has need to ask itself--Can we honestly say to those without, Come with us, and we will do you good? In order that there may be certainty on this point, should not every member of the Church be able to testify that the faith he has gives joy and peace, that his fellowship with God is making life pure and strong and free?" (Watson)

iv. The father of Hobab was **Reuel**, also known as Jethro. "Some earlier scholars took the use of the two names Jethro and Reuel as an indication that Exodus 2:18 and 3:11 were from different Pentateuchal sources. But the use of dual names in the Bible and ancient Near Eastern texts has been demonstrated by C. H. Gordon and others to be a common practice in poetic and prose contexts." (Cole)

b. **Please do not leave**: Since Moses knew God could use Hobab in a significant way, he was willing to appeal to him – and not take an initial "no" as an answer. The first appeal was to Hobab's selfishness (**we will treat you well**). The second appeal – the successful appeal – was to his charity and helpfulness (**you can be our eyes**).

i. "We are very prone to make our appeal to selfishness – granted, on a high level, but still to selfishness. Would not the appeal that calls to service and sacrifice to the heroic be far more forceful? One thing is certain, and that is this was the supreme note in Christ's call to men in the days of His flesh." (Morgan)

ii. "In the Book of Judges we find traces of the presence of Hobab's descendants as incorporated among the people of Israel. One of them came to be somebody, the Jael who struck the tent-peg through the temples of the sleeping Sisera, for she is called 'the wife of Heber the Kenite.' Probably, then, in some sense Hobab must have become a worshipper of Jehovah, and have cast in his lot with his brother-in-law and his people." (Maclaren)

4. (33-36) The departure from Sinai: **Rise up, O LORD!**

So they departed from the mountain of the LORD on a journey of three days; and the ark of the covenant of the LORD went before them for the three days' journey, to search out a resting place for them. And the cloud of the LORD *was* above them by day when they went out from the camp. So it was, whenever the ark set out, that Moses said:

**"Rise up, O LORD!
Let Your enemies be scattered,
And let those who hate You flee before You."**

And when it rested, he said:

**"Return, O LORD,
To the many thousands of Israel."**

a. **And the cloud of the LORD was above them by day when they went out from the camp**: As they began the journey to the Promised Land, they were guided by God's presence, not by their own sense of direction. They followed the cloud no matter where God led them. If they were to camp in a rough place, they did it. If they were told to depart from a comfortable place, they did it. They allowed themselves to be guided by God, not by their own wisdom or desire for comfort and ease.

i. **For the three days' journey**: This was how far it was to Paran (Numbers 10:12). "This kind of phraseology was commonly used in the ancient Near East to indicate distance traveled by armies or caravans, in which the average distance was about fifteen miles per day…. Hence, the Israelites probably traveled forty to forty-five miles on this initial leg." (Cole)

b. **Rise up, O LORD! Let Your enemies be scattered, and let those who hate You flee before You**: This was the prayer of Moses when the presence of God led them forward.

i. The idea was simple: "God, go before us and take care of our enemies. It's too dangerous ahead unless You do this." This is a fitting prayer for every believer to pray, and that faith here displayed gives the sense that Canaan would soon be theirs.

ii. This is also a fitting prayer to remember the glory and strength of the resurrected Lord. When Jesus rose up, all His enemies were scattered. No one dared oppose Him. All our victory is found in His risen glory. Spurgeon noted the extent of Jesus' victory in a sermon on this verse:

- Sin was defeated and scattered at the cross.

- The hosts of hell were defeated and scattered at the cross.

- Death itself was defeated and scattered at the cross.

- The gods of the heathen were defeated and scattered at the cross.

iii. "Commanders must pray, as well as lead on their forces, as did Charles the Great, and that late brave King of Sweden, more addict to prayer than to fight." (Trapp)

iv. "I quote not this except as a picture and illustration of the history of the entire Church. Methinks, in a spiritual sense, when Luther first bowed his knee, the Church began to chant, 'Let God arise, and let his enemies be scattered.' When Knox in Scotland upheld the glory of Jesus' name, was it not once again, 'O God arise, let them that hate thee flee before thee'? When Whitefield and Wesley, seraphic evangelists of Jesus Christ, went through this land, was not this the very song of Israel, 'O God, arise, and let thine enemies be scattered?' And shall it not be ours to-day?" (Spurgeon)

v. Spurgeon also saw this as a good prayer for the front-line missionary and the one laboring in difficult places: "Are you serving God in some particular work where many are seeking to undo all that you can accomplish? Are you a City Missionary, and do you labour in the midst of a den of iniquity? Does it seem that what you do in one day is undone in one hour by others? Take it to the throne of grace. Say, 'Rise up, Lord, and let thine enemies be scattered.'" (Spurgeon)

vi. "The faith which Moses affirms so confidently stands in ironic contrast to what happens in the succeeding chapters: whereas Moses is sure God will do good to Israel, the people begin to complain of the evil (11:1) that he is doing them. Moses prays that all God's enemies will be scattered: the spies declare Israel will be defeated (chapter 13). This chapter's triumphant conclusion deepens the poignant tragedy of the succeeding scenes." (Wenham)

c. **Return, O LORD, to the many thousands of Israel**: This was the prayer of Moses when the cloud of God's presence stopped and indicated the place to camp. Moses then prayed, "Here we camp, LORD. Stay with us."

> i. "Will you and I go home and pray this prayer by ourselves, fervently laying hold upon the horns of God's altar? I charge you, my brethren in Christ, do not neglect this private duty. Go, each of you, to your chambers; shut to your doors; cry to him who hears in secret, and let this be the burden of your cry – 'Rise up, Lord; and let thine enemies be scattered.'" (Spurgeon)

Numbers 11 – The People Complain

A. The complaints of Israel and of Moses.

1. (1-3) The complaining heart of Israel.

Now *when* the people complained, it displeased the Lord; for the Lord heard *it*, and His anger was aroused. So the fire of the Lord burned among them, and consumed *some* in the outskirts of the camp. Then the people cried out to Moses, and when Moses prayed to the Lord, the fire was quenched. So he called the name of the place Taberah, because the fire of the Lord had burned among them.

a. **Now when the people complained**: In the first 10 chapters of Numbers, Israel was ordered, organized, cleansed, separated, blessed, taught how to give, reminded of God's deliverance, given God's presence and the tools to advance to the Promised Land. Now, having set out towards Canaan, after just a few days **the people complained**.

i. We might think it strange that a people so blessed could still complain. God did so much in and for Israel yet they still murmured against Him. They were still in the wilderness and their circumstances were not easy, but nothing good came of it **when the people complained**.

ii. According to Allen, **when the people complained** "could also be translated, 'Now the people became truly murmurous, an offense to Yahweh's ears.'"

iii. "What the cause of this complaining was, we know not.... But surely no people had ever less cause for murmuring; they had God among them, and miracles of goodness were continually wrought in their behalf." (Clarke)

b. **The people complained, it displeased the Lord**: Their complaining made God **displeased**. Complaining hearts often displease God, especially when they show little gratitude for what He did in the past, and little faith for what God could do at the moment.

98

i. We aren't told here exactly what Israel **complained** about. It is possible that it simply came from a generally dissatisfied heart. Sometimes we complain not for any one great reason, but because our hearts are dissatisfied.

c. **The fire of the LORD burned among them**: Israel had valued the pillar of God's fire present with them every night. Here, the fire and the presence of God became something of a two-edged sword. God's fire was present with Israel to comfort them, but it was also present to deal with their sin.

i. "The text does not make clear what was burnt on this occasion, whether it was just shrubs near the tents, or some of the tents themselves. However, the people realized the danger they were in and appealed to Moses to pray for them." (Wenham)

ii. "Either a supernatural fire was sent for this occasion, or the lightning was commissioned against them, or God smote them with one of those hot suffocating winds which are very common in those countries." (Clarke)

iii. **Consumed some in the outskirts of the camp**: "This purging fire was limited to the outskirts of the camp, a mercy of the Lord. He might have cast his fire into the very midst of the camp and killed many more persons than suffered this terrible judgment." (Allen)

d. **The people cried out to Moses**: Ideally, Israel would have cried out to God directly. Because they lacked a strong sense of relationship with God Himself, they brought their cry to Moses instead of bringing it to the LORD.

e. **When Moses prayed to the LORD, the fire was quenched**: Moses **prayed** for the people, and the fire was quenched. The place was named **Taberah** (burning) as a reminder of God's judgment of the complaining hearts among Israel.

2. (4) Israel complains about a lack of meat.

Now the mixed multitude who were among them yielded to intense craving; so the children of Israel also wept again and said: "Who will give us meat to eat?

a. **Now the mixed multitude who were among them**: Exodus 12:38 says that *a mixed multitude* went out of Egypt. This means that not everyone in the great crowd that came out of Egypt with Moses was ethnically Israelite. There were many Egyptians (and perhaps other non-Israelites) who went with them. This may be because they were also slaves in Egypt, and perhaps because the God of Israel showed Himself more powerful than the gods of the Egyptians.

i. We first read of the **mixed multitude** in Exodus 12:38: *A mixed multitude went up with them also, and flocks and herds—a great deal of livestock.* The statement in Exodus shows that they were wealthy, having 'flocks and herds, even very much cattle.' Perhaps that accounted for the willingness of the people of God to permit them to accompany them.

ii. "The fact that they, had such possessions would seem also to suggest that they were more than adventurers. They had a certain interest in the migration--one of curiosity, perhaps. The only thing that is certain is that they were not of the Theocracy; and not having true part or lot in the Divine movement, they fell a-lusting after the things of Egypt, and infected the people of God with the same unholy desire." (Morgan)

iii. There is also a spiritual sense in which Israel was a **mixed multitude**. That is, not all who were descended from Abraham, Isaac, and Jacob had a genuine, real relationship with God. This is also true of the visible church, which Jesus said would contain good and bad until the final harvest (Matthew 13:24-30, 36-43).

b. **Yielded to intense craving**: The Hebrew word here is *taavah*; it is also used in passages like Genesis 3:6, 1 Samuel 2:16, Job 33:20, and Psalm 10:3 for the strong desire for something pleasant, but perhaps (though not always) sinful.

i. The people of Israel had to *yield* to this intense craving; their sinful desire would not be fulfilled unless they cooperated with it. James 1:14 says *but each one is tempted when he is drawn away by his own desires and enticed.* The attraction to sin is present within us, yet we must still *yield* to that sinful desire in choosing to sin.

ii. Allen on **intense craving**: "The verb can be used for positive and proper desires but is especially fitting for feelings of (improper) lusts and bodily appetites."

c. **Who will give us meat to eat?** This was a strange question to ask, considering they had a God in heaven that met their every need. It seems that some in Israel looked for *another* provider because they were not satisfied with what came to them from the hand of God. They were so distraught over this that they **wept**.

i. Tears of repentance or sorrow over sin or experienced as joy in the LORD can be beautiful. However, it is also possible for people – even among God's people – to shed tears over childish disappointments.

ii. Israel *could* have provided meat for themselves. God did not prohibit them to hunt whatever animals they could in the wilderness. and they also had their flocks, which could be slaughtered for meat. Yet they did not want to do anything about their desire for meat, except to weep about it.

iii. "They had indeed flesh and cattle which they brought with them out of Egypt, but these were reserved for breed to be carried into Canaan, and were so few that they would scarce have served them for a month." (Poole)

3. (5-6) Israel remembers the foods of Egypt.

We remember the fish which we ate freely in Egypt, the cucumbers, the melons, the leeks, the onions, and the garlic; but now our whole being *is* dried up; *there is* nothing at all except this manna *before* our eyes!"

a. **We remember the fish we ate freely in Egypt**: About a year before this, God responded to Israel's complaints by providing miraculous food for Israel (Exodus 16:11-35), which they called **manna** (Exodus 16:31). After a year of eating mainly manna, Israel now longed for the foods they (sometimes) ate as slaves in Egypt. The first food mentioned was **the fish we ate freely in Egypt** because there were no fish in the wilderness.

i. They also mentioned **cucumbers, melons, leeks, onions**, and **garlic** – all juicy, crunchy, or flavorful foods they *sometimes* ate as slaves in Egypt. Exodus 16:3 records a similar complaint about a year earlier: *when we sat by the pots of meat and when we ate bread to the full!*

ii. "Goshen in the eastern Nile delta was practically the breadbasket of Egypt, lush with vegetation and abounding with natural and man-made canals whose waters teemed with fish and were replete with nutrients for abundant crop production. The foods listed were among the most commonly grown in the region." (Cole)

iii. As the people of Israel claimed to **remember** their supposedly good life in Egypt, they sinned with ingratitude, selective memory, and twisting the past to justify their present complaints. There were no doubt some good and pleasant times and meals for the Hebrew slaves in Egypt, but in general their Egyptian masters *made their lives bitter with hard bondage* (Exodus 1:14).

iv. In one sense, the memory of the **fish, cucumbers, melons, leeks, onions**, and **garlic** was not a lie. There were times they ate such things. Yet in a greater sense, this was a lie because they chose to remember one small, good aspect of their slavery in Egypt while ignoring the much greater bitter and hard bondage of their slavery. It can be a trap to remember only the good (or only the bad) of the past.

v. "They forgat their servitude. Discontent is ever harping upon wants, and enjoys nothing: no more than Haman did his honour, or Ahab his kingdom, when he longed for a salad out of Naboth's garden." (Trapp)

vi. Israel fell in love with an illusion from the past (the thought that their life in Egypt was wonderful). Instead, they should have looked for what God had for them in the future – the milk and honey of Canaan (Exodus 13:5). God's people should have the attitude later expressed by Paul in Philippians 3:13-14 – pressing forward, looking ahead, and not focused on the past.

b. **Nothing at all except this manna**: It seems Israel complained that **manna** was not exciting enough, that it was boring. This terrible lack of thankfulness was nothing less than to have *despised the* LORD (Numbers 11:20).

i. There were at least three distinct times when Israel complained about God's provision of food: Exodus 16:1-3, Numbers 11:4:3-4, and Numbers 21:4-9. In Exodus 16 they complained about the lack of food; in Numbers 11 they complained about the lack of variety, and in Numbers 21 they were again dissatisfied with manna.

ii. God is our provider; to despise what He provides is to despise Him. It is not God's job to entertain us, and we should be more than children who demand to be entertained and excited.

iii. "They could never be satisfied; even God himself could not please them, because they were ever preferring their own wisdom to his. God will save us in his own way, or not at all; because that way, being the plan of infinite wisdom, it is impossible that we can be saved in any other." (Clarke)

c. **Now our whole being is dried up**: These words sound over-dramatic from a people who were fed by the manna that came to them that morning. In their complaining, Israel not only romanticized the past, but they also exaggerated the problems of the present. To say, "**our whole being is dried up**" was a terrible exaggeration. God would not allow them to waste away in the wilderness. In fact, God provided their every need – though not their every desire.

i. Israel focused on what they *didn't have*. It was true – they didn't have the fish and several kinds of vegetables listed. However, they seemed to completely forget what they *did have* – daily, miraculous, nutritious provision from God that could feed a nation in the wilderness. Many people since that time have followed the same dangerous path of forgetting what God has provided and focusing on what they do not (yet) have.

4. (7-9) A description of manna.

Now the manna *was* like coriander seed, and its color like the color of bdellium. The people went about and gathered *it*, ground *it* on millstones or beat *it* in the mortar, cooked *it* in pans, and made cakes of it; and its taste was like the taste of pastry prepared with oil. And when the dew fell on the camp in the night, the manna fell on it.

a. **Now the manna *was* like coriander seed, and its color like the color of bdellium**: This passage and Exodus 16 give the most detail about what manna was like and how God provided it.

- "Manna" was Israel's name for this substance (Exodus 16:31), because they didn't know what it was (Exodus 16:15). God called it *bread from heaven* (Exodus 16:4, Psalm 78:24) and *angel's food* (Psalm 78:25).

- Manna was given by God to Israel as a test of their obedience (Exodus 16:4).

- Manna was given by God in double measure on the sixth day, so Israel could rest from collecting it on the seventh day (Exodus 16:5).

- Manna appeared in the morning, like **dew** on the ground (also in Exodus 16:13-14)

- Manna "melted" away later in the morning (Exodus 16:21).

- Manna was small, white, and fine as frost on the ground (Exodus 16:14), like a white **coriander seed** (also in Exodus 16:31) Some (such as Wenham) suggested that manna came as little white flakes.

- Manna was collected family by family (Exodus 16:16).

- Manna that was kept for the following day spoiled (Exodus 16:19-20), except for that which was gathered on the sixth day for the sabbath day (Exodus 16:23-26).

- Manna was prepared in a variety of ways (**ground it on millstones or beat it in the mortar, cooked it in pans, and made cakes of it**).

- Manna was sweet to the taste, like wafers made with honey (Exodus 16:31). It tasted like **pastry prepared with oil**.

- Manna was eaten by Israel for 40 years until they entered Canaan (Exodus 16:35).

b. **Its taste was like the taste of pastry prepared with oil**: In fact, manna was excellent provision. It was as tasty as a bread-like **pastry** that was cooked **with oil** (perhaps something like a modern donut or pancake). Yet, manna provided all the nutrition the people of Israel needed for a long journey through the wilderness.

5. (10-15) The complaint of Moses.

Then Moses heard the people weeping throughout their families, everyone at the door of his tent; and the anger of the LORD was greatly aroused; Moses also was displeased. So Moses said to the LORD, "Why have You afflicted Your servant? And why have I not found favor in Your sight, that You have laid the burden of all these people on me? Did I conceive all these people? Did I beget them, that You should say to me, 'Carry them in your bosom, as a guardian carries a nursing child,' to the land which You swore to their fathers? Where am I to get meat to give to all these people? For they weep all over me, saying, 'Give us meat, that we may eat.' I am not able to bear all these people alone, because the burden *is* too heavy for me. If You treat me like this, please kill me here and now; if I have found favor in Your sight; and do not let me see my wretchedness!"

a. **And the anger of the LORD was greatly aroused; Moses also was displeased**: The childish weeping of the people not only angered the LORD; it also **displeased** Moses. This frustration drove Moses to God, and he complained that he could never meet the needs of so many people.

i. Moses certainly had a *better* reason to complain to God; it wasn't as if he **yielded to intense craving** as the children of Israel did. Yet even his complaining was not good and showed a lapse in his trust in God.

ii. Perhaps Moses was caught off-guard, surprised that the people rebelled so quickly after such a strong warning at Taberah (Numbers 11:1-3). It's easy for a leader to do the wrong thing when they are caught off-guard.

b. **Why have You afflicted Your servant?** Moses responded to God the way many of us do in a time of trial. He essentially said, "God, here I am serving You. Why did You bring this upon me?" It's easy to say God did not bring this upon Moses – a carnal and ungrateful people did. Yet, though God did not directly afflict Moses with this, He ultimately allowed it.

i. God allowed this for the same reason God allows any affliction – to compel us to trust in Him more, to partner with Him in overcoming obstacles, and to love and praise Him more through our increased dependence on Him and the greater deliverance He brings. For these reasons and more, God sometimes appoints affliction for His people (1 Thessalonians 3:3).

ii. In the middle of our affliction it is easy to think God is against us, as Moses did (**Why have I not found favor in Your sight?**). God's response is ever the same: "It's because I do love you that I am training you, building you up in faith."

iii. "Whereas Moses assured Hobab that the LORD would treat Israel well, he was soon to ask, 'Why hast thou dealt ill with thy servant?' (10:32; 11:11)." (Wenham)

c. **Did I conceive all these people? Did I beget them**: When Moses likened himself to a mother and the children of Israel to his children, he used a fitting figure of speech – because Israel was acting like unsatisfied infants, complete with tears (**For they weep all over me**).

i. Moses, like many servants of God since his time, had to understand that as unpleasant as the work of leading God's people sometimes is, God uses such difficulties in the lives of His servants. "God does not remove annoyances out of the way even of His devoted servants. We remember how Paul was vexed and burdened while carrying the world's thought on into a new day." (Watson)

d. **I am not able to bear all these people alone**: Understanding that the job of leading Israel was too big for Moses was good. It could lead him to rely on God, and not try to do the work apart from God. Moses could not bear all these people alone; God will do it in him and through him.

i. To paraphrase John Trapp, the German reformer Philip Melanchthon said that the three most painful labors were those of God's ministers, civil leaders, and women giving birth.

ii. "The best service that all human leaders, helpers or lovers, can do us, is to confess their own insufficiency, and to point us to Jesus. All that men need is found in Him and in Him alone." (Maclaren)

e. **If You treat me like this, please kill me here and now**: Moses was greatly frustrated. He poured out his emotion, pain, and frustration to the LORD. This wasn't a proper thing to ask God to do, but we understand the misery of Moses. He did the right thing in pouring out his heart and complaint before the LORD.

i. God did not say "yes" when Moses asked, "**please kill me here and now**." Yet, God helped the overwhelmed Moses, who knew that the job of leading God's people was too big for him to do without God's help.

ii. **And do not let me see my wretchedness**: In a sense, God wanted Moses to see his **wretchedness** – his inability to do what God called him to do in his *own* strength. As the Apostle Paul later learned, God's strength is made perfect in weakness (2 Corinthians 12:9).

B. God answers the complaints of Israel and Moses.

1. (16-17) God helps Moses by sending elders to assist him.

So the LORD said to Moses: "Gather to Me seventy men of the elders of Israel, whom you know to be the elders of the people and officers over them; bring them to the tabernacle of meeting, that they may stand there with you. Then I will come down and talk with you there. I will take of the Spirit that *is* upon you and will put *the same* upon them; and they shall bear the burden of the people with you, that you may not bear *it* yourself alone.

> a. **Gather to Me seventy men of the elders of Israel**: God told Moses to gather men to help in the work of leading Israel. These **seventy men** would *first* be gathered to God (**Gather to Me**) before they were gathered to *Moses*. Their loyalty was first to God, not to Moses.

> > i. "Here, say some, began the Sanhedrim, that is, the great council of the Jews, consisting of seventy seniors and one president. It continued till the time of Herod the Great." (Trapp)

> b. **Whom you know to be the elders of the people**: Moses was not to pick men whom he thought might *become* elders; he was to pick men who were already known as elders because of their wisdom, conduct, and ministry to others. Elders are made by God but recognized by men.

> c. **That they may stand there with you**: These were called to simply **stand there with** Moses, before the LORD. They were a support and strength to Moses just by their presence.

> d. **I will take of the Spirit that is upon you and will put the same upon them**: The elders needed the same heart, the same vision, and the same **Spirit** that was on Moses. If not, there would be no agreement among the leadership of the nation and disaster could come to Israel.

> e. **They shall bear the burden of the people with you**: The elders were there to help Moses carry the spiritual load – to help him care for and minister to the people, and to be a support for him in the ministry. God's help was going to come to Moses through the support of godly men. This is a customary way for God to meet our needs.

2. (18-20) God promises to provide meat for Israel.

Then you shall say to the people, 'Consecrate yourselves for tomorrow, and you shall eat meat; for you have wept in the hearing of the LORD, saying, "Who will give us meat to eat? For *it was* well with us in Egypt."

Therefore the LORD will give you meat, and you shall eat. You shall eat, not one day, nor two days, nor five days, nor ten days, nor twenty days, but *for* a whole month, until it comes out of your nostrils and becomes loathsome to you, because you have despised the LORD who is among you, and have wept before Him, saying, "Why did we ever come up out of Egypt?""

a. **For you have wept in the hearing of the LORD**: God heard the weeping of Israel and knew these were the tears of ungrateful and complaining people. God heard their claim, **it was well with us in Egypt**, and knew their words were based upon a few selective memories and twisting the past to justify their complaints.

b. **Therefore the LORD will give you meat, and you shall eat**: This was not a blessing. God promised to answer the desire of Israel's heart but not in a way that would be a blessing to Israel. Sometimes God disciplines His people by giving them what they ask for – what their *intense craving* cries out for.

c. **Until it comes out of your nostrils and becomes loathsome to you**: God promised to give them so much meat that they would become sickened by it. This was because they denied and doubted the goodness of God's deliverance. It isn't good for the people of God to deny the goodness of God's deliverance in their lives.

3. (21-23) Moses reacts to God's promise to provide meat for Israel.

And Moses said, "The people whom I *am* among *are* six hundred thousand men on foot; yet You have said, 'I will give them meat, that they may eat *for* a whole month.' Shall flocks and herds be slaughtered for them, to provide enough for them? Or shall all the fish of the sea be gathered together for them, to provide enough for them?"

And the LORD said to Moses, "Has the LORD's arm been shortened? Now you shall see whether what I say will happen to you or not."

a. **The people whom I am among are six hundred thousand men on foot**: Moses reacted as we often do – trying to understand how God would perform His promise. Moses couldn't understand how God could do this, but God never asked him to understand it. God would provide from His inexhaustible resources.

i. "Moses reminds God (!) of the numbers involved: six hundred thousand men on foot…. A marching force of this size suggests a total population of over two million people." (Allen)

ii. "You will see, my brethren, right readily the mistake which Moses made. He looked to the creature instead of the Creator. Doth the

Creator expect the creature to fulfil his promise? No; he that makes fulfils. If he speaks, it is done—done by himself." (Spurgeon)

b. **Has the LORD's arm been shortened?** God had not suddenly become weak or limited. God had resources that Moses knew nothing about. God would meet Israel's need in a completely unexpected way.

4. (24-25) The Spirit of the LORD comes upon the seventy elders.

So Moses went out and told the people the words of the LORD, and he gathered the seventy men of the elders of the people and placed them around the tabernacle. Then the LORD came down in the cloud, and spoke to him, and took of the Spirit that *was* upon him, and placed *the same* upon the seventy elders; and it happened, when the Spirit rested upon them, that they prophesied, although they never did *so* again.

a. **He gathered the seventy men of the elders of the people and placed them around the tabernacle**: Before God provided the meat for Israel (which they asked for, but *didn't* really need), He first provided them with more leadership and oversight (which they didn't ask for, but really *did* need).

b. **And took of the Spirit that was upon him, and placed the same upon the seventy elders**: For this expanded leadership to do the job, they needed to have an outpouring of the Holy Spirit – and they needed to have the same spirit that was on Moses. They needed to have his vision, his heart, and his attitude.

i. If a man does not have the Holy Spirit's power flowing in his life, and the same spirit as those he serves the LORD under or serves with, he is unequipped to serve as he should. That man will end up being a hindrance, not a blessing.

c. **When the Spirit rested upon them, that they prophesied**: It is difficult to picture exactly what this was like. Perhaps they each spontaneously spoke a word from God or divinely inspired praises to God. Whatever exactly happened, it was a clear sign that the Spirit of the LORD had come upon them.

i. "As with Saul, the prophecy described here was probably an unintelligible ecstatic utterance, what the New Testament terms speaking in tongues, not the inspired, intelligible speech of the great Old Testament prophets and the unnamed prophets of the early church." (Wenham)

d. **Although they never did so again**: Apparently, the prophetic gift was given to these elders in a unique, one-time experience. They **prophesied** this once but did not become prophets. It was meant to be visible evidence of the Holy Spirit's equipping them for the office of elder, not the role of prophet.

i. Like the tongues of fire on Pentecost in Acts 2, the prophetic gift of these elders did not continue – but their Spirit-empowered service did.

5. (26-30) The Spirit of the LORD upon Eldad and Medad, and upon all God's people.

But two men had remained in the camp: the name of one *was* Eldad, and the name of the other Medad. And the Spirit rested upon them. Now they *were* among those listed, but who had not gone out to the tabernacle; yet they prophesied in the camp. And a young man ran and told Moses, and said, "Eldad and Medad are prophesying in the camp." So Joshua the son of Nun, Moses' assistant, *one* of his choice men, answered and said, "Moses my lord, forbid them!" Then Moses said to him, "Are you zealous for my sake? Oh, that all the LORD's people were prophets *and* that the LORD would put His Spirit upon them!" And Moses returned to the camp, he and the elders of Israel.

a. **Yet they prophesied in the camp**: The operation of the Holy Spirit was not limited to only one place. Even these two men (**Eldad** and **Medad**) who were not at the tabernacle with the rest of the seventy elders were also filled with the Holy Spirit, evidenced by the prophetic gift.

i. Joshua was first introduced as leading the battle against the Amalekites in Exodus 17:8-13. When he learned of what **Eldad** and **Medad** did, Joshua hoped to support Moses. His first concern was for Moses' ministry and he feared that this unusual display of the Spirit might in some way undermine it. Perhaps **Eldad** and **Medad** would become rivals to Moses.

b. **Oh, that all the LORD's people were prophets *and* that the LORD would put His Spirit upon them!** Moses probably appreciated that Joshua was **zealous** for his **sake**, but Moses did not fear these men as rivals. Instead, Moses longed that all God's people would receive this gift of **His Spirit**.

i. That broad outpouring of the Spirit of God upon all the people of God waited for a better covenant, a new covenant. Under the new covenant, God promised to pour out His Spirit upon all His people (Ezekiel 36:27, Joel 2:28-29).

ii. "This one saying proves the incomparable greatness of Moses' character. Little souls are monopolists. They like to be good and gifted, because it gives them a kind of superiority to others; but they dislike to see a levelling-up process at work by which the Eldads and Medads are lifted to stand by their side." (Meyer)

6. (31-35) God brings meat to Israel.

Now a wind went out from the LORD, and it brought quail from the sea and left *them* fluttering near the camp, about a day's journey on this side and about a day's journey on the other side, all around the camp, and about two cubits above the surface of the ground. And the people stayed up all that day, all night, and all the next day, and gathered the quail (he who gathered least gathered ten homers); and they spread *them* out for themselves all around the camp. But while the meat *was* still between their teeth, before it was chewed, the wrath of the LORD was aroused against the people, and the LORD struck the people with a very great plague. So he called the name of that place Kibroth Hattaavah, because there they buried the people who had yielded to craving.

From Kibroth Hattaavah the people moved to Hazeroth, and camped at Hazeroth.

a. **Now a wind went out from the LORD, and it brought quail**: Miraculously, God directed a huge number of **quail** to the camp of Israel, where they were killed and could be eaten. Quail migrate over the Sinai wilderness every year; it has been recorded that Arabs living near this region could catch between one and two million quails during their autumn migration, using nets.

i. The quail came **all around the camp** – that is, on the perimeter. When the Holy Spirit was poured out, it drew men into the center of the camp – right into the middle of the people of God. To get the quail, they had to go outside of the camp – away from the people of God.

ii. "The scene must have been similar to a riot: people screaming, birds flapping their wings, everywhere the pell-mell movement of a meat-hungry people in a sea of birds." (Allen)

iii. The Spirit was given to the elders to help Moses (Numbers 11:25, 29), and the wind brought the quail (Numbers 11:31) – using the same word in Hebrew for both "spirit" and "wind" (*ruah*).

b. **While the meat was still between their teeth, before it was chewed, the wrath of the LORD was aroused against the people**: The people, with great effort and excitement, gathered the quail and prepared it for eating. But when they ate – **while the meat was still between their teeth**, the LORD sent a plague among them and many died.

i. *He also rained meat on them like the dust, feathered fowl like the sand of the seas; and He let them fall in the midst of their camp, all around their dwellings. So they ate and were well filled, for He gave them their own desire. They were not deprived of their craving; but while their food was still in their mouths, the wrath of God came against them, and slew the stoutest of them, and struck down the choice men of Israel.* (Psalm 78:27-31)

ii. *They soon forgot His works; they did not wait for His counsel, but lusted exceedingly in the wilderness, and tested God in the desert. And He gave them their request, but sent leanness into their soul.* (Psalm 106:13-15)

iii. When we allow ungodly cravings to rule our lives, God may send what we crave – and *leanness* into our souls as well. Better to have a well-fed soul and to be deprived of ungodly cravings.

iv. "There are times when God grants an unwarranted request in order that men may learn through experience the folly of their desires." (Morgan)

v. This was a strict judgment, but it was a *help* to Israel because it taught them to not be ruled by their desires. If the lesson was learned, it was a huge help to the nation. To inherit the land of Canaan – God's Promised Land for Israel – they had to be ruled by more than their physical or emotional appetites.

c. **So he called the name of that place Kibroth Hattaavah**: They named the place **Kibroth Hattaavah** – which means "Graves of Craving." Spiritually speaking, many people are killed by their unrestrained desires.

i. Jesus proclaimed that He was God's true or ultimate bread from heaven (John 6:29-35). Like the manna in the wilderness, this was God's provision and there was nothing else to eat. Israel was sustained only by manna in the wilderness, and the disciple is sustained only by Jesus and nothing else.

Numbers 12 – The Dissension of Miriam and Aaron

A. Miriam and Aaron bring an accusation against Moses.

1. (1) Miriam and Aaron criticize Moses' wife and marriage.

Then Miriam and Aaron spoke against Moses because of the Ethiopian woman whom he had married; for he had married an Ethiopian woman.

a. **Then Miriam and Aaron spoke against Moses**: **Miriam** and **Aaron** were the sister and brother of Moses. Their disapproval of Moses and his **Ethiopian** wife was an example of a principle later stated by Jesus: that it is not unusual for a prophet to find no honor among his own people (Matthew 13:57).

> i. According to Allen, **Miriam** took the lead in this criticism. "The feminine singular verb that initiates the chapter (lit., 'and she spoke,' v.1) and the placement of her name before that of Aaron indicate that Miriam is the principal in the attack against Moses."

> ii. "Her discontent might arise from this, that, being a prophetess, she was not one of those seventy that were chosen to be helps in government." (Trapp)

b. **Because of the Ethiopian woman whom he had married**: This was the reason for their criticism. Some regard this as a problem passage because Exodus 2:16-22 says that the wife of Moses (named Zipporah) was the daughter of a man from Midian (not Ethiopia).

> i. Some think that Zipporah died, and this was a second wife Moses took after Zipporah's death. Remember that Moses had a remarkably long life and was more than 81 at this time. It is certainly possible he survived more than one wife.

> ii. Others think that Moses took a second wife in addition to Zipporah; this is possible but doesn't seem likely.

iii. Still others suggest that Jethro, Zipporah's father, was actually from Ethiopia but had moved to Midian, making Zipporah an Ethiopian by birth but one who had lived in Midian.

iv. It may also be possible that **Ethiopian** here was a derogatory term used to criticize Zipporah because of her dark complexion.

c. **For he had married an Ethiopian woman**: Interestingly, they criticized Moses and his wife for something she had no control over – her appearance, either because she was an Ethiopian (a black or dark African) or had a dark complexion as an Ethiopian.

i. As the following verses will show, the complaint over Moses' wife was not the real issue. Many people are criticized for things that are not the real issue, or about things they have no control over.

2. (2) A challenge to Moses' spiritual authority.

So they said, "Has the LORD indeed spoken only through Moses? Has He not spoken through us also?" And the LORD heard *it*.

a. **Has the LORD indeed spoken only through Moses?** This question was meant to tear Moses down, asked with the assumption that Moses was spiritually proud. The idea was that Moses arrogantly presented himself as the only spokesman of God to Israel. Though it was presented in the form of a question, it was in fact an attack against the authority of Moses, and the God who appointed Moses.

i. In one sense, the proper answer to their question was *no*, the LORD had not **spoken only through Moses**.

- God spoke to the people through Aaron in Exodus 4:30.
- God again spoke to and through Aaron in Exodus 12:1.
- Miriam spoke words inspired by God in Exodus 15:20-21.
- On one other occasion, in some way, God spoke through the elders of Israel in Numbers 11:24-25.

ii. In another sense, the answer to their question was *yes* – God had **spoken only through Moses**. God appointed Moses as the foremost leader of Israel, and God used Moses as His spokesman to Israel.

iii. Aaron and Miriam reasoned like this: "We are spiritually gifted, and God has spoken through us. Therefore, Moses should share his place of authority over the congregation of Israel with us." They didn't understand that being spiritually gifted or being used by God in themselves did not justify receiving the responsibility and authority of leading the people of God.

b. **Has He not spoken through us also?** In one sense, this was a strange question. God had **spoken through** Aaron and Miriam in Exodus 4:30, 12:1, and 15:20-21. This wasn't really a question, but an attempt to lift Miriam and Aaron up. They wanted some of the authority and attention Moses received by God's appointment.

i. By God's design, Moses had a singular position of leadership over Israel, and the people were not led by a congress or committee. This type of leadership is often seen in the Bible, shown in leaders such as Joshua, David, Daniel, James, Peter, Paul, Timothy, and Titus. The greatest example of this kind of leadership was Jesus Christ, whose leadership style we are commanded to imitate.

ii. "Every now and then we hear some simpleton or other talking against a 'one-man ministry,' when it has been a one-man ministry from the commencement of the world to the present day; and whenever you try to have any other form of ministry, except that of each individual saint discharging his own ministry, and doing it thoroughly and heartily and independently and bravely in the sight of God, you very soon run upon quicksands." (Spurgeon)

c. **And the LORD heard it:** Of course, God **heard it**. God always does, and He hears according to truth, not according to mere appearance. Miriam and Aaron accused Moses of pride, the very same sin that motivated them to make the accusation.

3. (3) The humble heart of Moses.

(Now the man Moses *was* very humble, more than all men who *were* on the face of the earth.)

a. **Now the man Moses was very humble:** Moses did not have a significant problem with pride; he **was very humble**. Quite the contrary – his accusers were the ones with a pride problem.

i. If the genuinely humble man Moses was accused of pride and a dictatorial manner, it shows that accusations of pride and authoritarian manner are sometimes untrue. In this case the accusation was false, even though it was made by those close to the accused.

b. **More than all men who were on the face of the earth:** This statement, if written by Moses, seems to be self-contradictory. It doesn't seem to be proper for a **very humble** man to write of his great humility. Though Moses wrote the first five books of the Bible, it is likely that someone added this comment after the death of Moses – perhaps Joshua, who would have known Moses well.

i. Another portion of the books of Moses that was completed by a later, inspired editor was the account of Moses' death in Deuteronomy 34. Perhaps Joshua was also the editor who added Deuteronomy 34.

ii. It is important to see Moses didn't start out as the humblest man on earth. As a prince of Egypt, Moses grew up proud and confident in his abilities. It was only time – desert time, lowly time – that made him a humble man, able to be greatly used by God.

c. **Moses was very humble**: Other commentators suggest that **humble** is better understood as "low" or "miserable," and this describes a low point in Moses' life.

i. **Humble**: "It is a word that elsewhere is used only in poetry. It sometimes refers to those in real poverty, or those who are weak and liable to be exploited (Amos 2:7; Isa. 11:4). Such people must look to God for aid, because they are unable to help themselves." (Wenham)

ii. "The word 'miserable' could hardly be more fitting in the context of this chapter. Moses has been under assault from every front." (Allen)

iii. Moses was "miserable" because "of the great burden he had to bear in the care and government of this people, and because of their ingratitude and rebellion both against God and himself: of this depression and affliction, see the fullest proof in the preceding chapter. The very power they envied was oppressive to its possessor, and was more than either of *their* shoulders could sustain." (Clarke)

B. God answers the accusation of Miriam and Aaron against Moses.

1. (4-5) God's dramatic appearance to Miriam and Aaron.

Suddenly the LORD said to Moses, Aaron, and Miriam, "Come out, you three, to the tabernacle of meeting!" So the three came out. Then the LORD came down in the pillar of cloud and stood *in* the door of the tabernacle, and called Aaron and Miriam. And they both went forward.

a. **Suddenly**: There was no long delay. Many of God's judgments are long in coming, at least from a human perspective – but on occasion, God brings His justice **suddenly**.

b. **Come out, you three, to the tabernacle of meeting**: In what seems to have been an audible voice, God called for all three to come before the tabernacle of meeting. Perhaps Miriam and Aaron thought that God would use this situation to correct Moses, whom they claimed was proud and dictatorial.

c. **Then the LORD came down in the pillar of cloud**: God took a personal, powerful interest in this important matter. The LORD wanted to make His will plainly known.

2. (6-9) God's vindication of Moses.

Then He said,

"Hear now My words:
If there is a prophet among you,
***I,* the LORD, make Myself known to him in a vision;**
I speak to him in a dream.
Not so with My servant Moses;
He *is* faithful in all My house.
I speak with him face to face,
Even plainly, and not in dark sayings;
And he sees the form of the LORD.
Why then were you not afraid
To speak against My servant Moses?"

So the anger of the LORD was aroused against them, and He departed.

a. **I speak with him face to face**: The basis of the complaint of Miriam and Aaron was essentially, "What's so special about Moses?" God here explained exactly what was so special about him. Most prophets receive revelation through a dream or in a vision, but God spoke with Moses **face to face**.

i. We understand the phrase **face to face** to mean great and unhindered closeness in relationship; we do not take this to mean that Moses literally saw a material or physical face of God. In the sense of seeing the material or physical face of God in glory, what God declared in Exodus 33:20 is true: *You cannot see My face; for no man shall see Me, and live.*

ii. This is also demonstrated by the phrase, **and he sees the form of the LORD**. This is what Moses had actually seen of God with his physical eyes – only **the form of the LORD**, nothing specific or material, because he could not see the LORD and live.

iii. This clarity of revelation from God made Moses unique. "Only Moses could approach the holy mountain and gaze on the Divine Person. Only his face radiated following these encounters. Others might hear the words; only Moses sees God's person.... At the very least, these words speak of an unprecedented level of intimacy between God and Moses." (Allen)

iv. "The word 'form' is used of visual representations, pictures, or images, of earthly and heavenly beings (Exodus. 20:4). Job saw someone's form, but could not identify the person from it (Job 4:16)." (Wenham)

b. **My servant Moses; he is faithful in all My house. I speak with him face to face, even plainly, and not in dark sayings**: Moses enjoyed remarkably close communion with God, and it is worth considering why.

i. It was because God *needed* a man this close to Him, to be a vessel of revelation and a proper leader for the nation through this remarkable time of the Exodus. This close relationship was a gift of the sovereign God to Moses.

ii. It was because Moses was a **humble** man. Only the **humble** – those who are genuinely others-centered – can be trusted with such communion with God.

iii. It was because Moses, according to God, was **faithful in all My house**: His walk of righteousness and purity, demonstrated over forty years in obscure service to God in the smallest things, revealed the faithful heart that God saw in Moses. "The vision of God is not given to great intellectual ability or mental gift; but to those who as servants are faithful in the administration of God's Household.... Such are they that enjoy the face-to-face fellowship, and the mouth-to-mouth speech." (Meyer)

iv. **Faithful in all My house**: The author of Hebrews quoted this idea in Hebrews 3:5-6, making a contrast between Moses and Jesus. Moses was a servant **faithful in all** God's **house**, but Jesus was, and is, the Son of God; builder of His own house (the church). Also, "Moses saw God's form and heard his word, but Jesus was the Word and in the form of God (John 1:14–18; Phil. 2:6)." (Wenham)

c. **Why then were you not afraid to speak against My servant Moses?** As much as Miriam and Aaron did not want to recognize it, Moses *did* have a unique calling and equipping from the LORD. They did not speak against Moses as the leader of Israel as much as they spoke against Moses the servant of *God*.

i. It was not that Moses was beyond criticism. Moses was not to be simply obeyed and praised, and never held to account or asked difficult questions. In fact, another relative of Moses, his father-in-law Jethro, did confront Moses and ask him difficult questions, and Jethro was greatly used of God when he did this (Exodus 18:12-24).

ii. Miriam and Aaron should have been **afraid to speak against** Moses because their criticism was petty and about something that didn't matter or was beyond control: the nationality or appearance of Moses' wife.

iii. Miriam and Aaron should have been **afraid to speak against** Moses because their criticism was simply not true. Moses was not a proud man, but the humblest man on earth.

iv. Miriam and Aaron should have been **afraid to speak against** Moses because their criticism was prompted by their own self-interest; they were jealous of all the attention Moses was receiving and wanted some of it for themselves.

v. Leaders in the house of God must be held to account, and they must be open to criticism and questioning. But they don't need to make themselves quiet targets for those who bring petty, false, and self-motivated criticism.

d. **So the anger of the LORD was aroused against them, and He departed**: After making His anger evident, the remarkable presence of God departed. This left an extremely uncomfortable pause for Miriam and Aaron.

C. God's punishment for Miriam and Aaron.

1. (10) Miriam is made a leper.

And when the cloud departed from above the tabernacle, suddenly Miriam *became* leprous, as *white as* snow. Then Aaron turned toward Miriam, and there she was, a leper.

a. **Suddenly Miriam became leprous, as white as snow**: Leprosy was a disease where the body rotted and decayed. It was considered a "walking death" – and Miriam had an advanced case of leprosy (**white as snow**) instantly. At this moment, God caused her body to reflect her heart.

i. "Though 'leprosy' is the traditional translation of the Hebrew root 𝕏*ara*, it is inaccurate. True leprosy (Hansen's disease) did not reach the Middle East until New Testament times at the earliest. Nor does true leprosy spontaneously disappear, as the various complaints listed in Leviticus 13–14 may do. Rather, biblical leprosy is a patchy, scaly skin complaint, such as psoriasis or severe eczema. It may be that the flaking, peeling scales associated with such complaints prompts the comparison with snow and a still-born infant." (Wenham)

b. **Then Aaron turned toward Miriam, and there she was, a leper**: It seems that Miriam did not immediately know this; Aaron noticed it first as he turned and looked at his sister.

2. (11-12) Aaron's apology.

So Aaron said to Moses, "Oh, my lord! Please do not lay *this* sin on us, in which we have done foolishly and in which we have sinned. Please do not let her be as one dead, whose flesh is half consumed when he comes out of his mother's womb!"

a. **Oh, my lord! Please do not lay this sin on us, in which we have done foolishly and in which we have sinned**: Aaron was easily influenced. When the people of Israel wanted an idol, he was persuaded to provide it (Exodus 32:1-6). He was influenced by his sister (who seemed to be the greater troublemaker, because she was named first and was first struck with leprosy). Now Aaron was quickly influenced back to a humble submission before Moses.

i. Adam Clarke considered one possible reason Miriam was afflicted with leprosy and Aaron was not: "Had he [Aaron] been smitten with the leprosy, his sacred character must have greatly suffered, and perhaps the *priesthood* itself have fallen into contempt. How many priests and preachers who deserved to be exposed to reproach and infamy, have been spared for the sake of the holy character they bore, that the ministry might not be blamed! But the just God will visit their transgressions in some other way, if they do not deeply deplore them and find mercy through Christ. Nothing tends to discredit the work of God so much as the transgressions and miscarriages of those who minister in holy things."

ii. **Done foolishly**: "The Hebrew *yaal* is a rare term used in Isaiah 19:13 and Jeremiah 5:4 and 50:36 to refer to a person who acts in a delusional manner as a result of ignorance, of one lacking knowledge of God and his ways." (Cole)

iii. "Himself trembling as one who had barely escaped, Aaron could not but confess his share in the transgression." (Watson)

b. **Oh my lord! Please do not lay this sin on us**: Aaron called Moses his master (**my lord**), and he attributed to Moses the power to strike Miriam with leprosy. Aaron also confessed his previous criticism as foolish and sinful (**we have done foolishly...we have sinned**).

i. Sadly, we can't seem to separate Aaron's immediate and dramatic change of heart from the threat that he might be the next victim of God's judgment. His confession seemed to be full of self-interest.

3. (13) Moses prays for Miriam.

So Moses cried out to the LORD, saying, "Please heal her, O God, I pray!"

a. **So Moses cried out to the LORD**: This was the first word spoken by Moses in this chapter. He had not spoken the entire time he was accused, leaving it up to God to answer his critics.

i. When a leader perceives accusations are petty, false, or self-motivated, often the right thing to do is to ignore them, leave them up to God, and keep busy with what the LORD has called the leader to do. Jesus did this, as described in Isaiah 53:7: *He was oppressed and He was afflicted, yet He opened not His mouth.*

b. **Please heal her, O God, I pray**: When Moses finally did speak, it was in prayer *for* his accusers.

4. (14-16) The restoration of Miriam.

Then the LORD said to Moses, "If her father had but spit in her face, would she not be shamed seven days? Let her be shut out of the camp seven days, and afterward she may be received *again*." So Miriam was shut out of the camp seven days, and the people did not journey till Miriam was brought in *again*. And afterward the people moved from Hazeroth and camped in the Wilderness of Paran.

a. **Let her be shut out of the camp seven days, and afterward she may be received again**: God did heal Miriam. If she were still a leper, she would not have been allowed to remain in the camp of Israel, and she was **received again**. Yet, God allowed her to live with the outward display of her inward heart for seven days – and allowed the whole nation to know it.

b. **So Miriam was shut out of the camp seven days**: This was appropriate because Miriam had done something even more shameful than her own father spitting in her face. She tried to bring down a leader of God's people with petty, false, and self-interested criticism.

i. **Afterward the people moved from Hazeroth**: "While Miriam was going through her required period of separation and ritual purification, the Israelite camp remained at Hazeroth. This delay was perhaps out of some respect or admiration for Miriam and her noble place within the community leadership. But also Israel would not disembark on the next stage of the journey to the Promised Land until the Lord would lead them by the cloud. Hence the seriousness of the rebellion of one of Israel's leaders is magnified, and the consequences of such an act would affect the entire community." (Cole)

c. **Camped in the Wilderness of Paran**: After leaving Mount Sinai (Numbers 10:11-12), now Israel came to the staging ground for the invasion and conquest of Canaan. They were on the threshold of the Promised Land, with God inviting them to take the land by faith.

i. "The Desert of Paran was the staging area for the attack on the land of Canaan.... Now was the time for regrouping, for reconnaissance and evaluation, for placing strategy in place, and for mounting the assault of victory over the Canaanite peoples." (Allen)

Numbers 13 – Spies Are Sent into Canaan

A. Spies are chosen and commissioned.

1. (1-3) The sending of the spies.

And the LORD spoke to Moses, saying, "Send men to spy out the land of Canaan, which I am giving to the children of Israel; from each tribe of their fathers you shall send a man, every one a leader among them." So Moses sent them from the Wilderness of Paran according to the command of the LORD, all of them men who *were* heads of the children of Israel.

a. **Send men to spy out the land of Canaan**: These men were sent on a reconnaissance mission. They were to examine the land of Canaan and bring back a report to the nation. They would investigate the path to Canaan, see if the land was a good land to live in, and learn the military strength of the Canaanites.

i. This was a strategic time for the tribes of Israel. "Given all the experiences that the people have gone through in the previous months of preparation and journey, at last—at long last—it was time to claim God's word, to believe in his power, to march in his name, and to enter his land." (Allen)

b. **From each tribe of their fathers you shall send a man, every one a leader among them**: These spies were chosen from among the people. According to Deuteronomy 1:20-25, the plan to send spies did not first come from Moses, but the idea came from the people.

i. Deuteronomy 1:21 records the words of Moses when Israel came to Kadesh Barnea in the Wilderness of Paran: *Look, the LORD your God has set the land before you; go up and possess it, as the LORD God of your fathers has spoken to you; do not fear or be discouraged.* Moses told them simply to go and take the land God had promised. According to Ezekiel 20:6,

God had already searched out the land for them. They didn't need to do it themselves.

ii. In response, the people suggested this plan to Moses (*every one of you came near to me and said*, Deuteronomy 1:22). However, Moses agreed with the plan of the people saying, *the plan pleased me well* (Deuteronomy 1:23).

iii. This mission of the spies had a bad result. It could be said that Moses was wrong in agreeing to this suggestion of the people. Perhaps the accusations of Miriam and Aaron (petty, false, and self-interested as they were) had made Moses hesitant to take strong leadership.

iv. Since the people of Israel initiated this excursion, perhaps Moses only came to God asking *how* to send out the spies, not *if* he should send out the spies. Still, God directed them on how to do it: **from each tribe of their fathers you shall send a man, every one a leader among them** describes the *method* of sending the spies.

c. **According to the command of the LORD**: Nevertheless, in the larger picture this was in the plan of God. God used the report of the spies as a test of Israel's faith.

2. (4-16) The men chosen as spies.

Now these *were* their names: from the tribe of Reuben, Shammua the son of Zaccur; from the tribe of Simeon, Shaphat the son of Hori; from the tribe of Judah, Caleb the son of Jephunneh; from the tribe of Issachar, Igal the son of Joseph; from the tribe of Ephraim, Hoshea the son of Nun; from the tribe of Benjamin, Palti the son of Raphu; from the tribe of Zebulun, Gaddiel the son of Sodi; from the tribe of Joseph, *that is,* from the tribe of Manasseh, Gaddi the son of Susi; from the tribe of Dan, Ammiel the son of Gemalli; from the tribe of Asher, Sethur the son of Michael; from the tribe of Naphtali, Nahbi the son of Vophsi; from the tribe of Gad, Geuel the son of Machi. These *are* the names of the men whom Moses sent to spy out the land. And Moses called Hoshea the son of Nun, Joshua.

a. **Now these were their names**: One man was chosen from each tribe, so the spies would represent the entire community of Israel.

b. **Caleb the son of Jephunneh**: This was the representative from the tribe of Judah. The name **Caleb** is very similar to the Hebrew word for a *dog* (*keleb*).

i. Allen speculates that despite the often-negative association with dogs in the Old Testament, "the name of this heroic companion of Joshua is indeed a word that means 'dog'—but in a positive sense. Perhaps we may term him 'a dog of God' in the most honorable sense this phrase may convey."

c. **And Moses called Hoshea the son of Nun, Joshua**: Joshua was chosen as the leader of the group. His name was first listed as **Hoshea**, meaning "salvation." Here we learn that Moses gave him the name he is more commonly known by: *Ya-Hoshea* meaning, "Yahweh is salvation." This is the Hebrew way of saying the name "Jesus."

i. One might build an imaginary conversation of when Moses first met Joshua:

Moses: "What's your name?"
Joshua: "I'm Hoshea" (or, "I'm salvation").
Moses: "No, Ya-Hoshea!" (or, "Yahweh is salvation").
Joshua: "Then just call me Joshua."

3. (17-20) Moses commissions the spies.

Then Moses sent them to spy out the land of Canaan, and said to them, "Go up this *way* into the South, and go up to the mountains, and see what the land is like: whether the people who dwell in it *are* strong or weak, few or many; whether the land they dwell in is good or bad; whether the cities they inhabit *are* like camps or strongholds; whether the land *is* rich or poor; and whether there are forests there or not. Be of good courage. And bring some of the fruit of the land." Now the time *was* the season of the first ripe grapes.

a. **See what the land is like**: Moses' direction to the spies was a subtle example of unbelief. When God first commissioned Moses, He told him that the land was *a good and large land...a land flowing with milk and honey* (Exodus 3:8). Moses told Israel that it was a good land (Exodus 13:5). There is at least a small sense here that Moses sent the spies to see if God was truthful in describing the land.

i. Nevertheless, this was an entirely *reasonable* thing for Moses to do, and it reflected the *curiosity* of all of Israel. After all, they had never seen this land, nor had almost any Israelite for some 400 years.

b. **Whether the people who dwell in it are strong or weak**: In some sense, this was a dangerous question to ask. If they thought the people of Canaan were **strong**, they might be afraid to go into the land and conquer them. If they thought they were **weak**, they might enter trusting in their own strength.

i. **Now the time was the season of the first ripe grapes**: "*The season of the first ripe grapes* (20) is late July, approximately two months after the departure from Sinai (10:11)." (Wenham)

B. The report of the spies.

1. (21-25) The twelve spies in the Promised Land.

So they went up and spied out the land from the Wilderness of Zin as far as Rehob, near the entrance of Hamath. And they went up through the South and came to Hebron; Ahiman, Sheshai, and Talmai, the descendants of Anak, *were* there. (Now Hebron was built seven years before Zoan in Egypt.) Then they came to the Valley of Eshcol, and there cut down a branch with one cluster of grapes; they carried it between two of them on a pole. *They* also *brought* some of the pomegranates and figs. The place was called the Valley of Eshcol, because of the cluster which the men of Israel cut down there. And they returned from spying out the land after forty days.

a. **So they went up and spied out the land**: As these spies toured the land, they saw some of the people and the produce of the land. This spectacular produce included clusters of grapes so big that they had to be carried between two men **on a pole**. This was a good land.

i. Adam Clarke gave several historical citations noting the large size of grapes in the region and added this: "I myself once cut down a bunch of grapes nearly twenty pounds in weight. Those who live in cold climates can scarcely have any conception to what perfection both grapes and other fruits grow in climates that are warm, and where the soil is suitable to them."

b. **And came to Hebron**: God promised all the land of Canaan to Abraham, but the only piece he owned (in the eyes of the Canaanites) was the burial cave in Hebron. They came to Hebron, but no mention is made of the tombs of Abraham, Sarah, Isaac, Rebekah, Jacob, and Leah.

i. "The narrator knew these traditions, and he assumes the spies did and that the reader does. It is essential that they be borne in mind as the rest of the story unfolds." (Wenham)

ii. **Hebron was built seven years before Zoan in Egypt**: "This seems to be noted to confront the Egyptians, who vainly boasted of the antiquity of their city Zoan above all places." (Poole)

c. **The descendants of Anak, were there**: This is the first Biblical mention of these people. They were a people of great stature (Numbers 13:33) and thought to be fierce warriors (Deuteronomy 9:2).

i. They saw the **descendants of Anak** in **Hebron**. "Instead of looking to the patriarchs and the promises, the spies noticed sizes of buildings and statures of persons.... they averted their glance from the tombs of the fathers, and they neglected the promise of God; they were too preoccupied with the sandal sizes of three huge men who lived in Hebron." (Allen)

ii. "In Joshua 11:21–22 the Anakim were noted as having lived in the Hebron region, as well as to the west in the Shephelah in such cities as Gath, and in the coastal plain in Gaza and Ashdod. Some have suggested that the famous Goliath, who was defeated by David, was one of the surviving descendants of these exceptionally tall individuals. Four others were killed by David's men in a battle recounted in 2 Samuel 21:15–22." (Cole)

d. **And they returned from spying out the land after forty days**: The discovery tour covered some 250 miles (400 kilometers) and took **forty days**. In the Bible, a period of **forty** (such as forty days or forty years) is often associated with testing.

2. (26-29) The report regarding the land.

Now they departed and came back to Moses and Aaron and all the congregation of the children of Israel in the Wilderness of Paran, at Kadesh; they brought back word to them and to all the congregation, and showed them the fruit of the land. Then they told him, and said: "We went to the land where you sent us. It truly flows with milk and honey, and this *is* its fruit. Nevertheless the people who dwell in the land *are* strong; the cities *are* fortified *and* very large; moreover we saw the descendants of Anak there. The Amalekites dwell in the land of the South; the Hittites, the Jebusites, and the Amorites dwell in the mountains; and the Canaanites dwell by the sea and along the banks of the Jordan."

a. **They brought back word to them and to all the congregation, and showed them the fruit of the land**: The returning spies both spoke and showed all Israel what they saw in the land. This included the huge cluster of grapes mentioned in verse 23.

b. **We went to the land where you sent us**: The spies seemed to sense they were more on a mission from Israel than on a mission from God.

c. **It truly flows with milk and honey**: What God had promised about the land was indeed true. The fruit they brought back – grapes, pomegranates, and figs – showed how fruitful and blessed Canaan was agriculturally.

d. **Nevertheless**: The word (according to Wenham and Cole) is a strong way to make a contradictory statement. **Nevertheless** means "despite all of that." The message from most of the spies was, "The land is as wonderful as God promised, but we can't conquer it."

- Despite God's faithful promise, **the people who dwell in the land are strong**.

- Despite God's faithful promise, **the cities are fortified and very large**.

- Despite God's faithful promise, **we saw the descendants of Anak there**.

- Despite God's faithful promise, **the Amalekites dwell...the Hittites, the Jebusites, and the Amorites dwell...and the Canaanites dwell** in the land, and there isn't any room for the people of Israel.

  i. **Fortified**: "The term *besurot* (NIV, 'fortified') is used in 2 Kings 18:13 of inaccessible cities and in Jeremiah 33:3 of inaccessible things. The cities of Canaan were said to be beyond the reach of the people of Israel." (Allen)

  ii. It is hard to imagine a report *more* unbelieving and unfaithful to God than this. This report recognized the faithfulness of God's promise, the truth of His word, and yet said, "Despite all that, we can't conquer the land."

  iii. If the faith of the spies was tested over this 40-day tour of the land, they failed the test. They didn't believe God could or would fulfill His promise to give Israel this land, as stated in the covenant God made with Abraham, Isaac, and Jacob.

  iv. "Presumably they left in confidence, with a spirit of divine adventure; but they returned in fear, groveling before men, no longer fearful of God." (Allen)

3. (30) Caleb's faith-filled objection.

Then Caleb quieted the people before Moses, and said, "Let us go up at once and take possession, for we are well able to overcome it."

   a. **Then Caleb quieted the people**: Caleb commanded the people to immediately (**at once**) trust God, obey God, and take the land. He understood that in the LORD they were **well able to overcome it**.

   b. **Let us go up at once and take possession**: It took great courage for this man to stand against the tide of unbelief and doubt. Caleb had the spirit of Romans 3:4: *Let God be true but every man a liar.*

4. (31-33) The other spies respond to Caleb.

But the men who had gone up with him said, "We are not able to go up against the people, for they *are* stronger than we." And they gave the children of Israel a bad report of the land which they had spied out,

saying, "The land through which we have gone as spies *is* a land that devours its inhabitants, and all the people whom we saw in it *are* men of *great* stature. There we saw the giants (the descendants of Anak came from the giants); and we were like grasshoppers in our own sight, and so we were in their sight."

a. **But the men who had gone up with him said**: Their unbelieving response was a strong combination of truth, lies, and exaggeration.

- It was true from a human perspective that **they are stronger than we** – but to say, **we are not able to go up against the people** was a lie.

- It was true that they had gone through the land – but to say, **a land that devours its inhabitants** was a lie.

- Each of the statements, **All the people whom we saw in it are men of great stature** or **the giants** and **we were like grasshoppers** were all terrible exaggerations – meaning they were lies.

  i. "Note, too, the exaggerations of terror. 'All the people' are sons of Anak now. The size as well as the number of the giants has grown; 'we were in our own sight as grasshoppers.' No doubt they were gigantic, but fear performed the miracle of adding a cubit to their stature." (Maclaren)

  ii. F.B. Meyer compared the perspective of the ten unbelieving spies to that of the two faithful spies, Caleb and Joshua: "They saw the same spectacles in their survey of the land; but the result in the one case was *panic*, in the other *confidence and peace*. What made the difference? It lay in this, that the ten spies compared themselves with the giants, whilst the two compared the giants with God."

  iii. "The fate they feared they would meet in Canaan actually overtakes them in the desert (Numbers 14:3, 29–34)." (Wenham)

b. **The land through which we have gone as spies**: The unbelieving spies appealed to their authority as those who had seen the strong cities and people of Canaan themselves. They thought and said that the facts and practical realities were on their side. Yet the most fact-based and practical thing the believer can do is to trust the promises of the living God. Ultimately, their unbelief was not according to the facts, but despite the facts.

  i. Significantly, two groups of men could see the same things – the same grapes, the same Canaanites, the same land, and the same cities. One group (Caleb and Joshua) came away strong in faith, and the other ten spies had a sense of certain doom. Ultimately, faith or unbelief is not rooted in circumstances or environment. Faith is rooted in a heart that trusts God and His promises.

ii. "The remarkable fact is that in their report there was no reference to God. They would seem to have lost sight of Him completely for the time being." (Morgan)

iii. "The evil report prevailed. Ten fearful men can out-shout, and certainly out-scare, two brave men." (Allen)

Numbers 14 – The People Reject Canaan

A. The rebellion of Israel at Kadesh Barnea.

1. (1) Israel's sorrow at facing the choice between faith and unbelief.

So all the congregation lifted up their voices and cried, and the people wept that night.

> a. **So all the congregation lifted up their voices and cried**: The tribes of Israel were confronted with two reports regarding the Promised Land. Two of the twelve spies (Caleb and Joshua) said, *Let us go up at once and take possession, for we are well able to overcome it* (Numbers 13:30). The message of the other ten spies was, "What God promised about the land is true; nevertheless, the natives of the land are too mighty, and we cannot overcome them, despite what God has promised" (as in Numbers 13:31-33).

> > i. The twelve spies were sent as representatives of the twelve tribes (Numbers 13:2). In this way, they truly represented the people of Israel. The lack of faith of most of the spies represented a lack of faith among most of Israel.

> > ii. They wept because all of Canaan seemed like a strong, unconquerable fortress. They completely forgot that God defeated *Egypt* to free them from their slavery, a nation far mightier than the Canaanites.

> > iii. In this section the idea of *all the people* is often repeated:

> > - **All the congregation** (14:1).
> > - *All the children of Israel* (14:2).
> > - *The whole congregation* (14:2).
> > - *All the congregation* (14:7).
> > - *All the congregation* (14:10).
> > - *All the children of Israel* (14:10).

Those who refused to trust God and His promise were not a minority or even a slight majority. Unbelief spread among God's people like an epidemic, infecting virtually all of Israel. This was crowd psychology working in an evil, destructive way.

iv. "Terror is more contagious than courage, for a mob is always more prone to base than to noble instincts." (Maclaren)

b. **And the people wept that night**: The unbelief of the ten spies accurately represented the unbelieving heart of the nation. Israel **wept that night** when they heard that the enemies in Canaan were strong. Their tearful grief had at least four distinct aspects.

i. *They mourned because God would not make it all "easy."* We often expect this of God and therefore we often resent adversity. This is to forget the example of Jesus, who faced great difficulty in life and ministry. We may forget that we, as disciples, are not above Jesus our Master.

ii. *They mourned with resentment against God*, putting the blame on Him. In doing this, they denied that the LORD is a loving Father who cares for His children.

iii. *They mourned and gave in to the feeling of unbelief and fear.* This sorrow allowed their feelings to overwhelm their thinking and actions, instead of being directed by a thinking faith in the living God. This was a sinful and unbelieving trust in the feelings of fear and sorrow.

iv. *They mourned over a loss.* We often mourn because something has died. They felt the promise of Canaan had died, becoming impossible. Instead, God wanted them to "die" to their unbelief and their trust in self.

c. **And the people wept that night**: As God invited Israel to take the land of Canaan, they rebelled against Him through their mourning. Unbelief made them think that God's good for them (the gift of the Promised Land) was an evil thing.

i. This shows the great tragedy of unbelief. Less than two years out of Egypt, Israel here stood on the threshold of the Promised Land. Over the first ten chapters of Numbers Israel was fully prepared to live and go forward as people suited for God's Promised Land. They had been ordered and organized; cleansed and purified; set apart and blessed; taught how to give and how to function as priests. In that period, Israel was made to remember judgment spared and deliverance brought; they were given God's presence as a guide, and the tools needed to lead the people. Yet, *unbelief* prevented this otherwise prepared people from receiving God's promises.

2. (2-3a) Israel rebels by murmuring.

And all the children of Israel complained against Moses and Aaron, and the whole congregation said to them, "If only we had died in the land of Egypt! Or if only we had died in this wilderness! Why has the LORD brought us to this land to fall by the sword, that our wives and children should become victims?"

a. **All the children of Israel complained against Moses and Aaron**: Their murmuring was directed first **against Moses and Aaron**, but since these were the LORD's leaders, they really murmured against the LORD. Here, the goal of Moses and Aaron (to lead Israel to the Promised Land) was the LORD's goal. Their complaint was against the LORD, even if they wanted to hide this by directing the complaint **against Moses and Aaron**.

i. There were probably some among Israel who *claimed* to truly trust God, and *claimed* their problem was with Moses and Aaron, not with God. Yet, since Moses and Aaron were properly directed towards God's goal for Israel, on this point to complain against them was to complain against God.

ii. Joshua and Caleb understood this was rebellion against Yahweh: *Only do not rebel against the LORD* (Numbers 14:9). The LORD Himself understood this was a rebellion against Him: *How long will these people reject Me?* (Numbers 14:11)

b. **If only we had died**: The challenge of faith before the people seemed so great – and so dreadful – that they would rather have **died** than go on with what the LORD planned for them.

i. "Often in a state of rebellion against God, one loses the benefit of spiritual mooring, whereby wisdom and discernment become elusive and proper decision making is made extremely difficult. Worry and fear dominate one's thought patterns." (Cole)

ii. Tragically for this generation of Israelites, God would give them what their rebellious, unbelieving hearts wanted. They would die in the desert, never making it to the Promised Land.

c. **Why has the LORD brought us to this land to fall by the sword**: Here, they directly accused the Almighty of sin and of doing evil to them. They were angry with God, accusing Him of plotting to murder them and their **wives and children**.

i. This was a deep state of rebellion. God, who can do no evil, and with Whom there is no shadow of turning, was called *evil* and a *murderer* by His own people.

ii. Later, God would comment on these events in Psalm 95. God described this as *the rebellion* (Psalm 95:8), as when Israel *tested* and *tried* God, despite seeing His mighty works (Psalm 95:9). The writer of Hebrews used these events to solemnly warn against unbelief (Hebrews 3:7-13, 3:16-19).

iii. According to the advice that some give, it is a healthy thing to be angry with God, to express your anger against God, so that God and you can be reconciled. While it is true that one may be angry with God, and true that one should take every such feeling to God, it is wrong to ever assume or imply that such feelings are justified. If we are angry at God, *we* are in sin, because God has never done anything that deserves our anger with Him. We should honestly bring such sin before God, but never for a moment feel it to be justified.

d. **That our wives and children should become victims**: The unbelieving among Israel justified their unbelief based on concern for their **wives and children**. Tragically, because of their unbelief, they would die in the wilderness and their **children** – a new generation of faith – would inherit the Promised Land.

i. "Only their children—whom they claimed outrageously that God desired dead—would be able to enter the land." (Allen)

ii. "So, my brethren, let us strip our discouragements and murmurings of all their disguises, and see them in their true character, and they will appear in their own naked deformity as discrediting God. It is true the difficulty before us may appear great, but it cannot be great to the Lord, who has promised to make us more than conquerors." (Spurgeon)

3. (3b-4) Israel rebels by longing to return to Egypt.

Would it not be better for us to return to Egypt?" So they said to one another, "Let us select a leader and return to Egypt."

a. **Would it not be better for us to return to Egypt?** This was *not* better. In the first ten chapters of Numbers, God led Israel through a process intended to transform them from a slave-minded people to those suited for His Promised-Land. Here, they completely revert to what could be called a slave mentality. They professed to prefer their Egyptian slavery over the walk of faith God intended.

i. Israel rejected a *life of faith*. If God intended to lead them into a deeper trust than before, they wanted no part of it. If God gave them the Promised Land without having to receive it by faith and faith-filled actions, that was fine with Israel – but they did not want a walk of *faith*.

ii. We often think that the experience of the miraculous builds faith, but it rarely does. In the two years previous to Numbers 14 the people of Israel experienced countless dramatic miracles, including the daily miracles of manna and God's presence in the pillars of fire and cloud. Yet when it came to trusting God's promise in a critical moment, they failed.

iii. Certainly, the unbelieving in Israel would claim that they *did* believe God for many things. They believed His presence would be with them in the pillars of cloud and fire. They believed He would provide manna daily. They believed that He would provide water as needed. At many points they did believe, but not here, at this most critical point, at the need of the moment. We have a way of believing everything good about God *except* at the particular point where we are being challenged.

iv. When we distrust and doubt God, we should ask which attribute of His we think will fail. Do we think God has lost His power? His goodness? His honesty? His faithfulness? His love?

b. **Let us select a leader and return to Egypt**: This was pure rebellion. They said that they did not want God's plan, they did not want God's leaders, and they did not want God's land. Here, Israel believed that they knew better than God.

i. "This time they actually propose returning to Egypt, thereby completely rejecting the whole plan of redemption." (Wenham)

ii. Their rebellion was *man-centered*. **They said to one another**, means that the decision was made among themselves, believing their majority vote had more wisdom than God. **Let us select**, means that they didn't like God's selection, so they wanted a leader who would truly represent them – including representing their rebellion against God.

4. (5-9) The reaction of Moses, Aaron, Joshua, and Caleb to the rebellion of the people.

Then Moses and Aaron fell on their faces before all the assembly of the congregation of the children of Israel. But Joshua the son of Nun and Caleb the son of Jephunneh, *who were* among those who had spied out the land, tore their clothes; and they spoke to all the congregation of the

children of Israel, saying: "The land we passed through to spy out *is* an exceedingly good land. If the LORD delights in us, then He will bring us into this land and give it to us, 'a land which flows with milk and honey.' Only do not rebel against the LORD, nor fear the people of the land, for they *are* our bread; their protection has departed from them, and the LORD *is* with us. Do not fear them."

a. **Then Moses and Aaron fell on their faces**: Moses and Aaron were older and wiser and therefore knew how bad the situation was. They simply bowed down in prayer, not saying a word to the people (perhaps sensing it would do no good). They knew that they must cry out to God for a miracle if Israel was to be spared.

> i. "No wonder *Moses and Aaron fell on their faces*, not to plead for their lives, but to express their awe at the sacrilegious blasphemy of the people. To fall on one's face is the Old Testament's ultimate mark of religious worship and awe (Gen. 17:3; Lev. 9:24). But in Numbers it usually anticipates some great act of judgment (cf. 16:4, 22, 45; 20:6)." (Wenham)

b. **But Joshua the son of Nun and Caleb the son of Jephunneh**: Joshua and Caleb, the two faithful spies, were younger and more optimistic, so they attempted to persuade the people.

> i. Joshua and Caleb showed how serious the situation was when they **tore their clothes**, demonstrating deep grief and mourning. They acted as if someone had died – or was about to die.

> ii. Joshua and Caleb reminded the people that **the land...is an exceedingly good land**. The LORD promised that Canaan would be good, and it was – Joshua and Caleb saw it with their own eyes. If God promised Israel could take possession of the land, they could also trust that promise.

> iii. When the people of God looked at the enormous clusters of grapes (13:23, 26-27), a few said: "These huge grapes show us what a good land God has promised us. God said the land would be good, and it is." Most of them said, "Giant grapes mean there must be giant people in the land, people too mighty for us to overcome."

> iv. "These men saw all the others saw, and more. They had clear apprehension of the goodness of the land; they were by no means blind to the formidable nature of the difficulties that stood between them and that possession. But they saw God. They started with that vision, and saw everything else in its light." (Morgan)

v. **They are our bread**: "We shall destroy them as easily as we do our bread or common food." (Poole)

vi. **Their protection has departed**: "The word translated 'protection' is *sel* often rendered 'shadow' or 'shade.' In the hot and arid regions of the Middle East, the notion of a shadow or shade is a symbol of grace and mercy, a relief from the searing heat (cf. Ps 91:1)." (Allen)

vii. Joshua and Caleb warned the people, saying **only do not rebel against the LORD, nor fear the people...the LORD is with us**. Their fear and unbelief were willful rebellion. Therefore, Joshua and Caleb appealed to the will of the people, asking them to decide to give up their rebellion and return to the LORD. Israel did not have to give in to their feelings of fear, of anger against the LORD, of unbelief. By God's grace they could choose to submit to Him and trust Him.

5. (10) Two responses to the appeal of Joshua and Caleb.

And all the congregation said to stone them with stones. Now the glory of the LORD appeared in the tabernacle of meeting before all the children of Israel.

a. **All the congregation said to stone them with stones**: This was the response of the people. Rebellious, unbelieving men cannot endure the men of faith, who come with the challenge of faith. They wanted to *kill* Joshua and Caleb for calling them to forsake their unbelief and to trust God.

i. Those who live in rebellion and unbelief often find those who live in faith and submission to God to be aggravating and disturbing. This is especially true if those who live in faith try to correct or guide the rebellious and unbelieving.

b. **The glory of the LORD appeared**: This was the response of the LORD. Verse 10 does not yet say what the glory of the LORD would do, but it isn't hard to understand. The actions and feelings of the ten unbelieving spies and the great majority of Israel were not consistent with the glory of the LORD.

- It was not consistent with the glory of the LORD to be unbelieving.

- It was not consistent with the glory of the LORD to mourn because the walk of faith was difficult.

- It was not consistent with the glory of the LORD to long for death.

- It was not consistent with the glory of the LORD to accuse God of plotting murder.

- It was not consistent with the glory of the LORD to desire to go back to the slavery of Egypt.

- It was not consistent with the glory of the LORD to reject God's leaders.

- It was not consistent with the glory of the LORD to threaten to kill those who called them to a deeper trust in God.

B. Moses' remarkable intercession for the children of Israel.

1. (11-12) God's charge against Israel and offer to Moses.

Then the LORD said to Moses: "How long will these people reject Me? And how long will they not believe Me, with all the signs which I have performed among them? I will strike them with the pestilence and disinherit them, and I will make of you a nation greater and mightier than they."

a. **The LORD said to Moses**: Here, God did not speak to Israel as a nation. God knew they were past hearing Him. The LORD spoke to Moses directly.

i. Many a child of God in rebellion wonders why they do not hear the voice of God anymore, why God does not speak to them in the Bible as before. Yet, when we reject what God has already said, we often close our ears to what He may continue to speak to us through the Bible.

b. **How long will these people reject Me?** God had been only good to Israel and had demonstrated His loving strength towards them countless times. Israel's rejection of God made no sense. It was right for God to ask, **"how long?"**

c. **I will strike them...and disinherit them**: In this, God said He would give rebellious Israel what they deserved: judgment. The judgment would be what they said they wanted in Numbers 14:2 – to die in the wilderness.

d. **I will make of you a nation greater and mightier**: This was an astonishing offer God made to Moses. God offered to fulfill His promises of a land, a nation, and a blessing to Abraham, Isaac, and Jacob through Moses, and *not* through the twelve tribes of Israel as a whole.

i. This was an impressive proposal for Moses. God offered Him the status of "patriarch," to become a father for Israel in the same way Abraham, Isaac, and Jacob were. Moses certainly knew of their greatness and fame; God used Moses to compile their stories in the book of Genesis.

ii. We must regard this as a genuine proposal from God; the LORD does not speak make-believe words. If Moses were to do nothing, this plan of God would go into effect. The presently constituted people of Israel would perish, and God would make a new people of Israel descended from Moses. God even promised Moses that this new **nation** would be **greater and mightier** than the present one.

iii. About a year before this, God made a similar offer to Moses, proposing to make a "great nation" of him after God judged Israel as it was at the time (Exodus 32:9-10).

2. (13-16) Moses intercedes for Israel, appealing to God's glory.

And Moses said to the LORD: "Then the Egyptians will hear *it,* for by Your might You brought these people up from among them, and they will tell *it* to the inhabitants of this land. They have heard that You, LORD, *are* among these people; that You, LORD, are seen face to face and Your cloud stands above them, and You go before them in a pillar of cloud by day and in a pillar of fire by night. Now *if* You kill these people as one man, then the nations which have heard of Your fame will speak, saying, 'Because the LORD was not able to bring this people to the land which He swore to give them, therefore He killed them in the wilderness.'"

a. **And Moses said to the LORD**: It seems that Moses did not consider God's proposal for a moment. Instead, Moses pleaded for the nation and loved them despite their rebellion.

i. Adam Clarke wrote that the words of Moses' prayer "are full of simplicity and energy; his arguments with God (for he did reason and argue with his Maker) are pointed, cogent, and respectful; and while they show a heart full of humanity, they evidence the deepest concern for the glory of God."

b. **Then the Egyptians will hear it, for by Your might You brought these people up from among them**: Moses asked God to spare the present nation of Israel for *His own* glory and reputation. Moses knew that if God struck and disinherited the present nation and started again with Moses (Numbers 14:12), it would be a mark against His reputation before the nations – especially Egypt.

i. Perhaps then the nations could claim that **the LORD was not able to bring this people to the land**. The pagan nations could say that the sin and rebellion of man were greater than the power and goodness of God.

ii. "Here God offered Moses a private fortune, which he prudently refuseth, because God should be a loser by it." (Trapp)

c. **Which He swore to give them**: Moses brought God's promise before Him. He begged God to not give the pagan nations any opportunity to think God had not been true to His word.

3. (17-19) Moses intercedes for Israel, appealing to God's power and promise.

"And now, I pray, let the power of my LORD be great, just as You have spoken, saying, 'The LORD is longsuffering and abundant in mercy, forgiving iniquity and transgression; but He by no means clears *the guilty,* visiting the iniquity of the fathers on the children to the third and fourth *generation.'* Pardon the iniquity of this people, I pray, according to the greatness of Your mercy, just as You have forgiven this people, from Egypt even until now."

a. **Let the power of my LORD be great**: Moses glories in the power of God but asks that God would use His power by showing mercy and longsuffering to a rebellious Israel.

b. **Just as You have spoken**: The list of Numbers 14:18-19 is almost a quote from the words of self-revelation God spoke to Moses in the dramatic encounter Moses had with God in Exodus 34:6-8.

i. **Longsuffering and abundant in mercy, forgiving iniquity and transgression; but He by no means clears the guilty**: Each of these is mentioned first in Exodus 34:6-8.

ii. Moses basically said: "LORD, You have revealed Yourself to me by Your word. Your word declares who You are. Now LORD, please act towards Israel according to who You have declared Yourself to be in Your word."

c. **Pardon the iniquity of this people, I pray, according to the greatness of Your mercy**: Moses knew God's power and appealed to it; Moses knew God's promise and appealed to it, and Moses knew God's glory and appealed to it. This was a spectacular example of intercession.

i. What made this intercession spectacular was not primarily the method Moses used (appealing to God's glory, power, and promise) but the heart of Moses in prayer. Here, Moses was totally others-centered, not concerned for his own glory, but only for Israel. He displayed that he shared the heart of God towards His people, and that was what made the intercession of Moses spectacular.

ii. "Moses here may be taken as a dim shadow of Christ. 'Moses was faithful in all his house,' but Jesus is the true Mediator, whose intercession consists in presenting the constant efficacy of His sacrifice, and to whom God ever says, 'I have pardoned according to Thy word.'" (Maclaren)

C. The fate of Israel after the rebellion at Kadesh Barnea.

1. (20) God's promise of pardon in response to Moses' intercession.

Then the LORD said: "I have pardoned, according to your word;

a. **I have pardoned**: The heart of Moses and his method of intercession were successful. These are sweet words for any sinner to hear.

b. **According to your word**: This means that Moses' prayer *mattered*. Some people may wonder if prayer is an elaborate game, where God threatens to do a thing He would never do anyway, believers respond with prayer, pretending to believe God would do what He threatened. Then, when God hears the believer pray, He forgets His idle threat and does what He was going to do anyway. Prayer does not work that way.

i. We don't understand the relationship between the eternal, sovereign plan of God and our prayers; but we know it is no game. God never wanted Moses to think of it as a game and wanted Moses to at least think that his prayers had directly affected the outcome: **I have pardoned, according to your word**! We should pray as if life and death, heaven and hell, would be decided by our prayers!

2. (21-25) The fate of the rebels and the fate of the faithful.

"But truly, as I live, all the earth shall be filled with the glory of the LORD; because all these men who have seen My glory and the signs which I did in Egypt and in the wilderness, and have put Me to the test now these ten times, and have not heeded My voice, they certainly shall not see the land of which I swore to their fathers, nor shall any of those who rejected Me see it. But My servant Caleb, because he has a different spirit in him and has followed Me fully, I will bring into the land where he went, and his descendants shall inherit it. Now the Amalekites and the Canaanites dwell in the valley; tomorrow turn and move out into the wilderness by the Way of the Red Sea."

a. **But truly, as I live, all the earth shall be filled with the glory of the LORD**: God's response to Israel would be full of, and be reflective of, His glory. He would show mercy and pardon, but in a way consistent with His glory.

i. "The people who have behaved so intolerably will not be put to death, but neither can things go back to the way they were on the day before the rebellion. The words of God in v.21 are forceful and direct; as surely as he lives, as surely as his glory fills the earth, there is a sentence to be paid." (Allen)

ii. **Put Me to the test now these ten times**: "God spoke of the Israelites testing him 'these ten times,' an expression that denotes consistent action over a long period of time. Though the Babylonian Talmud delineated ten specific occasions of Israelite sedition, the number probably was used figuratively and in contrast to the ten plagues that God brought against the Egyptians." (Cole)

b. **They certainly shall not see the land of which I swore to their fathers, nor shall any of those who rejected Me see it**: Therefore, those who put God to the test and rebelled against His promise, would not see the Promised Land. An exception was made for the few faithful like Caleb and Joshua.

c. **My servant Caleb...he has a different spirit in him...[he] has followed Me fully...I will bring into the land**: God praised Caleb, who (together with Joshua) stood on the side of faith while almost all of Israel did not believe in God's promise or goodness.

i. Caleb was God's **servant**, an honored title. When all of Israel went in one direction, Caleb had **a different spirit in him** and remained faithful to the LORD.

ii. **Has followed Me fully**: According to Clarke and others, the literal sense of this Hebrew phrase is *he filled after Me*. Caleb was complete, full, in his following of the LORD, leaving nothing out.

iii. Caleb received a great and appropriate reward. "Caleb would be granted a tract of land within the tribal allocation for the Judahites, in the region of Hebron, the town mentioned explicitly in the text as the abode of the giant Anakites and the area near where the enormous cluster of grapes was procured." (Cole)

d. **Tomorrow turn and move out into the wilderness**: God had brought them to the threshold of the Promised Land, but they rebelled against Him and did not enter – so God will send them back to the wilderness.

i. Israel has demonstrated they were still slave-minded; they did not think like people suited for God's Promised Land. It will take more wilderness training until the new generation became a people ready to live in the Promised Land.

ii. "Far greater hardships and pains are met on the road of departure from God, than any which befall His servants. To follow Him involves a conflict, but to shirk the battle does not bring immunity from strife." (Maclaren)

3. (26-35) The death sentence upon the rebels.

And the Lord spoke to Moses and Aaron, saying, "How long *shall I bear with* this evil congregation who complain against Me? I have heard the complaints which the children of Israel make against Me. Say to them, 'As I live,' says the Lord, 'just as you have spoken in My hearing, so I will do to you: The carcasses of you who have complained against Me shall fall in this wilderness, all of you who were numbered, according to your entire number, from twenty years old and above. Except for Caleb the son of Jephunneh and Joshua the son of Nun, you shall by no means enter the land which I swore I would make you dwell in. But your little ones, whom you said would be victims, I will bring in, and they shall know the land which you have despised. But *as for* you, your carcasses shall fall in this wilderness. And your sons shall be shepherds in the wilderness forty years, and bear the brunt of your infidelity, until your carcasses are consumed in the wilderness. According to the number of the days in which you spied out the land, forty days, for each day you shall bear your guilt one year, *namely* forty years, and you shall know My rejection. I the Lord have spoken this; I will surely do so to all this evil congregation who are gathered together against Me. In this wilderness they shall be consumed, and there they shall die.'"

a. **All of you who were numbered...from twenty years old and above**: God gave the message to the nation – this generation must die in the wilderness and would never see the Promised Land. It was as if God said to them, "You didn't want it when it was offered to you, so now you will never have it."

i. They said, *If only we had died in this wilderness!* (Numbers 14:2). God will now give them that desire. If they preferred death to a walk of faith, God would make that their destiny.

ii. **Carcasses**: "The term used here for their dissipated bodies...often is used to describe human corpses that would be scattered on the ground after a great battle." (Cole)

b. **Except for Caleb...and Joshua**: These men of faith were the glorious exceptions. They would enter the land of promise because they had the hearts and minds of new men.

i. Not even Moses and Aaron were excepted. They would also not enter the Promised Land, each for their own reasons. But we remember that Moses was not guiltless in this whole tragedy, having agreed to the request of the people to send out spies instead of simply boldly taking the land by faith.

c. **But your little ones**: When excusing their unbelief, Israel had claimed concern for their children (Numbers 14:3), accusing God of bringing them to the wilderness to kill their wives and children. In an ironic twist, God said it would be their **little ones** who would inherit the land, while unbelieving adults perished in the wilderness.

i. **Bear the brunt of your infidelity**: The sense of **infidelity** is that of harlotry, and in this context, spiritual adultery – unfaithfulness to God by the allegiance to idols. We aren't told of any obvious idols that Israel was given over to in Numbers 14. Surely, they battled against some of the idols we do today – idols of comfort, safety, and the refusal to risk anything upon God's promise.

d. **The land which you have despised**: If the generation of unbelief did not trust God to give them the good land of Canaan, it was as if they **despised** it. The Promised Land was a land to take in faith, and the unbelieving and rebellious **despised** God's good promise and the land.

e. **Forty days...forty years**: The spies, representing all Israel, failed in the test of 40 days. Now the nation would be tested for 40 years – and they would come from that time purified, ready to inherit the Promised Land, but only after the generation of unbelief and rebellion perished in the wilderness.

i. This failure to take God's promise by faith was a turning point in Israel's history, and is recalled in Numbers 32, Deuteronomy 1, Nehemiah 9, Psalms 95 and 106, Amos chapters 2 and 5, 1 Corinthians 10, and Hebrews 3-4.

ii. There is a spiritual analogy to make with life in Jesus under the new covenant. The old man, the man still slave-minded to sin, can *never* enter God's promises. The old man must die and the believer must reckon this as done in Jesus Christ (Romans 6:6).

iii. This turning point in Israel's history is an essential lesson for every believer as described in Psalm 95:7-11: *Today, if you will hear His voice: Do not harden your hearts, as in the rebellion, as in the day of trial in the wilderness, when your fathers tested Me; they tried Me, though they saw My work. For forty years I was grieved with that generation, and said, "It is a people who go astray in their hearts, and they do not know My ways." So I swore in My wrath, "They shall not enter My rest."*

iv. Psalm 106:24-27 adds this: *Then they despised the pleasant land; they did not believe His word, but complained in their tents, and did not heed the voice of the LORD. Therefore He raised up His hand in an oath against them, to overthrow them in the wilderness, to overthrow their descendants among the nations, and to scatter them in the lands.*

v. Centuries later, the leaders of Israel recognized this sinful episode in a prayer: *But they and our fathers acted proudly, hardened their necks, and did not heed Your commandments. They refused to obey, and they were not mindful of Your wonders that You did among them. But they hardened their necks, and in their rebellion they appointed a leader to return to their bondage.* (Nehemiah 9:16-17)

vi. Hebrews 3:7-4:16 makes it clear that God has a place of rest and promise for every believer to enter into, and it can only be entered by faith. The man of unbelief, self-reliance, and self-focus can never enter God's rest and abundance.

4. (36-38) An immediate death sentence upon the ten unfaithful spies.

Now the men whom Moses sent to spy out the land, who returned and made all the congregation complain against him by bringing a bad report of the land, those very men who brought the evil report about the land, died by the plague before the LORD. But Joshua the son of Nun and Caleb the son of Jephunneh remained alive, of the men who went to spy out the land.

a. **Now the men whom Moses sent to spy out the land...died by the plague before the LORD**: If the death of the unbelieving generation would take some 38 years (the number of years left to make the total time of the exodus forty years), the death of the ten unfaithful spies happened immediately.

i. **Those very men who brought the evil report**: Adam Clarke used the judgment upon the unfaithful spies who gave the evil report as an occasion to warn unfaithful preachers who prevent people from entering into God's eternal promises: "Let preachers of God's word take heed how they straiten the way of salvation, or render, by unjust description, that way perplexed and difficult which God has made plain and easy."

b. **Died by the plague before the LORD**: This was a strong and fearful judgment against these ten unbelieving spies. Their sin was greater than their own fear and unbelief; they influenced all of Israel to follow them in their sinful unbelief.

5. (39-40) Israel's insincere and superficial repentance.

Then Moses told these words to all the children of Israel, and the people mourned greatly. And they rose early in the morning and went up to the

top of the mountain, saying, "Here we are, and we will go up to the place which the LORD has promised, for we have sinned!"

a. **The people mourned greatly**: When Israel heard God's response to their unbelief and the judgment on the ten unbelieving spies, they knew that they had made a bad, fear-filled, faith-denying choice. They **mourned**, knowing they would suffer 38 years of death in the wilderness because of that choice.

b. **They rose early...went up to the top of the mountain..."Here we are, and we will go up...we have sinned!"** Israel hoped they could undo the consequences of the terrible choice made because of fear and unbelief. Here, they did many good things.

- They were energetic (**they rose up early** and **went up to the top of the mountain**).
- They presented themselves to Moses and to God (**Here we are**).
- They claimed a commitment to go forward in faith (**we will go up to the place which the LORD has promised**).
- They offered a confession of sin (**for we have sinned**).

  i. Yet, God did not accept these many good things and take back His solemn judgment that this generation would wander and die in the wilderness. This was an imitation of true repentance.

6. (41-43) Moses warns Israel that their superficial repentance will not grant them God's favor.

And Moses said, "Now why do you transgress the command of the LORD? For this will not succeed. Do not go up, lest you be defeated by your enemies, for the LORD *is* not among you. For the Amalekites and the Canaanites *are* there before you, and you shall fall by the sword; because you have turned away from the LORD, the LORD will not be with you."

a. **Why do you transgress the command of the LORD?** Moses saw there was something wrong with these superficial and insincere words and actions. They expressed regret for the consequences of their sinful fear and unbelief, not true repentance for the actual sins.

  i. One can sense that Israel's repentance was not a response to the conviction of the Holy Spirit. This was on their initiative, a way of attempting God's will *their* way instead of God's way.

b. **This will not succeed**: Moses spoke for God, warning Israel that they could not escape the consequences of their sin on the previous day. If they attempted to go into Canaan *before* God led them in by faith, **the LORD** would **not be with** them and they would fail. Sometimes we have a narrow window of opportunity for faith, and when the opportunity passes, it is gone.

i. "Sometimes the consequences of sin and rebellion are irreversible, and one must endure the experience of God's judgment before a new course of action brings blessing." (Cole)

7. (44-45) The unsuccessful attempt to conquer Canaan.

But they presumed to go up to the mountaintop; nevertheless, neither the ark of the covenant of the LORD nor Moses departed from the camp. Then the Amalekites and the Canaanites who dwelt in that mountain came down and attacked them, and drove them back as far as Hormah.

a. **They presumed to go up the mountaintop**: Israel hoped to conquer Canaan without God's presence and help (**neither the ark of the covenant of the LORD nor Moses departed from the camp**).

i. "This short episode underlines the message of the whole spy story. Israel still does not take God seriously, or listen to Moses his appointed representative. They will not enter Canaan until they learn their lesson, and that may take a long time." (Wenham)

b. **The Canaanites who dwelt in that mountain came down and attacked them, and drove them back as far as Hormah**: Their attempt to conquer Canaan in their own wisdom and strength quickly failed. They made a futile attempt in the flesh to accomplish what they had refused to accomplish by faith, and it ended in defeat.

i. Ironically, when God *was* with Israel, they did not think it was enough to conquer Canaan. When God *was not* with Israel, they thought they could conquer Canaan.

ii. "Nature, poor, fallen human nature, is ever running into extremes. This miserable people, a short time ago, thought that though they had Omnipotence with them they could not conquer and possess the land! Now they imagine that though God himself go not with them, yet they shall be sufficient to drive out the inhabitants, and take possession of their country!" (Clarke)

Numbers 15 – Various Laws and Provisions

A. Grain, drink, and wave offerings.

1. (1-5) The sacrifice of a lamb to be accompanied with grain and wine.

And the LORD spoke to Moses, saying, "Speak to the children of Israel, and say to them: 'When you have come into the land you are to inhabit, which I am giving to you, and you make an offering by fire to the LORD, a burnt offering or a sacrifice, to fulfill a vow or as a freewill offering or in your appointed feasts, to make a sweet aroma to the LORD, from the herd or the flock, then he who presents his offering to the LORD shall bring a grain offering of one-tenth *of an ephah* of fine flour mixed with one-fourth of a hin of oil; and one-fourth of a hin of wine as a drink offering you shall prepare with the burnt offering or the sacrifice, for each lamb.

    a. **Speak to the children of Israel, and say to them**: Israel was at one of the lowest points in its history. They had just rebelliously rejected God's promise to bring the nation into Canaan. God sentenced them to wander in the wilderness for 38 years until the unbelieving generation had perished in the wilderness and a new generation of faith could take the Promised Land. Yet, immediately after this stinging rebellion and the chastisement from the LORD, Israel received valuable examples of God's mercy, care, and help to Israel.

        i. The style of chapter 15 is like many passages of the first ten chapters of Numbers. There is a sense in which this chapter takes the disobedient, unbelieving people of chapter 14 and makes a new start with them from the beginning. Starting over means the whole process will take much longer. "Although much has happened, nothing has happened. The land still awaits the people, but the people must now wait for the land." (Allen)

b. **When you have come into the land**: God cared for Israel. These were commands that could only be fulfilled in the Promised Land. These laws had the built-in promise that God *would* lead them there and would *not* leave them in the wilderness forever.

i. God said, **When you have come into the land you are to inhabit, which I am giving to you**. He said, **when** you come into the land, and not *if* you come into the land. God had not and would not give up on Israel. Many a believer under the rod of God's correction has felt abandoned by God as if the LORD had given up on them, but God is always near to the believer under correction.

c. **And you make an offering by fire to the LORD, a burnt offering or a sacrifice**: God's mercy to Israel is seen in these instructions for offerings to cover sin and to express gratitude. Israel, at their point of failure, needed to be reminded of sacrificial atonement, and their need to give thanks.

i. Many people think that the command to bring **grain**, **oil**, and **wine** with the **burnt offering** of a lamb was a way to express *thanksgiving*. After the tragic unbelief and judgments of chapter 14, Israel still needed to think about showing gratitude to God for His goodness to them.

ii. According to Allen, **fine flour** was the food of luxury, used in "dainty cooking" (Ezekiel 16:13) and fit for royalty (1 Kings 4:22).

iii. **One-tenth of an ephah** was about two quarts (two liters), and **one-fourth of a hin** was about one quart (one liter).

2. (6-7) The sacrifice of a ram to be accompanied with grain and wine.

Or for a ram you shall prepare as a grain offering two-tenths *of an ephah* of fine flour mixed with one-third of a hin of oil; and as a drink offering you shall offer one-third of a hin of wine as a sweet aroma to the LORD.

a. **For a ram you shall prepare as a grain offering**: When Israel came into the land, the offering of a ram was also to include a **grain offering** made with **flour**, **oil**, and **wine**. These were required in larger measure than with the sacrifice of a lamb (15:1-5).

b. **A sweet aroma to the LORD**: This phrase is repeated for the sacrifice of the lamb, the ram, and the bull. In Leviticus, this phrase is repeated often as a description of a pleasing or "successful" sacrifice. Sacrifice performed as God commanded (here including flour, oil, and wine) pleased God as a **sweet aroma** pleases the senses. The Bible specifically tells us that Jesus Christ fulfilled this sacrifice with His own offering, perfectly pleasing God in laying down His life at the cross: *As Christ also has loved us and given*

Himself for us, an offering and a sacrifice to God for a sweet-smelling aroma. (Ephesians 5:2)

> i. The ultimate sacrifice of Jesus Christ to come would be perfectly **sweet** and pleasing to God, and therefore be offered once-for-all (Hebrews 7:27, 9:12, 10:10).

3. (8-10) The sacrifice of a bull to be accompanied with grain and wine.

And when you prepare a young bull as a burnt offering, or as a sacrifice to fulfill a vow, or as a peace offering to the LORD, then shall be offered with the young bull a grain offering of three-tenths *of an ephah* of fine flour mixed with half a hin of oil; and you shall bring as the drink offering half a hin of wine as an offering made by fire, a sweet aroma to the LORD.

> a. **When you prepare a young bull as a burnt offering**: When Israel came into the land, the offering of a bull (made to **fulfill a vow** or as a **peace offering**) was also to include a **grain offering**.

> b. **Fine flour mixed with half a hin of oil**: The offering of a lamb required a one-tenth measure of flour, a ram required two-tenths, and a bull required three-tenths. If one takes the flour, oil, and wine of the grain offering to speak of joy and gratitude, this points to a principle: the greater our offering, the more joy and gratitude we should bring with it.

4. (11-16) The universal character of these laws.

'Thus it shall be done for each young bull, for each ram, or for each lamb or young goat. According to the number that you prepare, so you shall do with everyone according to their number. All who are native-born shall do these things in this manner, in presenting an offering made by fire, a sweet aroma to the LORD. And if a stranger dwells with you, or whoever *is* among you throughout your generations, and would present an offering made by fire, a sweet aroma to the LORD, just as you do, so shall he do. One ordinance *shall be* for you of the assembly and for the stranger who dwells *with you,* an ordinance forever throughout your generations; as you are, so shall the stranger be before the LORD. One law and one custom shall be for you and for the stranger who dwells with you.'"

> a. **Thus it shall be done for each**: *Everyone* who made a sacrifice had to bring it with the thanksgiving of grain and the joy of wine. God did not want reluctant, complaining people to bring sacrifices to Him. If one could not *serve the LORD with gladness* (Psalm 100:2), then God didn't want his service at all.

b. **For you…and for the stranger who dwells with you**: It was expected that those from other nations who lived in Israel (**the stranger**) would worship the LORD and offer sacrifices to Him. These laws of sacrifice were for all who brought sacrifices, and not the **native-born** only.

i. The **stranger** who lived among Israel was invited to worship the God of Israel according to God's command. The worship of strange and pagan gods was forbidden. "We shall see the absolute necessity of having but one *form* of *worship* in the land…. no others could be tolerated, because they were idolatrous. All *strangers*—all that came to *sojourn* in the land, were required to conform to it; and it was right that those who did conform to it should have equal rights and privileges with the Hebrews themselves." (Clarke)

ii. Even the reference to the **native-born** was a promise that they would come into Canaan and live there for generations.

5. (17-21) A heave offering of thanksgiving to the LORD.

Again the LORD spoke to Moses, saying, "Speak to the children of Israel, and say to them: 'When you come into the land to which I bring you, then it will be, when you eat of the bread of the land, that you shall offer up a heave offering to the LORD. You shall offer up a cake of the first of your ground meal *as* a heave offering; as a heave offering of the threshing floor, so shall you offer it up. Of the first of your ground meal you shall give to the LORD a heave offering throughout your generations.

a. **When you come into the land to which I bring you**: Once again, immediately after the failure to enter Canaan by faith, God gave Israel laws that were to be obeyed **when you come into the land**. God did not question *if* they would live in Canaan, and only spoke of **when**.

b. **Then it will be**: This set their minds *forward* to the promise. Even if a child of God isn't walking in the richness of God's promises now, they need to set their mind on heavenly places. Ephesians 2:6 says God has *raised us up together, and made us sit together in the heavenly places in Christ Jesus* – even if it doesn't feel like it now, set your mind on those heavenly places!

c. **A heave offering of the threshing floor**: Exodus 29:27-28 and Leviticus 10:14 speak of a heave offering of sacrificial meat. Here, as in Leviticus 7:14, the heave offering is made with grain (**a cake of the first of your ground meal…a heave offering of the threshing floor**).

i. Most commentators understand the **first of your ground meal** to be a portion of dough made from the first harvest of the season. Each household in Israel brought a **cake of the first of** its **ground meal** as a thanksgiving and firstfruits offering. Paul referred to this custom in Romans 11:16.

ii. "Even the most seemingly mundane daily practice of kneading dough for making bread was to be a time of worship and celebration of God's benevolence and faithfulness." (Cole)

iii. "After the fall of the second temple this custom was still maintained: pious Jews would throw a handful of the dough into the fire as a sort of mini-sacrifice, thereby making every hearth an altar and every kitchen a house of God." (Wenham)

iv. "The raising of the first cake of coarse grain is similar to the custom today in small businesses to frame the first dollar. The difference is potent as well; the cake was raised in gratitude to the Lord; such is less common in the framed dollar bill." (Allen)

B. Remedies for sin.

1. (22-29) Addressing unintentional sin, both for the nation and for individuals.

'If you sin unintentionally, and do not observe all these commandments which the LORD has spoken to Moses—all that the LORD has commanded you by the hand of Moses, from the day the LORD gave commandment and onward throughout your generations—then it will be, if it is unintentionally committed, without the knowledge of the congregation, that the whole congregation shall offer one young bull as a burnt offering, as a sweet aroma to the LORD, with its grain offering and its drink offering, according to the ordinance, and one kid of the goats as a sin offering. So the priest shall make atonement for the whole congregation of the children of Israel, and it shall be forgiven them, for it was unintentional; they shall bring their offering, an offering made by fire to the LORD, and their sin offering before the LORD, for their unintended sin. It shall be forgiven the whole congregation of the children of Israel and the stranger who dwells among them, because all the people *did it* unintentionally.

'And if a person sins unintentionally, then he shall bring a female goat in its first year as a sin offering. So the priest shall make atonement for the person who sins unintentionally, when he sins unintentionally before the LORD, to make atonement for him; and it shall be forgiven him. You shall have one law for him who sins unintentionally, *for* him who is native-born among the children of Israel and for the stranger who dwells among them.

a. **If you sin unintentionally**: Significantly, the Bible talks about sins **unintentionally committed**. It is often thought that if an action is unintentional, it cannot be a sin. But many of the worst sins are committed with the best of intentions. Good intentions don't excuse a sinful result.

i. Throughout history, many atrocities and much terror has come from those dedicated to honorable causes. One of the stated goals of communism is to establish a just, fair economic system where everyone works according to his ability and receives according to his need. Despite these good intentions, the goals of communism were used to justify the murder of tens of millions of people in the 20th century – perhaps up to 100 million.

ii. Among God's people, there are many gossips, many talebearers, and many divisive people who will claim the best of intentions. Even if they mean well, they still may be in serious sin. The same applies to many other sins we may be ready to ignore or think lightly of because we think that good intentions excuse sin. A sacrifice for those who sin **unintentionally** shows that good intentions do not excuse sin.

b. **That the whole congregation shall offer one young bull as a burnt offering**: Unintentional sins needed a blood atonement. A **young bull** had to be sacrificed when the nation was guilty, and a **female goat** had to be sacrificed when an individual was guilty.

c. **You shall have one law for him who sins unintentionally**: There was to be no exception. Sin is sin, and must be accounted as such, even if the motive seems to be good.

i. **For the stranger**: "As in the earlier legislation of vv. 13–16, the efficaciousness of the ritual act was extended to the resident alien as well as the native Israelite, for the community of faith is viewed holistically and harmoniously rather than ethnically divided." (Cole)

2. (30-31) Addressing presumptuous sin.

'**But the person who does *anything* presumptuously, *whether he is native-born or a stranger*, that one brings reproach on the LORD, and he shall be cut off from among his people. Because he has despised the word of the LORD, and has broken His commandment, that person shall be completely cut off; his guilt *shall be* upon him.'"**

a. **But the person who does anything presumptuously**: Literally, to sin **presumptuously** means to sin "with a high hand." This speaks of an open, unashamed rebellion against God, the law of Moses, and the nation.

i. "The sinner with a high hand feels no guilt; therefore the offense is not sacrificially expiable. The one who sins defiantly may not feel the guilt of his violation, but he is nonetheless guilty before God and man." (Cole)

b. **That person shall be completely cut off; his guilt shall be upon him**: Such sin was not to be tolerated in Israel. This command was a judicial and cultural tool for addressing such sins and confirming that such arrogant defiance of public morality would not be rewarded.

i. This contrasts with modern culture where notorious, defiant sinners are sometimes rewarded with fame and fortune. Instead of **his guilt shall be upon him**, our culture often puts guilt on anyone who would judge or confront defiant sinners and their works.

3. (32-36) The execution of a Sabbath violator.

Now while the children of Israel were in the wilderness, they found a man gathering sticks on the Sabbath day. And those who found him gathering sticks brought him to Moses and Aaron, and to all the congregation. They put him under guard, because it had not been explained what should be done to him. Then the LORD said to Moses, "The man must surely be put to death; all the congregation shall stone him with stones outside the camp." So, as the LORD commanded Moses, all the congregation brought him outside the camp and stoned him with stones, and he died.

a. **They found a man gathering sticks on the Sabbath day**: This was an immediate example of dealing with someone who sinned presumptuously (15:30-31). All Israel knew the Sabbath law, but perhaps this man thought himself a courageous social reformer, trying by his example to free the nation from the bondage of heaven's law.

i. "It seems likely that the following story of the sabbath breaker illustrates what sinning with a high hand means." (Wenham)

ii. "The point of the story is that Sabbath breaking is the act of a raised fist in defiance of the Lord; the offense strikes at the very center of Israel's responsibility before the Lord. By his action (v.32) this man was thumbing his nose at God." (Allen)

b. **The man must surely be put to death**: God commanded the execution of this presumptuous sinner, that all might fear. This was so all would know that the social order and law of God are more important than any individual's "right" to attack or destroy that social order or law of God.

i. **Stoned him**: "Stoning was prescribed, a punishment which involved a large body of people, the *congregation* (36), thereby symbolizing the community's rejection of this offence. Since the sabbath was a sign of

the covenant, its desecration was particularly serious (Deut. 5:15)."
(Wenham)

4. (37-41) Reminders for a holy people.

Again the LORD spoke to Moses, saying, "Speak to the children of Israel: Tell them to make tassels on the corners of their garments throughout their generations, and to put a blue thread in the tassels of the corners. And you shall have the tassel, that you may look upon it and remember all the commandments of the LORD and do them, and that you *may* not follow the harlotry to which your own heart and your own eyes are inclined, and that you may remember and do all My commandments, and be holy for your God. I *am* the LORD your God, who brought you out of the land of Egypt, to be your God: I *am* the LORD your God."

a. **Tassels on the corners of their garments and blue thread in the tassels of the corners**: These were intended to remind Israel to Whom they belonged; they were God's people. Such reminders can be effective in helping to keep believers from sin and making believers mindful of God.

i. Perhaps a **blue thread** was commanded because the ark of the covenant was covered with a blue cloth, blue curtains adorned the tabernacle, and blue was part of the high priest's garments. Blue, as a color, was associated with holy reminders.

ii. "That cord of blue was a symbol of the deepest truth in their national life, that they were under the direct government of heaven. Every time the eye rested on that simple sign the heart was to be reminded of the sublime truth." (Morgan)

iii. "This was practised by the Pharisees in Christ's time, who are noted for making their borders larger than ordinary, Matt. 23:5; and by Christ himself, as may [be] gathered from Luke 8:44." (Poole)

b. **That you may look upon it and remember all the commandments of the LORD and do them**: We might imagine an Israelite being tempted to sin, and then catching sight of his own distinctive clothing. These could remind him of who he is and remind him that others can see who he is: a child of God, and not a child of the sin he is contemplating.

i. In this sense, Christian-themed clothing, jewelry, and other items can serve a purpose. Such things can remind us of who we are and provide a kind of accountability for our conduct.

ii. However, man's instinctive pride always has a way of perverting such good and holy commands of God. Jesus directly rebuked the abuse of this command among the religious elite, speaking of how they would *enlarge the borders of their garments* (Matthew 23:5), making the tasseled area as conspicuous as possible, as a proud display of their "holiness." The same can also be said of today's Christian themed clothing and jewelry; it can also be abused in the same self-righteous, hypocritical manner.

iii. **I am the** L<small>ORD</small> **your God who brought you out of the land of Egypt, to be your God:** "Though I am justly displeased with you for your frequent and horrid rebellions, for which also I will keep you forty years in the wilderness, yet I will not utterly cast you off, but will continue to be your God, to preserve and provide for you there, and after that time to bring you into Canaan." (Poole)

Numbers 16 – Korah's Rebellion

A. Korah and his followers oppose the leadership of Moses.

1. (1-3) The accusation against Moses and Aaron.

Now Korah the son of Izhar, the son of Kohath, the son of Levi, with Dathan and Abiram the sons of Eliab, and On the son of Peleth, sons of Reuben, took *men*; and they rose up before Moses with some of the children of Israel, two hundred and fifty leaders of the congregation, representatives of the congregation, men of renown. They gathered together against Moses and Aaron, and said to them, *"You take* too much upon yourselves, for all the congregation *is* holy, every one of them, and the LORD *is* among them. Why then do you exalt yourselves above the assembly of the LORD?"

> a. **Now Korah the son of Izhar**: This rebellion, like all rebellions, had a leader and followers. This leader was **Korah**, descended from **Kohath**. Both Moses and Korah were descended from Kohath but by different sons. Moses was from the family of Amram (Numbers 26:58-59), and Korah from the family of **Izhar**.
>
> > i. Among the three divisions of the tribe of Levi, the Kohathites had the most prestigious duty. Their responsibility was to carry and care for the most holy things of the tabernacle after Aaron and his sons had covered them with the specially prepared coverings (Numbers 4:15).
> >
> > ii. **Dathan**, **Abiram**, and **On** were from the tribe of **Reuben**. In the arrangement of the tribes, the Levitical family of Kohath was placed near the tribe of Reuben. It's not a surprise that the complaint and dissatisfaction of Korah spread to these three Reubenites.
> >
> > iii. Korah perhaps said, "I'm also from the tribe of Levi, and Aaron is my cousin. Why does he get to be the priest and I don't?" Dathan and Abiram perhaps said, "Reuben was the firstborn of Israel, so our tribe should lead. Why does Moses get to lead, and we don't?"

b. **You take too much upon yourselves, for all the congregation is holy**: Korah accused Moses of pride (**too much upon yourselves**) and love of power refusing to let others lead (**all the congregation is holy**). It is likely that Korah wanted some of the power and position that God had appointed to Moses.

> i. It was significant that this accusation was made publicly, in front of **two hundred and fifty leaders of the congregation…men of renown**. Korah played to an audience, hoping to draw a following after himself.

c. **You take too much upon yourselves, for all the congregation is holy, every one of them, and the LORD is among them**: This was a clever attack. Korah acted as if he represented the people and fought for their interests. It is more likely that Korah wanted for himself some of the power and position God gave to Moses.

> i. It was as if Korah said, "Moses, you shouldn't be the leader. Let everyone be a leader. God can speak to everyone."

> ii. Significantly, Korah proclaimed the holiness of the people (**all the congregation is holy**) and regarded strong leadership as unnecessary (**You take too much**) at the very time when the nation was *not* holy and desperately needed strong leadership. Korah completely misread the condition of God's people because he was not a true shepherd.

d. **Why then do you exalt yourselves above the assembly of the LORD?** Korah accused Moses (and Aaron) of pride and self-seeking. The truth was that Moses didn't become leader of Israel by ambition or desire, but by the direct calling of God. Moses had a clear, God-appointed position of leadership, but he was not a proud man who saw himself **above the assembly of the LORD**.

> i. "The attitude taken up by those who organized the movement was plausible and popular. It was democratic in its expression: 'All the congregation are holy, every one of them, and Jehovah is among them.' It was a plea for equal rights, and for independence of action." (Morgan)

e. **Two hundred and fifty leaders of the congregation, representatives of the congregation, men of renown**: On a human level, Korah was successful because these **two hundred and fifty leaders** followed him. These men did not lead the rebellion, but they did not have the discernment to oppose Korah, and instead followed him. It is a big problem when 250 prominent **leaders** support a man like Korah.

i. These 250 were **leaders**, but they were not the *elders* of Israel, appointed in Numbers 10:14-27. The distinction between these **leaders** and the elders of Israel is made clear by verse 25.

2. (4-11) The response of Moses to Korah and his company.

So when Moses heard *it*, he fell on his face; and he spoke to Korah and all his company, saying, "Tomorrow morning the Lord will show who *is* His and *who is* holy, and will cause *him* to come near to Him. That one whom He chooses He will cause to come near to Him. Do this: Take censers, Korah and all your company; put fire in them and put incense in them before the Lord tomorrow, and it shall be *that* the man whom the Lord chooses *is* the holy one. *You take* too much upon yourselves, you sons of Levi!" Then Moses said to Korah, "Hear now, you sons of Levi: *Is it* a small thing to you that the God of Israel has separated you from the congregation of Israel, to bring you near *to Himself*, to do the work of the tabernacle of the Lord, and to stand before the congregation to serve them; and that He has brought you near to Himself, you and all your brethren, the sons of Levi, with you? And are you seeking the priesthood also? Therefore you and all your company *are* gathered together against the Lord. And what *is* Aaron that you complain against him?"

a. **When Moses heard it, he fell on his face**: When Moses heard of the dangerous unbelief of Israel, he and Aaron fell on their faces before God (Numbers 14:5). Now, at the dangerous rebellion of Korah, Moses once again **fell on his face**, in a humble posture of prayer.

i. Being a humble man, Moses probably asked God if his critics were right or had something to teach him. Moses probably asked God what should be done in the situation. He certainly asked God to spare the nation and he asked God to not allow these divisive men to bring permanent harm to the people of God.

b. **Tomorrow morning the Lord will show who is His and who is holy**: We don't know how long Moses prayed, but after prayer he had a sense of God's direction for this crisis. He issued a challenge where Korah and his followers would come before the Lord, and Moses and Aaron would also come, so that the Lord would make His choice of leaders clear.

c. **You take too much upon yourselves, you sons of Levi!** This shows that Moses did not doubt the outcome of the test. He knew that God would prove Korah wrong. Moses was unafraid to put it to the test.

d. **Is it a small thing to you that the God of Israel has separated you from the congregation of Israel**: Moses reminded Korah that God gave them an honorable service that they now apparently regarded as a **small thing**. Their role in serving the priests, carrying, and caring for the holy articles of the tabernacle brought them **near to** God, but Korah wasn't content with his calling.

i. Even if Korah was right – if Moses had become proud and power-hungry – this was the wrong way to approach the problem. This public challenge was the wrong way to confront someone so obviously called and appointed to leadership as Moses was. Korah's use of ungodly methods (accusation, intimidation, the gathering of a rival following) was wrong.

e. **What is Aaron, that you complain against him?** We can only imagine what Aaron thought about all this. Aaron and his sister Miriam came against Moses before, as recorded in Numbers 12. That ended in ruin for Aaron and Miriam, and we might imagine that Aaron thought, "Korah, don't make the same mistake that I made."

3. (12-14) Dathan and Abiram speak for the rebels.

And Moses sent to call Dathan and Abiram the sons of Eliab, but they said, "We will not come up! "Is it a small thing that you have brought us up out of a land flowing with milk and honey, to kill us in the wilderness, that you should keep acting like a prince over us? Moreover you have not brought us into a land flowing with milk and honey, nor given us inheritance of fields and vineyards. Will you put out the eyes of these men? We will not come up!"

a. **Dathan** and **Abiram**: These were co-conspirators with Korah (Numbers 16:1). They would not meet with Moses, nor answer his challenge. Instead, they accused Moses of wanting to kill the people of God.

b. **You have brought us up out of a land flowing with milk and honey**: Dathan and Abiram *lied about the past*. They thought of *Egypt* as a land of **milk and honey**, even for the Hebrew slaves. Their lie about the past made Moses look as bad as possible.

c. **To kill us in the wilderness**: Dathan and Abiram *assigned an evil heart* to Moses. They spoke as if they had discovered a secret plot of Moses and Aaron: To lead Israel into the wilderness and kill them all. This was foolish.

d. **That you should keep acting like a prince over us**: Dathan and Abiram *refused to acknowledge progress* in Moses. Some 40 years before this, Moses was a **prince**, a self-confident man who thought he could deliver and lead Israel himself. God broke him of that self-confidence with 40 years of humble service in the wilderness (Exodus 2:15-3:10; 7:7). Yet Dathan and Abiram spoke as if Moses was still an arrogant **prince**.

e. **You have not brought us into a land flowing with milk and honey**: This shows that Dathan and Abiram *had unfair expectations* of Moses. It was true that Moses had not yet brought them to Canaan. Yet, it was wrong to blame Moses for this, and wrong to think that Korah could have done any better.

> i. It is easy for men like Korah to say, "If I led Israel, we would already be in Canaan." But Korah was not leading Israel, and men of his type rarely do. God seldom puts side-line critics in positions of real leadership – except as a punishment, to show them just how difficult leadership is, and to show them that perfect leadership, like perfect anything, is impossible.

> ii. Leaders should expect to be held to a *higher* standard but it is obviously unfair to hold a leader to a *perfect* standard.

f. **We will not come up**: Dathan and Abiram *considered themselves under no authority*. It was as if they said: "Moses, we have no respect for your authority. We will listen to God, but not to you. Your word means nothing to us, and **we will not come up**." Apparently, the 250 other leaders agreed with Dathan and Abiram; not one of those 250 raised an opposing voice to their harsh accusations.

> i. "It is difficult to believe the level of acrimony that we find in Dathan and Abiram. They are not even willing to come to appear before Moses to face charges. Twice they refuse absolutely." (Allen)

4. (15-19a) Moses restates his challenge.

Then Moses was very angry, and said to the LORD, "Do not respect their offering. I have not taken one donkey from them, nor have I hurt one of them." And Moses said to Korah, "Tomorrow, you and all your company be present before the LORD; you and they, as well as Aaron. Let each take his censer and put incense in it, and each of you bring his censer before the LORD, two hundred and fifty censers; both you and Aaron, each *with* his censer." So every man took his censer, put fire in it, laid incense on it, and stood at the door of the tabernacle of meeting with Moses and Aaron. And Korah gathered all the congregation against them at the door of the tabernacle of meeting.

a. **Then Moses was very angry, and said to the LORD**: After the words of Dathan and Abiram, Moses was angry – **very angry**. He knew he had done nothing to deserve such accusations, and Moses did the right thing. Moses left the situation to God.

> i. Moses was a man of political power who had soldiers and something like the police at his command. He was able to have Korah, Dathan,

Abiram, and their followers arrested and executed. Instead, Moses trusted God to resolve this rebellion.

ii. Sometimes people are offended that a man like Moses was **angry** with men like Dathan and Abiram. They think a gentle, easy love is the proper response. Such thinking is understandable, but wrong. Shepherds are gentle with wayward sheep who might injure themselves, but they are passionate against wolves who would injure the flock.

b. **I have not taken one donkey from them, nor have I hurt one of them**: Moses declared that he was a man of integrity and service to the people. He could rest with his clean conscience before God.

i. This reminds us of Paul's testimony before the Ephesian elders in Acts 20: *Therefore I testify to you this day that I am innocent of the blood of all men. For I have not shunned to declare to you the whole counsel of God.... I have coveted no one's silver or gold or apparel.... I have shown you in every way, by laboring like this, that you must support the weak* (Acts 20:26-27, 33, 35). When a leader is troubled by rebellious and divisive persons, they should be able to take refuge in a clean conscience.

c. **Let each take his censer and put incense in it, and each of you bring his censer before the LORD**: This specified the challenge. God would approve or disapprove of the 250 men gathered with censers of incense before the door of the tabernacle.

i. There was a good reason for God to use the censers with fire and incense in this test. A **censer** is a metal pot used to burn **incense**, and they were used in the priestly service of Israel. Since Korah and his companions questioned Moses and Aaron's right to lead the nation and lead the priesthood, each group would come to the LORD as worshipping priests, and the LORD would show which group He accepted.

ii. Moses allowed the rebels to take the position they desired – the position of priest. Sometimes the best judgment on the divisive and rebellious is to let them lead.

iii. Humanly speaking, the odds were against Moses and Aaron. Two men stood against more than 250 others, in the presence of **all the congregation**. Yet God would make this choice, and not popular opinion.

iv. "*Korah gathered the congregation*, that they might be witnesses of the event, and, upon their success, which they doubted not of, might fall upon Moses and Aaron with popular rage, and destroy them." (Poole)

B. God affirms Moses' leadership over the nation of Israel.

1. (19b-21) God announces judgment on the rebels.

Then the glory of the LORD appeared to all the congregation. And the LORD spoke to Moses and Aaron, saying, "Separate yourselves from among this congregation, that I may consume them in a moment."

a. **The glory of the LORD appeared to all the congregation**: This was the presence of the *shekinah*, the cloud of God's glory. God would address this controversy in a strong, direct, clear way.

b. **Separate yourselves from among this congregation**: It is as if God said, "Moses and Aaron, will you please move away? I'm going to destroy all these rebels in an instant, and I don't want you to get hurt."

c. **That I may consume them in a moment**: God decided to make His choice immediately evident. Sometimes this is not the case when God deals with those who rebel and divide, but it was the way God worked on this occasion.

2. (22) The intercession of Moses and Aaron for Korah and the rebels.

Then they fell on their faces, and said, "O God, the God of the spirits of all flesh, shall one man sin, and You be angry with all the congregation?"

a. **Then they fell on their faces**: Once again, Moses and Aaron humbled themselves before God. With great love, they asked God to spare **all the congregation**.

i. Perhaps one reason God allowed Moses and Aaron to experience this painful rebellion was to allow them to display this kind of love for **all the congregation**. Such love for the undeserving shows that Moses and Aaron were growing in love and being transformed into the image of Jesus – before Jesus ever walked the earth.

ii. Again, the importance of prayer is emphasized. It seems that if there were no prayer, then the rebellious congregation would be destroyed. We should think that Moses' prayer was essential.

b. **Shall one man sin, and You be angry with all the congregation?** Even though more than 250 leaders opposed Moses and Aaron, they rightly understood this to be the work of **one man**. Korah was the center of all this.

3. (23-27) God warns of the judgment soon to come upon Korah and his companions.

So the LORD spoke to Moses, saying, "Speak to the congregation, saying, 'Get away from the tents of Korah, Dathan, and Abiram.'"

Then Moses rose and went to Dathan and Abiram, and the elders of Israel followed him. And he spoke to the congregation, saying, "Depart now from the tents of these wicked men! Touch nothing of theirs, lest you be consumed in all their sins." So they got away from around the tents of Korah, Dathan, and Abiram; and Dathan and Abiram came out and stood at the door of their tents, with their wives, their sons, and their little children.

a. **Get away from the tents of Korah, Dathan, and Abiram**: This was God's mercy. The LORD told Moses to warn the people of Israel to separate themselves from the rebellion of Korah, so that they would not be caught up in the judgment soon to come against them.

b. **The elders of Israel followed him**: This was glorious. God had appointed elders back in Numbers 10:14-27, in response to a previous attack on Moses' leadership. These elders were to be men with the same spirit and vision as Moses, men to help him bear the burden, men to stand with Moses. Here they did exactly what God appointed them to do.

c. **Lest you be consumed in all their sins**: Moses, in response to God's command to get away from the tents of the leaders of the rebellion (Korah, Dathan, and Abiram), pleaded with the people to separate themselves from the divisive persons. The people did this (**they got away from around the tents**).

i. The same attitude should be among God's people today. They should stay away from divisive, argumentative, contentious people in God's family. There should be an appropriate fear of being caught in the same judgment or correction that they will bring upon themselves.

ii. The New Testament also speaks of this same principle:

- *Reject a divisive man after the first and second admonition, knowing that such a person is warped and sinning, being self-condemned.* (Titus 3:10-11)

- *Now I urge you, brethren, note those who cause divisions and offenses, contrary to the doctrine which you learned, and avoid them. For those who are such do not serve our Lord Jesus Christ, but their own belly, and by smooth words and flattering speech deceive the hearts of the simple.* (Romans 16:17-18)

iii. Divisive and contentious people will never *claim* to be divisive and contentious. They always consider their work a noble cause. Therefore, God's people need discernment to look at what others *do*, not only at what they *say*.

4. (28-35) God's judgment on Korah and his companions.

And Moses said: "By this you shall know that the LORD has sent me to do all these works, for *I have* not *done them* of my own will. If these men die naturally like all men, or if they are visited by the common fate of all men, *then* the LORD has not sent me. But if the LORD creates a new thing, and the earth opens its mouth and swallows them up with all that belongs to them, and they go down alive into the pit, then you will understand that these men have rejected the LORD."

Now it came to pass, as he finished speaking all these words, that the ground split apart under them, and the earth opened its mouth and swallowed them up, with their households and all the men with Korah, with all *their* goods. So they and all those with them went down alive into the pit; the earth closed over them, and they perished from among the assembly. Then all Israel who *were* around them fled at their cry, for they said, "Lest the earth swallow us up *also!*"

And a fire came out from the LORD and consumed the two hundred and fifty men who were offering incense.

a. **By this you shall know**: God gave Moses supernatural insight to know that a special judgment (**a new thing**) would come upon Korah, Dathan, and Abiram. The earth would swallow them up, as evidence that these men **have rejected the LORD**.

b. **The ground split apart under them, and the earth opened its mouth and swallowed them up**: This was God's judgment upon Korah, Dathan, Abiram, and their families.

i. It is not comfortable for us to see their families also judged, but this shows that the families of the rebellious, divisive, contentious people suffer also – often greatly.

c. **Went down alive into the pit**: Literally, they went alive into *Sheol*. This was the Hebrew concept of the realm of the dead, under the earth's surface (where the dead were buried). These were not buried; they **went down alive into the pit**. There was no need to dig graves; God dug their graves and sent them straight to the realm of the dead.

i. There was an unusual mercy shown to a remnant in this. "It turns out that there are survivors of Korah's family who extend all the way to the time of David and beyond. Numbers 26:10–11 tells us that Korah was among those whom the earth swallowed but that his sons did not die with him. His descendants would later become the temple singers, responsible for the crafting of numerous psalms." (Allen)

d. **A fire came out from the LORD and consumed the two hundred and fifty men**: God appointed judgment for those who walked in agreement with Korah. Korah and his close associates were **swallowed...up** by the earth, but the **two hundred and fifty men** were destroyed by fire. Their worship was not received.

i. "By fire they sinned, and by a fire they suffer." (Trapp)

ii. "Thus there were *two* distinct punishments, the *pit* and the *fire*, for the *two divisions* of these rebels." (Clarke)

5. (36-40) A bronze covering for the altar.

Then the LORD spoke to Moses, saying: "Tell Eleazar, the son of Aaron the priest, to pick up the censers out of the blaze, for they are holy, and scatter the fire some distance away. The censers of these men who sinned against their own souls, let them be made into hammered plates as a covering for the altar. Because they presented them before the LORD, therefore they are holy; and they shall be a sign to the children of Israel." So Eleazar the priest took the bronze censers, which those who were burned up had presented, and they were hammered out as a covering on the altar, *to be* a memorial to the children of Israel that no outsider, who *is* not a descendant of Aaron, should come near to offer incense before the LORD, that he might not become like Korah and his companions, just as the LORD had said to him through Moses.

a. **Pick up the censers out of the blaze, for they are holy.... let them be made into hammered plates as a covering for the altar**: The censers were beaten flat and used to cover the main altar of sacrifice. The censers of the rebels were **holy** and preserved because even though Korah and his followers worshipped wrongly, they worshipped the right God.

i. "Can you imagine the scene? True priests are picking among the bodies, charred flesh, stench, smoke, smoldering embers, and twisted parts. They are to make a count. There were 250 censers; not one is to be lost. Each one is recorded, each one cleansed, each one holy." (Allen)

ii. In the end, each one of the 250 was identified with Korah. Perhaps that wasn't what they intended. We can imagine some among the 250 saying, "I don't agree with everything Korah says, but he's got some good points." Before God, all those distinctions were lost. All the censers were hammered together, and the group was collectively titled: **Korah and his companions**.

b. **Scatter the fire some distance away**: The fire that the 250 leaders presented was *not* holy and was to be scattered away. It was a strange fire – not accepted by God at all.

c. **They were hammered out as a covering on the altar, to be a memorial to the children of Israel**: The censers were thus memorialized and served as an important reminder. God appoints His leaders, and no one should be a divisive rebel like Korah. The flattened censers were a **sign** to Israel, a solemn warning – like the remains of a smashed automobile can warn others to drive safely.

> i. If Christians today encounter ungodly, divisive leaders or would-be leaders, they should take care not to imitate the errors of Korah and his companions. Often (not always), the proper approach is to protect one's own safety and leave it to God to deal with arrogant and abusive leadership, as David later did with Saul.

> ii. In the Hebrew edition of the Old Testament, Numbers 16:36 begins a new chapter (chapter 17).

C. The people murmur against Moses and Aaron.

1. (41) The accusation is made: **You have killed the people of the LORD.**

On the next day all the congregation of the children of Israel complained against Moses and Aaron, saying, "You have killed the people of the LORD."

> a. **On the next day all the congregation of the children of Israel complained against Moses and Aaron**: Poor Moses! He probably hoped that all the trouble was over when the rebels were judged. But now he had to deal with those who were sympathetic to the divisive people and who felt sorry for them.

> b. **You have killed the people of the LORD**: Their accusation against Moses was bizarre. Moses certainly did not kill them. When the earth opened and swallowed more than 250 people, it was evidently the hand of God, not of Moses.

2. (42-45) The threat of judgment on the children of Israel for their sympathy for Korah.

Now it happened, when the congregation had gathered against Moses and Aaron, that they turned toward the tabernacle of meeting; and suddenly the cloud covered it, and the glory of the LORD appeared. Then Moses and Aaron came before the tabernacle of meeting. And the LORD spoke to Moses, saying, "Get away from among this congregation, that I may consume them in a moment." And they fell on their faces.

a. **The cloud covered it, and the glory of the LORD appeared**: Once again, the *shekinah* glory of God appeared and would defend Moses.

b. **Get away from among this congregation, that I may consume them in a moment**: God reacted the same way towards the sympathizers among the **congregation** as He did towards Korah and his company. Evidently, these people *deserved* to be judged.

c. **And they fell on their faces**: Once again, Moses and Aaron humbled themselves before God. This showed that they took the threat of judgment seriously. They understood that it was no small thing for the congregation to sympathize with the divisive, contentious people who opposed Moses and Aaron.

3. (46-50) Aaron's intercession stops the plague of judgment upon the children of Israel.

So Moses said to Aaron, "Take a censer and put fire in it from the altar, put incense *on it*, and take it quickly to the congregation and make atonement for them; for wrath has gone out from the LORD. The plague has begun." Then Aaron took *it* as Moses commanded, and ran into the midst of the assembly; and already the plague had begun among the people. So he put in the incense and made atonement for the people. And he stood between the dead and the living; so the plague was stopped. Now those who died in the plague were fourteen thousand seven hundred, besides those who died in the Korah incident. So Aaron returned to Moses at the door of the tabernacle of meeting, for the plague had stopped.

a. **Take a censer and put fire in it from the altar, put incense on it, and take it quickly to the congregation and make atonement for them**: God had promised judgment in verse 45 (*that I may consume them in a moment*). Therefore, Moses told Aaron, as the high priest among God's people, to immediately offer incense to **make atonement** for the congregation.

i. "Aaron took the true priestly censer and used it to bring atonement and purification on behalf of the Israelite camp so that the plague brought on by the insurrection could be averted." (Cole)

ii. **Fire…from the altar**: The fire that went into the censers of Korah and his companions did *not* come from the altar – it was strange fire, unauthorized fire. When Moses told Aaron to offer incense to stop the plague, he specifically told him to take the **fire…from the altar**.

b. **Then Aaron took it as Moses commanded, and ran into the midst of the assembly**: As the plague swept through the people like a wildfire, the high priest Aaron **ran into the midst** of the danger, to rescue those who wanted him and Moses dead.

i. We have no reason to think that Korah or his group would have shown the same mercy to Moses. They might have passively said, "God, go ahead and give them what they deserve. I knew they deserved it." Korah and the complainers didn't have the same shepherd's heart for Israel that Moses and Aaron did.

c. **So he put in the incense and made atonement for the people**: A censer filled with burning incense was used to stop the plague. Incense is a picture of prayer in the Bible (as in Revelation 8:3-4), because the sweet-smelling smoke of incense ascends to heaven illustrating prayer that pleases God. This was a dramatic picture of Aaron, as high priest, interceding for God's people.

d. **And he stood between the dead and the living; so the plague was stopped**: The plague stopped where Aaron prayed. Intercessors do the same thing today; they stand between the dead and the living, begging for God's mercy, preserving and promoting life with their prayer.

i. To stand **between the dead and the living** speaks of how *serious* the matter of prayer is. It is no casual pursuit, no fatalistic exercise in self-improvement. Prayer moves the hand of God and moves it to stop death and to give life.

e. **Those who died in the plague were fourteen thousand seven hundred**: This is a large number, but not compared to the consuming of the whole nation. This was another step in the passing of the generation of unbelief in the wilderness, so a new generation of faith and boldness could be raised up to take the Promised Land.

i. Aaron and his high priestly work here form a picture of our High Priest Jesus Christ, and His work on our behalf. We were guilty sinners deserving judgment and we were rightly plagued.

- Our Savior was sent on a mission to save.
- Our Savior was unjustly accused and attacked.
- Our Savior rescued those who wanted Him dead.
- Our Savior prayed on our behalf.
- Our Savior "ran" to save us.
- Our Savior did this work alone – Moses the lawgiver did not help Him. All the law could do is say, "Something must be done," but the law was powerless to rescue. Only the High Priest could stop this deathly plague.

- Our Savior stood between death and life for us.
- Our Savior is the only chance of salvation.
- Our Savior is the dividing line between death and life.

ii. "Aaron wisely puts himself in the pathway of the plague. It came on, cutting down all before it, and there stood Aaron the interposer with arms outstretched and censer swinging towards heaven, interposing himself between the darts of death and the people. 'If there be darts that must fly,' he seemed to say, 'let them pierce me; or let the incense shield both me and the people.'" (Spurgeon)

iii. "If Aaron the high priest, with his censer and incense, could disarm the wrath of an insulted, angry Deity, so that a guilty people, who deserved nothing but destruction, should be spared; how much more effectual may we expect the great atonement to be which was made by the Lord Jesus Christ, of whom Aaron was only the *type!* The *sacrifices* of living animals pointed out the *death* of Christ on the cross; the *incense,* his *intercession.* Through his *death* salvation is purchased for the world; by his *intercession* the offending children of men are spared." (Clarke)

iv. God would not allow a "second priesthood" under Korah or anyone else. God appointed *one way* of atonement and salvation and would make none other. "The way of God's own appointment, the agony and death of Christ, is the only way in which souls can be saved. His is the *priesthood,* and *his* is the only available sacrifice. All other modes and schemes of salvation are the inventions of men or devils, and will in the end prove ruinous to all those who trust in them." (Clarke)

Numbers 17 – The Budding of Aaron's Rod

A. The test commanded.

1. (1-3) Gathering rods, identified with each tribe.

And the LORD spoke to Moses, saying: "Speak to the children of Israel, and get from them a rod from each father's house, all their leaders according to their fathers' houses; twelve rods. Write each man's name on his rod. And you shall write Aaron's name on the rod of Levi. For there shall be one rod for the head of *each* father's house.

    a. **Get from them a rod from each father's house**: **A rod** was a symbol of authority because shepherds would use a rod to guide and correct the sheep (Psalm 23:4).

        i. Moses, as a shepherd, had **a rod** in his hand when tending sheep in the wilderness (Exodus 4:2). This rod later became known as *the rod of God* (Exodus 4:20), a symbol of the authority God gave to Moses.

        ii. This same **rod** held by Moses demonstrated his authority in action. The rod of God in the hand of Moses:

- Miraculously became a serpent, and then became a rod again (Exodus 7:9-10).
- Turned the waters of the Nile into blood (Exodus 7:17).
- Brought plagues of frogs (Exodus 8:5), lice (Exodus 8:16-17), hail (Exodus 9:23), and locusts (Exodus 10:13).
- Was raised over the Red Sea when it was to be parted (Exodus 14:16).
- Was raised in prayer over Israel in victorious battle (Exodus 17:9).
- Struck the rock and brought water (Numbers 20:11).

iii. The **rod** is also a picture of God's authority over man (Psalm 2:9, 23:4, 89:32; Isaiah 10 24; 11:4, Ezekiel 20:37). Jesus, in His divine authority, was given the title the *Rod* (Isaiah 11:1 and Micah 6:9). The rod was also an emblem of an apostle's authority in the church (1 Corinthians 4:21).

b. **Write each man's name on his rod. And you shall write Aaron's name on the rod of Levi**: After the gathering of the rods, inscribing each with the name of a tribe, and inscribing Aaron's name on the rod of Levi, God would declare which tribe possessed priestly authority by choosing one of the rods. This was the issue at hand considering Korah's rebellion.

i. All this happened because of what the LORD **spoke to Moses**: "If the words in this introductory clause mean what they seem to mean, then we have a constant punctuation throughout the Book of Numbers (in over 150 instances!) that Yahweh has spoken and that he has spoken principally to Moses." (Allen)

2. (4-5) The rods to be placed in the tabernacle for God's choosing.

Then you shall place them in the tabernacle of meeting before the Testimony, where I meet with you. And it shall be *that* **the rod of the man whom I choose will blossom; thus I will rid Myself of the complaints of the children of Israel, which they make against you."**

a. **The rod of the man whom I choose will blossom**: Not only would this obviously be a miraculous sign; the blossoming of dead wood spoke of fruitfulness. Fruitfulness – *miraculous* fruitfulness – is present when godly authority and leadership are being practiced.

b. **Thus I will rid Myself of the complaints**: This did not mean that after this, the children of Israel would never complain again. But God, having demonstrated more than sufficient evidence to the murmurers, would no longer regard their murmuring. Indeed, He would then judge their murmuring.

i. Murmurers (complainers) are rarely satisfied by evidence or the resolution of one issue. Complainers are usually not issue-motivated, though they may claim to be and appear to be. More often they are heart-motivated. They sometimes murmur because they have complaining, discontented hearts. The complaining heart is demonstrated when people murmur about one issue after another, never being satisfied.

ii. So, God would give them an unmistakable answer to this matter of contention – then **rid** Himself **of the complaints**.

B. The test vindicates Aaron as God's priestly leader.

1. (6-7) The rods are placed before the LORD in **the tabernacle of witness**.

So Moses spoke to the children of Israel, and each of their leaders gave him a rod apiece, for each leader according to their fathers' houses, twelve rods; and the rod of Aaron *was* among their rods. And Moses placed the rods before the LORD in the tabernacle of witness.

> a. **Twelve rods; and the rod of Aaron**: Some (such as Cole) believe that there was a total of twelve rods, with the two tribes of Joseph (Ephraim and Manasseh) represented by one rod. Others (such as Poole) believe that Aaron's rod was added to the twelve rods.

> b. **Moses placed the rods before the LORD in the tabernacle**: Moses and the tribes of Israel did just as God commanded in the previous passage. Several commentators (such as Allen and Cole) believe the rods were placed in the Holy of Holies, the Most Holy Place. However, they may have been placed just outside the veil that separated the holy place from the Most Holy Place.

2. (8-9) The budding of Aaron's rod.

Now it came to pass on the next day that Moses went into the tabernacle of witness, and behold, the rod of Aaron, of the house of Levi, had sprouted and put forth buds, had produced blossoms and yielded ripe almonds. Then Moses brought out all the rods from before the LORD to all the children of Israel; and they looked, and each man took his rod.

> a. **And behold, the rod of Aaron**: When Moses checked on the rods the next day, Aaron's rod – and only **the rod of Aaron** – had **sprouted**. It had not only sprouted, but it had also **put forth buds**. It had not only put forth buds, but it had also **produced blossoms**. It had not only produced blossoms, but it had also **yielded...almonds**. It had not only yielded almonds, but it had also yielded **ripe** almonds.

> > i. This was a place where a relatively small miracle would have been convincing. After all, God could have merely made a little green sprout come from Aaron's rod alone, and that would have, or should have, been enough.

> > ii. But God gave, as in the words of Acts 1:3, *many infallible proofs*, to demonstrate His approval of Aaron's leadership. God gives us *more* than enough evidence; our problem is a lack of willingness to see what He has made clear.

iii. "We are probably to understand that some parts were in bud, others in bloom and others had fruited." (Wenham) Fruit from a godly leader may come in all different stages.

iv. There is nothing remarkable about a piece of wood with buds, blossoms, or fruit on it. But a piece of dead wood with all these things appearing in one night after sitting in a tent is remarkable. "Miracles in the Bible are often of this sort: natural events in unnatural conditions, timing, and placement." (Allen)

b. **Behold, the rod of Aaron, of the house of Levi, had sprouted**: God's choice of Aaron's rod did not mean that Aaron was the most spiritual man in the nation. God's chosen leaders will have godly character according to the principles of 1 Timothy 3:1-13 and Titus 1:5-9, but this wasn't a contest to determine the most spiritual man among them.

i. It also did not mean that Aaron *had* not and *would* not sin or fail significantly. God's chosen leaders may fail or sin, but they must set things right when they do.

ii. The clear choice of Aaron meant that he was God's chosen priest and the nation was required to recognize it.

iii. Aaron's rod was chosen, and it was *chosen to bear fruit*. Those whom God chooses should have evident fruit as a mark of their election. Aaron's rod had both fruit (the almond) and the promise of future fruit.

c. **Each man took his rod**: This was a dramatic scene. Each murmurer from the different tribes took his rod, and clearly saw that his *had not* budded or borne fruit, and that Aaron's had.

i. We can imagine Moses carefully inspecting the other rods, noting that there was nothing on them resembling a sprout, bud, or blossom.

ii. This confirmed God's choice of Aaron, Aaron's authority as assigned by God, and that the authority of God's appointed high priest is fruitful.

iii. The difference between Aaron's rod and the others could be attributed to *God alone*. It was a miracle that only God could do. This should have made Aaron humbler; what God did to affirm the choice of Aaron was something that had *nothing* to do with Aaron himself. Bearing fruit should give us both a sense of authority *and* humility.

3. (10-11) The command to preserve Aaron's rod in the ark of the covenant.

And the LORD said to Moses, "Bring Aaron's rod back before the Testimony, to be kept as a sign against the rebels, that you may put

their complaints away from Me, lest they die." Thus did Moses; just as the LORD had commanded him, so he did.

a. **To be kept as a sign against the rebels**: The rod of Aaron was to be kept as a museum piece, to remind the children of Israel that God had chosen a priesthood, and nothing would change that – Aaron's priesthood would always be Aaron's priesthood.

> i. The *unfruitful* rods were given back to their owners. The *fruitful* rod was kept before the LORD.

> ii. "Only he [Aaron] can draw near to God. Only he can make atonement for Israel's sin. Israel must acknowledge his unique place in the scheme of salvation by not usurping his prerogatives and by supporting his ministry financially." (Wenham)

> iii. If God demonstrated His choice of Aaron and *his* descendants as priests for Israel, how can Jesus be our High Priest, as Hebrews 2:17 says? Because Jesus is a high priest of the order of Melchizedek, not the order of Aaron (as explained in Hebrews 7).

b. **Bring Aaron's rod back before the Testimony**: Aaron's rod was to be kept in the ark of the covenant, as another example of Israel's failure and rebellion. When God looked down from heaven into the ark, He saw emblems of Israel's sin: The tablets of the law that they broke, the manna that they complained about, and Aaron's rod which was the answer to their rebellion. The covering blood of sacrifice was applied to the lid covering over these reminders of Israel's sin, so God "saw" the blood "covering" their sin, and atonement was made.

c. **That you may put their complaints away from Me**: God noted that their murmuring and complaining against Aaron was actually murmuring and complaining against Himself.

> i. Yet Trapp noted that this did not end all of Israel's complaining, "Which yet would hardly be done.... Many men's lips, like rusty hinges, for want of the oil of grace and gladness, move not without murmuring and complaining."

> ii. At the same time, there was not another direct rebellion against Aaron's authority as the high priest in Israel after this. "The sign was efficacious; for while the spirit of rebellion manifested itself subsequently in other ways, it may safely be said that any complaint against the rights of the God-appointed priesthood ceased from this time." (Morgan)

4. (12-13) The reaction of the children of Israel.

So the children of Israel spoke to Moses, saying, "Surely we die, we perish, we all perish! Whoever even comes near the tabernacle of the LORD must die. Shall we all utterly die?"

a. **Surely we die, we perish, we all perish**: This shows that the people of Israel were clearly convicted of their sin. They now clearly knew that it was wrong to contest the priestly leadership of Aaron.

> i. **Surely we die**: According to Adam Clarke's comment, perhaps they described something like the shortness of breath that comes with a panic or anxiety attack. "...*gavaenu* signifies not so much to *die* simply, as *to feel an extreme difficulty of breathing*, which, producing *suffocation*, ends at last in death."

> ii. "Every thing in this miracle is so far beyond the power of nature, that no doubt could remain on the minds of the people, or the envious chiefs, of the Divine appointment of Aaron, and of the especial interference of God in this case." (Clarke)

b. **Whoever even comes near the tabernacle of the LORD must die**: Much in chapter 16 during the rebellion of Korah gave these Israelites who resisted the leadership of Aaron reason to be afraid.

- The leaders (Korah, Dathan, and Abiram) were judged and destroyed.

- Their 250 followers among the leading men of Israel were judged and destroyed.

- The censers from the 250 were recovered, flattened, and used to cover the altar.

- A plague was used to judge and destroy 14,700 of those who sympathized with Korah and his followers.

c. **Shall we all utterly die?** Considering the miraculous confirmation of Aaron's priesthood, the people feared they were next to be judged and destroyed, and this was not an unreasonable fear.

> i. This kind of feverish fear doesn't necessarily mean their hearts were changed. This will not be the last account of a complaining, murmuring Israel. This shows that dramatic events don't take away our complaining and rebelliousness. The heart must be changed by God.

Numbers 18 – Laws Pertaining to Priests and Levites

A. Responsibilities of the priests and the Levites.

1. (1) The priests are accountable for the sanctuary and the priesthood.

Then the LORD said to Aaron: "You and your sons and your father's house with you shall bear the iniquity *related to* the sanctuary, and you and your sons with you shall bear the iniquity *associated with* your priesthood.

> a. **You and your sons and your father's house**: The priests – that is, Aaron, his sons, and their descendants – **shall bear the iniquity related to the sanctuary**, and the priesthood. They were accountable to God.

> b. **You shall bear the iniquity**: This was the other side of Aaron's privilege as the chosen priest of God, as demonstrated with the budding of the rod in Numbers 17. Aaron had authority from God as the appointed high priest, but he also had great accountability.

>> i. God never gives authority without accountability; the two always go together. If someone is in leadership at God's providential direction and others are expected to submit to him, then God also has a special accountability for that person.

2. (2-7) The Levites are God's chosen helpers for the priests in their ministry at the altar and the tabernacle.

Also bring with you your brethren of the tribe of Levi, the tribe of your father, that they may be joined with you and serve you while you and your sons *are* with you before the tabernacle of witness. They shall attend to your needs and all the needs of the tabernacle; but they shall not come near the articles of the sanctuary and the altar, lest they die—they and you also. They shall be joined with you and attend to the needs of the tabernacle of meeting, for all the work of the tabernacle;

but an outsider shall not come near you. And you shall attend to the duties of the sanctuary and the duties of the altar, that there *may* be no more wrath on the children of Israel. Behold, I Myself have taken your brethren the Levites from among the children of Israel; *they are* a gift to you, given by the LORD, to do the work of the tabernacle of meeting. Therefore you and your sons with you shall attend to your priesthood for everything at the altar and behind the veil; and you shall serve. I give your priesthood *to you* as a gift for service, but the outsider who comes near shall be put to death."

a. **Bring with you your brethren of the tribe of Levi**: Aaron himself was of the tribe of Levi. While only he and his descendants were given the priesthood, the whole tribe of Levi had a special calling to help Aaron and the priests (Numbers 3:5-10).

b. **That they may be joined with you and serve you**: The Levites were called to support the work of the priests. They didn't have the same prominent position as the priests, but they were important for their service.

i. The Levites are described as serving the priests (Numbers 18:2), the congregation of Israel (Numbers 16:9), and God (Deuteronomy 10:8). Both were true and each area was within their legitimate calling.

c. **They shall not come near the articles of the sanctuary and the altar**: The Levites were not allowed to do what the priests did, **lest they die**. Korah is an example of a Levite who dared to **come near the articles of the sanctuary and the altar** and who died as a result (Numbers 16:16-19, 31-33).

i. **An outsider**: "The term 'stranger'…which often speaks of a foreign national, is used to describe all other people in the Holy Place. The only people who have a right to work in the shrine are the Levites under the supervision of the priests. All others are 'foreigners.'" (Allen)

d. **You shall attend to the duties of the sanctuary and the duties of the altar**: If it was wrong for the Levites to envy or covet the work Aaron and his sons did as priests, it was also sin for Aaron and his sons to neglect the work God gave them to do. Though they had the **gift** of help from Levites, Aaron and his sons must **attend to the priesthood for everything at the altar and behind the veil**.

i. "The Levites were never to be regarded as 'priests in training.' They had a serious 'career ceiling' in their vocation. The sanctity of the Holy Place is not to be underestimated." (Allen)

ii. In a similar way, the New Testament says we are all different "parts" of the body, each with gifts and callings (1 Corinthians 12:4-7). We shouldn't envy or covet the gifts and callings of others.

iii. **I give your priesthood to you as a gift for service**: "Among the rest these words, 'I give you the priesthood as a service of gift,' emphasized again the fact that these priests, and these people, had done nothing to merit the provision. It was wholly one of grace, a gift from God." (Morgan)

B. The privileges of the priests and the Levites.

1. (8-20) The firstborn and the devoted portions belong to the priest.

And the LORD spoke to Aaron: "Here, I Myself have also given you charge of My heave offerings, all the holy gifts of the children of Israel; I have given them as a portion to you and your sons, as an ordinance forever. This shall be yours of the most holy things *reserved* from the fire: every offering of theirs, every grain offering and every sin offering and every trespass offering which they render to Me, *shall be* most holy for you and your sons. In a most holy *place* you shall eat it; every male shall eat it. It shall be holy to you.

"This also *is* yours: the heave offering of their gift, with all the wave offerings of the children of Israel; I have given them to you, and your sons and daughters with you, as an ordinance forever. Everyone who is clean in your house may eat it.

"All the best of the oil, all the best of the new wine and the grain, their firstfruits which they offer to the LORD, I have given them to you. Whatever first ripe fruit is in their land, which they bring to the LORD, shall be yours. Everyone who is clean in your house may eat it.

"Every devoted thing in Israel shall be yours.

"Everything that first opens the womb of all flesh, which they bring to the LORD, whether man or beast, shall be yours; nevertheless the firstborn of man you shall surely redeem, and the firstborn of unclean animals you shall redeem. And those redeemed of the devoted things you shall redeem when one month old, according to your valuation, for five shekels of silver, according to the shekel of the sanctuary, which *is* twenty gerahs. But the firstborn of a cow, the firstborn of a sheep, or the firstborn of a goat you shall not redeem; they *are* holy. You shall sprinkle their blood on the altar, and burn their fat *as* an offering made by fire for a sweet aroma to the LORD. And their flesh shall be yours, just as the wave breast and the right thigh are yours.

"All the heave offerings of the holy things, which the children of Israel offer to the LORD, I have given to you and your sons and daughters with you as an ordinance forever; it *is* a covenant of salt forever before the LORD with you and your descendants with you."

Then the LORD said to Aaron: "You shall have no inheritance in their land, nor shall you have any portion among them; I *am* your portion and your inheritance among the children of Israel."

a. **Here, I Myself have also given you charge of My heave offerings**: The **heave offerings** were brought to God as part of the peace offering (Exodus 29:28 and Leviticus 7:14), for a Nazirite's consecration offering (Numbers 6:20), and for thanksgiving (Numbers 15:19-21). In the heave offering, a choice portion of the animal (the breast or the thigh) was *heaved* or *waved* before the LORD.

i. Afterwards, that choice portion of the meat was for the priest and his family and was considered holy – so it had to be eaten in the **holy place**.

ii. **My heave offerings**: "Something was regarded as holy, not because of some mysterious inner quality, but because it has been presented to the Lord for his use." (Allen)

iii. **All the wave offerings of the children of Israel**: "By holding up grain or produce and waving it back and forth in the air in a respectful manner, the offeror was marking out the Lord as the source of his plenty. Since this food was not put to fire, it was then given over to the priests for their own family use." (Allen)

b. **Every offering of theirs**: The priest also received portions from the **grain offering** and **sin offering** and **trespass offering**; gifts of **oil**, **wine**, **grain**, and **ripe fruit** from the firstfruits offerings were given to the priests. This was how the priesthood was supported in Israel.

i. "The cereal grain offering, as described in [Leviticus] 2:1-13 and 6:14-23, was an unleavened mixture of fine flour, oil, and incense. A memorial portion was burned on the altar as a sweet aroma to the Lord, and the remainder was eaten by the Aaronic priests." (Cole)

c. **Everything that first opens the womb of all flesh**: When the firstborn was brought to the tabernacle, either to be given or redeemed with money, it also belonged to the priest.

i. It was important to make clear that God did not want human sacrifice of any kind. **The firstborn of man** was never to be sacrificed to God but redeemed – an amount of money was given to God's work instead of the sacrifice.

d. **I have given to you and your sons and daughters with you as an ordinance forever**: All these parts of these sacrifices belonged to the priests, and it was important for Israel to fulfill their obligation to bring them. This is emphasized as God called it **a covenant of salt forever**.

i. Salt speaks of *purity*, of *preservation*, and of *expense*. So, a covenant of salt is a *pure* covenant (salt stays a pure chemical compound), a covenant of salt is an *enduring* covenant (salt preserves things and makes them endure), and a covenant of salt is a *valuable* covenant (salt was expensive).

ii. Spurgeon on the **covenant of salt**: "By which was meant that it was an unchangeable, incorruptible covenant, which would endure as salt makes a thing to endure, so that it is not liable to putrefy or corrupt."

iii. According to some ancient customs, a bond of friendship was established through the eating of salt. It was said that once you had eaten a man's salt, you were his friend for life.

e. **You shall have no inheritance in their land**: While by God's command the priests received much material support from Israel (and a lot of meat), they also were deprived of **inheritance in their land**. The priests had no permanent portion of land given to them because God said **I am your portion and your inheritance**.

i. Many of God's people through the generations could say with David in Psalm 16, *O LORD, You are the portion of my inheritance and my cup; You maintain my lot* (Psalm 16:5). They could say with Asaph in Psalm 73, *My flesh and my heart fail; but God is the strength of my heart and my portion forever* (Psalm 73:26). They could agree with David in Psalm 142, *I cried out to You, O LORD: I said, "You are my refuge, my portion in the land of the living"* (Psalm 142:5).

ii. When God is our portion, He is our inheritance – our hope, the one whom we trust for our future. We are satisfied in Him. Since we are all a royal priesthood (1 Peter 2:9), we all have the LORD for our portion.

2. (21-24) Tithes given to the Levites.

"Behold, I have given the children of Levi all the tithes in Israel as an inheritance in return for the work which they perform, the work of the tabernacle of meeting. Hereafter the children of Israel shall not come near the tabernacle of meeting, lest they bear sin and die. But the Levites shall perform the work of the tabernacle of meeting, and they shall bear their iniquity; *it shall be* **a statute forever, throughout your generations, that among the children of Israel they shall have no inheritance. For the tithes of the children of Israel, which they offer up** *as* **a heave offering**

to the LORD, I have given to the Levites as an inheritance; therefore I have said to them, 'Among the children of Israel they shall have no inheritance.'"

a. **I have given the children of Levi all the tithes in Israel**: While the priests were supported by their portions of the sacrifices brought to God's altar (18:8-20), God commanded that the Levites be supported by the tithes of Israel (a giving of ten percent of income). The tithes *belong* to God (He says **I have given**, so they are His to give), but God then gave them to the Levites.

i. When an Israelite did not give their tithe, they did not rob the Levite, even though the money went to the Levites. They robbed God (Malachi 3:8-10), because God received the tithe from the giver, and God gave it to the Levite.

ii. Some today think the tithe commanded here is most like modern-day taxes paid to governments. This is because these tithes were to support the Levites who were, in a sense, government workers in ancient Israel. Those who hold this idea often claim that free-will giving mentioned in the Old Testament answers to the New Testament emphasis on giving. We can say that the New Testament nowhere specifically *commands* tithing, but it certainly does speak of it in a *positive* light if, and only if, it is done with the right heart (Luke 11:42).

iii. It is also important to understand that tithing is not a principle that depended on the Mosaic law. Hebrews 7:5-9 explains that tithing was practiced and honored by God *before* the Law of Moses.

iv. What the New Testament does speak with great clarity on is the principle of *giving*. The New Testament tells us that giving should be regular, planned, proportional, and private (1 Corinthians 16:1-4). It says that giving must be generous, voluntary, and cheerful (2 Corinthians 9).

v. Since the New Testament doesn't emphasize tithing, one might not advocate a strict standard, even though some Christians argue against tithing because of self-interest. But since giving is to be proportional (as in 1 Corinthians 16:2), believers today should give according to *some* percentage. Based on the Old Testament description of the tithe, perhaps one could say that ten percent is a good goal or practice for the modern believer's generosity. However, one should not regard ten percent as a hard limit to our generosity; surely God would have some give much more, as He has blessed and prospered them.

vi. If our question is, "How little can I give and still be pleasing to God?" it demonstrates that our heart isn't in the right place. We should have the attitude of some early Christians, who essentially said: "We are not under the tithe – we can give *more!*" Giving and financial management are *spiritual* issues, not merely financial matters (Luke 16:11).

b. **In return for the work which they perform**: The tithes were also given by God as *pay* to the Levites, not as gifts. Because the Levites had dedicated themselves to the service of God, the people of God, and the things of God, it was right that they were supported by God – through the tithes of the children of Israel.

i. "The assignment of the tithe to the tribe of Levi is something new. Tithing, giving a tenth of one's agricultural produce, was an ancient institution in the Near East. Both Abraham and Jacob gave tithes (Gen. 14:20; 28:22). Leviticus 27:30–33 regulates the redemption of tithes, evidently presupposing their existence, but it does not state who would receive them. This law, looking forward to the settlement in Canaan when tithing would become possible, lays it down that the Levites are to receive them." (Wenham)

ii. **In return for the work which they perform** means the Levites had the "right" to expect to be supported through the tithe. Paul presents the same principle for ministers of the gospel in the New Testament (1 Corinthians 9:7-14). Yet in his words and in his life Paul also showed that when it was better for the gospel, this right should be willingly given up for God's glory and the progress of His kingdom (1 Corinthians 9:15).

iii. However, once every three years, the tithe was collected and distributed not only to the Levites but also to the poor and needy among Israel (Deuteronomy 14:28-29).

iv. "These payments were an acknowledgment of the enormous importance of the ministry of the tribe of Levi, representing the nation to God and God to the nation. Through their mediation the people were saved from the danger of extermination. Similarly, Jesus and Paul expected those who heard the gospel to recognize its worth by paying its ministers adequately (Matt. 10:9–10; 1 Cor. 9:3–10; 16:2; cf. Matt. 23:23)." (Wenham)

v. According to Numbers 2:32, there were 603,550 men who could fight as soldiers among the 12 tribes of Israel (excluding the tribe of Levi). Numbers 3:39 says there were 22,000 men among the Levites. If we consider these counted men to be heads of households, then the tithes of 603,550 families supported 22,000 families among the Levites.

vi. This was potentially generous support. Every Levite family was supported by roughly 27 Israelite families from the other tribes. It's difficult to make comparisons from our modern economy to an ancient agrarian society, but if for the sake of comparison, we said that each Israelite family averaged an income of $10,000 and tithed from it, the tithe (10%) of their income from the 603,550 families would total $603,550,000 – more than $603 million. If one-tenth went to the priests (as commanded by Numbers 18:25-32) and of the remaining, one-third was given to the poor in Israel (as in Deuteronomy 14:28-29), then the average Levite family would receive more than $16,000 ($16,460) – more than 160% of the income of the average Israelite family. Yet this was only true *if* every Israelite family properly paid their tithe.

vii. Since we have no evidence that the Levitical families were rich or lived wealthy lifestyles, it was probably the case that many Israelites never properly paid their tithes, as later described and rebuked in Malachi 3:8-10. Perhaps as few ancient Israelites actually gave God a tithe of their income as do believers today. It may be that God's system "accounted" for Israel's disobedience. In some sense, it was not "necessary" for every Israelite to pay their tithe to support the Levites, but it was *necessary for their obedience* and it was *necessary to guard their hearts against greed and materialism*.

c. **The Levites shall perform the work of the tabernacle of meeting, and they shall bear their iniquity**: This shows that the Levites also had a special responsibility. If they were to be supported through the tithe, they had to do the job, and do it with diligence.

i. There are probably few things worse than someone who is supported through the gifts of God's people but is lazy at his job. If a man robs his employer by laziness, how much more does a lazy minister rob God and His people?

d. **Among the children of Israel they shall have no inheritance**: Just as with the priests, this was a trade-off. The Levites did not have the best of both worlds; they did not have a personal inheritance of land as the other tribes did.

i. Those who are supported through the giving of God's people should expect that they would not have the best of both worlds; they will not be wealthy in this life, though if possible, they should be comfortable. It is wrong for the congregation to keep the pastor "humble" through poverty, and just as wrong for the pastor to use the gifts of God's people to live above God's people.

3. (25-32) The Levites tithe to the priests.

Then the LORD spoke to Moses, saying, "Speak thus to the Levites, and say to them: 'When you take from the children of Israel the tithes which I have given you from them as your inheritance, then you shall offer up a heave offering of it to the LORD, a tenth of the tithe. And your heave offering shall be reckoned to you as though *it were* **the grain of the threshing floor and as the fullness of the winepress. Thus you shall also offer a heave offering to the LORD from all your tithes which you receive from the children of Israel, and you shall give the LORD's heave offering from it to Aaron the priest. Of all your gifts you shall offer up every heave offering due to the LORD, from all the best of them, the consecrated part of them.' Therefore you shall say to them: 'When you have lifted up the best of it, then** *the rest* **shall be accounted to the Levites as the produce of the threshing floor and as the produce of the winepress. You may eat it in any place, you and your households, for it** *is* **your reward for your work in the tabernacle of meeting. And you shall bear no sin because of it, when you have lifted up the best of it. But you shall not profane the holy gifts of the children of Israel, lest you die.'"**

a. **A tenth of the tithe**: The Levites themselves were not excused from tithing. They were also to give a **tenth of the tithe**, and the **best of them** given as the tenth. This was **due to the LORD**, and the LORD gave it to the priests.

i. It was important for the Levites to also learn how to be givers. Just because they were supported through the giving of God's people, it did not mean they were excused from giving. We all need to learn how to be givers, because God is a giver, and God wants His people to imitate Him.

ii. **From all the best of them**: "The tribute from the Levites was from the very best, literally 'its fat' *(heleb)*, the same word used to describe the best of the oil, grain, and wine processing in v. 12." (Cole)

iii. "There is a tendency, then and now, for persons to believe that if their lives are spent in the Lord's work, then they are exempt from contributing to that work. This leads to a concept, lamentably more and more observed in our own day, that payment for ministry is something deserved and is something to be demanded." (Allen)

b. **Of all your gifts you shall offer up every heave offering due to the LORD:** We are not told if the *priests* were to tithe from what they received. Presumably, they did not – because what belonged to the priests was considered holy, and not to be used by others outside the priestly families.

i. This chapter clearly shows that the obligation of the Israelite to give was far more than just the tithe (the giving of ten percent). The Israelite also had to give *firstfruits* (Numbers 18:12) of all their produce and the *firstborn* (Numbers 18:15) of their flocks and herds. These were portions that went to the priests and/or the Levites.

ii. To give the firstborn of the flock and the firstfruits of the field was something of a risk; it was giving in faith. This was because the cow that gave birth to a calf or the ewe that gave birth to a lamb might not give birth again. The field that produced grain or the vineyard that gave grapes might not give much more. The giving of firstfruits and the firstborn was a way to give God the first and the best, and to give God the priority. God promised to bless this giving of the firstfruits and firstborn in faith: *Honor the LORD with your possessions, and with the firstfruits of all your increase; so your barns will be filled with plenty, and your vats will overflow with new wine* (Proverbs 3:9-10). We are so accustomed to giving out of what is left over – giving from our surplus – that many of us are unfamiliar with the principle of the giving of the firstborn or the firstfruits.

iii. This wasn't the end of Israel's required giving. They were also told to leave a portion of their fields unharvested so the poor could eat from those portions (Leviticus 19:9-10). A Passover sacrifice was required from each family every year (Exodus 12:43-47). Sometimes a temple tax was required (Nehemiah 10:32-33), or a special tribute (Numbers 31:28-29).

iv. It is hard to estimate exactly how much the firstfruits and firstborn obligations amounted to; it would differ from family to family. But the actual required giving of Israel was far more than ten percent (the tithe).

v. Some say that Deuteronomy 12:6 speaks of an additional ten percent given (sometimes called the "festival tithe"), but in context Deuteronomy 12 speaks only of *where* to bring the tithe, and does not command an additional tithe. As well, some claim that Deuteronomy 14:28-29 commands an additional tithe every three years (sometimes called the "poor tithe"). Yet, since Deuteronomy 14:28 speaks of *the tithe*, and since it also went to the Levite and not only to the poor, it is best to understand that this was not an additional tithe, but a command that once every three years, the tithe was also available to the poor, not only to the Levite.

vi. Besides the required giving, Israel was asked to give free-will offerings: This chapter speaks of willingly given sacrifices, of which the heave offering went to the priests (Numbers 18:9-11).

vii. This wasn't the end of Israel's voluntary giving. Israel was asked to give for special projects like the building of the tabernacle (Exodus 35:4-9), and free-will giving to the poor.

Numbers 19 – The Red Heifer and the Cleansing Waters

A. Provision for purification – the ashes from the sacrifice of a red heifer.

1. (1-2) The taking of a **red heifer**.

Now the LORD spoke to Moses and Aaron, saying, "This *is* the ordinance of the law which the LORD has commanded, saying: 'Speak to the children of Israel, that they bring you a red heifer without blemish, in which there *is* no defect *and* on which a yoke has never come.

a. **That they bring you a red heifer**: This introduces a different kind of offering, unique in the Old Testament. This **red heifer** would not be killed to drain and offer its blood at the altar. Instead, it would be wholly burned, and the remaining ashes were added to water to be used for ritual cleansing.

> i. A **heifer** is a cow which has never been pregnant, and thus cannot yet give milk. The Hebrew text does not specifically state that this had to be a **heifer**, simply a young female cow, **red** in color.

> ii. "*Heifer* (RSV) is more accurately rendered 'cow' by the NEB. However, if it had never been used for ploughing or pulling a cart (2), it must have been relatively young, hence the traditional English translation." (Wenham)

> iii. When it came to choosing an animal used for sacrifice in ancient Israel, "Normally the animal's colour did not matter. This one had to be red to resemble blood." (Wenham)

b. **Without blemish, in which there is no defect and on which a yoke has never come**: These requirements made this animal even rarer. This red heifer, therefore, would be valuable, rare, and in some sense pure, having never been mated.

i. "The heifer was to be *without spot* – having no mixture of any other colour. Plutarch remarks…that if there was a *single hair* in the animal either *white* or *black*, it marred the sacrifice." (Clarke)

2. (3-10) The sacrifice, burning, and gathering of ashes from the red heifer.

You shall give it to Eleazar the priest, that he may take it outside the camp, and it shall be slaughtered before him; and Eleazar the priest shall take some of its blood with his finger, and sprinkle some of its blood seven times directly in front of the tabernacle of meeting. Then the heifer shall be burned in his sight: its hide, its flesh, its blood, and its offal shall be burned. And the priest shall take cedar wood and hyssop and scarlet, and cast *them* into the midst of the fire burning the heifer. Then the priest shall wash his clothes, he shall bathe in water, and afterward he shall come into the camp; the priest shall be unclean until evening. And the one who burns it shall wash his clothes in water, bathe in water, and shall be unclean until evening. Then a man *who is* clean shall gather up the ashes of the heifer, and store *them* outside the camp in a clean place; and they shall be kept for the congregation of the children of Israel for the water of purification; it *is* for purifying from sin. And the one who gathers the ashes of the heifer shall wash his clothes, and be unclean until evening. It shall be a statute forever to the children of Israel and to the stranger who dwells among them.

a. **That he may take it outside the camp, and it shall be slaughtered before him**: This was more of a *slaughtering* than a *sacrifice*. Most of the blood of this heifer remained with the animal at its burning. A small amount of blood was sprinkled in the direction of the **front of the tabernacle of meeting**, as the animal was slaughtered **outside the camp**.

i. The procedure for this offering was dramatically different than every other under the Law of Moses. It was a sacrifice, but it was a unique kind of sacrifice in many ways.

- This offering demanded an animal of a specific color.
- This offering demanded a female cow, not a male bull.
- This offering was slaughtered, not sacrificed.
- This offering was killed outside the camp, not at the altar.
- This offering was burned whole, not cut into pieces.
- This offering's blood was not drained from the animal.
- This offering's blood was not applied to the altar but sprinkled toward the tabernacle.

ii. **Its blood...shall be burned**: Unlike every other sacrifice in the Old Testament, the blood of the red heifer was burnt along with the sacrifice, instead of being completely drained out at the neck and poured out at the altar. Blood was included in the ashes remaining from the burning of the carcass of the red **heifer**.

b. **And the priest shall take cedar wood and hyssop and scarlet, and cast them into the midst of the fire burning the heifer**: When the red heifer was burnt, the priest would also put **cedar wood and hyssop and scarlet** into the fire. The ashes remaining from **the midst of the fire** included the carcass of the animal, its blood, and the **wood and hyssop and scarlet**.

i. In Leviticus 14:4-6, each of these three items was used in the cleansing ceremony for a leper and each has special significance.

ii. **Cedar wood** is resistant to disease and rot and is well known for its quality, preciousness, and fragrant aroma. These properties may be the reason for including it here – as well as a symbolic reference to the wood of the cross. Some suppose the cross Jesus was crucified on was made of cedar wood.

iii. Because **hyssop** was used for the cleansing ceremony for lepers, when David asked God *purge me with hyssop* in Psalm 51:7, he associated himself with the leper who needed cleansing. As well, on the cross Jesus was offered a drink from a hyssop branch (John 19:29).

iv. **Scarlet**, the color of blood, was used in the veil and curtains of the tabernacle (Exodus 26:31), in the garments of the high priest (Exodus 28:5-6), and for the covering for the table of showbread (Numbers 4:8). **Scarlet** was the sign of Rahab's salvation (Joshua 2:21), and the color of the "king's robe" mockingly set on Jesus by Roman soldiers (Matthew 27:28).

v. "According to Maimonides, the cedar wood was taken in logs and bound round with hyssop, and then afterwards the whole enveloped in scarlet; so what was seen by the people was the scarlet which was at once the emblem of sin and its punishment." (Spurgeon)

c. **They shall be kept for the congregation of the children of Israel for the water of purification; it is for purifying from sin**: The residue from the burning of the carcass, the cedar, the hyssop, and the scarlet fabric together would produce a lot of ash. This ash was gathered and sprinkled in water bit by bit to make water suited for **purification** ceremonies.

i. The **water of purification** was only made effective when the ash remains of the red heifer (along with the cedar, hyssop, and scarlet) were added to the water.

ii. This **water of purification** was necessary because of sin and its many effects. "The most serious and obvious type of human uncleanness was that caused by death. Anyone who touched a corpse or a human bone or a grave, or entered the tent of a dead man, became unclean (14–16). Furthermore, this uncleanness was contagious: anything the unclean man touched would itself become unclean and infect others (22; cf. Lev. 15)." (Wenham)

iii. This **water of purification** showed God's kindness in providing another way of cleansing from ritual impurity. Leviticus gives a ritual for cleansing that included washing in water and waiting until evening (Leviticus 11:28, 11:39-40, 15:16-18). In more serious cases (such as contact with a dead body), one must wait seven days and then offer an animal sacrifice (Leviticus 14:10-32). This provides an alternative to the long and expensive ritual described in Leviticus 14. With the **water of purification**, instead of being cleansed by a sin offering, the unclean person was sprinkled with water that included all the ingredients of a sin offering.

iv. Taken together the offering of the red heifer and the water of purification associated with that offering are a powerful picture pointing to the perfect work of Jesus Christ.

- Like the red heifer, Jesus was "red" in His sacrifice, "Christ covered with his own blood." (Trapp)
- Like the red heifer, Jesus was pure and without spot.
- Like the red heifer, Jesus was never under the yoke (of sin).
- Like the red heifer, Jesus was sacrificed outside the camp.
- Like the red heifer, the sacrifice of Jesus was unique.
- Like the red heifer, Jesus was completely offered.
- Like the red heifer, the sacrifice of Jesus is effective for all who claim it, including the stranger and sojourner (v. 10).

v. The **water of purification** made with the ashes of the red heifer did not create a *different* purification from ritual uncleanness. In some sense, it did what the longer, more costly, and more elaborate ceremony of Leviticus 14 did. Instead, this water of purification made a better way (more accessible and virtually instant) to ritually purify even the most unclean ones among God's people. It did this by building on existing principles of sacrifice, but making a different offering, one that did not need to be constantly repeated, but only referred to again and again. One might say that the **water of purification** offered a better way to be made clean, something of a God-approved shortcut – but it wasn't easy for the red heifer. The red heifer and **water of purification** are a wonderful illustration of the perfect work of Jesus Christ on the cross, as a substitute for His people (Hebrews 9:13-14). In both cases, a better sacrifice replaced a previous system for cleansing.

vi. Sometimes there are modern news stories about rabbis searching for and (perhaps) finding a perfect red heifer, suitable for this ceremony in a restored priestly service and temple. While this is an interesting thought, it is helpful to remember that in the Bible, there is nothing *necessary* about the water of purification made by the ashes of the burning of the red heifer. What it accomplished had already been made possible by a longer and more costly routine described in Leviticus 14.

B. Other laws of purification.

1. (11-13) The worst kind of ritual impurity: touching a dead human body.

He who touches the dead body of anyone shall be unclean seven days. He shall purify himself with the water on the third day and on the seventh day; *then* he will be clean. But if he does not purify himself on the third day and on the seventh day, he will not be clean. Whoever touches the body of anyone who has died, and does not purify himself, defiles the tabernacle of the LORD. That person shall be cut off from Israel. He shall be unclean, because the water of purification was not sprinkled on him; his uncleanness *is* still on him.

a. **He who touches the dead body of anyone shall be unclean seven days**: After giving the provision of the cleansing water made with the ashes of the red heifer, God immediately mentioned the most extreme situation requiring ritual purification – contact with a dead human body.

i. To be ceremonially unclean was not "sin," as we might think of it. To be **unclean** in this sense meant that one was kept apart from the community of worship in Israel until they were ceremonially purified.

ii. Priests were made unclean by contact with the dead (Leviticus 22:1-4), and Nazirites could not go near a dead body (Numbers 6:6) or their vow would be ended. For those who were not priests or Nazirites, contact with a dead body made them unclean for seven days, when they had to live outside the camp (Leviticus 5:2-3).

iii. Adam Clarke observed that the time of uncleanness after touching a dead human body was longer than that of touching an animal carcass: "How low does this lay man! He who touched a dead *beast* was only unclean for *one day*, Lev. 11:24, 27, 39; but he who touches a dead *man* is unclean for *seven days.* This was certainly designed to mark the peculiar impurity of man, and to show his sinfulness – *seven* times worse than the vilest animal!" (Clarke)

b. **If he does not purify himself…. that person shall be cut off**: One who was unclean needed purification and could not ignore their condition. However, they were still part of the nation – unless they refused to address their unclean condition.

i. A parallel to this idea is found in John 13:5-11. When Peter asked Jesus to wash him completely, Jesus said *He who is bathed needs only to wash his feet, but is completely clean* (John 13:10).

ii. "The feet want constant washing. The daily defilement of our daily walk through an ungodly world brings upon us the daily necessity of being cleaned from fresh sin, and that the mighty Master supplies to us." (Spurgeon)

c. **Defiles the tabernacle of the LORD**: These laws were relevant to all of Israel, but especially to priests, who had the potential to defile the tabernacle of the LORD. Under the new covenant, the Christian also has a special call to purity because an impure believer may defile the dwelling place of God (1 Corinthians 6:19-20).

2. (14-16) More on ritual uncleanness from a dead body.

This *is* the law when a man dies in a tent: All who come into the tent and all who *are* in the tent shall be unclean seven days; and every open vessel, which has no cover fastened on it, *is* unclean. Whoever in the open field touches one who is slain by a sword or who has died, or a bone of a man, or a grave, shall be unclean seven days.

a. **This is the law when a man dies in a tent**: The practice of quarantining all those who contacted a dead body was also a helpful public health measure. Those who were potentially contaminated would be set aside until it could be seen whether they had contracted a disease from the dead body.

b. **Every open vessel, which has no cover fastened on it, is unclean**: In fact, this principle extended to **every open vessel** – which could potentially carry disease-causing organisms. If near a dead body, those vessels were declared unclean and thus destroyed, reducing the danger of contagious disease.

c. **Shall be unclean**: One reason a dead body was considered unclean was to communicate the idea that death is the result of sin and the positive proof of sin (Genesis 2:15-17, Romans 5:12). Death is something like *sin made visible.*

i. If someone touched the carcass of a dead animal, he was unclean for less than one day (Leviticus 11:24, 27, 39). But if someone touched a dead human, he was unclean for seven days. In the Law of Moses, there was more potential contamination from death among humans than among animals.

ii. Spiritually speaking, our contact with a dead body also makes us unclean. In Romans 7:24, Paul cried out in frustration at his defeat by sin: *Who will deliver me from this body of death?* We can only be delivered from the body of death if we receive and walk in the precious work of Jesus for us.

3. (17-19) The application of the cleansing water made with the ashes of the read heifer.

And for an unclean *person* they shall take some of the ashes of the heifer burnt for purification from sin, and running water shall be put on them in a vessel. A clean person shall take hyssop and dip *it* in the water, sprinkle *it* on the tent, on all the vessels, on the persons who were there, or on the one who touched a bone, the slain, the dead, or a grave. The clean *person* shall sprinkle the unclean on the third day and on the seventh day; and on the seventh day he shall purify himself, wash his clothes, and bathe in water; and at evening he shall be clean.

a. **They shall take some of the ashes of the heifer**: The ashes of the red heifer (19:9) were sprinkled in fresh **running water**, and this water was used for the ceremonies of purification.

i. **Running water**: "Special care was to be exercised that only living water, or water from a flowing stream, should be used for this purpose." (Watson)

ii. Together, the ashes and the water are "Signifying the ashes of Christ's merit, and the water of his Spirit." (Trapp)

iii. In this picture, it can be observed that the **running water** alone, by itself, did not have the power to cleanse. It had to be joined with the **ashes of the heifer**. This illustrates the truth that reference to the work of the Holy Spirit or the word of God *alone*, without reference to the offering of Jesus Christ on the cross, is empty (1 Corinthians 1:23, 2:2). As well, the presentation of the work of Jesus is of little use without the power of the Holy Spirit. We need *both* the work of Jesus and the work of the Spirit with the word of God.

b. **And at evening he shall be clean**: Thus, ashes of the red heifer combined with water to bring ceremonial cleansing. It could cleanse even the uncleanness brought about by death.

i. This was a powerful prophetic picture of the work of Jesus under the new covenant. One can say that the ashes of the red heifer point to the work of Jesus (see the explanation on 19:3-10). The water points to the work of the word of God and Spirit of God (Ephesians 5:26, John 7:38-39). The person and work of Jesus Christ, together with the work of God's Spirit through the word of God, bring cleansing – even from the power and impurity of death.

ii. The work of Jesus can cleanse the conscience from dead works: *For if the blood of bulls and goats and the ashes of a heifer, sprinkling the unclean, sanctifies for the purifying of the flesh, how much more shall the blood of Christ, who through the eternal Spirit offered Himself without spot to God, cleanse your conscience from dead works to serve the living God?* (Hebrews 9:13-14)

4. (20-22) The nature of uncleanness.

But the man who is unclean and does not purify himself, that person shall be cut off from among the assembly, because he has defiled the sanctuary of the LORD. The water of purification has not been sprinkled on him; he *is* unclean. It shall be a perpetual statute for them. He who sprinkles the water of purification shall wash his clothes; and he who touches the water of purification shall be unclean until evening. Whatever the unclean *person* touches shall be unclean; and the person who touches *it* shall be unclean until evening.

a. **The man who is unclean and does not purify himself**: This shows that uncleanness cannot correct itself. The unclean man will not just become clean over time. He must do something, and he must do what God says must be done to be clean. His own plans or efforts to cleanse mean nothing.

b. **He who sprinkles the water of purification**: Those who help others to become clean must walk in cleanness themselves. The one who regards the water of cleansing as a common thing (**he who touches the water of purification**) will himself be regarded as unclean.

c. **Whatever the unclean person touches shall be unclean**: Uncleanness was easily transmitted, but cleanness had to be deliberately sought.

i. These laws of ritual purity communicated many important and enduring principles.

- The distinction must be made between the clean and the unclean. This means that not everything is the same; there is a difference between the clean and the unclean.

- Ritual uncleanness is the individual's responsibility, but it matters to the whole community.

- Ritual impurity must be recognized and dealt with.
- One can be polluted by the uncleanness of the world.
- God graciously offered an immediate and "easy" way to be cleansed (it wasn't "easy" for the red heifer).
- The cleansing comes by reference back to a past offering.
- The cleansing comes both by the remains of the past offering and by running, living water.
- The ashes of the red heifer and the entire sacrificial system look forward to the perfect work of Jesus Christ (Hebrews 9:13-14).

ii. "As the men of the old covenant had in this ritual an ever-ready means of bodily purification, so we are reminded that 'the blood of Jesus cleanses us from all sin' (1 John 1:7)." (Wenham)

iii. "We should perpetually seek fresh cleansing in the precious blood of Christ. He is represented in this heifer without spot, slain in its prime, whose ashes were mingled in running water to testify their perpetual efficacy and freshness." (Maclaren)

iv. "From all the sins I ever shall commit there is a purification laid by to cleanse me. The seven times sprinkled blood has put these sins away before the judgment-seat of God, and the ashes which are laid by shall put my sin away from my conscience, purging it from dead works." (Spurgeon)

Numbers 20 – The Beginning of the Last Year

A. Contention among the children of Israel.

1. (1) The death of Miriam.

Then the children of Israel, the whole congregation, came into the Wilderness of Zin in the first month, and the people stayed in Kadesh; and Miriam died there and was buried there.

> a. **The people stayed in Kadesh; and Miriam died there and was buried there**: Miriam died in Kadesh. Through the years of wandering in the wilderness, Israel came now to Kadesh. This is probably another place named Kadesh but presented to remind us of the failure of faith at the Kadesh of Numbers 13:26.

> > i. Numbers 13:26 associates Kadesh with the Paran Wilderness, and Numbers 20:1 associates Kadesh with the Wilderness of Zin. It's possible that there are two different places, each called **Kadesh** (Holy Place).

> b. **Miriam died there and was buried there**: Miriam's death was an important point in the journey from Egypt to Canaan. She was the first of Moses' siblings to die in the wilderness, and her death was a demonstration of the fulfillment of God's promise that the generation which refused to enter Canaan would die in the wilderness, and the new generation would enter instead (Numbers 14:29-34).

> > i. Miriam's death shows there were no special exceptions for the family of Moses. God said only Joshua and Caleb would survive from that generation (Numbers 14:30), and that included Miriam, Aaron, and even Moses himself. This chapter will show the frailty of each of these significant leaders.

> > ii. It is common for people to deceive themselves into thinking they have a special exception from God, with their own special arrangement

with the LORD. If Moses and his siblings had no special exception, we should not arrogantly think we have our own arrangement with God.

c. **Miriam died there and was buried there**: Miriam was a complicated character. She was commendable for her courage in helping Moses and his parents (Exodus 2:4-8), and admirable for leading Israel in praise (Exodus 15:20-21). Yet she was also disgraced for her rebellion against Moses (Numbers 12). That one incident of rebellion left a bad mark against her.

i. "Eusebius says that her tomb was to be seen at *Kadesh*, near the city of Petra, in his time." (Clarke)

2. (2-6) Israel contends with Moses and Aaron because of thirst.

Now there was no water for the congregation; so they gathered together against Moses and Aaron. And the people contended with Moses and spoke, saying: "If only we had died when our brethren died before the LORD! Why have you brought up the assembly of the LORD into this wilderness, that we and our animals should die here? And why have you made us come up out of Egypt, to bring us to this evil place? It *is* not a place of grain or figs or vines or pomegranates; nor *is* there any water to drink." So Moses and Aaron went from the presence of the assembly to the door of the tabernacle of meeting, and they fell on their faces. And the glory of the LORD appeared to them.

a. **There was no water for the congregation**: This was a legitimate need for the people and their livestock. Yet they could have trusted in the God who had daily provided for them and made a faith-filled appeal to Moses. Instead, they **gathered together against Moses and Aaron**.

b. **If only we had died when our brethren died before the LORD**: Their contention led them to make outrageous statements, and they spoke as those who have no trust in God. The older generation of unbelief was almost dead, and now the younger generation started to act like the unbelieving generation. They openly doubted God's promise that He *would* lead them into the land of promise.

i. "As the *fathers* murmured, so also did the *children*." (Clarke)

c. **Why have you brought up the assembly of the LORD into this wilderness, that we and our animals should die here?** Their contention led them to make outrageous accusations, accusing Moses and Aaron of plotting the death of the people (and their animals).

d. **Not a place of grain or figs or vines or pomegranates**: Their contention limited their vision. Instead of seeing the wilderness as the place of God's faithful and miraculous provision, they could only see the wilderness as the place that did not have the abundance of Canaan.

i. Ironically, they would never come into the abundance of the land of Canaan unless they learned to trust God in the wilderness.

e. **Moses and Aaron...fell on their faces**: They realized how serious this was. With Israel's contentious attitude, the new generation could turn out just as unbelieving and untrusting in God as the old generation. If that were true, they also would die in the wilderness.

i. "We have here the first act of a new epoch, and the question to be tried is whether the new men are any better than the old. It is this which gives importance to the event, and explains the bitterness of Moses at finding the old spirit living in the children." (Maclaren)

3. (7-8) God's command to Moses: Provide water for Israel.

Then the LORD spoke to Moses, saying, "Take the rod; you and your brother Aaron gather the congregation together. Speak to the rock before their eyes, and it will yield its water; thus you shall bring water for them out of the rock, and give drink to the congregation and their animals."

a. **Take the rod.... Speak to the rock before their eyes**: Specifically, God told Moses to **take the rod**, but not to use it. God promised to provide water for Israel when Moses would **speak to the rock**.

b. **And it will yield its water**: Back at Mount Sinai, God told Moses to strike the rock and water came out (Exodus 17:6). Here, God commanded Moses to only **speak** to the rock, holding the **rod** in his hand.

4. (9-11) Moses' contention with Israel and with the LORD.

So Moses took the rod from before the LORD as He commanded him. And Moses and Aaron gathered the assembly together before the rock; and he said to them, "Hear now, you rebels! Must we bring water for you out of this rock?" Then Moses lifted his hand and struck the rock twice with his rod; and water came out abundantly, and the congregation and their animals drank.

a. **So Moses took the rod from before the LORD as He commanded him**: Moses began by doing exactly what the LORD had told him to do. He **took the rod** and **gathered** the people of Israel.

b. **Hear now, you rebels! Must we bring water for you out of this rock?** God told Moses to simply take the rod and speak to the rock (verses 7-8). God never told Moses to lecture the people of Israel, especially in this harsh and angry manner. There were times when Moses had to be the messenger of God's anger, but this was not one of those times.

i. It was bad for Moses to lecture Israel; it was worse for him to do it with an angry attitude, filled with bitter contempt against them. On previous occasions when Israel contended against Moses, he reacted differently.

- At Kadesh, Moses fell on his face before God when the people rebelled (Numbers 16:4).

- At Marah, Moses cried out to the LORD, not against the people (Exodus 15:22-25).

- At Massah and Meribah, Moses confronted the people (Exodus 17:1-7), but seemingly without the edge of anger, contempt, and bitterness seen here.

ii. There were many reasons to explain the sinful reaction of Moses, but there were no adequate excuses. He was provoked, but he responded in sin, as later described in Psalm 106:32-33: *They angered Him also at the waters of strife, so that it went ill with Moses on account of them; because they rebelled against His Spirit, so that he spoke rashly with his lips.*

c. **Must we bring water for you out of this rock?** Since Moses and Aaron stood before the people (verses 6 and 10), **we** probably refers to them. Moses spoke to the people as if it were he and Aaron who would give the people water, not the LORD.

d. **Then Moses lifted his hand and struck the rock twice with his rod**: Moses disobeyed God directly, striking the rock instead of speaking to it. Not only did he strike it, but he struck it **twice**. When he struck the rock at the beginning of the Exodus journey, he only had to strike it once (Exodus 17:5-7). Here, out of anger and frustration, Moses **struck the rock twice**.

i. "The Palestinian Targum says very significantly, that at the first stroke the rock dropped blood, thereby indicating the tragic sinfulness of the angry blow." (Maclaren)

e. **Water came out abundantly**: Despite the failure of Moses in both attitude and action, God still provided **abundantly** for the people. Perhaps because water was successfully provided Moses thought God was pleased and all was well.

i. God's love for His people is so great that He uses imperfect instruments. The fact that God uses someone is not evidence that the person used is in a right relationship with God and serving according to God's heart.

ii. "Geographers and biblical interpreters have written for years of the extensive aquifers that exist beneath the surface rock strata of the Sinai peninsula…. So at the moment of Moses' sin in striking the rock, God caused the water to erupt from underground water source, more than amply supplying the needs of the Israelite population." (Cole)

5. (12-13) God's rebuke and correction of Moses.

Then the LORD spoke to Moses and Aaron, "Because you did not believe Me, to hallow Me in the eyes of the children of Israel, therefore you shall not bring this assembly into the land which I have given them." This *was* the water of Meribah, because the children of Israel contended with the LORD, and He was hallowed among them.

a. **Because you did not believe Me**: Moses' sinful attitude and action were rooted in unbelief. He didn't *really* believe God when the LORD told him to speak to the rock and not to strike it.

i. Unbelief has many forms. It was easy to see Israel's unbelief in Numbers 14 when they refused to trust God and enter Canaan. Here, Moses was also unbelieving, but in different circumstances. Moses did not trust God to correct His people, so he took it upon himself to do so at a time when God did not want to correct Israel. Moses acted more like an Egyptian prince than a servant of the LORD.

ii. Under the headings of **you did not believe Me** and a failure to **hallow** the LORD **in the eyes of the children of Israel**, there were many specific sins of Moses, sins that leaders among God's people must take special care to avoid:

- Acting rashly at a time of emotional vulnerability – it is possible that Moses suffered from unresolved grief over his sister's death.

- Simple disobedience – not doing what God told him to do.

- Being a bad example – not showing God as holy before the people.

- Not listening when God wanted to do something different – thinking the miraculous could be made mechanical.

- Annoyance from wounded personal importance.

- Taking credit for themselves for God's work.

- Thinking God's work *must* include something more than a word.

- Presenting God as angry with His people when God isn't angry.

- Giving in to personal anger with God's people.

- Giving in to fearing the worst about the unbelief and faithlessness of God's people.

- Failing to draw on God's strength to endure until the end.

- Being a bad illustration of Jesus.

iii. "Perhaps there is no story in all the Old Testament more searching for all who are called to lead the people of God, than this of the failure of Moses. What he did was most natural. Therein lay the wrong of it." (Morgan)

b. **To hallow Me in the eyes of the children of Israel**: What Moses did was an *unholy* thing. He made God look no different than an angry man or one of the moody pagan gods. He did not reflect the heart and character of God before the people.

c. **Therefore you shall not bring this assembly into the land**: God's correction of Moses was hard. This great leader of Israel would not lead them into Canaan. Even as a young man, Moses dreamed of being a deliverer for his people, and he would now not complete this work. Another person would finish the job.

i. We might have thought, Israel might have thought, and Moses might have thought he was exempt from the decree that all the generation that was of age when the Exodus began would perish in the wilderness. But Moses, great a leader as he was, was still a man subject to God and God's law.

d. **You shall not bring this assembly into the land which I have given them**: This may seem an unreasonably harsh punishment for Moses. With only one seemingly small error he now had to die short of Canaan. But God judged Moses by a stricter standard because of his leadership position with the nation, and because he had a uniquely close relationship with God.

i. It is unrighteous to hold teachers and leaders to a *perfect* standard, but it is right for teachers and leaders to be judged by a stricter standard (James 3:1).

ii. Most importantly, Moses ruined a beautiful picture of Jesus' redemptive work through the rock which provided water in the wilderness. The New Testament makes it clear this water-providing and life-giving rock was a picture of Jesus (1 Corinthians 10:4). Jesus, being struck once, provided life for all who would drink of Him (John 7:37). But it was unnecessary – and unrighteous – that Jesus would be struck again, because the Son of God needed only to suffer once (Hebrews 10:10-12). Jesus can now be approached with words of faith (Romans 10:8-10), as Moses should have only used words of faith to bring life-giving water to the nation of Israel. Moses "ruined" this picture of the work of Jesus that God intended.

e. **And He was hallowed among them**: At the end of it all, God *was* seen as holy among the children of Israel. Moses did not hallow God in this incident, but God hallowed Himself through the correction of Moses.

B. The start of the last stage of the journey to Canaan, the request to pass through Edom.

1. (14-17) Messengers to the king of Edom.

Now Moses sent messengers from Kadesh to the king of Edom. "Thus says your brother Israel: 'You know all the hardship that has befallen us, how our fathers went down to Egypt, and we dwelt in Egypt a long time, and the Egyptians afflicted us and our fathers. When we cried out to the LORD, He heard our voice and sent the Angel and brought us up out of Egypt; now here we are in Kadesh, a city on the edge of your border. Please let us pass through your country. We will not pass through fields or vineyards, nor will we drink water from wells; we will go along the King's Highway; we will not turn aside to the right hand or to the left until we have passed through your territory.'"

a. **Moses sent messengers from Kadesh to the king of Edom**: Much time had passed since Israel refused to enter Canaan by faith in Numbers 14. They were now ready to go closer to Canaan than ever before, going from **Kadesh** through **Edom** to Canaan. This section of Numbers 20 brings us to the fifth of five stages of Israel's exodus journey.

- Stage 1: From Egypt to Mount Sinai (Exodus 12:31-18:27).

- Stage 2: The sojourn at Mount Sinai (Exodus 19:1 to Numbers 10:10).

- Stage 3: The first approach to the Promised Land, beginning at Mount Sinai, but being aborted at Kadesh with the refusal to enter the Promised Land in faith (Numbers 10:11-14:45).

- Stage 4: The 38 years of wandering in the wilderness until the generation of unbelief had died (Numbers 15:1-20:13).

- Stage 5: The second and final approach to the Promised Land (Numbers 20:14 to Joshua 2:24).

b. **Thus says your brother Israel**: The nation of Israel was a **brother** nation to **Edom**, because the patriarch Israel (also known as Jacob) was brother to Esau (also known as Edom), as described in Genesis 25:19-34.

i. "The request was couched in the form of a diplomatic letter that closely conformed to the conventions of oriental scribal practice, known from the archives of Mari, Babylon, Alalakh and El-Amarna. It consists of several standard parts." (Wenham)

c. **You know all the hardship**: In his correspondence with the leader of Edom, Moses expected that he would know the general story of Israel's time in Egypt and their deliverance. He also expected that he would know something of the LORD, the **Angel** of the LORD accompanying them, and God's great faithfulness to Israel. One reason God delivered, guided, and provided for Israel was to glorify Himself before the nations.

d. **Please let us pass through your country**: Moses asked for permission to **pass through** the land of Edom, located on the eastern side of the south part of the Jordan River and the Dead Sea. Israel expected no provision from the Edomites because God provided for all their needs.

i. The passage through **Edom** indicates a new strategy. "When they came to Kadesh thirty-eight years before, it seemed that their plan of attack was to march northward through the land of Canaan, conquering as they would go. But the events of the evil reports of the spies and the rebellion of the people against the Lord changed all that. This time the plan appears to be one of circumventing the south of the land, traversing southern Transjordan, then bursting into the land from the east." (Allen)

ii. The **King's Highway** was the trade route linking Damascus, Egypt, Arabia, and the lands in between.

2. (18-21) The Edomites refuse passage to Israel.

Then Edom said to him, "You shall not pass through my *land*, lest I come out against you with the sword." So the children of Israel said to him, "We will go by the Highway, and if I or my livestock drink any of your water, then I will pay for it; let me only pass through on foot, nothing *more*." Then he said, "You shall not pass through." So Edom came out against them with many men and with a strong hand. Thus Edom refused to give Israel passage through his territory; so Israel turned away from him.

a. **You shall not pass through my land, lest I come out against you with the sword**: This was an unnecessary refusal. It would have cost Edom nothing and would have been a genuine gesture of goodwill. But the Edomites, perhaps out of suspicion or fear, refused.

i. "Though every king has a right to refuse passage through his territories to any strangers; yet in a case like this, and in a *time* also in which *emigrations* were frequent and universally allowed, it was both cruelty and oppression in Edom to refuse a passage to a comparatively unarmed and inoffensive multitude, who were all their own near *kinsmen*." (Clarke)

b. **So Israel turned away**: This refusal made the journey of the children of Israel much more discouraging and dangerous (Numbers 21:4-5), but there seems to be no record of God punishing Edom for this sin. In fact, Israel was still commanded to treat the Edomites as a brother nation (Deuteronomy 23:7).

i. Here, God showed through Israel how to leave the judgment of those who hurt us up to the LORD, and how to love those who have acted as enemies against us – even if they are brothers.

C. The death of Aaron.

1. (22-29) The preparation for the death of Aaron.

Now the children of Israel, the whole congregation, journeyed from Kadesh and came to Mount Hor. And the LORD spoke to Moses and Aaron in Mount Hor by the border of the land of Edom, saying: "Aaron shall be gathered to his people, for he shall not enter the land which I have given to the children of Israel, because you rebelled against My word at the water of Meribah. Take Aaron and Eleazar his son, and bring them up to Mount Hor; and strip Aaron of his garments and put them on Eleazar his son; for Aaron shall be gathered *to his people* and die there."

a. **Now the children of Israel, the whole congregation, journeyed from Kadesh and came to Mount Hor**: Along with verse 14, this is another marker indicating the final stage of Israel's journey in the wilderness. Numbers 33:38 says this happened in the fortieth year after Israel came out of Egypt.

i. There is little record of what happened during these years. The history of the period is compressed into only five and one-half chapters, while the single year at Mount Sinai is given almost 50 chapters. This was to demonstrate these years accomplished nothing, except the death of the generation of unbelief.

ii. During those 38 years, there was much movement – but no progress. Our walk with God can be the same way. "The larger part of the sojourn in the desert is left without record. This may be deliberate on Moses' part. It is as though the time of sojourn was time that did not really count in the history of salvation." (Allen)

iii. "Because Israel had rebelled, their life has run to waste ever since, and only now, after such a lapse of time, and after so much suffering, did Israel find itself in a position to recommence the march that was suspended at Kadesh. So it is with the churches which have reached a certain point, then rebelled against the voice of God. Their history runs to waste; they exist, but hardly live; there is indeed a movement in them, but it has no definite aim, it leads no where; they just end up in the same place all the time. Only after a long time (if God has mercy on them) do they find themselves once more in a position to start afresh, and with not one step further forward in all of those years. Even so it is with individuals who will not go resolutely on when they are called. They are spent and wasted in movement back and forth which is not progress. After many years perhaps – perhaps after a whole lifetime – of wandering in dry places they find themselves once more at the very point to which they had come before, and not one step closer." (Winterbotham)

b. **Aaron shall be gathered to his people, for he shall not enter the land**: Miriam died (verse 1). Moses was told he would die before entering Canaan (verse 12). Now, Aaron learns that he also would soon die and **shall not enter the land**. Aaron was given the gift of time and awareness to prepare for his death.

i. "*Gathered to his people*. This is the usual phrase to describe the death of a righteous man in a ripe old age. It is used of Abraham, Ishmael, Isaac, Jacob and Moses (Gen. 25:8, 17; 35:29; 49:33; Num. 31:2).... The phrase is more than a figure of speech: it describes a central Old Testament conviction about life after death, that in Sheol, the place of the dead, people will be reunited with other members of their family." (Wenham)

2. (27-29) Aaron on Mount Hor.

So Moses did just as the LORD commanded, and they went up to Mount Hor in the sight of all the congregation. Moses stripped Aaron of his garments and put them on Eleazar his son; and Aaron died there on the top of the mountain. Then Moses and Eleazar came down from the mountain. Now when all the congregation saw that Aaron was dead, all the house of Israel mourned for Aaron thirty days.

a. **Moses stripped Aaron of his garments and put them on Eleazar**: This was an important transition from Israel's first high priest to his son, his successor **Eleazar**. Now, Eleazar wore the priestly **garments** for glory and beauty (Exodus 28:2).

i. The man died, but the priesthood – together with its access and relationship with God – carried on. No one's relationship with God in Israel was to depend on Aaron, but on the high priest – whomever he was. In Jesus the Messiah, God has made sure there will always be a high priest for us (Hebrews 4:14-16), and we need not depend on any man for our relationship with God. If a priest never dies, then his priesthood remains forever – and the priesthood of Jesus remains forever.

b. **Aaron died there on the top of the mountain**: Aaron was a great, but complex figure, even more so than Miriam. He was used of God mightily, as Moses' partner (Exodus 4:27-31), to initiate the priesthood (Leviticus 8), and to plead with Moses for the people (Numbers 16-17). At the same time, he was instrumental in the outrageous idolatry of the golden calf (Exodus 32) and in challenging Moses' authority together with his sister Miriam (Numbers 12).

i. Among other things, Aaron's life shows us that the office is more important than the man himself. Aaron the man was not always worthy of respect, but Aaron the high priest always was worthy of honor.

ii. Both Aaron and Moses were buried on mountains that overlooked the land of Canaan. Miriam was buried at the oasis of Kadesh. They probably died all within the same 12-month period.

c. **Moses and Eleazar came down from the mountain**: The passing of Aaron was a significant landmark in the history of Israel. The high priest died, but the institution of the priesthood continued. It would continue through Aaron's descendants until it was fulfilled in Jesus the Messiah (Hebrews 2:17 and 3:1), and in Jesus' people (1 Peter 2:9).

i. When only Moses and Eleazar returned to the camp of Israel, and Eleazar wore his father's high priestly garments, all Israel knew that Aaron was dead and his son was the new high priest.

ii. Moses, who represented the law, could not lead them into the Promised Land. Miriam, who represented the prophets, could not lead them into the Promised Land. Aaron, who represented the priesthood, could not lead them into the Promised Land. Only Joshua, that is, JESUS, could lead them into the land of God's promise.

Numbers 21 – On the Way to Canaan

A. The serpent in the wilderness.

1. (1-3) Defeat of the king of Arad the Canaanite.

The king of Arad, the Canaanite, who dwelt in the South, heard that Israel was coming on the road to Atharim, then he fought against Israel and took *some* of them prisoners. So Israel made a vow to the LORD, and said, "If You will indeed deliver this people into my hand, then I will utterly destroy their cities." And the LORD listened to the voice of Israel and delivered up the Canaanites, and they utterly destroyed them and their cities. So the name of that place was called Hormah.

a. **The king of Arad, the Canaanite, who dwelt in the South, heard that Israel was coming**: As the new generation of Israel began their approach to Canaan, they met with their first hostile army led **Arad, the Canaanite**.

i. The description of **the king of Arad** presents a challenge with geography and chronology. The site recognized as Tel Arad is *west* of the Dead Sea, about halfway between Beer Sheva and the Dead Sea, and about 20 miles (32 kilometers) south of Hebron. This is much further north than we would expect Israel to be, putting them in the southern part of Canaan. We would not expect Israel to be in this part of Canaan until well into the book of Joshua. Also, the archeological evidence from Tel Arad is from an earlier period.

ii. The most likely explanation is that **the king of Arad** was, at this time, the leader of a nomadic group that roamed the area south of Tel Arad (**who dwelt in the South**). When he **fought against Israel** he traveled still further south, to where Israel camped.

b. **Then he fought against Israel and took some of them prisoners**: After having lost some men to Arad, Israel vowed to God that they would **utterly destroy** the cities of Arad. That is, they would devote the cities of Arad to

God by destroying them completely. God then granted them victory (**the LORD listened to the voice of Israel and delivered up the Canaanites**).

i. **Israel made a vow to the LORD**: "They did not depend upon their own prowess in war. God had enabled them to rout the Amalekites, and to defeat many other adversaries; but when this new foe appeared, they did not rely upon their own swords, or spears, or bows, but they went at once to the Lord, and spread their case before him. In humble, earnest prayer, they sought his aid." (Spurgeon)

ii. This was the beginning of Israel's wars of conquest and God's judgment against the Canaanites. Most of these battles are found in the book of Joshua. These were not only battles to take the land that God promised to Israel, but they were also part of a unique war of judgment against the Canaanites. They were a particularly sinful and depraved people, whom God literally gave hundreds of years to repent. Just as God sometimes used other nations to bring judgment against His people, in this period the LORD used His people to bring judgment against the Canaanites.

iii. Because this was a war of judgment, they were to receive no spoil from the battles – nothing at all. They were to **utterly destroy** everything. There were a few reasons for this, but one of the most important was that God did not want His people to profit, to gain, to be enriched by a war of judgment. Such wars are the holy expression of God's sorrow at the necessity of judgment, and He did not want His people to gain or to be happy about it. Therefore, Israel was strictly commanded that when they conquered a Canaanite city, none of the spoil could go to them. It didn't go to the tabernacle, to the priests, or to Moses. It was all to be destroyed, dedicated to God alone by making no use of it for anyone else.

c. **So the name of that place was called Hormah**: It was at **Hormah** that Israel was defeated in their ill-advised attempt to enter the Promised Land by force after refusing to enter it by faith (Numbers 14:45). God brought them back to the same place and gave them the victory.

i. "The victory over the Canaanites of Arad provided the new generation a foretaste of great things to come when they would enter the Promised Land under the power of God and the leadership of Joshua." (Cole)

2. (4-5) Israel, provoked by the difficult journey, speaks against God.

Then they journeyed from Mount Hor by the Way of the Red Sea, to go around the land of Edom; and the soul of the people became very discouraged on the way. And the people spoke against God and

against Moses: "Why have you brought us up out of Egypt to die in the wilderness? For *there is* no food and no water, and our soul loathes this worthless bread."

a. **To go around the land of Edom**: They had to go far out of their way because the Edomites refused them passage (Numbers 20:14-21). To go around the Edomites, they had to turn back towards the wilderness and away from Canaan. No wonder **the soul of the people became very discouraged on the way**.

i. This was a discouraging situation, but it was also an opportunity to trust God. The same God who just gave them victory at Hormah and provided all their needs would also guide them through this setback.

b. **The people spoke against God and against Moses**: Israel's new generation sounded like the old generation that died in the wilderness. If they continued in the steps of their fathers, the new generation would be no more able to conquer Canaan than the previous generation was.

i. One might say that in these early challenges the new generation's behavior was worse than their fathers. In eight previous passages (Exodus 15:24, 16:2, 17:3; Numbers 12:1, 14:2, 16:3, 16:41 and 20:2), the children of Israel were described as speaking *against Moses*. In those situations, Moses knew (Exodus 16:7-8) and the LORD knew (Numbers 14:27) that they were really speaking against God – but the people were not shameless enough to do it directly. Now they were bold enough because **the people spoke against God and against Moses**.

ii. This was a major problem. They were on the threshold of Canaan, closer to it than the previous generation of unbelief had been, and now they started to act with the same unbelief – or worse.

iii. "When the grumbling humour is on us we complain of anything and everything, as did these Israelites: they complained of God, they complained of Moses; they complained of the manna. They would have been ready to complain of Aaron; but, fortunately for him, he had been dead a month or so, and so they poured the more gall upon Moses. To men in this state nothing is right: nothing can be right." (Spurgeon)

c. **Our soul loathes this worthless bread**: Like the generation of their fathers, this generation despised God's provision of manna, calling it **worthless bread**. Their complaining against the "bread of heaven" (Psalm 78:23-24) was the sin of ingratitude against the God who miraculously sustained them in the wilderness.

i. "When a person's heart is intent on rebellion and beset by discontent, even the best of gifts from the Lord can lose their savor; nothing will fully satisfy until the heart is made right." (Cole)

3. (6) The LORD sends fiery serpents.

So the LORD sent fiery serpents among the people, and they bit the people; and many of the people of Israel died.

a. **The LORD sent fiery serpents among the people**: Some people think these **serpents** were **fiery** in the sense that they were red, like the color of fire. Others believe their bite caused an intense burning, so they were called **fiery serpents**.

i. There was a connection between their despising of manna (21:5) and these fiery, poisonous snakes.

- They despised the bread from heaven; God gave them serpents from the earth.

- They despised God's blessings; God gave them burning poison.

- They despised the life God sustained for them; God gave them death.

ii. "Several species of snakes have been posited as the possible identity of these fiery serpents. T. E. Lawrence described his encounters with horned vipers, puff-adders, cobras, and black snakes in eastern Jordan. The 'carpet viper' (*Echis carinatus* or *Echis coleratus*) is a highly poisonous viper known from Africa and the Middle East and thus is a likely candidate." (Cole)

b. **The LORD sent fiery serpents**: These came from God, to get the nation's attention at this critical place in their journey to Canaan. If they continued in the unbelief of the previous verses, they would never take the land.

c. **Many of the people of Israel died**: Probably, these victims were mostly those of the older generation of unbelief. This was God's final way of fulfilling His promise that they would perish in the wilderness, and not enter His Promised Land.

4. (7-9) Deliverance through looking at the bronze serpent.

Therefore the people came to Moses, and said, "We have sinned, for we have spoken against the LORD and against you; pray to the LORD that He take away the serpents from us." So Moses prayed for the people. Then the LORD said to Moses, "Make a fiery *serpent,* and set it on a pole; and it shall be that everyone who is bitten, when he looks at it, shall live." So Moses made a bronze serpent, and put it on a pole; and so it was, if

a serpent had bitten anyone, when he looked at the bronze serpent, he lived.

a. **We have sinned, for we have spoken against the LORD and against you**: If the new generation was capable of deeper sin (such as quickly and openly complaining against the LORD in Numbers 21:5), they also had hearts softer and quicker to repent. Here, they quickly humbled themselves before the LORD and Moses, confessing their sin in a worthy way.

i. "Their quick recognition of its source and purpose, and their swift repentance, are to be put to their credit. It is well for us when we interpret for ourselves God's judgments, and need no Moses to urge us to humble ourselves before Him." (Maclaren)

b. **Pray to the LORD**: In their humility, they asked Moses to pray for them. This was an expression of trust in Moses and in the LORD.

c. **Make a fiery serpent, and set it on a pole; and it shall be that everyone who is bitten, when he looks at it, shall live**: God commanded Moses to make a serpent (and **Moses made a bronze serpent**), to set it on pole, so that those who looked upon it could be saved – and they were.

i. Even among miracles, this was unusual. There was no immediate logical connection between merely looking at a serpent on a pole and living, or refusing to look and dying. But God commanded that such an unusual thing – even a foolish thing – be used to bring salvation to Israel.

d. **Moses made a bronze serpent, and put it on a pole**: Jesus referred to this remarkable event in John 3:14-15: *And as Moses lifted up the serpent in the wilderness, even so must the Son of Man be lifted up, that whoever believes in Him should not perish but have eternal life.* Jesus clearly said there is a similarity between what Moses did here and what Jesus did on the cross.

i. The **serpent** is often used in the Bible to represent evil (Genesis 3:1-5, Revelation 12:9). However, in the Bible **bronze** is associated with judgment because it is made with fire. In a sense, **bronze** receives the fire of judgment as it is made.

ii. So, a **bronze serpent** speaks of evil; but evil having been judged. Jesus, who knew no sin, became sin for us on the cross, and our sin was judged in Jesus. A **bronze serpent** is a picture of evil judged and dealt with.

iii. "Men dying in sin are saved by the dead body of a man suspended on the cross. Just as physical contact was impossible between those bitten by snakes and the copper snake, so sinners are unable to touch the life-giving body of Christ. Yet in both situations the sufferers must appropriate God's healing power themselves: by looking at the copper snake or 'believing in the Son of man' (John 3:15)." (Wenham)

iv. If the serpent lay horizontally on the vertical pole, this would also be a *visual* representation of the cross. However, many traditions show the serpent being wrapped around the pole. This concept is the source for the ancient figure of healing and medicine – a serpent wrapped around a pole.

v. "The pole resembled the cross upon which Christ was lift up for our salvation; and looking up to it designed our believing in Christ." (Poole)

e. **If a serpent had bitten anyone, when he looked at the bronze serpent, he lived**: The people were saved not by *doing* anything, but by simply *looking* to the bronze serpent. They had to trust that something that seemed to be as foolish as looking at a serpent on a pole was enough to save them. It is likely that some in Israel perished because they thought it was too simple, too foolish to simply look and live.

i. When the new generation of Israel complained and doubted earlier in this chapter, they were not looking to the LORD. They looked to themselves, to their difficult circumstances, to the challenges ahead – but not to their God. Here, God put them in a situation where they *had to* look to Him.

ii. If God had willed it, the healing effect of the serpent might have come through contact – if one rubbed the serpent, they would be healed. It might have come through a priest. It might have come with a ceremony or a ritual. But God chose none of those; all one had to do was look and live.

iii. If any life still remained in the poisoned person, they could look and live. Some who had been just bitten looked and lived; some who were almost dead looked and lived. There was no case too difficult so that someone who looked would not live.

iv. The saving power represented by the serpent could not be exhausted. There was no limit to the number of those who could look and live.

v. This idea is later found in Isaiah 45:22: *Look to Me, and be saved, all you ends of the earth! For I am God, and there is no other.* We might be willing to *do* a hundred things to earn our salvation, but God commands us to only trust in Him – to look to Him.

vi. "They that looked upon their sores, and not upon the sign, died for it; as those that looked on the sign, though but with one eye, though with but a squint eye, or but with half an eye, they were healed presently. So they that fix their eyes upon their sins only, and not upon their Saviour, despair and die; but those that look to Christ, being faithful in weakness, though weak in faith, are sure to be saved." (Trapp)

vii. The great preacher of Victorian England, Charles Spurgeon, gave his life to Jesus Christ after hearing a message on Isaiah 45:22, and hearing that text connected to this account of Moses lifting up the serpent in the wilderness, with the people looking and living. Spurgeon was so impressed by this picture of the gospel and salvation in the book of Numbers that he chose an engraving of Moses lifting up the serpent in the wilderness as a logo for his publications.

viii. Spurgeon showed by his own example that we don't just look to Jesus at the beginning of our life in Jesus; we continue to look to Him: "Beloved, when I first came to Christ as a poor sinner and looked to him, I thought him the most precious object my eyes had ever lit upon; but this night I have been looking to him while I have been preaching to you, in remembrance of my own discouragements, and my own complaining, and I find my Lord Jesus dearer than ever. I have been seriously ill, and sadly depressed, and I fear I have rebelled, and therefore I look anew to him, and I tell you that he is fairer in my eyes to- night than he was at first."

f. **So Moses made a bronze serpent**: God commanded Moses to make an image of a serpent, even though such images were otherwise forbidden by Exodus 20:4. Actually, Exodus 20:4 forbids the making of idols, and this was no idol – it was a symbol, commanded by God, that they could look to in faith and be saved.

i. Sadly, even this God-ordained symbol was made into an idol. In the reforms of King Hezekiah, he *broke in pieces the bronze serpent that Moses had made; for until those days the children of Israel burned incense to it, and called it Nehushtan* (2 Kings 18:4). Fallen man can take any good and glorious thing from God and find an idolatrous use for it.

ii. "From excavations at Timna about 15 miles (25 km) north of Eilat has come remarkable confirmation of the biblical story, or at least of its origin in the wilderness period. At the foot of one of the Pillars of Solomon in Timna, Rothenberg found a temple of the Egyptian god, Hathor, used in the 13th century BC. When abandoned by the Egyptians about 1150 BC, it was taken over by the Midianites who covered it with curtains to make a tent shrine, somewhat like the tabernacle. Inside this tent temple in the holy place was found a copper snake 5 in. (12 cm) long." (Wenham)

B. On the way to the Promised Land.

1. (10-20) The journey towards Moab.

Now the children of Israel moved on and camped in Oboth. And they journeyed from Oboth and camped at Ije Abarim, in the wilderness which *is* east of Moab, toward the sunrise. From there they moved and camped in the Valley of Zered. From there they moved and camped on the other side of the Arnon, which *is* in the wilderness that extends from the border of the Amorites; for the Arnon *is* the border of Moab, between Moab and the Amorites. Therefore it is said in the Book of the Wars of the LORD:

"Waheb in Suphah,
The brooks of the Arnon,
And the slope of the brooks
That reaches to the dwelling of Ar,
And lies on the border of Moab."

From there *they went* to Beer, which *is* the well where the LORD said to Moses, "Gather the people together, and I will give them water." Then Israel sang this song:

"Spring up, O well!
All of you sing to it—
The well the leaders sank,
Dug by the nation's nobles,
By the lawgiver, with their staves."

And from the wilderness *they went* to Mattanah, from Mattanah to Nahaliel, from Nahaliel to Bamoth, and from Bamoth, *in* the valley that *is* in the country of Moab, to the top of Pisgah which looks down on the wasteland.

a. **Now the children of Israel moved on and camped**: Besides the names of the places Israel passes through on their way towards the Promised Land, brief passages of poetry are also recorded, giving the sense of elation they must have felt. There was thankful joy for the ways God provided water for the people (**brooks of the Arnon…the slope of the brooks…. I will give them water**). Israel was trusting God and God provided for them.

i. The last time we heard of Israel singing was back at the Red Sea (Exodus 15). That was a long time ago, about 40 years. Once again, they sang joyful songs.

ii. **The Arnon** is the modern Wadi al Mujib in Jordan, on the east of the Dead Sea. It marked the border between the land of the Amorites and the land of the Moabites. Israel was making progress northward up the eastern side of the Jordan River.

b. **The Book of the Wars of the LORD**: Some have used mentions of books like this in the Bible as an argument that the Bible is an incomplete book and must be supplemented – by something like the book of Mormon. But the mere mention of a book in the Bible doesn't mean that the book belongs in our Bibles. We would love to see and read such ancient literature lost to history, but anything in such books that is inspired and important is recorded for us in passages like Numbers 21:14-15.

i. "This book was presumably an ancient collection of songs of war in praise of God." (Allen)

ii. Paul quoted from a pagan poet in Acts 17:28. It certainly doesn't mean that everything that pagan poet wrote was inspired by God, or that our Bibles are incomplete without the full text of what that pagan poet wrote.

c. **Spring up, O well**: This joyful song refers back to an occasion when the leaders of Israel (**the nation's nobles**) helped dig wells, even using their **staves** (rods or staffs).

i. "They digged the well, and they digged it with their staves—not very first-class tools. Would not the mattock and the spade have been better? Ay, but they did as they were told. They digged with their staves. These, I suppose, were simply their rods, which, like the sheiks in the East, they carried in their hands as an emblem of government, somewhat similar to the crook of the shepherd." (Spurgeon)

ii. "We must dig as we can. We must use what abilities we have. It is every Christian's duty to try to know as much and get as much talent as he can, but if you have but one talent, use that one talent." (Spurgeon)

iii. Alexander Maclaren used this as a way to point to the work of Jesus for His people: "Jesus dug the well with the staff of His cross; but we wish that the Spirit, who is as a fountain of living water, fed from eternity and returning to its source, may spring up within it with greater volume and force."

2. (21-23) The challenge of the Amorites.

Then Israel sent messengers to Sihon king of the Amorites, saying, "Let me pass through your land. We will not turn aside into fields or vineyards; we will not drink water from wells. We will go by the King's Highway until we have passed through your territory." But Sihon would not allow Israel to pass through his territory. So Sihon gathered

all his people together and went out against Israel in the wilderness, and he came to Jahaz and fought against Israel.

> a. **Sihon would not allow Israel to pass through his territory**: As was the case with the Edomites, the **Amorites** would not let Israel pass through their land – even though the Israelites promised it would be of no expense or trouble to the Amorites.

> b. **So Sihon gathered all his people together and went out against Israel**: The Edomites threatened Israel and gathered their army, but they did not attack Israel (Numbers 20:18-21). The Amorites were different. They attacked Israel and King **Sihon** led the battle.

> > i. This incident is even more interesting when we consider Deuteronomy 2:30: *But Sihon king of Heshbon would not let us pass through, for the LORD your God hardened his spirit and made his heart obstinate, that He might deliver him into your hand.* God hardened the heart of Sihon, so he would provoke the battle, so he would lose, and so Israel could gain his land.

> > ii. It was not unrighteous of God to harden Sihon because he was *not* originally favorable towards Israel. God did not *change* Sihon's heart to make him attack Israel. God simply gave Sihon over to what his evil heart desired.

3. (24-32) King Sihon and the Amorites defeated by Israel.

Then Israel defeated him with the edge of the sword, and took possession of his land from the Arnon to the Jabbok, as far as the people of Ammon; for the border of the people of Ammon *was* fortified. So Israel took all these cities, and Israel dwelt in all the cities of the Amorites, in Heshbon and in all its villages. For Heshbon *was* the city of Sihon king of the Amorites, who had fought against the former king of Moab, and had taken all his land from his hand as far as the Arnon. Therefore those who speak in proverbs say:

"Come to Heshbon, let it be built;
Let the city of Sihon be repaired.
For fire went out from Heshbon,
A flame from the city of Sihon;
It consumed Ar of Moab,
The lords of the heights of the Arnon.
Woe to you, Moab!
You have perished, O people of Chemosh!
He has given his sons as fugitives,
And his daughters into captivity,

To Sihon king of the Amorites.
But we have shot at them;
Heshbon has perished as far as Dibon.
Then we laid waste as far as Nophah,
Which *reaches* to Medeba."

Thus Israel dwelt in the land of the Amorites. Then Moses sent to spy out Jazer; and they took its villages and drove out the Amorites who *were* there.

a. **Then Israel defeated him with the edge of the sword, and took possession of his land**: We now better understand God's favor and mercy to Israel. Before they faced the hardened warriors of Canaan, God gave them smaller foes and smaller battles to fight. We see how foolish the unbelief of the previous generation was.

b. **Thus Israel dwelt in the land of the Amorites**: Though this was still on the eastern side of the Jordan River, it was the first land Israel possessed in coming out of Egypt. For the first time, they could dwell in **cities**, the conquered **cities of the Amorites**. Later this land became the allotment of the tribes of Reuben, Gad, and half the tribe of Manasseh (Numbers 32).

c. **Fire went out from Heshbon.... Woe to you Moab**: This quotes an ancient song of the Amorites, celebrating when **Sihon** defeated **Moab**. The idea is that if **Sihon** defeated **Moab** and Israel defeated **Sihon** and the **Amorites** (as in 21:24), then surely Israel could and would defeat the Moabites.

i. This "is the so-called song of Heshbon, a very old poem apparently composed by Amorite bards to celebrate Sihon's defeat of Moab. It is probably inserted here to justify Israel's right to hold the land." (Wenham)

ii. What seemed the certain defeat of Moab prepares the reader for the story of Balak and Balaam in the following chapters. "Moab was next, and their defeat seemed imminent. Thus Balak king of Moab wished to transfer the battle arena from the field of men to the realm of the gods." (Allen)

iii. The Moabites were called **the people of Chemosh** because he was the idol they worshipped.

iv. **Moses sent to spy out Jazer**: "These spies must have done as they were instructed, in contrast to the rebellious spies of chapters 13-14." (Allen)

4. (33-35) The defeat of King Og and the land of Bashan.

And they turned and went up by the way to Bashan. So Og king of Bashan went out against them, he and all his people, to battle at Edrei. Then the LORD said to Moses, "Do not fear him, for I have delivered him into your hand, with all his people and his land; and you shall do to him as you did to Sihon king of the Amorites, who dwelt at Heshbon." So they defeated him, his sons, and all his people, until there was no survivor left him; and they took possession of his land.

a. **Og king of Bashan went out against them**: This was another battle that Israel did not provoke. Yet, Israel was more than up to the challenge, and through their God they won a glorious victory.

b. **Do not fear him, for I have delivered him into your hand**: This was a needed encouragement because **Og** of **Bashan** was noted for his size and strength. Deuteronomy 3:11 says, *For only Og king of Bashan remained of the remnant of the giants.*

c. **And they took possession of his land**: This land also becomes part of Israel, and a portion of the inheritance of tribes that settled east of the Jordan.

i. This chapter saw the new generation of Israel start in unbelief. But, after the bronze serpent incident, Israel trusted God and saw many victories and the beginning of their possession of the land. Yet, there remained many challenges.

Numbers 22 – Balak and Balaam

A. Balak's evil desire.

1. (1-4) Balak, king of Moab, fears an advancing Israel.

Then the children of Israel moved, and camped in the plains of Moab on the side of the Jordan *across from* Jericho.

Now Balak the son of Zippor saw all that Israel had done to the Amorites. And Moab was exceedingly afraid of the people because they *were* many, and Moab was sick with dread because of the children of Israel. So Moab said to the elders of Midian, "Now this company will lick up everything around us, as an ox licks up the grass of the field." And Balak the son of Zippor *was* king of the Moabites at that time.

a. **Then the children of Israel moved**: Israel was, at this point, on the move. They had basically finished their 38-year exile in the wilderness, and then progressed towards Canaan, coming closer than the previous generation of unbelief. They would remain in this general area (**the plains of Moab...across from Jericho**) for about a year, when the book of Joshua describes their crossing the Jordan and attack on Jericho.

i. The present generation also had the blessing of victory, God preparing them to fight the mighty Canaanites by a series of battles against the southern Canaanites (Numbers 21:1-3), the Amorites (Numbers 21:23-24), and the Bashanites (Numbers 21:33-35).

ii. "The geographical setting of 'the plains of Moab along the Jordan across from Jericho' would be that of the remainder of the Book of Numbers, as well as that of Deuteronomy." (Cole)

b. **Moab was sick with dread because of the children of Israel**: As Israel advanced towards Moab, Balak, the king of Moab **was exceedingly afraid**. This was because of the size of Israel and because of their victories over neighboring nations.

i. **Sick with dread**: "Rabbi Hirsch explains that this verb is a word that causes such violent emotion within that it may provoke one to vomit." (Allen)

c. **Now this company will lick up everything around us, as an ox licks up the grass of the field**: In one sense, Balak's fear made sense. On the other hand, if he had only known and believed God's word, he would have had nothing to fear. God commanded Israel to not harass Moab because He did not intend to give Israel the land of the Moabites (Deuteronomy 2:9).

i. It was significant that Balak met with the **elders of Midian**. Balak's later strategy against Israel would involve some Midianite women (Numbers 25:6-9).

ii. "The proverbial figure of an ox licking the grass is particularly fitting for a pastoral people.... The image of Israel as an ox is an emphatic symbol of her strength and power." (Allen)

2. (5-6) Balak's invitation to Balaam.

Then he sent messengers to Balaam the son of Beor at Pethor, which *is* near the River in the land of the sons of his people, to call him, saying: "Look, a people has come from Egypt. See, they cover the face of the earth, and are settling next to me! Therefore please come at once, curse this people for me, for they *are* too mighty for me. Perhaps I shall be able to defeat them and drive them out of the land, for I know that he whom you bless *is* blessed, and he whom you curse is cursed."

a. **He sent messengers to Balaam the son of Beor at Pethor**: A man named **Balaam** suddenly appears in Numbers. We do not know how he came to be regarded as a prophet or a man with spiritual powers, but King Balak certainly knew Balaam's reputation.

i. Balaam was definitely not an Israelite; he came from **Pethor** which was **near the River**. Earlier commentators took the **River** as a reference to the Euphrates, placing **Pethor** (ancient Pitru) in modern Syria (near Kobani). This was more than 400 miles (640 km) from Moab. However, since the 1967 discovery of the Deir Alla Inscription – which may mention Balaam by name – the case has been made for **Pethor** to be modern Deir Alla in Jordan, and **the River** to be the Jordan River. This was close to Moab.

ii. "The recovery of prophetic texts of Balaam in Aramaic from the sixth century at Deir-Allah in Jordan shows how very famous this man was in the ancient Near East, even centuries after his death." (Allen)

iii. As the account continues, it will be clear that Balaam had some knowledge of the true God, the God of Israel, that went beyond a vague spiritual connection (such as the specific mention of the LORD in Numbers 22:8). How Balaam came to know the true God is unclear; he was (in this regard) like Melchizedek (Genesis 14:18) and Jethro (Exodus 18), men who were not Israelites, but they came to some knowledge of the true God.

iv. "Balaam is not a good prophet who went bad or a bad prophet trying to be good. He is altogether outside Israel's prophetic tradition. He is a pagan, foreign national whose mantic acts center on animal divination, including the dissection of animal livers, the movement of animals, and the flight of birds. He believed that he had a way with the gods, a hold on them. To him Yahweh was not the Lord of heaven but just another deity whom he might manipulate. He was in for the surprise of his life." (Allen)

b. **Therefore please come at once, curse this people for me**: King Balak wanted Balaam to **curse** Israel, to cripple them spiritually so they could be defeated in battle. Balak seemed to know the strength of Israel was spiritually rooted, and they had to be cut off from their source of power if they were to be conquered.

i. Balaam was known as a mighty man in spiritual things. As far as Balak was concerned, when Balaam cursed or blessed a man or a people, it came to pass.

ii. "He wants Balaam to invoke a divine curse upon Israel that would weaken both them and their God enough to allow him to gain victory and drive them from his territory." (Cole)

B. Balaam's two meetings with Balak's representatives.

1. (7-8) Balak sends men to hire Balaam's services as a prophet.

So the elders of Moab and the elders of Midian departed with the diviner's fee in their hand, and they came to Balaam and spoke to him the words of Balak. And he said to them, "Lodge here tonight, and I will bring back word to you, as the LORD speaks to me." So the princes of Moab stayed with Balaam.

a. **The diviner's fee**: This suggests a standard fee for the work of a prophet. They took this standard fee in hand and approached Balaam.

i. "Whoever went to consult a prophet took with him a present, as it was on such gratuitous offerings the prophets lived; but here more than a mere present is intended, perhaps every thing necessary to provide materials for the *incantation*. The *drugs*, &c., used on such occasions were often very expensive. It appears that Balaam was very *covetous*, and that he loved the wages of unrighteousness, and probably lived by it; see 2 Pet. 2:15." (Clarke)

b. **Lodge here tonight, and I will bring back word to you**: Either out of customary hospitality or in hope of the **diviner's fee**, Balaam invited the men to **lodge here tonight**, so he could hear from God regarding their offer.

i. It was clearly wrong – then and now – to be a prophet for hire. Balaam said, "Let me seek God about this" regarding a matter that was clearly a sin and God's will was clear. He cared far more about **the diviner's fee** than about God's will.

ii. Immediately, the heart of Balaam was revealed. Though he was obviously a man with significant spiritual gifts, he was not a man with a genuine heart after God. He was "seeking God's will" regarding something that was plainly not His will.

iii. Balaam began on a dangerous course – entertaining, planning, setting his heart on something he knew to be sin, and looking for a spiritual excuse to pursue the sin. Because of his love for money, Balaam tried to manipulate God into granting him a special exception.

2. (9-12) God's response to Balaam.

Then God came to Balaam and said, "Who *are* these men with you?"

So Balaam said to God, "Balak the son of Zippor, king of Moab, has sent to me, *saying*, 'Look, a people has come out of Egypt, and they cover the face of the earth. Come now, curse them for me; perhaps I shall be able to overpower them and drive them out.'"

And God said to Balaam, "You shall not go with them; you shall not curse the people, for they *are* blessed."

a. **Then God came to Balaam**: God had no obligation to respond to a greedy, self-seeking heart like Balaam's. But in mercy God did respond, warning Balaam to have nothing to do with these men.

b. **Who are these men with you?** God knew the answer to this question, and He asked it because *Balaam* did not know. Balaam *did* know these were evil men who had come for an evil purpose – to hire a prophet – but Balaam did not act accordingly.

c. **You shall not go with them; you shall not curse the people, for they are blessed**: God's word to Balaam was clear. He said, "Balaam, do **not go**, and do **not curse**."

i. "Balaam is thus trapped between the demands of Balak and the commands of God. It is this conflict that sustains the whole drama that follows." (Wenham)

ii. **You shall not curse the people**: "He would not curse in words, but he did it in another way—by means of Baal-peor." (Maclaren)

3. (13-15) Balaam's reply to the elders of Moab and Midian.

So Balaam rose in the morning and said to the princes of Balak, "Go back to your land, for the LORD has refused to give me permission to go with you."

And the princes of Moab rose and went to Balak, and said, "Balaam refuses to come with us."

Then Balak again sent princes, more numerous and more honorable than they.

a. **Go back to your land**: Balaam said the right words. He told his guests, the elders from Moab and Midian (Numbers 22:7) to return without him.

b. **The LORD has refused to give me permission to go with you**: Though Balaam told his guests to go, he said it in a way that told them that Balaam *wanted* to go, but God wouldn't let him. The message from Balaam was, "**Go back to your land**. I would really like to go with you, but God won't allow me."

i. It was as if Balaam told them, "God doesn't want me to do this, but I can be persuaded." The message would be clear to King Balak.

c. **Then Balak again sent princes, more numerous and more honorable than they**: The response of Balak shows that Balaam effectively communicated the message, "God told me no, but perhaps you can persuade me." King Balak sent messengers **more numerous and more honorable**, with the promise of greater reward.

4. (16-17) Balak's messengers increase the offer to Balaam.

And they came to Balaam and said to him, "Thus says Balak the son of Zippor: 'Please let nothing hinder you from coming to me; for I will certainly honor you greatly, and I will do whatever you say to me. Therefore please come, curse this people for me.'"

a. **I will certainly honor you greatly**: No longer did they merely carry with them *the diviner's fee* of Numbers 22:7; now they also brought a promise of great riches.

b. **Therefore please come, curse this people for me**: Balaam refused to decisively put away a temptation the first time it came to him. Now the temptation came back to him stronger than it was before.

5. (18-19) Balaam entertains the offer from Balak's messengers.

Then Balaam answered and said to the servants of Balak, "Though Balak were to give me his house full of silver and gold, I could not go beyond the word of the LORD my God, to do less or more. Now therefore, please, you also stay here tonight, that I may know what more the LORD will say to me."

a. **Though Balak were to give me his house full of silver and gold**: We can imagine Balaam's tone of voice and expression when he said this. With a sense of longing, Balaam found a way to suggest a big offer from these richer messengers of Balak.

b. **I could not go beyond the word of the LORD my God, to do less or more**: Even so, Balaam knew the character of true prophecy. It did not come from his own initiative but from the LORD. Even though he wanted to do what they asked, he could not.

i. "Balaam's words echo the reality that he had indeed had an encounter with the God of Israel, through which the true Elohim had confronted and revealed himself to the pagan diviner. Yahweh God of Israel will use whatever means he desires to reveal himself to humanity." (Cole)

c. **Stay here tonight**: This was proof that Balaam continued to entertain this sin. There was no need to seek God again when the will of God was clear both from his moral conscience (which troubled him from the beginning) and from the clear revelation of God (spoken in Numbers 22:12).

d. **That I may know what more the LORD will say to me**: These words sound spiritual but were not at all. It sounded godly to say, "Let me seek the LORD about this one," but God had clearly spoken. Balaam was like a child who, having once heard the father's answer, will ask again, hoping the father's will might change.

6. (20-21) God allows Balaam to go with Balak's messengers.

And God came to Balaam at night and said to him, "If the men come to call you, rise *and* go with them; but only the word which I speak to you; that you shall do." So Balaam rose in the morning, saddled his donkey, and went with the princes of Moab.

a. **Rise and go with them**: God did not change His mind. Balaam would not now be *in* the will of God if he went with Balak's messengers.

i. We can say that God did *not* change His will. God had clearly spoken His will, and Balaam had decisively rejected it. Now God prepared Balaam for judgment, to both test and reveal the wickedness of Balaam's heart.

ii. We know that sometimes, God says "no" to the prayers of His people, because He loves them. But sometimes God also says "yes" to the desires of the wicked because He will judge them.

iii. "He was first forbidden, and afterwards commanded to go. The only explanation that is satisfactory is that, while attempting to maintain an external obedience to this supreme will of God, his heart was lusting after the riches offered to him by Balak." (Morgan)

iv. God's word to Balaam, **rise and go with them** was no more evidence of God's approval of Balaam's greed than the words of Jesus to Judas in John 13:27 (*What you do, do quickly*) were an approval of the actions of Judas.

b. **Balaam rose in the morning**: No doubt, he woke up at the break of dawn. He could not wait to do the wrong his heart desired, and he was so happy God was "blessing" him by allowing him to go.

i. Perhaps Balaam became all gloomy and sad when God said "no" by speaking to his conscience and giving a clear word. Yet as he **rose in the morning**, he was happy and excited, believing he had convinced God to say "yes" – with no idea what God was really doing.

C. Balaam, the donkey, and the Angel.

1. (22-27) God's message to Balaam through the Angel of the LORD.

Then God's anger was aroused because he went, and the Angel of the LORD took His stand in the way as an adversary against him. And he was riding on his donkey, and his two servants *were* with him. Now the donkey saw the Angel of the LORD standing in the way with His drawn sword in His hand, and the donkey turned aside out of the way and went into the field. So Balaam struck the donkey to turn her back onto the road. Then the Angel of the LORD stood in a narrow path between the vineyards, *with* a wall on this side and a wall on that side. And when the donkey saw the Angel of the LORD, she pushed herself against the wall and crushed Balaam's foot against the wall; so he struck her again. Then the Angel of the LORD went further, and stood in a narrow place where there *was* no way to turn either to the right hand or to the left. And when the donkey saw the Angel of the LORD, she lay down under

Balaam; so Balaam's anger was aroused, and he struck the donkey with his staff.

a. **God's anger was aroused because he went**: Some people think this was unfair because God told Balaam to go (verse 20) and then was angry because he went. But Balaam only went because he had first rejected God's voice, spoken to his conscience and clearly commanded, and God *should* be angry about that.

i. "God does not make the wrong way smooth for one who has extorted permission to follow it." (Watson)

b. **The Angel of the LORD took His stand in the way as an adversary against him**: To give an additional warning to stubborn Balaam, the **Angel of the LORD** blocked the path of Balaam as he rode on his donkey.

i. Yet, at this point, Balaam did not see **the Angel of the LORD**. "Which Balaam saw not; his eyes were put out with the dust of covetousness, or dazzled at least with the glittering of the promised promotions." (Trapp)

c. **The donkey saw the Angel of the LORD**: The donkey was more spiritually perceptive than the prophet. The donkey had no spiritual gifts, but at least acknowledged his Creator. The prophet had wonderful spiritual gifts but also had a disobedient heart and life.

i. "When God granted *visions*, those alone who were particularly interested saw them, while others in the same company saw nothing; see Dan. 10:7; Acts 9:7." (Clarke)

ii. "We see the prophet Balaam as a blind seer, seeing less than the dumb animal." (Allen)

iii. "Up to this point Balaam has been portrayed as a man of great spiritual stature, who can meet with God when he wants and whose words have tremendous effects on the fate of nations. Here his spiritual blindness and powerlessness are disclosed. He cannot see the angel of the LORD standing in his path, though his donkey can." (Wenham)

d. **The donkey turned aside out of the way**: The donkey, responding to the **Angel of the LORD**, turned one way, then another, then finally sat down to avoid judgment. The turns of the donkey **crushed Balaam's foot against the wall**, so as the disobedient prophet suffered, he made the donkey suffer as he **struck the donkey** several times.

i. The donkey is a perfect picture of a simple, unspectacular, yet obedient servant of God. The donkey was sensitive to God's direction, a thorn to the disobedient, and a victim of the wrath of the ungodly.

e. **When the donkey saw the Angel of the LORD, she lay down under Balaam**: The unusually difficult circumstances of this journey might have suggested to Balaam that his trip was not of God. Yet Balaam probably took it all as being an attack by a spiritual adversary and used the circumstances to strengthen his hope that God *wanted* him to work as a prophet for hire.

i. This shows the great difficulty of judging God's will by circumstances. Most circumstances can be interpreted two ways – if not more.

ii. F.B. Meyer reflected on the gracious ways God may hinder our path: "You were intent on pursuing your own way, and obtaining the rewards of unrighteousness, when suddenly you were stayed in your course. Another step would have brought you to the edge of the precipice; but you were suddenly arrested by that which forbade advance. Do not curse the hindering obstacle. Beneath it is God's gentlest angel, endeavoring to turn you from your evil purpose."

2. (28-30) God's message to Balaam through the donkey.

Then the LORD opened the mouth of the donkey, and she said to Balaam, "What have I done to you, that you have struck me these three times?"

And Balaam said to the donkey, "Because you have abused me. I wish there were a sword in my hand, for now I would kill you!"

So the donkey said to Balaam, *"Am* I not your donkey on which you have ridden, ever since *I became* yours, to this day? Was I ever disposed to do this to you?" And he said, "No."

a. **Then the LORD opened the mouth of the donkey**: God miraculously gave the donkey the ability to speak, and she did; and she rebuked the prophet for his cruelty (**What have I done to you, that you have struck me these three times?**).

i. We don't know the actual mechanism by which God gave the donkey the apparent mind and voice to speak, but the doing of it was certainly within the capability of the Creator.

ii. "And where is the wonder of all this? If the *ass* had opened *her own mouth*, and reproved the rash prophet, we might well be astonished; but when *God opens the mouth*, an *ass* can speak as well as a *man*." (Clarke)

b. **And Balaam said to the donkey**: Balaam was so irrational and angry that he answered back without hesitation. He seemed to be unimpressed by a donkey that carried on an intelligent conversation with him.

c. **For now I would kill you**: These were cruel words from a wicked prophet. Before and after the time of Balaam, the ungodly have threatened to kill God's messengers for telling the truth and seeking to hinder the evil of the ungodly.

> i. **I wish there were a sword in my hand**: Balaam complained because he didn't have a sword close at hand. There was a sword very close to him, but he couldn't see it or the Angel of the LORD holding it.

d. **And he said, "No"**: Balaam admitted that the donkey got the better of him in this conversation. Balaam had to humble himself before the donkey, admitting that she had not acted this way before, so perhaps there was good reason for her to act the way she did.

3. (31-33) God's message to Balaam through seeing the Angel of the LORD.

Then the LORD opened Balaam's eyes, and he saw the Angel of the LORD standing in the way with His drawn sword in His hand; and he bowed his head and fell flat on his face. And the Angel of the LORD said to him, "Why have you struck your donkey these three times? Behold, I have come out to stand against you, because *your* way is perverse before Me. The donkey saw Me and turned aside from Me these three times. If she had not turned aside from Me, surely I would also have killed you by now, and let her live."

a. **The Angel of the LORD standing in the way with His drawn sword in His hand**: The stance and the sword made the will of God clear. In this action of the **Angel of the LORD**, God told Balaam, "Don't go to Balak, turn back now." But Balaam would not listen.

b. **Why have you struck your donkey these three times?** God noticed Balaam's cruel treatment of his animal and demanded an accounting for it. God cares about how we treat animals.

> i. *A righteous man regards the life of his animal, but the tender mercies of the wicked are cruel.* (Proverbs 12:10)

c. **Your way is perverse before Me**: The Angel of the LORD rebuked Balaam for the cruel treatment of his donkey, but especially because Balaam's **way** was **perverse**. The word **perverse** carries the idea of "going the wrong way in a rash manner." This was exactly Balaam's problem.

> i. Since this was the **Angel of the LORD**, and the Angel of the LORD told Balaam that his sin was against Him personally (**your way is perverse before Me**), this indicates that this was an Old Testament appearance of God the Son – the Second Person of the Trinity, Jesus, before His incarnation as a baby in Bethlehem. For a specific Divine purpose, Jesus was temporarily present in the appearance of a human or an angel.

d. **Surely I would also have killed you by now, and let her live**: The Angel of the Lord had the ability and the authority to bring God's judgment against Balaam, and almost did. In a sense, the donkey rescued the prophet from judgment.

4. (34-35) Balaam's small repentance and sinful course.

And Balaam said to the Angel of the Lord, "I have sinned, for I did not know You stood in the way against me. Now therefore, if it displeases You, I will turn back."

Then the Angel of the Lord said to Balaam, "Go with the men, but only the word that I speak to you, that you shall speak." So Balaam went with the princes of Balak.

a. **I have sinned**: This sounds humble enough, but it was obvious and easy to say when the Angel of the Lord stood before Balaam with a drawn sword in hand. The threat of immediate judgment humbles most people.

i. Watson on Balaam's confession of sin: "It is the sullen acquiescence of a foiled adventurer, who at the very outset is made to understand the terms and narrow limits of his power."

b. **If it displeases You I will turn back**: Balaam seemed undecided as to if he was displeasing God. God made His will clear to Balaam many times, yet Balaam still sought for the answer he *wanted* from God. Through this, Balaam made it plain that he did not want what God had already clearly revealed.

i. 2 Peter 2:15-16 speaks of Balaam's attitude, telling us he had gone astray, he loved the wages of unrighteousness, was full of iniquity, and was not in his right mind.

ii. The root of Balaam's sin was a love for money. Jude 1:11 calls it *the error of Balaam for profit*. He was willing to disobey God and curse God's people if he could do it for money.

c. **Go with the men**: In response to Balaam's hard heart, God gave Balaam over to his sinful desire. God did not change His mind. Because of Balaam's hard heart, God allowed Balaam to continue on a path of judgment.

i. Romans 1:24, 1:26, and 1:28 explain how sometimes God's judgment is expressed in giving people over to the sin they desire. Since sin is destructive, when God gives a person over to their sin, it is a way that they end up destroying themselves. This would eventually be Balaam's fate.

5. (36-41) Balaam meets with Balak, king of Moab.

Now when Balak heard that Balaam was coming, he went out to meet him at the city of Moab, which *is* on the border at the Arnon, the boundary of the territory. Then Balak said to Balaam, "Did I not earnestly send to you, calling for you? Why did you not come to me? Am I not able to honor you?"

And Balaam said to Balak, "Look, I have come to you! Now, have I any power at all to say anything? The word that God puts in my mouth, that I must speak." So Balaam went with Balak, and they came to Kirjath Huzoth. Then Balak offered oxen and sheep, and he sent *some* to Balaam and to the princes who *were* with him.

So it was, the next day, that Balak took Balaam and brought him up to the high places of Baal, that from there he might observe the extent of the people.

a. **He went out to meet him**: This showed how happy Balak was to have Balaam visit, so that this so-called prophet could curse Israel. Normally, rulers have people come to them. This time, Balak took the trouble to **meet** Balaam and pointed this out to him (**Look, I have come to you!**).

i. **He went out to meet him**: "Balak's pleasure at Balaam's arrival is demonstrated by his journey to meet him at the Moabite border." (Wenham)

b. **Am I not able to honor you?** The **honor** Balak had in mind was money. With almost his first words, Balak told Balaam what he wanted to hear – that he would be paid a lot of money to curse Israel.

c. **The word that God puts in my mouth, that I must speak**: Balaam again warned Balak that the ability to curse Israel was not in his control. Perhaps he really believed and understood this, or perhaps this was his way of protecting himself in case he failed. Then he could say that it was God's fault, and not his.

d. **Balak took Balaam and brought him up to the high places of Baal**: After a bit of sacrifice (**oxen and sheep**), Balak then called upon Balaam to do what he hired him to do – to curse Israel, to rob them of their spiritual strength, so they could be defeated in battle.

i. **The high places of Baal**: "*Bamoth-baal*, literally 'the high places of Baal', is presumably identical with Bamoth (21:19–20) and was in the vicinity of Heshbon and Dibon, according to Joshua 13:17 (cf. Num. 21:25–26)." (Wenham)

ii. "He hoped that the sight of such a numerous host ready to break in upon his country would stir up his passion and further his charms." (Poole)

Numbers 23 – The Prophecies of Balaam

A. The first oracle – a prophetic word through Balaam.

1. (1-3) Sacrifice and preparation.

Then Balaam said to Balak, "Build seven altars for me here, and prepare for me here seven bulls and seven rams." And Balak did just as Balaam had spoken, and Balak and Balaam offered a bull and a ram on *each* altar. Then Balaam said to Balak, "Stand by your burnt offering, and I will go; perhaps the LORD will come to meet me, and whatever He shows me I will tell you." So he went to a desolate height.

a. **Build seven altars for me here**: These were many altars ready to receive many bulls and rams. King Balak of the Moabites was ready to do whatever Balaam asked for, so long as he would curse Israel.

i. Because Balaam sought to turn Yahweh against Israel, these **seven altars** and their sacrifices were intended to appease the LORD. But God never told Balaam to build an altar to Him, much less seven altars with seven sacrifices on seven different high places. These seven altars and burnt offerings were Balaam and Balak's idea, not God's.

b. **Whatever He shows me I will tell you**: In the Numbers account, Balaam was a corrupt prophet but not a false prophet. He was greedy and ready to receive riches for trying to curse Israel. At the same time, he could not or would not create his own prophecies. He could only say, **whatever the LORD shows me, I will tell you**.

i. We might imagine a conversation between Balak and Balaam:

"I want you to get the gods to curse Israel. Ask Baal or some other god to do it."

"It doesn't work like that. Yahweh, the God of Israel, is greater than all those gods. If Israel is going to be cursed, Yahweh has to do it."

"Then let's get the God of Israel to curse them."

"We can try – but I can tell you only what the God of Israel tells me."

c. **So he went to a desolate height**: Balak went to the top of a hill to stand beside one of the altars. Altars were often on the tops of hills, upon the *high places* (1 Kings 3:2, 12:31, 13:2).

2. (4-6) God meets Balaam and sends him back to Balak.

And God met Balaam, and he said to Him, "I have prepared the seven altars, and I have offered on *each* altar a bull and a ram." Then the Lord put a word in Balaam's mouth, and said, "Return to Balak, and thus you shall speak." So he returned to him, and there he was, standing by his burnt offering, he and all the princes of Moab.

a. **Then the Lord put a word in Balaam's mouth**: God spoke to and through someone as obviously corrupt as Balaam. This shows us that spiritual giftedness does not equal spiritual maturity or holiness of life. God spoke through a donkey in the previous chapter and now He **put a word in Balaam's mouth**.

i. "Despite the pagan and unsavory actions of this ungodly man, the Lord deigns to meet with him and to speak through him. This is utterly remarkable. We often say that God will never use an unclean vessel. This is not quite accurate. God may use whatever vessel he wishes; the issue concerns what happens to an unclean vessel when God has finished using it for his purposes. It appears that such vessels are tossed aside, dashed on the road." (Allen)

ii. "The words thus put into his mouth, do but pass from him; they are not polluted by him, because they are not his!.... Balaam did not 'eat' God's word as Jeremiah did, (Jeremiah 15:16) nor believe what he had spoken, as David, and after him St Paul did. (Psalm 116:10, 2 Corinthians 4:13)." (Trapp)

b. **So he returned to him, and there he was, standing by his burnt offering, he and all the princes of Moab**: When Balaam returned, Balak and all the princes of Moab were ready. They were ready to learn what their money bought them from Balaam.

3. (7-10) Balaam's first oracle – Israel can't be cursed.

And he took up his oracle and said:

**"Balak the king of Moab has brought me from Aram,
From the mountains of the east.
'Come, curse Jacob for me,
And come, denounce Israel!'**

"How shall I curse whom God has not cursed?
And how shall I denounce *whom* the Lord has not denounced?
For from the top of the rocks I see him,
And from the hills I behold him;
There! A people dwelling alone,
Not reckoning itself among the nations.

"Who can count the dust of Jacob,
Or number one-fourth of Israel?
Let me die the death of the righteous,
And let my end be like his!"

a. **And he took up his oracle and said**: This begins the first of seven "oracles" or prophecies that Balaam spoke regarding the people of Israel. These start at Numbers 23:7, 23:18, 24:3, 24:15, 24:20, 24:21, and 24:23.

b. **Come, curse Jacob for me, and come, denounce Israel**: This was what Balak asked for. He wanted a spiritual curse against Israel so that they could be defeated in battle.

i. "Cursing was a very solemn business in the ancient world and often thought to be automatically effective: the words themselves contained the power to affect those who heard them and disregarded them (cf. Deut. 27:15ff.; 1 Sam. 14:24ff.)." (Wenham)

c. **How shall I curse whom God has not cursed?** Yet, Balaam or any other prophet could not curse Israel if God had not cursed them. Balak could not bribe God to curse Israel.

i. "Balaam would have reversed the blessing into a curse, had he been able.... Is not this also the despair of Satan? God hath blessed us with all spiritual blessings in Christ Jesus, and he cannot reverse them." (Meyer)

d. **Not reckoning itself among the nations**: Israel was different from all other nations, chosen by God for a special role in His unfolding plan of redemption for the world. Israel was different because their God was different.

i. **A people dwelling alone**: "They shall ever be preserved as a *distinct* nation. This prophecy has been literally fulfilled through a period of 3300 years to the present day. This is truly astonishing." (Clarke)

e. **Who can count the dust of Jacob, or number one-fourth of Israel?** Through Balaam God promised to *bless* Israel by making them a singular nation and blessing them with great size. We sense that Balaam looked down upon Israel, saw their vast camp, and was amazed at their size and the blessing of their fruitfulness and prosperity.

i. The **dust of Jacob** is a clear reference to the promise God made to Abraham and his covenant descendants (Genesis 13:16).

f. **Let me die the death of the righteous, and let my end be like his!** Balaam concluded his **oracle** (another word for a prophecy) with this longing. Balaam was one of the many who long to die the **death of the righteous** yet have no desire to live the life of the righteous. The actual death of Balaam (Numbers 31:8) gives no hope for the fulfillment of this wish. His wish wasn't wrong, but neither was it enough.

i. "They are not only happy above other nations in this life, as I have said, and therefore in vain should I curse them, but they have this peculiar privilege, that they are happy after death; their happiness begins where the happiness of other people ends; and therefore I heartily wish that my soul may have its portion with theirs when I die." (Poole)

ii. Those who seek to separate living the life of the righteous and dying the **death of the righteous** hope to break an unbreakable chain: "They would break God's chain, sunder happiness from holiness, salvation from sanctification, the end from the means; they would dance with the devil all day, and then sup with Christ at night; live all their lives long in Delilah's lap, and then go to Abraham's bosom when they die." (Trapp)

iii. "Behold the vanity of mere desires. Balaam desired to die the death of the righteous, and yet was slain in battle fighting against those righteous men whom he envied." (Spurgeon)

4. (11-12) Balak's disappointment.

Then Balak said to Balaam, "What have you done to me? I took you to curse my enemies, and look, you have blessed *them* bountifully!" So he answered and said, "Must I not take heed to speak what the LORD has put in my mouth?"

a. **What have you done to me?** The king of Moab was understandably disturbed. He paid good money for a curse against Israel, and the prophet blessed them instead.

b. **Must I not take heed to speak what the LORD has put in my mouth?** Balaam spoke as a *true* prophet, but a *corrupt* prophet. We sense that he was disappointed that he couldn't please the king who promised him lots of money. Balaam had already told Balak that he could only speak what the LORD told him (Numbers 22:38).

B. The second oracle – a prophetic word through Balaam.

1. (13-17) Preparation before the prophecy.

Then Balak said to him, "Please come with me to another place from which you may see them; you shall see only the outer part of them, and shall not see them all; curse them for me from there." So he brought him to the field of Zophim, to the top of Pisgah, and built seven altars, and offered a bull and a ram on *each* altar. And he said to Balak, "Stand here by your burnt offering while I meet *the L*ORD over there." Then the LORD met Balaam, and put a word in his mouth, and said, "Go back to Balak, and thus you shall speak." So he came to him, and there he was, standing by his burnt offering, and the princes of Moab were with him. And Balak said to him, "What has the LORD spoken?"

a. **Please come with me to another place…you shall see only the outer part of them**: Balak wanted to change the word Balaam spoke over Israel from a blessing to a curse. Balak hoped that by changing the **place** where Balaam stood and changing the *perspective* he had as he looked out on Israel, then the prophecy would change. Because Balaam seemed so impressed by the size of Israel in the first oracle (23:10), Balak thought it was better to put him in a place where he could only see a portion of Israel for the second oracle.

b. **Built seven altars**: Balak so badly wanted Israel to be cursed that he was willing to build **seven** more **altars** and supply sacrifices for each of those altars.

c. **Then the LORD met Balaam, and put a word in his mouth**: Once again, Balaam could only speak the word that God put **in his mouth**. Balaam either could not or would not create his own message and claim it was from the LORD simply to please King Balak.

2. (18-24) Balaam's second oracle – the unchanging God blesses Israel.

Then he took up his oracle and said:

**"Rise up, Balak, and hear!
Listen to me, son of Zippor!**

**"God *is* not a man, that He should lie,
Nor a son of man, that He should repent.
Has He said, and will He not do?
Or has He spoken, and will He not make it good?
Behold, I have received *a command* to bless;
He has blessed, and I cannot reverse it.**

"He has not observed iniquity in Jacob,
Nor has He seen wickedness in Israel.
The LORD his God *is* with him,
And the shout of a King *is* among them.
God brings them out of Egypt;
He has strength like a wild ox.

"For *there is* no sorcery against Jacob,
Nor any divination against Israel.
It now must be said of Jacob
And of Israel, 'Oh, what God has done!'
Look, a people rises like a lioness,
And lifts itself up like a lion;
It shall not lie down until it devours the prey,
And drinks the blood of the slain."

a. **Rise up Balak, and hear**: In this message, God rebuked Balak, and taught him about the Divine nature.

- God is **not a man**, and can't be bribed or impressed with riches (as Balaam was).

- God does not **lie**, and He does not change His mind (**that He should repent**) as man does.

- God always performs His word. If God has spoken, He will perform it (**Has He said, and will He not do?**)

- God has all strength, and has the power to perform what He promises – He will **make it good**.

b. **He has blessed, and I cannot reverse it**: It was not within *Balaam's* power to either bless or curse Israel. All Balaam could do was report what God said. If God said Israel was **blessed**, Balaam must say so, no matter how much money Balak gave him.

i. "God's blessing is so powerful and irrevocable that even the most renowned divination expert of the day could not counter its effectiveness. Only God could rescind his blessing upon Israel." (Cole)

c. **He has not observed iniquity in Jacob nor has He seen wickedness in Israel**: One reason that God declared Israel to be **blessed** was because they were, in their present season, not walking in obvious or significant **iniquity** or **wickedness**. Therefore, **the LORD his God is with him** and **there is no sorcery against Jacob, nor any divination against Israel**. To put it in the later language of Romans 8:31, if God is *for* Israel, then no one can be *against* them.

i. One important feature of the Mosaic covenant was its promise of blessing and cursing (as in Leviticus 26). God promised to bless a generally obedient Israel, and curse a generally or significantly disobedient Israel. When Balaam noted that God had **not observed iniquity in Jacob nor has He seen wickedness in Israel**, it was a way to say "Therefore, under God's covenant with them, they will be blessed."

ii. "At this time, when Balak hired Balaam, there was no *peccatum flagrans*, no foul sin of that people, flaming in the eyes of God, or stinking in his nostrils; and therefore there could be no enchantment against them." (Trapp)

iii. This observation also hinted at a principle. If Israel could be enticed into general or significant sin, then perhaps they would – under the covenant they made with the LORD – bring a curse upon themselves.

iv. "For as Balaam knew that none but Israel's God could curse or destroy Israel, so he knew that nothing but their sin could move him so to do; and therefore he took a right, though wicked, course afterwards to tempt them to sin, and thereby to expose them to ruin, Numbers 25." (Poole)

v. **The shout of a King is among them**: This is the first specific mention of Yahweh as King among His people in the Bible. "Such joyful and triumphant shouts as those wherewith a people congratulate the approach and presence of their king when he appears among them upon some solemn occasion, or when he returns from battle with victory and spoils. The expression implies God's being their King and Ruler, and their abundant security and just confidence in him as such." (Poole)

d. **God brings them out of Egypt**: As Allen and others note, the verb tense here describes an *ongoing action*. God's great power and favor for Israel is seen in that He delivered them **out of Egypt** and that He *continues* to deliver them, bringing them into Canaan as He promised to do.

e. **He has strength like a wild ox**: The phrase **wild ox** (Numbers 23:22 and 24:8) is translated "unicorn" in the King James Version. The Hebrew word here (*reem*) occurs nine times in the Old Testament. The idea behind the Hebrew word is either of *one horn* or a *mighty horn*. Some think it refers to a rhinoceros, others to a wild ox, or a strong goat.

i. "The KJV 'unicorn' was wrong from the beginning; the Hebrew expression speaks of two horns (dual), which the NIV paraphrases as 'strength.'" (Allen)

ii. "The creature referred to is either the *rhinoceros*, some varieties of which have *two* horns on the nose, or the wild *bull, urus*, or *buffalo;* though some think the beast intended is a species of *goat;* but the *rhinoceros* seems the most likely." (Clarke)

f. **For there is no sorcery against Jacob, nor any divination against Israel**: This was a strong and direct way for God to say to Balak (and Balaam), "You can't curse Israel. Your sorcery can have no effect." Instead of being defeated by sorcery or divination, Israel was like the lion that will devour its prey.

3. (25-26) Balak's disappointment.

Then Balak said to Balaam, "Neither curse them at all, nor bless them at all!" So Balaam answered and said to Balak, "Did I not tell you, saying, 'All that the LORD speaks, that I must do'?"

a. **Neither curse them at all, nor bless them at all**: Balak was very frustrated and essentially said, "If you can't curse them, then at least don't go and bless them!"

b. **All that the LORD speaks, that I must do**: Balaam is again presented as *corrupt*, but not a *false* messenger or prophet. Balaam's greed and corruption were not a good example. Yet his commitment to faithfully report what God had said is an example that many modern Bible preachers and teachers should learn from. Balaam simply *could not* shape God's message to please his audience.

The last four verses of Numbers 23 are considered in the commentary on Numbers 24.

Numbers 24 – The Prophecies of Balaam (continued)

A. The third oracle – a prophetic word through Balaam.

1. (23:27-24:2) Preparation for the prophecy.

Then Balak said to Balaam, "Please come, I will take you to another place; perhaps it will please God that you may curse them for me from there." So Balak took Balaam to the top of Peor, that overlooks the wasteland. Then Balaam said to Balak, "Build for me here seven altars, and prepare for me here seven bulls and seven rams." And Balak did as Balaam had said, and offered a bull and a ram on *every* **altar.**

Now when Balaam saw that it pleased the LORD to bless Israel, he did not go as at other times, to seek to use sorcery, but he set his face toward the wilderness. And Balaam raised his eyes, and saw Israel encamped according to their tribes; and the Spirit of God came upon him.

a. **I will take you to another place; perhaps it will please God that you may curse them for me from there**: Even after two unsuccessful attempts to cause Balaam to curse Israel, Balak was still willing to try again. This shows both his desperation and his thought that it was just a matter of persuading a reluctant deity to get what he wanted. Balak thought that maybe **another place** would give him the results he wanted.

i. **To the top of Peor**: "The locale is also known as Baal Peor, at which the familiar northwestern Semitic deity Baal was worshiped, probably as a result of some perceived theophany of Baal in earlier antiquity (Num 25:3; Deut 4:3; Ps 106:28; Hos 9:10)." (Cole)

b. **Build for me here seven altars, and prepare for me here seven bulls and seven rams**: At the suggestion of Balaam, Balak offered another seven bulls and seven rams. By now, he had borne the expense of offering 21 bulls and 21 rams, plus Balaam's pay. This third time, they selected another place to make the prophecy again.

c. **When Balaam saw that it pleased the LORD to bless Israel**: If Balak had not yet learned that God was for Israel and not against them, Balaam seems to have, at this point, been convinced of this truth.

d. **He did not go as at other times, to seek to use sorcery**: Because he was finally convinced God wanted to **bless Israel** and not curse them, Balaam did not **use sorcery** in the following oracle. Perhaps this means that in the first two oracles Balaam followed traditional customs of discerning the will of the gods through examining the entrails of the sacrificed animals. He stopped the false and artificial methods of the pagans, and just listened to the voice of the LORD.

i. It may be that Balaam did use these pagan methods for the first two oracles, and God – in great mercy and willingness to meet sinful and superstitious humanity – still spoke His word to and through Balaam. This was God speaking despite such methods, not because of them.

ii. The third and following oracles would come from a man who had a true revelation from God. "As Saul had his experience on the road to Damascus, so Balaam had his experience on the road to Moab." (Allen)

2. (3-9) Balaam's third oracle – Israel blessed with beauty and strength.

Then he took up his oracle and said:

"The utterance of Balaam the son of Beor,
The utterance of the man whose eyes are opened,
The utterance of him who hears the words of God,
Who sees the vision of the Almighty,
Who falls down, with eyes wide open:

"How lovely are your tents, O Jacob!
Your dwellings, O Israel!
Like valleys that stretch out,
Like gardens by the riverside,
Like aloes planted by the LORD,
Like cedars beside the waters.
He shall pour water from his buckets,
And his seed *shall be* **in many waters.**

"His king shall be higher than Agag,
And his kingdom shall be exalted.

"God brings him out of Egypt;
He has strength like a wild ox;
He shall consume the nations, his enemies;
He shall break their bones
And pierce *them* with his arrows.
He bows down, he lies down as a lion;
And as a lion, who shall rouse him?

"Blessed *is* he who blesses you,
And cursed *is* he who curses you."

a. **The utterance of him who hears the words of God**: This oracle was different. Balaam did not receive this word in the circumstances of pagan superstitions. Balaam spoke as **the man whose eyes are opened** and who **sees the vision of the Almighty**.

> i. **The man whose eyes are opened**: "At first the eyes of Balaam were *shut*, and so closely too that he could not *see* the angel who withstood him, till God *opened* his eyes; nor could he see the gracious intentions of God towards Israel, till the *eyes of his understanding were opened* by the power of the Divine Spirit." (Clarke)

> ii. "Many scholars interpret Balaam's words as indicating that he entered into some kind of trance or ecstatic state as the Spirit of God came upon him, as with Saul in 1 Samuel 10:6–13, but the precise nature of this activity remains unclear." (Cole)

b. **How lovely are your tents, O Jacob!** This beautiful prophecy speaks of Israel's blessed abundance, strength, and their dominance over neighboring nations God would give to Israel. Under God's blessing, Israel has an abundance of water, stretching out all over the land and bringing fruitfulness (**his seed shall be in many waters**). Under God's blessing, Israel has **strength like a wild ox** and the superiority of **a lion**.

> i. "Balaam compares Israel's future settlements in Canaan to strong trees growing by life-giving streams of water, *Like valleys that stretch afar*." (Wenham)

> ii. **His seed shall be in many waters**: "By an elegant and chaste metaphor all this is applied to the *procreation of a numerous posterity*." (Clarke)

c. **His king shall be higher than Agag**: Either **Agag** was a common name among Amalekite kings, or this was a predictive prophecy of something to happen hundreds of years later (1 Samuel 15:32-33).

> i. "It is probably thought by the Jewish and other interpreters, that Agag was the common name of the Amalekitish kings, as Abimelech

was of the Philistines, and Pharaoh of the Egyptians, and Caesar of the Romans." (Poole)

d. **Blessed is he who blesses you, and cursed is he who curses you**: Most of all, this prophecy speaks of the abiding blessing of God on Israel, and directly rebukes Balak for trying to curse Israel (**cursed is he who curses you**). This is a deliberate echo of the blessing God gave to Abraham and his covenant descendants in Genesis 12:1-3.

3. (10-13) Balak's frustration with Balaam.

Then Balak's anger was aroused against Balaam, and he struck his hands together; and Balak said to Balaam, "I called you to curse my enemies, and look, you have bountifully blessed *them* these three times! Now therefore, flee to your place. I said I would greatly honor you, but in fact, the LORD has kept you back from honor."

So Balaam said to Balak, "Did I not also speak to your messengers whom you sent to me, saying, 'If Balak were to give me his house full of silver and gold, I could not go beyond the word of the LORD, to do good or bad of my own will. What the LORD says, that I must speak'?

a. **I called you to curse my enemies…you have bountifully blessed them these three times!** Over the period of the first three prophecies, things had become worse for Balak.

- In the first oracle, Balaam failed to curse Israel.

- In the second oracle, Balaam blessed Israel.

- In the third oracle, Balaam cursed Balak and blessed Israel again.

b. **I would greatly honor you, but in fact, the LORD has kept you back from honor**: The money used to hire Balaam, to build 21 altars, and to sacrifice 21 bulls and 21 rams was not well spent. Knowing this, Balak said that he would not pay Balaam. There is a sense in which it was true that **the LORD** had **kept** Balaam **back from honor**. What Balaam's corrupt heart most wanted (a lot of pay for being a prophet) he would not receive, and it was the LORD's doing.

c. **What the LORD says, that I must speak**: Balaam tried his best to excuse himself, and to blame God. But he knew that he would not receive the reward he hoped for because he failed to please his employer.

i. Perhaps at that moment Balaam saw the greater wisdom of God in telling him not to go, because now it seemed the whole trip would be a wasted endeavor.

B. The last four oracles – prophetic words through Balaam.

1. (14) Introduction.

And now, indeed, I am going to my people. Come, I will advise you what this people will do to your people in the latter days."

> a. **And now, indeed, I am going to my people**: It seemed as if Balaam was finished. He had failed to curse Israel and was now denied his reward from Balak. Balaam was ready to head home when God compelled him to give Balak more than he wanted or ever asked for. Balaam saved his best – or, from Balak's perspective, his worst – for last.

> b. **Come, I will advise you**: There was no preparation needed for this prophecy. Since Balak was not going to pay Balaam, Balaam would answer with a free prophecy, one that would show just how blessed and victorious (**what this people will do to your people**) Israel would be both now and in **the latter days**.

> > i. "Balaam's final speeches are explicitly said to concern the distant future: *in the latter days* (14). Though this phrase may simply mean 'in future' (e.g. Jer. 23:20), it can also mean 'the final days', whatever the period that constitutes the particular prophet's time horizon." (Wenham)

2. (15-19) Balaam's fourth oracle – a Star and a Scepter out of Israel.

So he took up his oracle and said:

**"The utterance of Balaam the son of Beor,
And the utterance of the man whose eyes are opened;
The utterance of him who hears the words of God,
And has the knowledge of the Most High,
Who sees the vision of the Almighty,
Who falls down, with eyes wide open:**

**"I see Him, but not now;
I behold Him, but not near;
A Star shall come out of Jacob;
A Scepter shall rise out of Israel,
And batter the brow of Moab,
And destroy all the sons of tumult.**

**"And Edom shall be a possession;
Seir also, his enemies, shall be a possession,
While Israel does valiantly.
Out of Jacob One shall have dominion,
And destroy the remains of the city."**

a. The utterance of him who hears the words of God: This repeat of 24:3-4 emphasizes that in this fourth prophecy, as in the third prophecy, Balaam spoke with no connection to pagan superstitions. Balaam spoke as **the man whose eyes are opened** and who **sees the vision of the Almighty**.

i. The last four oracles of Balaam are curses – the kind of oracles that Balak wanted Balaam to deliver against Israel. Instead, they are spoken against Israel's enemies.

b. A Star shall come out of Jacob; a Scepter shall rise out of Israel: Speaking again by the inspiration of the Holy Spirit, this strange and unlikely prophet of Yahweh described One glorious (like a **Star**) and with the authority to rule (pictured by a **Scepter**).

i. Previously Balaam prophesied of the beauty, strength, and blessedness of Israel; now God uses him to speak of the culmination of all Israel's beauty, strength, and blessedness – the Messiah, Jesus Christ. Israel's ultimate blessedness comes from Jesus, their Messiah.

ii. Early Jewish writers understood this as a reference to the Messiah. "The Dead Sea scrolls (c. 1st century BC) take the star and the sceptre as the messiahs of Aaron and Israel, i.e. the priestly and kingly messiahs. Rabbi Akiba, hailing the leader of the second Jewish revolt (AD 132–135) as the messiah, called him Bar-Kocheba, i.e. Son of the star." (Wenham)

iii. Early Christian writers understood this as a reference to the Messiah. Justin Martyr (*First Apology*, chapter 32) and Athanasius the Great (*On the Incarnation of the Word*, section 33) both saw this **Star** as a reference to Jesus Christ.

iv. Martin Luther had a hard time seeing this as a messianic prophecy because Balaam was such an unworthy prophet of such a glorious message. Yet, "The truth of the Scripture could never be dependent on the worthiness of the writer or the personal piety of the speaker. Else we would have gradations in inspiration and shadings in trustworthiness. I say this reverently but strongly; the words of Balaam the pagan mantic, *when he was speaking under the control of the Holy Spirit of God* were as sure as the words of the Savior Jesus in a red-letter edition of the NT." (Allen)

v. "A blind man may bear a torch in his hand, whereby others may receive benefit, though himself receive none; so here." (Trapp)

vi. "The New Testament does not cite the prophecies of Balaam explicitly, but there are probable allusions to it in Luke 1:78; Revelation

2:26–28; 22:16 and, of course, Christ's birth was announced by a star (Matt. 2:1–10)." (Wenham)

c. **And batter the brow of Moab, and destroy all the sons of tumult**: The Messiah will eventually rule over all nations that surround Israel. Here, and in the following verses, God spoke about the neighboring nations of Israel (Moab, Edom, Amalek, and the Kenites) and their future through Balaam. Balak, the king of the Moabites, must have been both grieved and outraged to hear his paid-for prophet speak these words against **Moab**, cursing them instead of Israel.

> i. Israel's deliverer – their **Star** and **Scepter** – would lead them in triumph over both **Moab** and **Edom**. "In the distant future both peoples would be conquered, captured, and eventually disappear from being distinctive ethnic groups. The phraseology of 'crushing of the head' is a symbol of defeating one's enemies in Egyptian, Ugaritic, and Hebrew literature." (Cole)

> ii. "This prediction of Moab's total defeat at the hand of a future Israelite king is an appropriate point for Balaam to end. He had been called in so that through his curse Balak, king of Moab, might defeat Israel; Balaam declares that the reverse will be the case: Moab will be destroyed by a coming king of Israel." (Wenham)

3. (20) Balaam's fifth oracle – the fall of Amalek.

Then he looked on Amalek, and he took up his oracle and said:

**"Amalek *was* first among the nations,
But *shall be* last until he perishes."**

a. **Then he looked on Amalek**: Balaam then turned his attention to the Amalekites, a nomadic people often hostile to Israel.

> i. **Amalek was first among the nations**: "*The first*, Hebrew, *the first-fruits;* so called either, 1. Because they were the first of all the neighbouring nations which were embodied together in one government. Or, 2. Because they were the most powerful and eminent of them." (Poole)

b. **But shall be last until he perishes**: The people of **Amalek** were at one time in a prestigious position, but the Star and Scepter, the Messiah prophesied by Balaam will subdue them.

4. (21-22) Balaam's sixth oracle – the captivity of the Kenites.

Then he looked on the Kenites, and he took up his oracle and said:

**"Firm is your dwelling place,
And your nest is set in the rock;**

Nevertheless Kain shall be burned.
How long until Asshur carries you away captive?"

a. **He looked on the Kenites**: The **Kenites** were another nomadic tribe that at times appears in Israel's history (Judges 4:11, 1 Samuel 15:6, 27:10).

i. "Why the Kenites come under attack here is not sure, except that it is possible that they became associated with the Midianites who come under the scourge of Israel (Numbers 31)." (Allen)

ii. **Firm is your dwelling place**: "The Kenites put their faith in the security afforded them by their geographical positioning, nestled in the rocky highlands of southern Canaan or the northeastern quadrant of the Sinai region." (Cole)

b. **Kain shall be burned**: The Kenites and their important city of **Kain** shall be subdued under Israel. Despite the desire of Balak, Israel would be lifted above her neighbors.

5. (23-24) Balaam's seventh oracle – the judgments of the God of Israel.

Then he took up his oracle and said:

"Alas! Who shall live when God does this?
But ships *shall come* from the coasts of Cyprus,
And they shall afflict Asshur and afflict Eber,
And so shall *Amalek*, until he perishes."

a. **Who shall live when God does this?** Balaam's seventh and final oracle begins with a reminder that this strength of Israel and the subduing of their neighbors would be the work of **God**. It wasn't to Israel's glory, but to God's glory.

i. Of the seventh oracle, the specifics are cloudy, but the general direction is clear – Israel's ultimate triumph through the power of their Star and Scepter; their deliverer.

b. **Ships shall come from the coasts of Cyprus**: Some of the affliction promised against Israel's neighbors would come from afar, from the **coasts of Cyprus** and presumably elsewhere.

i. **Cyprus** here is literally *Kittim*. "The identification of Kittim in the early period of Israel's history seems to be Cyprus. But ultimately the word was applied to Rome, as in Qumran (see, e.g., 1QM, VII, 'From of old Thou hast announced to us the time appointed for the mighty deed of Thy hand against the Kittim') and perhaps also (prophetically!) in Daniel (e.g., 11:30)." (Allen)

6. (25) Balaam and Balak depart.

So Balaam rose and departed and returned to his place; Balak also went his way.

a. **So Balaam rose and departed**: Undoubtedly, both were disappointed and perhaps angry, each because Israel had not been weakened spiritually and therefore made ready for defeat in battle. Balak wanted Israel defeated, and Balaam wanted Balak's money, but each wanted Israel spiritually cursed – and God would not curse Israel.

i. "Balak had not his will, nor Balaam his wages; God fooled them both, pulling the morsel out of their mouths, that they had well-nigh devoured." (Trapp)

ii. Meyer saw in Balaam a warning to see the difference between unction and union; between gift and grace, and between vision and realization. "Balaam saw truly, but he perished miserably.... He wished to die the death of the righteous, but was overtaken in that of the apostate. How near we may come to the gates of salvation, and yet perish miserably without!" (Meyer)

b. **Balak also went his way**: Balak deserves credit for understanding where the strength of Israel was. He did not seek to defeat Israel through military strategy or new weapons. He knew it was a spiritual battle, and if Israel won the spiritual battle, they would certainly win the military battle.

i. We should walk in the same awareness. If we did, we would give more time and attention to building our spiritual strength, in having a close walk with Jesus. We should not allow Balak to be more perceptive about spiritual things than we are.

Numbers 25 – Israel Bows to Baal

A. Sexual immorality, idolatry, and the aftermath.

1. (1-3) Israel's harlotry with the women of Moab.

Now Israel remained in Acacia Grove, and the people began to commit harlotry with the women of Moab. They invited the people to the sacrifices of their gods, and the people ate and bowed down to their gods. So Israel was joined to Baal of Peor, and the anger of the LORD was aroused against Israel.

> a. **And the people began to commit harlotry with the women of Moab**: The women of Moab, coming among the men of Israel, seduced them to both sexual sin and idolatry (**and bowed down to their gods**). The two were commonly connected in perverse forms of idol worship in the ancient world.

> > i. "The verb used to describe the action of the men [**commit harlotry**] is one normally used to describe the behavior of a loose woman, a harlot. Here the people, as a man, bewhore themselves with foreign, pagan women. Always in the ancient Near Eastern context, references to sexual imagery such as this suggest interconnecting circles of sexual immorality tied to sacral rites of prostitution, essential parts of pagan religious systems of the day." (Allen)

> > ii. "Whose fashion was, as soon as their sacrifice was ended, to step aside into the grove of their god, and there, like brute beasts, promiscuously to satisfy their lusts." (Trapp)

> > iii. Israel's sin at Baal-Peor also carries a strong sense of *ingratitude*. God had just wonderfully protected Israel against the best efforts of Balaam and Balak to curse them – instead, blessing Israel and cursing her enemies. Their **harlotry**, both sexual and spiritual, was their ungrateful response.

iv. In this chapter, the women and their people are sometimes described as Midianites and sometimes as Moabites. This is because the Midianites were a nomadic group, and in this period, they were in high numbers among the Moabites.

v. **Acacia Grove**: "Josephus identified the site with Abila of his day, a site located seven miles east of the Jordan and about five miles north of the Dead Sea. This general area just a few miles northeast of the Dead Sea, also referred to several times by the description 'on the plains of Moab by the Jordan across from Jericho,' was to be the geographical setting for the remainder of the Israelite sojourn prior to entering the Promised Land." (Cole)

b. **Israel was joined to Baal of Peor**: Baal was the great Canaanite fertility god, and the worship of Baal was a constant temptation for the children of Israel. Balaam prophesied from *the high places of Baal* (Numbers 22:41), possibly from this same place – Baal Peor. Here, Israel was **joined to** – that is, yoked with or partnered with – the Canaanite god Baal.

i. To this point in the whole story of the exodus, Israel has sinned in many ways. They murmured, grumbled, and complained, not being grateful for God's generous provision. They worshipped Yahweh in a false way, claiming an image of a golden calf could represent Him. They sinned by their unbelief, refusing to trust God and His promise. But before this, they had never plainly worshiped another god. This was a sin of idolatry unlike any previously seen in the exodus.

ii. "In doing this they were violating the principle of Balaam's first vision of them as a people dwelling alone. It was an act of rebellion against God and so a corruption of the Covenant." (Morgan)

iii. This is the first recorded encounter of Israel with Baal and sets a tragic pattern for Israel's later dealings with this pagan deity popular among the Canaanites. Enticing the people of Israel to idolatry through sexual liaisons with pagan women was such a powerful temptation that it even captured Solomon, Israel's king famous for his wisdom (1 Kings 11:1-10).

iv. It is not until Numbers 31:16 that we learn that this happened *through the counsel of Balaam*. In a sense, it was through Balaam's counsel that Baal worship first came to Israel.

c. **The anger of the LORD was aroused against Israel**: Balak could never pay enough money to Balaam to make God curse Israel. In the previous chapter, Balaam tried to curse Israel and could not – instead, by the inspiration of the LORD, Balaam blessed Israel and cursed her enemies. Yet now, at Baal of Peor, Israel was cursed by having **the anger of the Lord** turned against them because of their sin against the Lord.

i. **The anger of the Lord was aroused against Israel**: According to Allen, this is literally "a reddening of His nose," a metaphor used to describe a flashing of rage. We learn later in the chapter that **the anger of the Lord** showed itself in a plague that began to strike down thousands among Israel and seemed as if it would continue until the whole nation was consumed.

ii. What an enemy could never accomplish against Israel, Israel did to itself through disobedience. The same principle works among the people of God today. The mightiest attack of Satan against us can never do as much damage as our own sin and rebellion against the Lord.

iii. "The sword of no stranger, the curse of no stranger had the power to damage Israel. Only it itself could bring misfortune, by seceding from God and his Law." (Rabbi Hirsch, cited in Allen)

iv. "The Moabites being now neighbours to the Israelites, and finding themselves unable to effect their design against Israel by war and witchcraft, they now fell another way to work." (Poole) In the same way, Satan's violence and sorcery can have no lasting influence on the believer; but if he can lead us into sin, we can be destroyed.

d. **The anger of the Lord was aroused against Israel**: Balaam did his best to curse Israel – but was unsuccessful. Yet, his love for money wouldn't let the matter end without pleasing the man who hired him, Balak the king of Moab. Balaam's greed motivated him to be persistent in finding a way to help Balak bring **the anger of the Lord** against Israel.

i. 2 Peter 2:15 speaks of Balaam the man *who loved the wages of unrighteousness*. Revelation 2:14 makes the connection between Balaam's unsuccessful attempt to curse Israel and this subsequent idolatry: *Balaam, who taught Balak to put a stumbling block before the children of Israel, to eat things sacrificed to idols, and to commit sexual immorality.*

ii. Essentially, after his failure to curse Israel, Balaam said something like this to Balak: "I cannot curse these people. But you can get them to curse themselves by luring them to rebel against their God. Send your most provocative girls among them and tell them to tempt the men of Israel to immorality and idolatry." And it worked.

iii. Balaam, through his wicked counsel to Balak, got what he wanted – but he also ended up dead among the enemies of God (Numbers 31:7-8). He only enjoyed his wages for a short time.

2. (4-5) God's judgment on the offenders.

Then the LORD said to Moses, "Take all the leaders of the people and hang the offenders before the LORD, out in the sun, that the fierce anger of the LORD may turn away from Israel."

So Moses said to the judges of Israel, "Every one of you kill his men who were joined to Baal of Peor."

a. **Take all the leaders and the people and hang the offenders before the LORD**: God thought it important that the offenders be judged openly; this was not a sin to be kept hidden. Such open sin had to be dealt with openly.

i. Considering the strong sense of disgrace associated with unburied corpses, this was truly a severe judgment. "Moses was to round up all the tribal leaders, those representatives of the people who presumably should have either prevented the idolatrous activities or carried out the punishment of the guilty members of their tribes, and execute them by impaling them on poles such that their bodies would hang out in the open in broad daylight." (Cole)

b. **Every one of you kill his men who were joined to Baal of Peor**: This responsibility was given to **all the leaders of the people**. They would find those among them who had committed the sins of idolatry and immorality with the Moabite women. The penalty was to be death (**every one of you kill his men**).

i. "As if he had said, 'Assemble the chiefs and judges, institute an inquiry concerning the transgressors, and hang them who shall be found guilty *before the Lord*, as a matter required by his justice.'" (Clarke)

ii. This was severe judgment, but consistent with what God promised Israel in the terms of the covenant He made with them at Mount Sinai. *Now therefore, go, lead the people to the place of which I have spoken to you. Behold, My Angel shall go before you. Nevertheless, in the day when I visit for punishment, I will visit punishment upon them for their sin.* (Exodus 32:34)

iii. When sin such as this is tolerated or even approved in a culture, it is a sure sign of decay, and the LORD – speaking through Moses – wouldn't accept that decay. He commanded the community (**the leaders and the people**) to bring the offenders to be judged, to show *they* would not accept this kind of sin in their midst.

B. A flagrant sin judged.

1. (6-9) Phinehas' stand for righteousness stops God's plague of judgment.

And indeed, one of the children of Israel came and presented to his brethren a Midianite woman in the sight of Moses and in the sight of all the congregation of the children of Israel, who *were* weeping at the door of the tabernacle of meeting. Now when Phinehas the son of Eleazar, the son of Aaron the priest, saw *it,* he rose from among the congregation and took a javelin in his hand; and he went after the man of Israel into the tent and thrust both of them through, the man of Israel, and the woman through her body. So the plague was stopped among the children of Israel. And those who died in the plague were twenty-four thousand.

a. **A Midianite woman in the sight of Moses and in the sight of all the congregation**: This was an especially offensive example of the sin that was happening all around Israel. A **man of Israel** and a **Midianite woman** were together near **the door of the tabernacle of meeting**.

i. Some commentators (such as Allen) believe this man was having sex with the Midianite woman right in front of the tabernacle, and the text tactfully obscures this, because it was so outrageous and offensive. "The man is a blasphemer in the strongest sense. His sin is a deliberate provocateur of the wrath of the Lord, flaunting and taunting holiness in an almost unbelievable crudity." (Allen)

b. **Now when Phinehas the son of Eleazar, the son of Aaron the priest, saw it, he rose from among the congregation**: Phinehas was one among those in Israel who would not accept this widespread rebellion against God. He brought God's judgment by thrusting through the **man of Israel** and the **Midianite woman** with a spear – seemingly, during their immoral act.

i. In the presence of such shocking and outrageous sin, it is common for onlookers to freeze in stunned disbelief. One man did not remain motionless. Phinehas – a grandson of Aaron (Exodus 6:25) – was the one man who acted boldly against this outrage. "His anger mirrored the divine anger." (Wenham)

ii. Phinehas was not a vigilante, and his bold act (and God's praise of it) do not justify vigilantism. Numbers 3 and 4 explain that the priests were responsible for the security of the tabernacle, guarding it against intruders, and killing those who dared to trespass. Phinehas carried out this responsibility as an authorized protector of the tabernacle, and this was an outrageous attack against the holiness of the sanctuary.

iii. "The positioning and the ability to thrust the spear through both bodies, the man's first and then the woman's, suggests that they had involved themselves immediately in sexual intercourse upon entering the tent." (Cole)

iv. The Hebrew of verse 6 has *the* Midianite woman, marking her as a person of some importance. "This suggests that this was not just one of the local sacred prostitutes but a person of prominence. I suggest that the article is used to mark her out as a pivotal player. Perhaps she is the high priestess of the religion at Baal Peor." (Allen)

c. **So the plague was stopped among the children of Israel**: Phinehas was probably not the only one to make such a stand for righteousness. But what he did received the credit for stopping the plague.

i. It is easy to think that the stand for righteousness made by one person makes no difference in the massive presence of sin in a community. But God can honor just one righteous act and cause it to make the difference. It could be said that through one righteous act, Jesus Christ is the Savior of the world (John 12:32).

ii. "Some Christian commentators have seen Phinehas as a type of Christ. In that he embodied the ideal of Israelite priesthood this is surely legitimate: our Lord was angry more than once with sin (e.g. Mark 3:5; 11:15ff.). Yet there is another side to it: whereas it was Phinehas' spear that pierced the sinners that made atonement for Israel, it was the nails and spear that pierced Jesus that made atonement for the sins of the whole world." (Wenham)

iii. "The account of the action of Phinehas the priest is a revelation of how one man in loyalty to God and jealous for His honor may stand against the false attitude of a people. Phinehas dared refuse to take part in these false conventionalities and visited with immediate and terrible punishment the two notorious wrongdoers." (Morgan)

d. **Twenty-four thousand**: This many died in the plague. This must have delighted Balak, king of Moab. He knew that Balaam had succeeded in cursing Israel – or, rather, in getting them to curse themselves.

i. **Those who died in the plague were twenty-four thousand**: It seems that Paul refers to this incident in 1 Corinthians 10:8, but Paul says it was 23,000 killed instead of 24,000. "The two places may be reconciled thus: 1000 men were slain in consequence of the examination instituted ver. 4, and 23,000 in consequence of the orders given ver. 5; making 24,000 in the whole. St. Paul probably refers only to the latter number." (Clarke)

2. (10-13) God honors Phinehas for his zeal.

Then the LORD spoke to Moses, saying: "Phinehas the son of Eleazar, the son of Aaron the priest, has turned back My wrath from the children of Israel, because he was zealous with My zeal among them, so that I did not consume the children of Israel in My zeal. Therefore say, 'Behold, I give to him My covenant of peace; and it shall be to him and his descendants after him a covenant of an everlasting priesthood, because he was zealous for his God, and made atonement for the children of Israel.'"

a. **Because he was zealous with My zeal among them, so that I did not consume the children of Israel in My zeal**: It wasn't only Phinehas' obedience God noticed; it was also that **he was zealous with My zeal among them**. Phinehas was passionate about the things God was passionate about. In this situation, Phinehas faithfully demonstrated the **zeal** of God against Israel's unfaithfulness to their covenant with God.

b. **It shall be to him and his descendants after him a covenant of an everlasting priesthood**: God blessed Phinehas with the promise that he would be the descendant of Aaron through whom the priesthood passed.

i. This was fitting because it was the zeal of Phinehas that **made atonement for the children of Israel**, just as a priest should be the one ministering atonement.

3. (14-18) God commands Israel to harass and attack the Midianites.

Now the name of the Israelite who was killed, who was killed with the Midianite woman, *was* Zimri the son of Salu, a leader of a father's house among the Simeonites. And the name of the Midianite woman who was killed *was* Cozbi the daughter of Zur; he *was* head of the people of a father's house in Midian.

Then the LORD spoke to Moses, saying: "Harass the Midianites, and attack them; for they harassed you with their schemes by which they seduced you in the matter of Peor and in the matter of Cozbi, the daughter of a leader of Midian, their sister, who was killed in the day of the plague because of Peor."

a. **Zimri the son of Salu.... Cozbi the daughter of Zur**: These were the names of the previously unnamed (verses 6 and 8) Israelite man and Moabite woman who so publicly and offensively sinned. This naming was to their everlasting shame. Both of them came from fathers who were leaders.

i. The name Zimri means "my remembrance," and he was remembered in the worst way. The name Cozbi means "my lie" or "deception," and it is possible that her name was deliberately changed to make it more appropriate to her disgrace.

ii. **Cozbi, the daughter of a leader of Midian**: "Likely she was a priestess of her religion, a prototype of Jezebel who would later be instrumental in bringing Baal and Asherah worship into the center of the life of Israel." (Allen)

iii. In Israel, only men could be priests. In most of the peoples surrounding Israel, women were often priests, and their priestly "service" was often associated with prostitution.

b. **Harass the Midianites, and attack them; for they harassed you with their schemes by which they seduced you in the matter of Peor**: God commanded Israel to show no tolerance towards the **Midianites**, who played a role in seducing Israel to these sins of immorality and idolatry. Israel was commanded to battle against the Midianites at every opportunity they had.

i. **Harass the Midianites, and attack them**: Numbers 31:1-20 records that "Twelve thousand Israelites attacked the Midianites, destroyed all their cities, slew their five kings, every male, and every grown up woman, and took all their spoils." (Clarke)

ii. "With the plague of Baal Peor the punishment of the first generation was complete, and the process of preparing the second generation to enter the Promised Land was at hand." (Cole)

Numbers 26 – The Second Census

A. The second census of Israel in the wilderness.

1. (1-4) The command to take the census.

And it came to pass, after the plague, that the LORD spoke to Moses and Eleazar the son of Aaron the priest, saying: "Take a census of all the congregation of the children of Israel from twenty years old and above, by their fathers' houses, all who are able to go to war in Israel." So Moses and Eleazar the priest spoke with them in the plains of Moab by the Jordan, *across from* **Jericho, saying:** *"Take a census of the people from twenty years old and above, just as the LORD commanded Moses and the children of Israel who came out of the land of Egypt."*

a. **It came to pass, after the plague**: The census of Numbers 26 came *after* the **plague** of judgment described in the previous chapter. That marked the conclusion of the passing of the generation that would die in the wilderness, with the single exception of Moses, whose death is recorded in Deuteronomy 34. Only two from that generation would not die in the wilderness: Joshua and Caleb.

> i. Numbers 26:64-65 makes it clear that the generation of unbelief had passed, that not one remained from that generation.

> ii. "The expression 'after the plague' is to be regarded as the turning point from the first generation to the second, the shift from the fathers and mothers to sons and daughters. God was about to begin a new work with a new people. The younger generation would begin to have their day." (Allen)

b. **Take a census of all the congregation of the children of Israel**: Some 38 years earlier, at the beginning of the book of Numbers, while Israel still camped at Mount Sinai, God commanded them to take a census (Numbers 1-3). This census was carried out by Moses and Eleazar (Numbers 26:63).

i. "By thus taking a census of his people, the Lord showed that he valued each one of them. They were registered by their families and by their names; thus were they personally enrolled in the family book of the living God, and he thus, in effect, said to each one of them, 'I have called thee by thy name; thou art mine.'" (Spurgeon)

ii. The first census was primarily for military organization. If they were to enter and take possession of the land of Canaan, they had to know how many troops they had, and how they should best be organized.

iii. Numbers 26:52-56 reveals an important second reason for this second census: to help in the fair apportioning of the land of Canaan so that the larger tribes would receive more land.

c. **All who are able to go to war in Israel**: The purpose of the second census was also made clear. They were to count those able to fight on behalf of Israel. This accounting, 38 years later, was also for military organization.

i. 38 years before Israel was *organized* enough; they just did not have enough *faith* to take Canaan. Organization is good, and the work of God can suffer from a lack of it, but even the *best* organization can never replace bold trust in God.

ii. Numbering those **able to go to war** meant something different now than it did 38 years previously. "Once, an easy entrance into the land of promise may have been expected; but that dream has long passed away. Now the Israelites are made clearly to understand that the last effort will require the whole warlike energy they can summon, the best courage of every one who can handle sword or spear." (Watson)

iii. "The wisdom which commanded the counting of Israel at the beginning of the wilderness journey, also determined to count them at the end of it. This would show that he did not value them less than in former years; it would afford proof that his word of judgment had been fulfilled to them; and, moreover, it would marshal them for the grand enterprise of conquering the land of Canaan." (Spurgeon)

iv. **From twenty years old and above, by their fathers' houses, all who are able to go to war in Israel**: Spurgeon took this principle and applied it spiritually to our congregations, wondering how many there are among us who can truly battle in the spirit: "If the numbers of our churches were taken in this fashion, would they not sadly shrink? We have many sick among us that need to be carried about, and nursed, and doctored.... To revise the church rolls so as to leave none but vigorous soldiers on the muster-roll would make us break our hearts over our statistics."

2. (5-11) The tribe of Reuben.

Reuben *was* the firstborn of Israel. The children of Reuben *were: of* Hanoch, the family of the Hanochites; *of* Pallu, the family of the Palluites; *of* Hezron, the family of the Hezronites; *of* Carmi, the family of the Carmites. These *are* the families of the Reubenites: those who were numbered of them were forty-three thousand seven hundred and thirty. And the son of Pallu *was* Eliab. The sons of Eliab *were* Nemuel, Dathan, and Abiram. These *are* the Dathan and Abiram, representatives of the congregation, who contended against Moses and Aaron in the company of Korah, when they contended against the LORD; and the earth opened its mouth and swallowed them up together with Korah when that company died, when the fire devoured two hundred and fifty men; and they became a sign. Nevertheless the children of Korah did not die.

a. **The children of Reuben were**: In the first census, Reuben counted 46,500 men ready for war (1:21, 2:11); 38 years later, they counted 43,730 – a loss of 2,770 men (6%).

i. If this census is compared with that given in Numbers 1, the difference is that the first census only gave the total number of men over 20 years of age in each tribe. The second census gives that number, but also the names of the major families or clans that make up each tribe.

b. **These are the Dathan and Abiram, representatives of the congregation, who contended against Moses**: Notable in the tribe of Reuben were **Dathan and Abiram**, who were co-leaders with Korah in the rebellion against the LORD and Moses described in Numbers 16. Perhaps one reason Dathan and Abiram resented Moses' leadership was that they were from the tribe of Israel's firstborn son (Reuben); yet Moses, who was descended from Levi (a younger son) was the leader of the nation.

i. **Who contended against Moses and Aaron…when they contended against the LORD**: "Further, the verb translated 'rebelled' [**contended**] against Moses and Aaron is rare, signifying a strong contest of wills. But ultimately they found they were struggling, not just with man, but with God." (Allen)

ii. **And they became a sign**: God's judgment of Dathan, Abiram, Korah and their followers in Numbers 16 surely was a sign, both to the generation in the wilderness and beyond.

iii. "The term employed for 'sign,' the Hebrew *nes*, typically is used to denote an ensign or banner around which people rally (Jer 50:2) or soldiers muster for battle (Jer 50:2).... But like Sodom and

Gomorrah, or Nadab and Abihu, Dathan and Abiram, or Korah, these individuals would serve as historical bywords for how God deals with revolutionaries." (Cole)

3. (12-14) The tribe of Simeon.

The sons of Simeon according to their families *were: of* Nemuel, the family of the Nemuelites; *of* Jamin, the family of the Jaminites; *of* Jachin, the family of the Jachinites; *of* Zerah, the family of the Zarhites; *of* Shaul, the family of the Shaulites. These *are* the families of the Simeonites: twenty-two thousand two hundred.

a. **The sons of Simeon**: In the first census, the tribe of Simeon counted 59,300 men ready for war (1:23, 2:13); 38 years later, they counted 22,200. This was a staggering loss of 37,100 men for this once-great tribe (a loss of 63%).

i. "It may be that the fall in Reuben and Simeon's population should be linked with these tribes' support for Dathan and Abiram (ch. 16) and Zimri (ch. 25), but it is hard to identify any factor that would account for the decline of the other tribes." (Wenham)

4. (15-18) The tribe of Gad.

The sons of Gad according to their families *were: of* Zephon, the family of the Zephonites; *of* Haggi, the family of the Haggites; *of* Shuni, the family of the Shunites; *of* Ozni, the family of the Oznites; *of* Eri, the family of the Erites; *of* Arod, the family of the Arodites; *of* Areli, the family of the Arelites. These *are* the families of the sons of Gad according to those who were numbered of them: forty thousand five hundred.

a. **The sons of Gad**: In the first census, the tribe of Gad counted 45,650 men ready for war (1:25, 2:15). 38 years later, they counted 40,500. This was a loss of 5,150 fighting men (11%).

5. (19-22) The tribe of Judah.

The sons of Judah *were* Er and Onan; and Er and Onan died in the land of Canaan. And the sons of Judah according to their families were: *of* Shelah, the family of the Shelanites; *of* Perez, the family of the Parzites; *of* Zerah, the family of the Zarhites. And the sons of Perez were: *of* Hezron, the family of the Hezronites; *of* Hamul, the family of the Hamulites. These *are* the families of Judah according to those who were numbered of them: seventy-six thousand five hundred.

a. **The sons of Judah**: In the first census, the tribe of Judah counted 74,600 men ready for war (1:27, 2:4). 38 years later, they counted 76,500. This was a gain of 1,900 (3%).

6. (23-25) The tribe of Issachar.

The sons of Issachar according to their families *were: of* **Tola, the family of the Tolaites; of Puah, the family of the Punites; of Jashub, the family of the Jashubites; of Shimron, the family of the Shimronites. These** *are* **the families of Issachar according to those who were numbered of them: sixty-four thousand three hundred.**

> a. **The sons of Issachar**: In the first census, the tribe of Issachar counted 54,400 men ready for war (1:29, 2:6). 38 years later, they counted 64,300. This was a gain of 9,900 (18%).

7. (26-27) The tribe of Zebulun.

The sons of Zebulun according to their families *were:* **of Sered, the family of the Sardites; of Elon, the family of the Elonites; of Jahleel, the family of the Jahleelites. These** *are* **the families of the Zebulunites according to those who were numbered of them: sixty thousand five hundred.**

> a. **The sons of Zebulun**: In the first census, the tribe of Zebulun counted 57,400 men ready for war (1:31, 2:8). 38 years later, they counted 60,500. This was a gain of 3,100 (5%).

8. (28-34) The tribe of Manasseh.

The sons of Joseph according to their families, by Manasseh and Ephraim, *were***: The sons of Manasseh: of Machir, the family of the Machirites; and Machir begot Gilead; of Gilead, the family of the Gileadites. These** *are* **the sons of Gilead:** *of* **Jeezer, the family of the Jeezerites; of Helek, the family of the Helekites;** *of* **Asriel, the family of the Asrielites;** *of* **Shechem, the family of the Shechemites;** *of* **Shemida, the family of the Shemidaites;** *of* **Hepher, the family of the Hepherites. Now Zelophehad the son of Hepher had no sons, but daughters; and the names of the daughters of Zelophehad** *were* **Mahlah, Noah, Hoglah, Milcah, and Tirzah. These** *are* **the families of Manasseh; and those who were numbered of them** *were* **fifty-two thousand seven hundred.**

> a. **The sons of Manasseh**: In the first census, the tribe of Manasseh counted 32,200 men ready for war (1:35, 2:21). 38 years later, they counted 52,700. This was a remarkable gain of 20,500 (64%).

9. (35-37) The tribe of Ephraim.

These *are* **the sons of Ephraim according to their families: of Shuthelah, the family of the Shuthalhites; of Becher, the family of the Bachrites; of Tahan, the family of the Tahanites. And these** *are* **the sons of Shuthelah: of Eran, the family of the Eranites. These** *are* **the families of the sons of**

Ephraim according to those who were numbered of them: thirty-two thousand five hundred. These *are* the sons of Joseph according to their families.

a. **These are the sons of Ephraim**: In the first census, the tribe of Ephraim counted 40,500 men ready for war (1:33, 2:19). 38 years later, they counted 32,500. This was a loss of 8,000 men (20%).

10. (38-41) The tribe of Benjamin.

The sons of Benjamin according to their families were: of Bela, the family of the Belaites; of Ashbel, the family of the Ashbelites; of Ahiram, the family of the Ahiramites; of Shupham, the family of the Shuphamites; of Hupham, the family of the Huphamites. And the sons of Bela were Ard and Naaman: *of Ard,* **the family of the Ardites; of Naaman, the family of the Naamites. These** *are* **the sons of Benjamin according to their families; and those who were numbered of them** *were* **forty-five thousand six hundred.**

a. **The sons of Benjamin**: In the first census, the tribe of Benjamin counted 35,400 men ready for war (1:37, 2:23). 38 years later, they counted 45,600. This was a gain of 10,200 men (29%).

11. (42-43) The tribe of Dan.

These *are* **the sons of Dan according to their families: of Shuham, the family of the Shuhamites. These** *are* **the families of Dan according to their families. All the families of the Shuhamites, according to those who were numbered of them,** *were* **sixty-four thousand four hundred.**

a. **These are the sons of Dan**: In the first census, the tribe of Dan counted 62,700 men ready for war (1:39, 2:26). 38 years later, they counted 64,400. This was a gain of 1,700 men (3%).

12. (44-47) The tribe of Asher.

The sons of Asher according to their families *were:* **of Jimna, the family of the Jimnites; of Jesui, the family of the Jesuites; of Beriah, the family of the Beriites. Of the sons of Beriah: of Heber, the family of the Heberites; of Malchiel, the family of the Malchielites. And the name of the daughter of Asher** *was* **Serah. These** *are* **the families of the sons of Asher according to those who were numbered of them: fifty-three thousand four hundred.**

a. **The sons of Asher**: In the first census, the tribe of Asher counted 41,500 men ready for war (1:41, 2:28). 38 years later, they counted 53,400 men. This was a gain of 11,900 (29%).

i. **The daughter of Asher was Serah**: The mention of Serah, daughter of Asher (v.46), is remarkable (and she is mentioned as well in Gen 46:17 and 1 Chronicles 7:30)." (Allen)

13. (48-50) The tribe of Naphtali.

The sons of Naphtali according to their families *were:* of Jahzeel, the family of the Jahzeelites; of Guni, the family of the Gunites; of Jezer, the family of the Jezerites; of Shillem, the family of the Shillemites. These *are* the families of Naphtali according to their families; and those who were numbered of them *were* forty-five thousand four hundred.

a. **The sons of Naphtali**: In the first census, the tribe of Naphtali counted 53,400 men ready for war (1:43, 2:30). 38 years later, they counted 45,400 men. This was a loss of 8,000 (15%).

14. (51) The total number of men able to go to war among Israel.

These *are* those who were numbered of the children of Israel: six hundred and one thousand seven hundred and thirty.

a. **These are those who were numbered**: In the first census, Israel counted 603,550 men ready for war (1:46, 2:32). 38 years later, they counted 601,730 men – a loss of 1,820 men (0.3%).

b. **Six hundred and one thousand seven hundred and thirty**: So, the total number of men ready for war during the wilderness stayed virtually the same over the 38-year period, when the generation of unbelief died in the wilderness.

i. In one respect, we see *stagnation*. The stagnation of population is reflective of Israel's spiritual condition during those 38 years. We should have expected them to grow, as is normal in the course of generations. Instead, they simply stayed where they were. The 38 years in the wilderness were years of no growth, no advance – of mere existence until the generation of unbelief had died and a generation of faith had replaced them, a generation that was bold enough to take the Promised Land.

ii. In another respect, we see God's *great mercy and blessing*. The wilderness did not kill the people of God. Under God's blessing and guidance – even accounting for His judgments upon them – they remained strong and vital through an entire generation in a difficult, inhospitable wilderness.

iii. "An inconsequential net decline of only 1,820 (0.3 percent), in spite of physical obstacles, spiritual failures, and harsh judgment from the Lord, confirms that the promise to Abraham of innumerable descendants remains in effect." (Cole)

iv. "Notwithstanding the amazing increase in some and decrease in other tribes, the same sort of proportion is preserved in the *east, west, north,* and *south* divisions, as before." (Clarke)

c. **Numbered of the children of Israel**: During this period, certain tribes enjoyed significant gains, and certain tribes suffered significant losses.

i. Of these twelve tribes of Israel, five suffered loss, and seven gained men. Half of the tribes had gains or losses of 15% or less, but Simeon lost 63% of their population, and Manasseh gained 64%. God was blessing or cursing certain tribes, no doubt related to their trust in God and obedience.

Tribes of Israel – First and Second Census (Numbers 1, 3 and 26)

TRIBE	1ST CENSUS	2ND CENSUS	CHANGE	PERCENT
Reuben	46,500	43,730	-2,770	-6%
Simeon	59,300	22,200	-37,100	-63%
Gad	45,650	40,500	-5,150	-11%
Judah	74,600	76,500	+1,900	+3%
Issachar	54,400	64,300	+9,900	+18%
Zebulun	57,400	60,500	+3,100	+5%
Manasseh	32,200	52,700	+20,500	+64%
Ephraim	40,500	32,500	-8,000	-20%
Benjamin	35,400	45,600	+10,200	+29%
Dan	62,700	64,400	+1,700	+3%
Asher	41,500	53,400	+11,900	+29%
Naphtali	53,400	45,400	-8,000	-15%
Levi	Not counted	Not counted		
Total	**603,550**	**601,730**	**-1,820**	**-0.3%**

B. Inheritance of the land of Canaan.

1. (52-56) The general principle of inheritance: larger tribes receive larger portions of land.

Then the LORD spoke to Moses, saying: "To these the land shall be divided as an inheritance, according to the number of names. To a large *tribe* you shall give a larger inheritance, and to a small *tribe* you shall give a smaller inheritance. Each shall be given its inheritance according to those who were numbered of them. But the land shall be divided by lot; they shall inherit according to the names of the tribes of their fathers. According to the lot their inheritance shall be divided between the larger and the smaller."

a. **To a large tribe you shall give a larger inheritance**: When Canaan was divided by lot, the lines were to be drawn according to this general principle. Larger tribes received a larger territory because they had more families to divide the land among.

b. **According to the lot their inheritance shall be divided**: The actual apportioning of land within a territory would be done **according to the lot**, with the idea that God guided the **lot** (Proverbs 16:33). The apportioned land would be an **inheritance**, remaining within the family and not to be permanently sold or transferred.

2. (57-62) The tribe of Levi and their inheritance.

And these *are* those who were numbered of the Levites according to their families: of Gershon, the family of the Gershonites; of Kohath, the family of the Kohathites; of Merari, the family of the Merarites. These *are* the families of the Levites: the family of the Libnites, the family of the Hebronites, the family of the Mahlites, the family of the Mushites, and the family of the Korathites. And Kohath begot Amram. The name of Amram's wife *was* Jochebed the daughter of Levi, who was born to Levi in Egypt; and to Amram she bore Aaron and Moses and their sister Miriam. To Aaron were born Nadab and Abihu, Eleazar and Ithamar. And Nadab and Abihu died when they offered profane fire before the LORD. Now those who were numbered of them were twenty-three thousand, every male from a month old and above; for they were not numbered among the other children of Israel, because there was no inheritance given to them among the children of Israel.

a. **For they were not numbered among the other children of Israel**: The Levites were not numbered in either the first or second census, because the men of their tribe were not to go to war.

b. **Because there was no inheritance given to them among the children of Israel**: A second reason to not count the Levites was that they were to receive no inheritance of land as the other tribes did. Their inheritance was greater than property – the LORD Himself (Numbers 18:20).

3. (63-65) The generation of unbelief had no inheritance.

These *are* those who were numbered by Moses and Eleazar the priest, who numbered the children of Israel in the plains of Moab by the Jordan, *across from* Jericho. But among these there was not a man of those who were numbered by Moses and Aaron the priest when they numbered the children of Israel in the Wilderness of Sinai. For the LORD had said of them, "They shall surely die in the wilderness." So there was not left a man of them, except Caleb the son of Jephunneh and Joshua the son of Nun.

a. **But among these there was not a man of those who were numbered by Moses and Aaron**: None of those counted in the first census were counted in the second. That was the old generation, the generation of unbelief, who perished in the wilderness. They obviously had no inheritance in the Promised Land (except for Caleb and Joshua).

i. "The census takers, Moses and Eleazar, bridge the generations. Moses has led the people of Israel mightily and valiantly through the Sinai and wilderness experiences, but he will not enter the Promised Land. Instead Eleazar will assume the responsibility of priestly leadership for the new generation." (Cole)

ii. **Except Caleb...and Joshua**: "Under the latter [**Joshua**] this new people of God would enter their inheritance. Through the ministry of a greater Joshua (Jesus is Greek for Joshua), the people of God in every generation are invited to enter into God's rest (Heb. 4:1–13)." (Wenham)

b. **There was not left a man of them**: It is good to take such words as reminders of our own mortality. Just as a generation passed in the wilderness, so we – if Jesus does not return for us first – will pass from this earth to eternity. It is good to soberly consider this and live as one prepared to die.

i. "On each of these unbelieving men the Divine sentence was executed.... Unless Christ come first, our turn will come. In Adam all die. We must all appear before the judgment-seat of Christ. Each was born alone, must die alone, and alone give an account to the King. Prepare, my soul, to meet Him!" (Meyer)

ii. "If we are now serving God, let us do so with intense earnestness, since only for a little while shall we have the opportunity to do so among men.... Live while you live. At the same time, lay plans for influencing the rising generation. Lay yourself out to work while it is called to-day." (Spurgeon)

Numbers 27 – Laws of Inheritance and the Next Leader

A. The case of Zelophehad's daughters.

1. (1-5) The request of Zelophehad's daughters.

Then came the daughters of Zelophehad the son of Hepher, the son of Gilead, the son of Machir, the son of Manasseh, from the families of Manasseh the son of Joseph; and these *were* the names of his daughters: Mahlah, Noah, Hoglah, Milcah, and Tirzah. And they stood before Moses, before Eleazar the priest, and before the leaders and all the congregation, *by* the doorway of the tabernacle of meeting, saying: "Our father died in the wilderness; but he was not in the company of those who gathered together against the LORD, in company with Korah, but he died in his own sin; and he had no sons. Why should the name of our father be removed from among his family because he had no son? Give us a possession among our father's brothers."

So Moses brought their case before the LORD.

> a. **Then came the daughters of Zelophehad**: In Israel, (as in all the Ancient Near East) land was normally passed on from fathers to their sons, not to the daughters. Because of this principle, there was a question regarding **the daughters of Zelophehad**, whose father had no sons.

> > i. The issue is presented here because at the end of the previous chapter the distribution of the land of Canaan was in view (26:52-56). It was natural for **the daughters of Zelophehad** to wonder what their place would be in the coming allotment of land.

> > ii. "In a sense this chapter is an extension of the genealogies of chapter 26, showing how complications may be worked out when the people come to inherit their share in the land of Canaan." (Allen)

iii. Though women did not normally find economic security apart from a husband's holdings through land inheritance, a woman typically received a dowry from her father as a wedding present. Usually, the father required his potential son-in-law to provide much, if not all, of the dowry. A dowry might consist of clothes, jewelry, money, furniture, and more. It was thought that the dowry could help provide for the woman if her husband left her or if he unexpectedly died.

iv. Spurgeon appealed to the daughters of Zelophehad as examples of those who boldly approached to receive an inheritance by faith: "Dost thou want a portion in heaven, sinner? Go straight away to Jesus, and Jesus will take thy cause, and lay it before the Lord."

b. **Why should the name of our father be removed from among his family**: This was how **the daughters of Zelophehad** presented the issue. Without sons to inherit his land and perpetuate his name, there was a sense in which denying inheritance to the only descendants of Zelophehad was to erase his name.

i. When there were sons born to a family, "A father's property was divided between his sons after his death, the eldest son receiving twice as much as his brothers (Deut. 21:15–17)." (Wenham)

c. **So Moses brought their case before the LORD**: Moses did what he should when faced with a new situation. Moses sought God.

i. "For it was a hard case; and though their plea seemed reasonable, yet Moses showed his humility and modesty, that he would not determine it himself without God's particular direction." (Poole)

ii. "These verses also give an indication how case law might have operated in Israel. The general laws would be promulgated. Then legitimate exceptions or special considerations would come to the elders and perhaps be brought to Moses himself. He then would await a decision from the Lord." (Allen)

2. (6-11) The settlement of the inheritance of the daughters of Zelophehad.

And the LORD spoke to Moses, saying: "The daughters of Zelophehad speak *what is* right; you shall surely give them a possession of inheritance among their father's brothers, and cause the inheritance of their father to pass to them. And you shall speak to the children of Israel, saying: 'If a man dies and has no son, then you shall cause his inheritance to pass to his daughter. If he has no daughter, then you shall give his inheritance to his brothers. If he has no brothers, then you shall give his inheritance to his father's brothers. And if his father has no brothers, then you shall give his inheritance to the relative closest to him in his family, and he

shall possess it.'" And it shall be to the children of Israel a statute of judgment, just as the LORD commanded Moses.

a. **The daughters of Zelophehad speak what is right**: God seemed pleased that the daughters of Zelophehad brought this issue before Moses. God declared that if a father had no sons, **the inheritance of their father** could then go to the daughters.

i. "Allowing daughters to inherit, where there were no sons in the family, created another problem though. When they married, they would take the family land with them, thus destroying the father's estate. To deal with this, chapter 36 brings in additional rules governing the marriage of heiresses." (Wenham)

b. **If he has no daughter, then you shall give his inheritance to his brothers**: However, if there were no daughters, the inheritance then went to the father's brothers. If there were no brothers, the inheritance went to **the relative closest to him in the family**.

i. **You shall surely give them**: "*Give them:* in Hebrew it is of the masculine gender, to show that women in this case should enjoy the man's privilege, and that the heavenly Canaan, whereof this was a type, did belong no less to women than to men." (Poole)

c. **And it shall be to the children of Israel a statute of judgment**: These laws were made in anticipation – in faith – of coming into the inheritance of land in Canaan. This was only an issue for the daughters of Zelophehad because they were women of faith, who really believed Israel would possess the land of Canaan.

i. This was also relevant because Israel had already begun the occupation of their lands east of the Jordan River, and the tribe of Manasseh would occupy some of those lands. The daughters of Zelophehad were from Manasseh, so the allotment of their land may have come sooner than the allotment of land for the tribes settling west of the Jordan River.

ii. The case of the daughters of Zelophehad further clarified the laws of inheritance for Israel.

- If a man had sons, they were first in line to inherit their father's property.

- If a man had no sons, his daughters would stand in the place of his sons.

- If there were no sons or daughters, the inheritance would pass to the closest family member – a brother, uncle, cousin, or other.

B. The passing of Moses and the appointment of a new leader.

1. (12-14) God tells Moses of his coming death.

Now the LORD said to Moses: "Go up into this Mount Abarim, and see the land which I have given to the children of Israel. And when you have seen it, you also shall be gathered to your people, as Aaron your brother was gathered. For in the Wilderness of Zin, during the strife of the congregation, you rebelled against My command to hallow Me at the waters before their eyes." (These *are* the waters of Meribah, at Kadesh in the Wilderness of Zin.)

a. **You also shall be gathered to your people**: Moses was first told he would die before coming to the Promised Land in Numbers 20. It was still many months until Moses would climb to the top of the mountain; able to see Canaan but not able to enter it (Deuteronomy 34). After seeing the land, Moses would die (**be gathered to your people**).

i. In Deuteronomy 3:23-25, Moses explained that he did – on some occasion – ask God to relent from His judgment that Moses would never set foot in the land of Canaan. God did not relent, and Moses made himself content with knowing he would see the land and be gathered to His God.

ii. "The expression 'gathered to your people' describes the Hebrew concept of unity and identity with the faithful forefathers (Genesis 15:15; 25:8; 35:29; 47:30), with whom they would rest and find peace." (Cole)

b. **You rebelled against My command to hallow Me**: God reminded Moses of the reason why he would not be allowed to enter Canaan, because of his sin of misrepresenting God at Meribah (Numbers 20:12-13).

i. "The account of his going is given at the end of Deuteronomy, but these words bring the facts before us in this book, which is the book revealing the Divine discipline of failing people; and it serves to keep before us the fact that the most faithful servants of God cannot escape the results of their failure in this life." (Morgan)

2. (15-17) Moses' response to God's announcement.

Then Moses spoke to the LORD, saying: "Let the LORD, the God of the spirits of all flesh, set a man over the congregation, who may go out before them and go in before them, who may lead them out and bring them in, that the congregation of the LORD may not be like sheep which have no shepherd."

a. **Let the LORD...set a man over the congregation**: After hearing of his coming fate, Moses did not try to change God's mind, and he did not complain. His only concern was for the congregation of Israel, for the people, not for himself.

i. **The LORD, the God of the spirits of all flesh**: "This is an expressive title of the Lord that speaks of his ultimate sovereignty over all peoples. If God is sovereign of all, then surely God will wish to show his sovereignty over his people in their evident need for a shepherd to follow Moses." (Allen)

b. **That the congregation of the LORD may not be like sheep which have no shepherd**: This was the picture used to describe a leaderless people. Sheep without a shepherd are in constant danger. They have trouble finding food and water, and they wander into dangerous places. God wants His sheep to have shepherds.

i. In the ultimate sense, this is fulfilled by Jesus Christ, who is the Good Shepherd, as was prophesied in the Old Testament (Micah 5:2-4) and revealed in the New Testament: *I am the good shepherd. The good shepherd gives His life for the sheep.* (John 10:11)

ii. In an additional sense, this is also fulfilled by the New Testament office of *pastor-teacher*. The ancient Greek word for *pastor* is the word for *shepherd* (Acts 20:28, 1 Peter 5:2). As 1 Peter 5:4 presents it, Jesus is the Chief Shepherd, and pastors are under-shepherds.

iii. The duty of shepherds was well understood. They were to feed (John 21:15-17), to lead (**lead them out and bring them in**), and to protect the sheep.

iv. Jesus was also moved with compassion when He saw the people as sheep without a shepherd (Mark 6:34); Moses prefigured the nature of Jesus by his concern that Israel not be left as sheep without a shepherd.

3. (18-23) Joshua chosen and given authority.

And the LORD said to Moses: "Take Joshua the son of Nun with you, a man in whom *is* the Spirit, and lay your hand on him; set him before Eleazar the priest and before all the congregation, and inaugurate him in their sight. And you shall give *some* of your authority to him, that all the congregation of the children of Israel may be obedient. He shall stand before Eleazar the priest, who shall inquire before the LORD for him by the judgment of the Urim. At his word they shall go out, and at his word they shall come in, he and all the children of Israel with him— all the congregation."

So Moses did as the LORD commanded him. He took Joshua and set him before Eleazar the priest and before all the congregation. And he laid his hands on him and inaugurated him, just as the LORD commanded by the hand of Moses.

a. **Take Joshua the son of Nun with you, a man in whom is the Spirit, and lay your hand on him**: Though Joshua was not of noble birth or a literal son of Moses, there were many things that qualified him to be the successor of Moses.

- Joshua had led the army of Israel against the Amalekites (Exodus 17:8-16).

- Joshua was an assistant to Moses (Exodus 24:13).

- Joshua helped Moses at the tabernacle after the golden calf disaster (Exodus 33:7-11).

- Joshua was zealous to preserve the authority and leadership of Moses (Numbers 11:28).

- Joshua was one of the two faith-filled spies among the total of twelve who spied out the land of Canaan (Numbers 13:30-14:38).

- Joshua was **a man in whom is the Spirit**, the most important qualification of all. The Holy Spirit would empower and enable him to fulfill the challenging role of leading the nation into Canaan.

  i. "This must certainly mean the *Spirit of God;* and because he was endued with this Spirit, therefore he was capable of leading the people. How miserably qualified is that man for the work of God who is not guided and influenced by the Holy Ghost! God never chooses a man to accomplish his designs but that one whom he himself has qualified for the work." (Clarke)

  ii. "The prayer was immediately answered and he had not only the satisfaction already referred to of appointing his successor, but, what was far more important to him, that of knowing that the one so appointed was the man of God's own choice." (Morgan)

b. **You shall give some of your authority to him**: This seems to have been immediate. From this point, Joshua shared some of the **authority** of Moses in leading Israel. Until the passing of Moses, there were some months of shared leadership and responsibility, a brief transitional period.

c. **He shall stand before Eleazar the priest**: The appointment of Joshua was not only made evident by Moses but also by **Eleazar the priest**. The priests would support Joshua's leadership, even though he (unlike Moses) did not come from the priestly tribe of Levi.

i. The explanation of the role of **Eleazar the priest, who shall inquire before the LORD for him**, indicates a difference in the place of Moses and the place of Joshua. "Whereas God spoke to Moses face to face (12:6–8), Joshua will be instructed by Eleazar the priest, who will use the Urim and Thummim, the sacred lot, to discover God's will." (Wenham)

d. **And he laid his hands on him and inaugurated him**: This public presentation and laying on of hands upon Joshua was important. It presented Joshua before all Israel as the next leader, the one who should expect to follow as God's appointed leader.

i. "Jacob placed his hands on his grandsons' heads to bless them (Gen. 48:14); the people placed their hands on the blasphemer's head to transfer their guilt incurred through hearing blasphemy to the blasphemer (Lev. 24:14); and all worshippers placed a hand on the head of the sacrificial animal to indicate it was taking their place in dying for their sin (Lev. 1:4, etc.)." (Wenham)

Numbers 28 – Sacrifices for Appointed Days and Feasts

A. Offerings related to appointed days.

1. (1-2) Introduction – the appointed offerings.

Now the LORD spoke to Moses, saying, "Command the children of Israel, and say to them, 'My offering, My food for My offerings made by fire as a sweet aroma to Me, you shall be careful to offer to Me at their appointed time.'

a. **My offering, My food for My offerings**: The sacrifices God told Israel to make belonged to Him. They were to be made according to His command, and not improvised.

i. Throughout these chapters, the sheer number of animals, grain, oil, and wine needed to fulfill what God commanded is impressive. All these sacrifices assume that Israel is not only in Canaan, but that they are blessed in the land – they have the agricultural prosperity to provide such offerings.

ii. Meyer on **My food**: "We often speak of ourselves as hungering for God. Do we sufficiently realize that He hungers for our love, our whole-hearted devotion, our fellowship with Him?.... If we really loved Jesus, we should be eager to give Him food in our prayers, and yearnings, and activities; and we should long with intense desire for Him to be satisfied."

b. **You shall be careful to offer to Me at their appointed time**: The following two chapters concern details of the sacrificial system God instituted as part of the covenant made with Israel at Mount Sinai. These sacrificial offerings include:

- The morning and evening offerings.
- The Sabbath offering.

- The monthly offering.
- Offerings at Passover and the Feast of Unleavened Bread.
- Offerings at the Feast of Weeks (Pentecost).
- Offerings at the Feast of Trumpets.
- Offerings on the Day of Atonement.
- Offerings at the Feast of Tabernacles.

    i. These feasts or occasions were previously commanded, but there was little detail given on what specific offerings should be made in honor of these daily, weekly, monthly, and annual occasions. Israel needed God at special times of the year, at the start of every month, the end of every week, and multiple times a day – and these offerings were an expression of this.

    ii. "So offerings pile on offerings, sometimes overlapping in what seems to us today to be a bewildering, benumbing collage. But these offerings were the perpetual reminders of who the people were, who their God is, and the enormity of their need to respond to him in overwhelming gratitude." (Allen)

    iii. As will be seen in the number of required sacrifices, it was a lot of work to be a priest and to fulfill God's commanded offerings. Every day, every week, every month, and many times a year required special sacrifices – beyond what any individual in Israel might bring to God's altar. The work of slicing and bleeding and cutting and dismembering and cleaning and presenting and burning was a lot to do. No wonder the priesthood of Jesus is remarkable in that He sat down, His work finished (Hebrews 10:11-12).

2. (3-8) The morning offering and evening offering.

"And you shall say to them, 'This *is* the offering made by fire which you shall offer to the LORD: two male lambs in their first year without blemish, day by day, as a regular burnt offering. The one lamb you shall offer in the morning, the other lamb you shall offer in the evening, and one-tenth of an ephah of fine flour as a grain offering mixed with one-fourth of a hin of pressed oil. *It is* a regular burnt offering which was ordained at Mount Sinai for a sweet aroma, an offering made by fire to the LORD. And its drink offering *shall be* one-fourth of a hin for each lamb; in a holy *place* you shall pour out the drink to the LORD as an offering. The other lamb you shall offer in the evening; as the morning grain offering and its drink offering, you shall offer *it* as an offering made by fire, a sweet aroma to the LORD.

a. **Day by day, as a regular burnt offering**: Israel was commanded to bring a male **lamb** to the LORD every morning and every evening. Each day began and ended with this statement of the need for atonement by sacrifice and expression of surrender and devotion to the LORD.

i. Cole lists five aspects of theological significance in the burnt offering: "(1) a total burnt offering is a method by which the physical sacrifice is rendered fully to the Lord, the visible is rendered into the world of the invisible, and the smoke enters symbolically the nostrils of God with a sweet aroma such that he is pleased; (2) the animal must be perfect and unblemished because God requires nothing short of absolute purity; (3) nothing is returned to the offerer, signifying God's complete ownership; (4) offerings are made publicly as expressions of faith and obedience by those who must be ritually pure before presentation of the object; and (5) blood, the symbol of life of the sacrifice, was poured out on the altar as a means of returning life to the giver of all life."

b. **Fine flour as a grain offering…pressed oil…. And its drink offering**: Together with the lambs for the morning and evening sacrifice, Israel was also commanded to bring these additional offerings. This was to happen every morning and every evening.

i. In these chapters grain, oil, and sometimes drink offerings were commanded for the days and festivals. "The flour is as important as the animal; the wine is as significant as the oil. The sacrifices will not be appropriate if any element is not acceptable or if any element is not in the right proportion." (Allen)

c. **You shall offer in the morning…you shall offer in the evening**: For God's people, it is appropriate to begin and end our day with a statement of trust in God's atonement and expression of our devotion to Him.

i. The psalmist set the example as he sought the LORD in the morning:

- *My voice You shall hear in the morning, O LORD; in the morning I will direct it to You, and I will look up.* (Psalm 5:3)

- *But to You I have cried out, O LORD, and in the morning my prayer comes before You.* (Psalm 88:13)

ii. The psalmist set the example as he sought the LORD in the evening:

- *When I remember You on my bed, I meditate on You in the night watches.* (Psalm 63:6)

- *Let my prayer be set before You as incense, the lifting up of my hands as the evening sacrifice.* (Psalm 141:2)

iii. The psalmist set the example as he sought the LORD all the time:

- *Evening and morning and at noon I will pray, and cry aloud, and He shall hear my voice.* (Psalm 55:17)

iv. Jesus is the example, the Lamb of God who died at the time of the evening sacrifice.

3. (9-10) The Sabbath offering.

'And on the Sabbath day two lambs in their first year, without blemish, and two-tenths *of an ephah* of fine flour as a grain offering, mixed with oil, with its drink offering—*this is* the burnt offering for every Sabbath, besides the regular burnt offering with its drink offering.

a. **And on the Sabbath day two lambs**: Every Sabbath day, a lamb was sacrificed in the morning and in the evening.

b. **Besides the regular burnt offering with its drink offering**: The Sabbath offering was in addition to the daily morning and evening offerings.

4. (11-15) The monthly, new moon offering.

'At the beginnings of your months you shall present a burnt offering to the LORD: two young bulls, one ram, and seven lambs in their first year, without blemish; three-tenths *of an ephah* of fine flour as a grain offering, mixed with oil, for each bull; two-tenths *of an ephah* of fine flour as a grain offering, mixed with oil, for the one ram; and one-tenth *of an ephah* of fine flour, mixed with oil, as a grain offering for each lamb, as a burnt offering of sweet aroma, an offering made by fire to the LORD. Their drink offering shall be half a hin of wine for a bull, one-third of a hin for a ram, and one-fourth of a hin for a lamb; this *is* the burnt offering for each month throughout the months of the year. Also one kid of the goats as a sin offering to the LORD shall be offered, besides the regular burnt offering and its drink offering.

a. **At the beginnings of your months you shall present a burnt offering to the LORD**: Israel marked months by the cycle of the moon. At the start of each month, there was an extensive **burnt offering**, indicating dedication to the LORD.

i. The new moon sacrifice "was an opportunity for family worship (1 Samuel 20:5–6; 2 Kings 4:23) and all trading ceased (Amos 8:5). Like the other Old Testament festivals it prefigured the new age inaugurated by Christ (Colossians 2:16–17; cf. Isaiah 66:23)." (Wenham)

ii. 1 Samuel 20:5-6 also gives an example of how this offering might become part of a monthly feast for the leaders of the nation.

iii. "From other passages it would appear that the trumpets were used on the occasion of every new moon; and there must have been a longer and more elaborate service of festival music to distinguish the seventh." (Watson)

b. **Two young bulls, one ram, and seven lambs**: These significant offerings were accompanied by a **grain offering** and a **drink offering**. This was a significant ceremony marking the start of each month. In addition, there was **one kid of the goats** sacrificed as **a sin offering**.

i. The **one kid of the goats** was to be offered **to the LORD**, "not unto the moon, to which the Gentiles offered it." (Poole)

ii. "Later in Israel's history, the New Moon festivals may have become opportunities for excess, for licentious behavior. In the Prophets there are times when God says to his erring people, 'I hate your New Moons' (cf. Isaiah 1:14)." (Allen)

iii. Isaiah 1:14 shows how these festivals became corrupted: *Your New Moons and your appointed feasts My soul hates; they are a trouble to Me, I am weary of bearing them.* Our observance of the things God commands can turn into empty rituals that weary God instead of honoring Him.

c. **Throughout the months of the year**: There was a progression in the number of sacrifices required – from the day to the week to the month. This was especially true when considering that no required sacrifice canceled out a previous one. Every Sabbath, the daily sacrifice was to be offered. If a new moon began a month on a Sabbath, then on that day all three sacrifices (daily, weekly, monthly) were required.

i. This was a dramatic declaration of the principle that *as time goes on, our need becomes greater, not less.* Our need to receive and respond to God's sacrificial system becomes greater and not less. Our need to surrender completely to the LORD through His appointed sacrifice becomes greater, not less.

ii. "Not only must the worshippers bring gifts – they must bring gifts which were ordained, and in which the necessity for expiation of sin was perpetually recognized. A glance over the whole ground again will show how an increase in the number of sacrifices, and a growing importance in the religious rites, is marked in the growth of time divisions." (Morgan)

B. Offerings related to seasonal feasts.

1. (16-25) Offerings at Passover and the Feast of Unleavened Bread.

'On the fourteenth day of the first month *is* the Passover of the LORD. And on the fifteenth day of this month *is* the feast; unleavened bread shall be eaten for seven days. On the first day *you shall have* a holy

convocation. You shall do no customary work. And you shall present an offering made by fire as a burnt offering to the LORD: two young bulls, one ram, and seven lambs in their first year. Be sure they are without blemish. Their grain offering shall be of fine flour mixed with oil: three-tenths *of an ephah* you shall offer for a bull, and two-tenths for a ram; you shall offer one-tenth *of an ephah* for each of the seven lambs; also one goat *as* a sin offering, to make atonement for you. You shall offer these besides the burnt offering of the morning, which *is* for a regular burnt offering. In this manner you shall offer the food of the offering made by fire daily for seven days, as a sweet aroma to the LORD; it shall be offered besides the regular burnt offering and its drink offering. And on the seventh day you shall have a holy convocation. You shall do no customary work.

a. **On the fourteenth day of the first month is the Passover of the LORD**: On Passover, each household in Israel was to offer a lamb and eat it together in a meal remembering their deliverance from Egypt.

i. "The Passover, the first great feast, a sacrament rather, is merely mentioned in this portion of Numbers. It was chiefly a domestic celebration--not priestly--and had a most impressive significance, of which the eating of the lamb with bitter herbs was the symbol." (Watson)

b. **On the fifteenth day of this month is the feast**: The day after Passover began the **feast** of **unleavened bread**. For seven days, they were to eat nothing that was made with yeast.

i. "The dual commemoration of Passover and Unleavened Bread reflect the dual aspects of the annual fetes, God's paramount salvation event in the deliverance of Israel from Egypt and his sustaining blessing in the spring barley harvest." (Cole)

c. **Two young bulls, one ram, and seven lambs**: These were to be offered **as a burnt offering** at God's altar at the tabernacle, together with a **grain offering** and **one goat as a sin offering** each day through the seven days of the Feast of Unleavened Bread. This was all in addition to **the regular burnt offering and its drink offering**.

d. **You shall have a holy convocation**: These days were marked by a sacred gathering of the people of Israel, and during those days they were to **do no customary work**.

2. (26-31) Offerings at the Feast of Weeks (Pentecost).

'Also on the day of the firstfruits, when you bring a new grain offering to the LORD at your *Feast of* Weeks, you shall have a holy convocation.

You shall do no customary work. You shall present a burnt offering as a sweet aroma to the LORD: two young bulls, one ram, and seven lambs in their first year, with their grain offering of fine flour mixed with oil: three-tenths *of an ephah* **for each bull, two-tenths for the one ram, and one-tenth for each of the seven lambs;** *also* **one kid of the goats, to make atonement for you. Be sure they are without blemish. You shall present** *them* **with their drink offerings, besides the regular burnt offering with its grain offering.**

a. **You shall have a holy convocation**: The **Feast of Weeks** (also known as Pentecost) was also a sacred gathering time for Israel, when they would **do no customary work**.

i. "The Feast of Weeks, also called the day of firstfruits of the wheat harvest (Exodus 34:22).... The highlight of the festival was the priest's waving of the two bread loaves of new grain and the two lambs of the fellowship offering (Leviticus 23:15–21)." (Cole)

b. **Two young bulls, one ram, and seven lambs**: The **Feast of Weeks** had a grain offering associated with it, in thankfulness for the harvest. In addition to that offering, these animals were presented as a **burnt offering**, together with a **grain offering** specifically divided for each sacrifice. Besides all that, they must also offer **one kid of the goats, to make atonement for you**.

i. Even with a feast focused on thanksgiving for the harvest, Israel was still to remember their complete commitment to God in the burnt offerings, and their need for atonement in the sin offerings. God wants His people to live in an ongoing state of dependence on His atoning sacrifice and in surrendered devotion to Him.

ii. **Be sure they are without blemish**: "This is to be understood as applying, not only to the animals, but also to the *flour, wine,* and *oil;* every thing must be *perfect* in its *kind.*" (Clarke)

Numbers 29 – Sacrifices for More of the Appointed Feasts

A. More offerings related to seasonal feasts.

1. (1-6) Offerings at the Feast of Trumpets.

'And in the seventh month, on the first *day* of the month, you shall have a holy convocation. You shall do no customary work. For you it is a day of blowing the trumpets. You shall offer a burnt offering as a sweet aroma to the LORD: one young bull, one ram, *and* seven lambs in their first year, without blemish. Their grain offering *shall be* fine flour mixed with oil: three-tenths *of an ephah* for the bull, two-tenths for the ram, and one-tenth for each of the seven lambs; also one kid of the goats *as* a sin offering, to make atonement for you; besides the burnt offering with its grain offering for the New Moon, the regular burnt offering with its grain offering, and their drink offerings, according to their ordinance, as a sweet aroma, an offering made by fire to the LORD.

a. **It is a day of blowing the trumpets**: The Feast of Trumpets was the third feast regarded as a sacred gathering (**a holy convocation**) and a day to **do no customary work**.

> i. "Later in Jewish tradition this feast became the time of the new year (Rosh Hashanah). The blowing of the trumpet on this feast is the blowing of the shophar, the ram's horn, rather than the silver trumpet of Numbers 10." (Allen)

b. **One young bull, one ram, and seven lambs**: These made up the **burnt offering** to be sacrificed on the Feast of Trumpets, together with a **grain offering** measured to each sacrificial animal and a **sin offering** of **one kid of the goats**.

c. **Besides the burnt offering...for the New Moon, the regular burnt offering**: The special sacrifices made on the Feast of Trumpets did not replace the daily, weekly, or monthly sacrifices mentioned earlier in Numbers 28. Special obligations did not replace normal obligations; they were added to them.

2. (7-11) Offerings on the Day of Atonement.

'On the tenth *day* of this seventh month you shall have a holy convocation. You shall afflict your souls; you shall not do any work. You shall present a burnt offering to the LORD *as* a sweet aroma: one young bull, one ram, *and* seven lambs in their first year. Be sure they are without blemish. Their grain offering *shall be of* fine flour mixed with oil: three-tenths *of an ephah* for the bull, two-tenths for the one ram, and one-tenth for each of the seven lambs; also one kid of the goats *as* a sin offering, besides the sin offering for atonement, the regular burnt offering with its grain offering, and their drink offerings.

a. **On the tenth day of this seventh month**: The sacrificial ceremonies for the Day of Atonement are described in Leviticus 16. The high priest was to sacrifice one bull, two rams, and two goats. In addition, God here commanded the sacrifice of **one young bull, one ram, and seven lambs** together with the appropriate **grain offering** and the offering of **one kid of the goats as a sin offering**. All this was **besides the sin offering for atonement** and the normal daily **burnt offering with its grain offering, and their drink offerings**.

b. **You shall afflict your souls**: The Day of Atonement was not a happy feast. It was a day to carefully consider the burden of sin, and to put it away on a national basis through the appointed sacrifice for that day.

i. The command to **afflict your souls** was to show the humility and repentance appropriate for those who need forgiveness. It was also an identification with the sacrifice for sin. Afflicting the soul brought the Israelite into sympathy with the afflicted sacrificial victim, even as the believer identifies with Jesus Christ on the cross. Throughout history and to the modern day, Jews who do observe the Day of Atonement (Yom Kippur) typically fast for that day to **afflict** the **soul**.

ii. "The term translated 'deny' [**afflict**] (*ana*) means 'to afflict, oppress, be humble, or be lowly' and is used occasionally in the context of fasting (Ezra 8:21). This latter means of self-denial became the principal means of individual participation during the late postexilic period, when the day became known as 'The Fast.'" (Cole)

iii. **Afflict your souls**: "i. e. yourselves, by fasting and abstinence from all delightful things, and by compunction and bitter sorrow for your sins, and the judgments of God either deserved by you or inflicted upon you for your sins." (Poole)

3. (12-39) Offerings at the Feast of Tabernacles.

'On the fifteenth day of the seventh month you shall have a holy convocation. You shall do no customary work, and you shall keep a feast to the LORD seven days. You shall present a burnt offering, an offering made by fire as a sweet aroma to the LORD: thirteen young bulls, two rams, *and* fourteen lambs in their first year. They shall be without blemish. Their grain offering *shall be of* fine flour mixed with oil: three-tenths *of an ephah* for each of the thirteen bulls, two-tenths for each of the two rams, and one-tenth for each of the fourteen lambs; also one kid of the goats *as* a sin offering, besides the regular burnt offering, its grain offering, and its drink offering.

'On the second day *present* twelve young bulls, two rams, fourteen lambs in their first year without blemish, and their grain offering and their drink offerings for the bulls, for the rams, and for the lambs, by their number, according to the ordinance; also one kid of the goats *as* a sin offering, besides the regular burnt offering with its grain offering, and their drink offerings.

'On the third day *present* eleven bulls, two rams, fourteen lambs in their first year without blemish, and their grain offering and their drink offerings for the bulls, for the rams, and for the lambs, by their number, according to the ordinance; also one goat *as* a sin offering, besides the regular burnt offering, its grain offering, and its drink offering.

'On the fourth day *present* ten bulls, two rams, *and* fourteen lambs in their first year, without blemish, and their grain offering and their drink offerings for the bulls, for the rams, and for the lambs, by their number, according to the ordinance; also one kid of the goats *as* a sin offering, besides the regular burnt offering, its grain offering, and its drink offering.

'On the fifth day *present* nine bulls, two rams, *and* fourteen lambs in their first year without blemish, and their grain offering and their drink offerings for the bulls, for the rams, and for the lambs, by their number, according to the ordinance; also one goat *as* a sin offering, besides the regular burnt offering, its grain offering, and its drink offering.

'On the sixth day *present* eight bulls, two rams, *and* fourteen lambs in their first year without blemish, and their grain offering and their drink offerings for the bulls, for the rams, and for the lambs, by their number, according to the ordinance; also one goat *as* a sin offering, besides the regular burnt offering, its grain offering, and its drink offering.

'On the seventh day *present* seven bulls, two rams, *and* fourteen lambs in their first year without blemish, and their grain offering and their drink offerings for the bulls, for the rams, and for the lambs, by their number, according to the ordinance; also one goat *as* a sin offering, besides the regular burnt offering, its grain offering, and its drink offering.

'On the eighth day you shall have a sacred assembly. You shall do no customary work. You shall present a burnt offering, an offering made by fire as a sweet aroma to the LORD: one bull, one ram, seven lambs in their first year without blemish, and their grain offering and their drink offerings for the bull, for the ram, and for the lambs, by their number, according to the ordinance; also one goat *as* a sin offering, besides the regular burnt offering, its grain offering, and its drink offering.

'These you shall present to the LORD at your appointed feasts (besides your vowed offerings and your freewill offerings) as your burnt offerings and your grain offerings, as your drink offerings and your peace offerings.'"

a. **Thirteen young bulls, two rams, and fourteen lambs**: This was the required offering on the first day of the Feast of Tabernacles, together with the **grain offering** and a **kid of the goats as a sin offering**. This was in addition to the **regular burnt offering, its grain offering, and its drink offering**.

i. "In the NT the Feast of Booths is mentioned in John 7:2, 37. It was on the last, the most significant day of the feast, that Jesus stood in the temple in Jerusalem and invited the spiritually thirsty to come to him (John 7:37–38)." (Allen)

b. **Twelve young bulls, two rams, and fourteen lambs**: This was the required offering on the second day of the Feast of Tabernacles. One less bull was required, but the same number of **rams**, **lambs**, and appropriate grain offerings. This number diminished by one for each day of the Feast of Tabernacles, until the **seventh day**, when **seven bulls** were presented. On the final day of the feast – the **eighth day – one bull, one ram**, and **seven lambs** were offered.

i. "Hereby the Holy Ghost might teach them their duty, to grow in grace and increase in sanctification, that their sins decreasing, the number of their sacrifices, whereby atonement was made for their sins, should also decrease daily. Or it might signify a diminishing and wearing away of the legal offerings." (Trapp)

c. **And their drink offerings**: This was commanded to be added to the offerings on the second day and continued to the eighth day. There is no clear reason why no mention was made of the drink offering for the first day (apart from the regular daily drink offering).

d. **On the eighth day you shall have a sacred assembly**: Both the first and eighth days of the Feast of Tabernacles were days of sacred gathering for the people of Israel.

i. **On the eighth day**: "In the first century A.D. the Pharisees practiced a ritual of carrying a large golden flagon of fresh spring water, drawn from the Pool of Siloam, paraded ceremonially through the city to the Temple, and where it was then poured out as a libation offering to God upon the sacrificial altar. In this ritual, water, which was a symbol of life throughout the ancient world, would be poured out unto God in thanksgiving for the rains of the past year and in prayerful anticipation of that with which he would bless the people. Jesus utilized the imagery conveyed in this ceremony to teach an amazing lesson regarding himself. He was the true source of life symbolized in the living water." (Cole)

ii. **The eighth day**: "This was the last and great day of the feast, as it is called John 7:37, and yet the sacrifices were fewer than any other day, to teach them not to trust to the multitude of their sacrifices, nor to expect remission of sins from them, but from the one and only sacrifice of Christ." (Poole)

e. **These you shall present to the LORD at your appointed feasts**: God required so many animals and such expensive sacrifices because the Feast of Tabernacles was a happy memorial of God's faithfulness to Israel during the Exodus. The sacrifice of so many animals was a demonstration of the richness of God's provision to them through the years in the wilderness.

B. The obedience of Israel.

1. (40a) Moses tells the children of Israel the words of the LORD.

So Moses told the children of Israel everything,

a. **So Moses told the children of Israel everything**: As Israel was now on the threshold of the Promised Land, they needed to be reminded of the essential place of sacrifice. As part of the covenant God made with Israel at Mount Sinai, it could not be ignored or rejected.

b. **Everything**: These commanded offerings bathed every day, week, month, and year in sacrificial submission, surrender, and honor to God.

i. "Thus the whole year was covered and conditioned by these solemn religious ceremonies. Every day as it broke and passed, every week as it began, every month as it opened, every year both as it commenced and closed was sealed with sacred matters which ever spoke to the people about the relation they bore to God, as based on sacrifice and expressing itself in service." (Morgan)

2. (40b) A costly obedience.

Just as the LORD commanded Moses.

a. **Just as the LORD commanded**: For Israel to obey what God commanded in Numbers 28 and 29, it meant that every year, the priests sacrificed at least 1,086 lambs, 113 bulls, 32 rams, more than a ton of flour, and some 1,000 bottles of oil and wine on behalf of the nation.

i. Numerically speaking, the most prominent animal of sacrifice was the lamb. This is an obvious prophetic reference to Jesus, who is *the Lamb of God who takes away the sin of the world.* (John 1:29)

ii. "All sacrifices—whether of the morning or evening, of Sabbath or New Moon—have their ultimate meaning in the death the Savior died. Apart from his death, these sacrifices were just the killing of animals and the burning of their flesh with attendant ceremonies." (Allen)

b. **Just as the LORD commanded**: All this sacrifice did not include the sacrifices made by individuals or households. The priests and Levites were clearly busy with the job of sacrifice, and it was fulfilled at considerable expense.

i. In the days of Jesus, there is a record of 255,600 Passover lambs being sacrificed at one Passover just by individuals and households.

ii. Significantly, *none of it was enough!* Not one of these hundreds of thousands of sacrifices over the centuries could ever take away a person's sin; that had to wait until a perfect sacrifice was offered – the sacrifice of Jesus.

Numbers 30 – The Keeping of Vows

A. The requirement to keep vows.

1. (1) Moses speaks to the leaders of the tribes.

Then Moses spoke to the heads of the tribes concerning the children of Israel, saying, "This *is* the thing which the LORD has commanded:

a. **Moses spoke to the heads of the tribes**: This instruction was given to the leaders of the tribes of Israel, for them to communicate to all the others in Israel.

2. (2) The command of the LORD regarding vows.

If a man makes a vow to the LORD, or swears an oath to bind himself by some agreement, he shall not break his word; he shall do according to all that proceeds out of his mouth."

a. **If a man makes a vow to the LORD**: A vow made to God is no small thing. God commanded that His people should be careful to keep their vows and to fulfill every oath they made. Psalm 15:4 describes the godly man as the one *who swears to his own hurt and does not change*.

i. "Vows either took the form of a promise to give something to God, usually a sacrifice, or a pledge to abstain from something." (Wenham)

ii. Some people believe, usually based on Matthew 5:34-37, that vows or oaths are not permitted for God's people today. But what Jesus said in the Sermon on the Mount regarding oaths was an emphasis on truth-telling and honesty, not an absolute prohibition of every oath. The Bible shows us that oaths are permitted under certain circumstances if they are not abused and used as a cover for deception.

- God Himself swears oaths: Hebrews 6:13 and Luke 1:73.

- Jesus spoke under oath in a court: Matthew 26:63-64.

- Paul made oaths: Romans 1:9, 2 Corinthians 1:23, Galatians 1:20, 1 Thessalonians 2:5.

iii. Wenham notes that vows are often made by people in the Bible (as in Genesis 28:20–22, Numbers 21:2, Judges 11:30ff., 1 Samuel 1:11 and 14:24, Jonah 1:16 and 2:9, Acts 18:18, and 21:23), sometimes in a plea for God's help. Wenham also notes the common tendency: "But when the crisis passes and the prayer is answered, there is a temptation to forget the vow."

iv. **If a man makes a vow to the LORD**: John Trapp observed that this shows that "God is the proper object of a vow," not angels or saints. In Trapp's words, to vow to such "is sacrilege, yea, it is idolatry."

b. **He shall not break his word; he shall do according to all that proceeds out of his mouth**: Because God holds us to account for the vows that we make, sometimes it is better not to make a vow (Ecclesiastes 5:4-5).

i. **He shall not break his word**: "Hebrew, *not pollute* or *profane his word*, as the same phrase is used, Psalm 55:20; 89:34, i. e. not render his word, and consequently himself, profane, or vile and contemptible in the eyes of others." (Poole)

ii. A commonly overlooked and unappreciated sin among God's people is the sin of *broken vows* – promising things to God and failing to live up to the vow. Under the old covenant, it was commanded to make an offering to atone for the breaking of vows (Leviticus 5:4). Therefore, those who honor God:

- Will not be quick to make vows to God, especially unwise vows.
- Will be serious about fulfilling vows that they do make.
- Will regard broken vows as sins to be confessed and to be repented of.

iii. There is a regular vow we all can and should make – a vow to praise God:

- *Vows made to You are binding upon me, O God; I will render praises to You.* (Psalm 56:12)
- *So I will sing praise to Your name forever, that I may daily perform my vows.* (Psalm 61:8)

B. Vows that may not be binding.

1. (3-5) A young woman within her father's household.

"Or if a woman makes a vow to the LORD, and binds *herself* by some agreement while in her father's house in her youth, and her father hears

her vow and the agreement by which she has bound herself, and her father holds his peace, then all her vows shall stand, and every agreement with which she has bound herself shall stand. But if her father overrules her on the day that he hears, then none of her vows nor her agreements by which she has bound herself shall stand; and the LORD will release her, because her father overruled her.

a. **If a woman makes a vow to the LORD**: This command refers to a woman who is young and unmarried, still living with her parents (**while in her father's house in her youth**).

b. **Her father holds his peace, then all her vows shall stand**: The vows of a young woman in such circumstances were subject to review or approval by **her father**. He could approve of her vow by silence, with silence being understood as agreement.

i. Significantly, women were able to make vows and have a direct dealing with God. Even young women (with the approval of their father) could make promises to God, vow offerings to Him, or pledge seasons of self-denial to the LORD. "The very fact that women were making vows in this antique age is a step of great significance." (Allen)

c. **If her father overrules her on the day that he hears, then none of her vows...shall stand**: The father of a young woman in such circumstances also had the right to disapprove of his daughter's vows, and to declare the vow invalid.

2. (6-8) A new wife's vow overruled by her husband.

"**If indeed she takes a husband, while bound by her vows or by a rash utterance from her lips by which she bound herself, and her husband hears *it,* and makes no response to her on the day that he hears, then her vows shall stand, and her agreements by which she bound herself shall stand. But if her husband overrules her on the day that he hears *it,* he shall make void her vow which she took and what she uttered with her lips, by which she bound herself, and the LORD will release her.**

a. **If indeed she takes a husband**: The woman considered in verses 3-5 is now considered as if she had become married. In such cases, her new husband had the right to approve **her vows** and he could accept them by his silence (**makes no response to her on the day that he hears**).

i. **If indeed she takes a husband** "suggests that the woman might have made a vow and then subsequently have become married. That she might be released from such a vow is greatly liberating both to her and to her husband. He might not want to take on a obligation that she

has entered into before they were married. This is a protective clause."
(Allen)

ii. "When she marries, she is removed into her husband's house, Ruth
1:9." (Poole)

b. **If her husband overrules her on the day that he hears it, he shall
make void her vow which she took**: If a husband objected to vows made
by his wife, he had the right to overrule her. God considered the wife
released from such disapproved vows (**the LORD will release her**).

i. **On the day that he hears it**: "And it is hereby intimated, that the day
or time he had for disallowing her vow was not to be reckoned from
her vowing, but from his hearing or knowledge of her vow." (Poole)

ii. "The husband, as the male authority figure in the relationship, may
choose from several courses of action: (1) permit the vow or oath to
remain in effect by default—no action, (2) negate the obligation, or
(3) affirm the commitment by word or deed." (Cole)

3. (9) A widow or a divorced woman is bound by her vows.

**"Also any vow of a widow or a divorced woman, by which she has bound
herself, shall stand against her.**

a. **Any vow of a widow or a divorced woman**: Here the case of a woman
who was neither in her father's house (as in verses 3-5) nor married (as in
verses 6-8) was considered.

i. That the **widow** and the **divorced woman** have the same status
regarding the making of vows is significant. "Some people claim
that divorce in biblical times was only a certain legal fiction, that the
woman was always to be considered the wife of the husband who
had dismissed her.... Yet this verse clearly indicates that a divorced
woman…has the legal status of one who is a widow (*almanah*). She has
become an independent agent. Like the widow, her former husband is
in a sense 'dead' to her." (Allen)

b. **By which she has bound herself**: Such vows made by a woman not
living with her parents and not married to a husband were considered
binding. Any vows she made **shall stand against her**.

i. "A woman who was no longer under the patriarchal authority of her
father or her husband, whether by his death or by divorce, possessed
the same status and responsibility of a man with regard to vows and
obligations." (Cole)

4. (10-16) A wife's vow confirmed by her husband.

"If she vowed in her husband's house, or bound herself by an agreement with an oath, and her husband heard *it*, and made no response to her *and* did not overrule her, then all her vows shall stand, and every agreement by which she bound herself shall stand. But if her husband truly made them void on the day he heard *them*, then whatever proceeded from her lips concerning her vows or concerning the agreement binding her, it shall not stand; her husband has made them void, and the LORD will release her. Every vow and every binding oath to afflict her soul, her husband may confirm it, or her husband may make it void. Now if her husband makes no response whatever to her from day to day, then he confirms all her vows or all the agreements that bind her; he confirms them, because he made no response to her on the day that he heard *them*. But if he does make them void after he has heard *them*, then he shall bear her guilt."

These *are* the statutes which the LORD commanded Moses, between a man and his wife, and between a father and his daughter in her youth in her father's house.

a. **If she vowed in her husband's house**: Verses 6-8 have in mind the vows that a newly married woman carried into her marriage. Verses 10-15 have in mind vows made by a woman in her married state. As before, if the husband confirmed his wife's vow (either by silence or by specific approval), then *he* was responsible to make sure the vow was fulfilled (**he shall bear her guilt**).

i. "Hannah, Samuel's mother, provides a classic example of a woman who took upon herself a Nazirite vow of dedication and self-denial, which Elkanah her husband allowed to come to fulfillment by taking no action. Her vow was completed when she presented her son to Eli the priest for service of the Lord and offered sacrifices of bull, flour, and wine (1 Sam 1:3–28)." (Cole)

ii. "*He shall bear her iniquity* means he will suffer for the broken vow as though it were his." (Wenham)

b. **Every vow and every binding oath to afflict her soul, her husband may confirm it, or her husband may make it void**: This was an outworking of the principle of headship. When God declares someone to be in a position of rightful authority and others are expected to submit to that authority, the head is accountable before God for the result. When God grants authority, He also commands accountability.

i. "These regulations establish the headship of the father and the husband in regard to matters which belong to religion. And the significance of them lies in this, that no intrusion of the priest is permitted…. the father or husband was the family head and the judge. No countenance whatever is given to any official interference." (Watson)

ii. "They are of the utmost importance, as they reveal the Divine conception of the necessity for the maintenance of the unity of the family. In no family must there be two supreme authorities; and here, as always in the Divine arrangement, the headship is vested in the husband and father. It can easily be seen how, were this otherwise, through religious vows and discord probably disruption in family life would ensue. The measure in which modern society has departed from this ideal, is the measure of its insecurity." (Morgan)

Numbers 31 – Vengeance on Midian

A. The command to destroy the Midianites and its fulfillment.

1. (1-2) God commands Israel to take vengeance on the Midianites.

And the LORD spoke to Moses, saying: "Take vengeance on the Midianites for the children of Israel. Afterward you shall be gathered to your people."

a. **Take vengeance on the Midianites**: The Midianites were a nomadic people associated with the people of Moab in Numbers 25. God commanded that they be attacked in retribution for their part in the seduction of Israel into sexual immorality and idolatry.

i. "The Midianites were a large confederation of tribes, associated with various smaller groups.... They roamed through the arid lands of the Sinai, the Negeb and Transjordan. Here it is those Midianites associated with Moab that are picked out for vengeance." (Wenham)

ii. The emphasis is on the fact that **the LORD spoke to Moses** in initiating this attack. This wasn't about personal revenge, the conquest of territory, or the lust for plunder. "The war is announced by the Lord, not Moses. The war was not regarded by Moses as motivated by petty jealousy. It was 'the Lord's vengeance' because of the wickedness of the Midianites, who caused the seduction of the Israelites in the pagan worship system of Baal of Peor." (Allen)

iii. Because it was specifically commanded by the LORD, this was also a test of Israel's obedience. "The second generation of Israel, now poised in the plains of Moab opposite Jericho, was facing the same moral, ethical, and spiritual dilemma that the first generation had faced in the wilderness. Would they be faithful to their unique covenant relationship with Yahweh their God or succumb to the temptations that lay ever before them?" (Cole)

iv. "The Moabites also were guilty, but God out of his own good pleasure, and in kindness to Lot, was pleased to spare them, the rather, because the measure of their iniquity was not yet full." (Poole)

b. **Take vengeance**: We are often uncomfortable with the idea of vengeance because it doesn't seem consistent with God's love. Yet, in the right context, **vengeance** is something good that God pursues.

i. The Scriptures repeatedly speak of the vengeance of *God* as a positive thing. Evil comes with the vengeance of *man*. "That Moses was directed by God to 'take vengeance' (NIV, NKJV) on the Midianites reflects one side of the Hebrew verb *nqm*, which can also mean 'vindication.' God directs his vengeance against the immoral, idolatrous, and unjust; and yet his vengeance is often self-limiting according to his great mercy." (Cole)

ii. In this circumstance, Israel was in a unique role – with a special call to be an instrument of God's vengeance upon the varied people of and near Canaan. This is something no individual, acting on their own authority, can rightly take upon themselves today. There is also no community defined as the people of God (such as a church congregation or denomination) that has the same unique place that ancient Israel had in God's plan.

iii. While God has not called the church as His instrument of vengeance, God has ordained certain instruments of society (such as government) to take vengeance on evildoers (Romans 13:1-4).

c. **Afterward you shall be gathered**: Moses did die some months after this. He did not die immediately **afterward**, but this was something that had to be accomplished before his work could be considered complete.

2. (3-5) Moses organizes the army to battle against the Midianites.

So Moses spoke to the people, saying, "Arm some of yourselves for war, and let them go against the Midianites to take vengeance for the LORD on Midian. A thousand from each tribe of all the tribes of Israel you shall send to the war."

So there were recruited from the divisions of Israel one thousand from *each* **tribe, twelve thousand armed for war.**

a. **Arm some of yourselves for war**: Moses promptly obeyed what God told Israel to do.

i. "Degrading idolatry was to be held in abhorrence, and those who clung to it suppressed. Now the time comes for an exterminating war. While hordes of Bedawin occupy the hills and the neighbouring desert, there can be no security either for morals, property, or life. Balaam is among them plotting against Israel; and his restless energy, we may suppose, precipitates the conflict." (Watson)

b. **A thousand from each tribe of all tribes of Israel you shall send to the war**: This was something God called Israel to do together as a people, not just a few individual tribes. God wanted them to think and act as a unified people, despite their tribal differences.

3. (6-11) The battle fought, Midian defeated, and spoil taken.

Then Moses sent them to the war, one thousand from *each* tribe; he sent them to the war with Phinehas the son of Eleazar the priest, with the holy articles and the signal trumpets in his hand. And they warred against the Midianites, just as the LORD commanded Moses, and they killed all the males. They killed the kings of Midian with *the rest of* those who were killed—Evi, Rekem, Zur, Hur, and Reba, the five kings of Midian. Balaam the son of Beor they also killed with the sword.

And the children of Israel took the women of Midian captive, with their little ones, and took as spoil all their cattle, all their flocks, and all their goods. They also burned with fire all the cities where they dwelt, and all their forts. And they took all the spoil and all the booty; of man and beast.

a. **He sent them to war with Phinehas the son of Eleazar the priest, with the holy articles and the signal trumpets in his hand**: Significantly, the priests went with the nation into this battle, and the priests went with **the holy articles**. This was unusual and marked this, in a unique way, as God's battle.

i. "Who then was general? *Joshua*, without doubt, though not here mentioned, because the battle being the Lord's, he alone is to have the supreme direction, and all the glory." (Clarke)

ii. **Holy articles**: "Commentators cannot decide whether this means 'with the ark' (cf. Joshua 6:6; 1 Samuel 4), or with *the trumpets of alarm* (10:1–10; Joshua 6), or 'wearing priestly garments' (*keli*, 'vessel' [**articles**], means 'garment' in Deuteronomy 22:5)." (Wenham)

b. **And they warred against the Midianites**: According to the custom of the day, all the males were killed, and the women and children were taken as slaves, with all the possessions being taken as spoil.

i. **Just as the LORD commanded Moses**: This phrase is repeated four times in this chapter (also in verses 31, 41, and 47). There is a strong emphasis on the idea that this was the LORD's battle, not Israel's.

ii. **Killed all the males**: "The report that they 'killed every man' does not necessarily mean that they killed every individual but that there was a complete defeat, with a focus on the males of the enemy army who were slain. Some of the enemies must have fled. The emphasis in this report is that they killed the men only." (Allen)

c. **Evi, Rekem, Zur, Hur, and Reba, the five kings of Midian**: The name of **Zur** is of some interest. He was the father of Cozbi (Numbers 25:15), the Midianite woman who so flagrantly drew an Israelite man into immorality and idolatry at the very tabernacle itself and was killed with a spear by Phinehas. Cozbi, coming from such a powerful family, was probably something of a priestess of Baal.

d. **Balaam the son of Beor they also killed with the sword**: Balaam, who had suggested the strategy to seduce Israel into sexual immorality and idolatry, and who did it all for money, was now dead. The vengeance of God judged him, and whatever money he gained was no longer of any benefit to him.

i. This was the *error of Balaam for profit* mentioned in Jude 1:11. Balaam was in *error* to do evil against God and His people for the sake of money. When the vengeance of God came against Midian, this error cost him his life.

ii. "Balaam's name, amid the recital of the names of the Midianite kings, suggests that he was their advisor, their spiritual guru. Always after a shekel, Balaam had a new gig." (Allen)

iii. In Numbers 23:10 Balaam spoke of this desire: *Let me die the death of the righteous, and let my end be like his!* But Balaam had no interest in living the life of the righteous, so he died the death of the wicked, in the company of those under God's judgment.

B. The division of the spoil.

1. (12-20) Moses becomes angry when Israel keeps the women of Midian, following the attack against Midian.

Then they brought the captives, the booty, and the spoil to Moses, to Eleazar the priest, and to the congregation of the children of Israel, to the camp in the plains of Moab by the Jordan, *across from* Jericho. And Moses, Eleazar the priest, and all the leaders of the congregation, went to meet them outside the camp. But Moses was angry with the officers of the army, *with* the captains over thousands and captains over hundreds, who had come from the battle.

And Moses said to them: "Have you kept all the women alive? Look, these *women* caused the children of Israel, through the counsel of Balaam, to trespass against the Lord in the incident of Peor, and there was a plague among the congregation of the Lord. Now therefore, kill every male among the little ones, and kill every woman who has known a man intimately. But keep alive for yourselves all the young girls who have not known a man intimately. And as for you, remain outside the camp seven days; whoever has killed any person, and whoever has touched any slain, purify yourselves and your captives on the third day and on the seventh day. Purify every garment, everything made of leather, everything woven of goats' *hair,* and everything made of wood."

a. **Have you kept all the women alive?** Moses was angry because the children of Israel failed to see the great danger of sexual immorality and idolatry posed by these women who before had led the men of Israel into these exact sins.

i. God's people may be deceived by things that *were* a threat, but do not seem to be a *present* danger. The Israelite **officers of the army** thought these women were safe, but they were more dangerous to Israel than an army of mighty warriors. Israel could overcome mighty warriors if they were spiritually strong; but if they were seduced into immorality and idolatry, they would certainly fall.

ii. "Moses was wroth with the officers, not because of the severity of the judgment they had executed on Midian, but rather because they had failed to carry out the judgment completely." (Morgan)

iii. We often think of many things as dangerous to us as the people of God – hostile government, secular humanism, academic attack, and so forth. But when God's people accept things among them that open the door to immorality and idolatry, this can be a much greater danger than any of those other things.

b. **Keep alive for yourselves all the young girls who have not known a man intimately**: Therefore, all the women who had **known a man intimately** were to be killed. But ones who were not related to the immorality and idolatry of the Midianites could be kept alive.

i. "Women who had known men sexually, whether Midianite or sinful Israelite men, were to be considered unclean, since they were the main instrument of Israel's demise at Baal Peor. Only the young girls would be allowed to live so that they may be taken as wives or slaves by the Israelite men, according to the principles of holy war (Deut 20:13–14; 21:10–14). By this they could be brought under the umbrella of the covenant community of faith." (Cole)

ii. **Who have not known a man**: "As far as they could conjecture by their age." (Trapp)

c. **Every male among the little ones**: These also had to be killed. This was harsh but done with the understanding that in that ancient culture, the boys would have grown into men with the solemn responsibility to avenge their fathers' death and to perpetuate Midianite culture – which was under God's judgment.

i. This was a strong, even harsh judgment against the Midianites. It did not wipe them out as a people, because they are often found later as enemies of Israel (as in Judges 6).

ii. God has the right to judge not only individuals but also communities of all different sizes. Such judgments go beyond punishing individuals for their personal guilt; judgment comes upon the society as a whole, including those who may not be personally and individually guilty (such as children; the **little ones**). Sometimes God sends these judgments directly (as in the Genesis flood or with Sodom and Gomorrah), and sometimes God sends nations as instruments of His judgment (as with the Assyrians against the northern kingdom of Israel and the Babylonians against the southern kingdom of Judah). In the broader conquest of Canaan, God uniquely used His people (Israel) as that instrument of judgment.

iii. This harsh judgment often makes us uncomfortable but is rooted in both God's fundamental right to judge (Psalm 9:8, 50:6), and in His merciful granting of much time for people to repent (Genesis 15:16). We can trust that God is a righteous judge (Genesis 18:25, Psalm 7:11).

iv. "For this action I account simply on the principle that God, who is the author and supporter of life, has a right to dispose of it *when* and *how* he thinks proper; and the Judge of all the earth can do nothing but what is *right*." (Clarke)

v. "The nations today are at risk from the judgment of God. This is true whether they acknowledge it or not. One day that judgment will come. At that time there will be no weeping over women and boys who died in ancient Midian three and a half millennia ago; at that time the judgment of God will transcend anything ever written in the harshest Scripture." (Allen)

d. **As for you, remain outside the camp seven days**: Israel's soldiers were triumphant and carried out God's will in attacking and defeating these Midianites. Yet, their carrying out of God's will involved much death, so the soldiers were commanded to wait **seven days** before coming back into the camp of Israel.

> i. "Over every war, however glorious its outcome from the victor's point of view, hangs the shadow of death. These purification rules reminded Israel that the death of one's fellow men was a catastrophic disruption of God's creation, even though in some cases it was the Creator himself who demanded the execution of the sinner." (Wenham)

e. **Purify every garment, everything made of leather, everything woven of goats' hair, and everything made of wood**: As well, anything of the Midianites and the spoil taken from them had to be purified. Then it could be used. This was also the case in some of Israel's later wars of judgment against the Canaanites – some of the plunder could be accepted, but not by individuals (Joshua 6:18-19).

> i. There is some application of this principle among the people of God today. They must properly discern what aspects of the culture can be "plundered," "purified," and used among God's people. They must also properly discern what aspects of the culture have no place at all among God's people and must be "destroyed."

2. (21-24) The purification of the spoil.

Then Eleazar the priest said to the men of war who had gone to the battle, "This *is* the ordinance of the law which the LORD commanded Moses: Only the gold, the silver, the bronze, the iron, the tin, and the lead, everything that can endure fire, you shall put through the fire, and it shall be clean; and it shall be purified with the water of purification. But all that cannot endure fire you shall put through water. And you shall wash your clothes on the seventh day and be clean, and afterward you may come into the camp."

a. **Everything that can endure fire, you shall put through the fire, and it shall be clean**: All the material spoil had to either be purified by fire or cleansed with water. Only then was it fit for use among the people of God.

> i. "The great aim of this enactment was to render these articles ceremonially clean. They had been in the use of the Midianites, and required cleansing, before they could be appropriated by Israel. But the cleansing processes were to be determined by their texture. Fire for what would stand fire; water for what could not stand fire." (Meyer)

b. **Fire...and it shall be purified with the water of purification**: Things that would be destroyed by passing through fire could be purified with **the water of purification**, which seems to be the water in which the ashes of the red heifer were sprinkled (Numbers 19).

i. This is a pattern of how God uses **fire** and **water** to purify His people today – the fire of pressing difficulty and the water of God's pure word.

ii. When God uses the fire of purification, we can say with Job: *When He has tested me, I shall come forth as gold* (Job 23:10). The fire purifies precious metal by causing the impurities (the dross) to rise to the top, where the refiner can skim them away. The refiner can tell when the gold is pure because he can then see his reflection in the pool of gold.

iii. When God wants to wash us clean, He not only uses the waters of baptism, but also the ministry of His word as described in Ephesians 5:26: *That He might sanctify and cleanse her with the washing of water by the word.*

3. (25-54) The spoil is divided among the soldiers and the nation at large.

Now the LORD spoke to Moses, saying: "Count up the plunder that was taken—of man and beast—you and Eleazar the priest and the chief fathers of the congregation; and divide the plunder into two parts, between those who took part in the war, who went out to battle, and all the congregation. And levy a tribute for the LORD on the men of war who went out to battle: one of every five hundred of the persons, the cattle, the donkeys, and the sheep; take *it* from their half, and give *it* to Eleazar the priest as a heave offering to the LORD. And from the children of Israel's half you shall take one of every fifty, drawn from the persons, the cattle, the donkeys, and the sheep, from all the livestock, and give them to the Levites who keep charge of the tabernacle of the LORD." So Moses and Eleazar the priest did as the LORD commanded Moses.

The booty remaining from the plunder, which the men of war had taken, was six hundred and seventy-five thousand sheep, seventy-two thousand cattle, sixty-one thousand donkeys, and thirty-two thousand persons in all, of women who had not known a man intimately. And the half, the portion for those who had gone out to war, was in number three hundred and thirty-seven thousand five hundred sheep; and the LORD's tribute of the sheep was six hundred and seventy-five. The cattle *were* thirty-six thousand, of which the LORD's tribute *was* seventy-two. The donkeys *were* thirty thousand five hundred, of which the LORD's tribute *was* sixty-one. The persons *were* sixteen thousand, of which the LORD's tribute *was* thirty-two persons. So Moses gave the tribute *which was* the LORD's heave offering to Eleazar the priest, as the LORD commanded Moses.

And from the children of Israel's half, which Moses separated from the men who fought—now the half belonging to the congregation was

three hundred and thirty-seven thousand five hundred sheep, thirty-six thousand cattle, thirty thousand five hundred donkeys, and sixteen thousand persons—and from the children of Israel's half Moses took one of every fifty, drawn from man and beast, and gave them to the Levites, who kept charge of the tabernacle of the LORD, as the LORD commanded Moses.

Then the officers who *were* over thousands of the army, the captains of thousands and captains of hundreds, came near to Moses; and they said to Moses, "Your servants have taken a count of the men of war who *are* under our command, and not a man of us is missing. Therefore we have brought an offering for the LORD, what every man found of ornaments of gold: armlets and bracelets and signet rings and earrings and necklaces, to make atonement for ourselves before the LORD." So Moses and Eleazar the priest received the gold from them, all the fashioned ornaments. And all the gold of the offering that they offered to the LORD, from the captains of thousands and captains of hundreds, was sixteen thousand seven hundred and fifty shekels. (The men of war had taken spoil, every man for himself.) And Moses and Eleazar the priest received the gold from the captains of thousands and of hundreds, and brought it into the tabernacle of meeting as a memorial for the children of Israel before the LORD.

a. **Divide the plunder into two parts, between those who took part in the war, who went out to battle, and all the congregation**: Customarily, the spoil belonged to the soldiers alone. Here, God commanded that the **plunder** be divided between the soldiers and the congregation, with a portion given to the LORD from each.

i. "The booty is equally divided between the people and the soldiers; a five-hundredth part being given to the Lord, and a fiftieth part to the Levites." (Clarke)

b. **The half belonging to the congregation was three hundred and thirty-seven thousand five hundred sheep, thirty-six thousand cattle**: This accounting of spoil from the defeat of the Midianites shows a remarkable amount of plunder. The numbers are so large that some commentators wonder if an error was made in the copying of the text. If this is the case or not, this was a significant bonus for Israel to gain as they prepared to enter Canaan.

i. "The listing of the plunder as a whole is given in vv.32–35. The numbers were enormous; the victory was staggering. This was just the beginning; on the other side of the Jordan lay the rest of the land of God's promise." (Allen)

ii. "It has been suggested that in all probability some of the actual numbers in this chapter are inaccurate, that in the process of translation and copying, mistakes have been made. That is quite possible. It is, however, a matter of no real moment." (Morgan)

c. **Your servants have taken a count of the men of war who are under our command, and not a man of us is missing**: Israel's officers made this remarkable report to Moses and Eleazar. They took 12,000 men to battle against the Midianites, and **not a man of** them was **missing**.

i. "This wondrous indication of Yahweh's providence and protection would provide the armies of Israel with assurance and confidence for the coming campaigns in the land of Canaan." (Cole)

ii. "We have no reason to believe that the protection of the lives of every soldier in the wars of Israel ever happened again. This must have been a solitary act in the history of Israel." (Allen)

d. **All the gold of the offering that they offered to the LORD**: This was a special gift from the officers, made in gratitude for God's remarkable protection of Israel's army. This generous gift belonged to the LORD and would be used as **a memorial** and in the service of the tabernacle. The new generation of Israel, soon to take the Promised Land, was showing itself to be generous – in contrast to the generation of their fathers that perished in the wilderness.

i. **Sixteen thousand seven hundred and fifty shekels**: "The total amount of the gold offered by Israel's commanders on behalf of their enumerated troops far exceeded the minimal requirement of one-half shekel per person.... Instead they presented almost 2.8 times the minimal amount." (Cole)

ii. **To make atonement for ourselves before the LORD**: "That is, to make an acknowledgment to God for the preservation of their *lives*. The gold offered on this occasion amounted to 16,750 shekels." (Clarke)

iii. **The persons were sixteen thousand, of which the LORD's tribute was thirty-two persons**: "As to the use to which the women would be put in the service of the priests… It is possible that they were given menial tasks to do in the service of the Lord, as many commentators suggest (see Exodus 38:8)." (Allen)

Numbers 32 – The Tribes Settling East of the Jordan

A. The request of the tribes of Reuben and Gad.

1. (1-5) The request to settle on the east side of the Jordan River.

Now the children of Reuben and the children of Gad had a very great multitude of livestock; and when they saw the land of Jazer and the land of Gilead, that indeed the region *was* a place for livestock, the children of Gad and the children of Reuben came and spoke to Moses, to Eleazar the priest, and to the leaders of the congregation, saying, "Ataroth, Dibon, Jazer, Nimrah, Heshbon, Elealeh, Shebam, Nebo, and Beon, the country which the LORD defeated before the congregation of Israel, *is* a land for livestock, and your servants have livestock." Therefore they said, "If we have found favor in your sight, let this land be given to your servants as a possession. Do not take us over the Jordan."

a. **If we have found favor in your sight, let this land be given to your servants as a possession**: Israel had conquered the Moabites and the Midianites, and the ideal grazing lands on the east side of the Jordan River were laid out before them. Seeing that **the region was a place for livestock**, the tribal leaders of Reuben and Gad were content with these lands and asked to be given them as their tribal inheritance.

i. "Unexpectedly the abundant gains in livestock resulting from successive victories over the Amorites Sihon of Heshbon and Og of Bashan, as well as the miraculous defeat of the Midianites, precipitated a crisis for the Israelites." (Cole)

ii. **A place for livestock**: "Extensive excavations and surface surveys have been done in these areas of Transjordan in the 1970s and 1980s. The consensus is that these were not regions of a high population density in the period of the Exodus (however this period may be dated); the biblical evidence of this chapter accords well with the archaeological evidence. This was an ideal place for the running of large flocks and herds." (Allen)

iii. **A land for livestock, and your servants have livestock**: "The repetition of the word 'livestock' (*miqneh*) is for emphasis; their herds must have been exceptionally large." (Allen)

iv. **The land of Gilead**: "*Gilead* designates a variety of areas in the Old Testament. Its primary meaning (as here) is the hilly district south of the Jabbok...and sometimes it designates the whole of the Transjordanian territory held by Israel (e.g. Joshua 22:9, 13, etc.). These high lands (c. 2500 ft) overlooking the Jordan valley enjoy a good rainfall and are therefore very fertile." (Wenham)

b. **Do not take us over the Jordan**: For some 400 years, the tribes of Israel longed to go **over the Jordan** into Canaan. Now, it seemed, that these two tribes were content to stop *short* of crossing the Jordan and they seemed to be satisfied with settling for less.

i. "That any Israelite tribe should consider settling outside the land promised to Abraham showed a disturbing indifference to the divine word, the word on which Israel's existence entirely depended." (Wenham)

ii. "But it was, in a sense, the fringe of the garment. It was not the heart and soul of the land. To settle in the fringes was a mixed blessing.... because they were somewhat removed from the center of the life of the land, they were the most prone to be influenced by outsiders." (Allen)

iii. G. Campbell Morgan was among those commentators who saw this desire of the tribes of Reuben and Gad as only a bad thing. There was certainly the potential for great evil to come of it, but here in Numbers 32 it seems that the eastern tribes adequately answered the concerns of Moses. Taking this land definitely expanded the territory of the tribes of Israel, and gave them a buffer against threats coming from the east.

2. (6-7) Moses reacts to the request of the tribes of Reuben and Gad.

And Moses said to the children of Gad and to the children of Reuben: "Shall your brethren go to war while you sit here? Now why will you discourage the heart of the children of Israel from going over into the land which the LORD has given them?

a. **Why will you discourage the heart of the children of Israel from going over into the land which the LORD has given them?** Moses feared that the attitude of the tribes of Reuben and Gad would keep the other tribes from going into Canaan. Their attitude said, "We've fought enough and have suffered enough already. Let's just settle down where we are."

i. The fear of Moses had a foundation. When we keep company with those who are satisfied with what they have, and have no desire to go deeper or press on further, their contentment often influences us. If these tribes were guilty of complacency, it could dangerously influence the other tribes.

ii. **The land which the LORD has given them**: "The phraseology referencing the Promised Land as 'the land the Lord has given them,' used here and in v. 9, recalls the language of Num 13:1; 14:8, 16, 30, as well as the other numerous promises of the land throughout the Pentateuch." (Cole)

b. **Shall your brethren go to war while you sit here?** Moses wanted them to know that there was a battle to fight and they had a responsibility to fight that battle together with the other tribes. Just because these tribes were content with staying where they were did not relieve them of the responsibility to share in the battle as their **brethren** went **to war**.

3. (8-15) Moses fears they are following in the footsteps of the previous generation of unbelief, the generation which perished in the wilderness.

Thus your fathers did when I sent them away from Kadesh Barnea to see the land. For when they went up to the Valley of Eshcol and saw the land, they discouraged the heart of the children of Israel, so that they did not go into the land which the LORD had given them. So the LORD's anger was aroused on that day, and He swore an oath, saying, 'Surely none of the men who came up from Egypt, from twenty years old and above, shall see the land of which I swore to Abraham, Isaac, and Jacob, because they have not wholly followed Me, except Caleb the son of Jephunneh, the Kenizzite, and Joshua the son of Nun, for they have wholly followed the LORD.' So the LORD's anger was aroused against Israel, and He made them wander in the wilderness forty years, until all the generation that had done evil in the sight of the LORD was gone. And look! You have risen in your father's place, a brood of sinful men, to increase still more the fierce anger of the LORD against Israel. For if you turn away from following Him, He will once again leave them in the wilderness, and you will destroy all these people."

a. **Thus your fathers did**: The generation that died in the wilderness didn't have the faith to boldly enter the Promised Land, and they decided they would rather stay where they were. Moses worried that this same unbelief was present among the tribes of Reuben and Gad.

i. Allen, Wenham, and Cole point out that there are many "word associations" with Numbers 32 and Numbers 13-14, the chapters describing the first generation's refusal to trust God to take the Promised Land by faith.

ii. "The nation stood poised to cross the Jordan and take up its inheritance, when suddenly three of the tribes announced their intention of opting out. It looked like the spy story (chapters 13–14) all over again." (Wenham)

iii. **For when they went up to the Valley of Eshcol and saw the land**: "In this preaching Moses presents an example of a biblical use of history for the instruction of the people of God. He speaks with specificity, with passion, with historical insights, and with a contemporary feel— the tying of the experience of the past into the present of his hearers. In some ways this section may be thought of as a model of biblical exhortation." (Allen)

b. **They discouraged the heart of the children of Israel**: Moses reminded the leaders of the tribes of Reuben and Gad why Israel failed to enter Canaan some 38 years before. The bad report of most of the spies so **discouraged the heart** of God's people that they lost their desire to take the land by faith.

i. It is a terrible sin to discourage the heart of another believer.

c. **Because they have not wholly followed Me**: This was why the discouragement of the ten unfaithful spies worked on the men of that generation. If they had **wholly followed** the LORD, the discouraging report would not have overly influenced them.

i. What made Joshua and Caleb different was that they **wholly followed the LORD**. They did not bend to the discouraging report of the ten unfaithful spies.

ii. When we have not **wholly followed the LORD**, we are much more likely to be influenced by the worldly-minded and discouraging people around us.

d. **If you turn away from following Him, He will once again leave them in the wilderness**: Perhaps this generation supposed that they had a guaranteed passage to inherit Canaan, thinking that the price had already been paid by the generation of unbelief. This was not true. If they failed to press in by faith, God would **once again leave them in the wilderness**.

i. **A brood of sinful men**: "In the phrase 'brood of sinners' (v.14), he is prescient of the preaching of Jesus (e.g., Matthew 12:34; cf. 3:7)." (Allen)

e. **You will destroy all these people**: It was as if Moses said, "Your discouragement of the nation would mean that *you* have destroyed them, just as the ten unfaithful spies destroyed the previous generation."

i. Moses perhaps felt that the tribes of Reuben and Gad made a bad choice for themselves; that is, they hurt themselves by settling on the lands east of the Jordan River. What concerned Moses was that their potential complacency would corrupt the other tribes. If a believer hurts themselves through unbelief and complacency it is bad; if they influence others by their unbelief and complacency, it is far worse.

B. The issue of the eastern tribes is settled.

1. (16-19) The tribal leaders of Reuben and Gad offer to send their troops to help conquer the land west of the Jordan River.

Then they came near to him and said: "We will build sheepfolds here for our livestock, and cities for our little ones, but we ourselves will be armed, ready *to go* before the children of Israel until we have brought them to their place; and our little ones will dwell in the fortified cities because of the inhabitants of the land. We will not return to our homes until every one of the children of Israel has received his inheritance. For we will not inherit with them on the other side of the Jordan and beyond, because our inheritance has fallen to us on this eastern side of the Jordan."

a. **We ourselves will be armed, ready to go before the children of Israel until we have brought them to their place**: This effectively answered the issue of discouragement. None of the tribes would envy Reuben or Gad, resting in ease, while the rest of them fought to conquer their territory. The men of Reuben and Gad would fight right beside them.

b. **We will not return to our homes until every one of the children of Israel has received his inheritance**: The leaders of Reuben and Gad promised that they would continue to fight with the other tribes on the west side of the Jordan River until the conquest of Canaan was complete.

2. (20-24) Moses receives their offer – providing they fulfill it.

Then Moses said to them: "If you do this thing, if you arm yourselves before the Lord for the war, and all your armed men cross over the Jordan before the Lord until He has driven out His enemies from before Him, and the land is subdued before the Lord, then afterward you may return and be blameless before the Lord and before Israel; and this land shall be your possession before the Lord. But if you do not do so, then take note, you have sinned against the Lord; and be sure your

sin will find you out. Build cities for your little ones and folds for your sheep, and do what has proceeded out of your mouth."

a. **If you do this thing**: If they did as they said, then they would **be blameless before the LORD and before Israel**. But if they did not, they would be guilty.

i. **Before the LORD**: "The phrase *lipne YHWH* ('before Yahweh') occurs four times in vv. 20–22 and is highlighted." (Cole)

b. **But if you do not do so, then take note, you have sinned against the LORD**: If they failed to do as they said, they would sin. The sin specifically spoken of here is the sin of *doing nothing*. Failing to serve their brethren, to fight on their behalf, to join in their struggle, would be a sin, the sin of doing nothing. This was something Moses wanted them to **take note** of.

i. If the tribes of Reuben and Gad did nothing – if they stayed at home while their brothers battled to take possession of the Promised Land – then their sin of doing nothing would surely **find** them **out**.

ii. "If you take the text as it stands, there is nothing in it about murder, or theft, or anything of the kind. In fact, it is not about what men do, but it is about what men do not do. The iniquity of doing nothing is a sin which is not so often spoken of as it should be." (Spurgeon)

iii. In his sermon titled *The Great Sin of Doing Nothing*, Charles Spurgeon mentioned several ways that doing nothing was and is a sin:

• This would be a sin of God's people, not of the pagan nations.

• This would be a sin of idleness and self-indulgence.

• This would be a sin of selfishness and unbrotherliness.

• This would be a sin of ingratitude.

• This would be a sin of untruthfulness, breaking a promise made.

• This would be a sin that caused serious injury to others.

iv. "Spiritual self-indulgence is a monstrous evil; yet we see it all around. On Sunday these loafers must be well fed. They look out for such sermons as will feed their souls. The thought does not occur to these people that there is something else to be done besides feeding…. These people want pleasant things preached to them. They eat the fat and drink the sweet, and they crowd to the feast of fat things full of marrow, and of wines on the lees well refined—spiritual festivals are their delight: sermons, conferences, Bible-readings, and so forth, are sought after, but regular service in ordinary ways is neglected." (Spurgeon)

v. "A do nothing professor is a merely nominal member, and a nominal member is a real hindrance. He neither contributes, nor prays, nor works, nor agonizes for souls, nor takes any part in Christian service, and yet he partakes in all the privileges of the church. Is this fair? What is the use of him? He sits and hears, and sometimes sleeps under the sermon. That is all." (Spurgeon)

c. **Be sure that your sin will find you out**: The sin of doing nothing would be exposed. In fact, there was something in that sin that would actively work to be exposed; in some sense the **sin** itself would **find you out**.

i. **Your sin will find you out**: "The language is striking: it is not just that their sin will be discovered but that their sin will be an active agent in discovering them." (Allen)

ii. "Sin is like the boomerang…it comes back on the hand that has launched it forth. The brethren accused Joseph of being a spy, and cast him into the pit; and on the same charge they were cast into prison. King David committed adultery and murder; so Absalom requited him." (Meyer)

iii. "The guilt will haunt you at heels, as a bloodhound, and the punishment will overtake you" (Trapp)

iv. Spurgeon suggested several ways in which our sin might find us out:

- We become ill at ease.
- We feel ourselves to be low and despicable.
- We become weakened by our own inaction.
- We have little joy in the progress and prosperity of the church.
- We lose our appetite for the gatherings of God's people.

v. "When sin comes to find you out, like a sleuthhound on the track of the criminal, be sure that it finds you in Jesus. 'That I may be found in Him.' Nothing will avail to intercept the awful execution of sin's vengeance, except the blood and righteousness of Jesus. Put Him between you and your sins, between you and your past, between you and the penalty of a broken law." (Meyer)

3. (25-27) The tribal leaders of Reuben and Gad agree.

And the children of Gad and the children of Reuben spoke to Moses, saying: "Your servants will do as my lord commands. Our little ones, our wives, our flocks, and all our livestock will be there in the cities of Gilead; but your servants will cross over, every man armed for war, before the LORD to battle, just as my lord says."

a. **Your servants will do as my lord commands**: This showed a surrendered, submitted attitude. The tribal leaders of Reuben and Gad did not try to negotiate with Moses and work a more favorable agreement.

b. **Our little ones, our wives, our flocks, and all our livestock will be there in the cities of Gilead**: This was also a step of faith. The other tribes had to trust God to fight the battles needed to occupy the land of Canaan. The tribes of Reuben and Gad had to trust God to preserve and protect their families while a substantial portion of their fighting men helped the tribes settling west of the Jordan River.

> i. Adam Clarke notes that more than a third of the available fighting men went to help the tribes on the western side of the Jordan. "Now from Joshua 4:13 we learn that of the tribes of Reuben and Gad, and the half of the tribe of Manasseh, only 40,000 armed men passed over Jordan to assist their brethren in the reduction of the land: consequently the number of 70,580 men were left behind for the defence of the women, the children, and the flocks."

4. (28-42) The agreement is settled, and cities are given to the tribes settling on the lands east of the Jordan River.

So Moses gave command concerning them to Eleazar the priest, to Joshua the son of Nun, and to the chief fathers of the tribes of the children of Israel. And Moses said to them: "If the children of Gad and the children of Reuben cross over the Jordan with you, every man armed for battle before the LORD, and the land is subdued before you, then you shall give them the land of Gilead as a possession. But if they do not cross over armed with you, they shall have possessions among you in the land of Canaan."

Then the children of Gad and the children of Reuben answered, saying: "As the LORD has said to your servants, so we will do. We will cross over armed before the LORD into the land of Canaan, but the possession of our inheritance *shall remain* with us on this side of the Jordan."

So Moses gave to the children of Gad, to the children of Reuben, and to half the tribe of Manasseh the son of Joseph, the kingdom of Sihon king of the Amorites and the kingdom of Og king of Bashan, the land with its cities within the borders, the cities of the surrounding country. And the children of Gad built Dibon and Ataroth and Aroer, Atroth and Shophan and Jazer and Jogbehah, Beth Nimrah and Beth Haran, fortified cities, and folds for sheep. And the children of Reuben built Heshbon and Elealeh and Kirjathaim, Nebo and Baal Meon *(their names being changed)* and Shibmah; and they gave *other* names to the cities which they built.

And the children of Machir the son of Manasseh went to Gilead and took it, and dispossessed the Amorites who *were* in it. So Moses gave Gilead to Machir the son of Manasseh, and he dwelt in it. Also Jair the son of Manasseh went and took its small towns, and called them Havoth Jair. Then Nobah went and took Kenath and its villages, and he called it Nobah, after his own name.

a. **If the children of Gad and the children of Reuben cross over the Jordan with you…then you shall give them the land of Gilead as a possession**: The possession of the **land of Gilead** was on the condition of their faithfulness to their promise. Moses told Eleazar to make sure they honored their promise before granting them Gilead.

> i. "The listing of towns such as Dibon, Ataroth, Aroer, Atroth Shophan, Jazer, and the like are important, not just for cartography, but for theology. This land was now really theirs. The cities that had been destroyed were now being rebuilt, and in some cases they were being renamed (v.38)." (Allen)

b. **So Moses gave to the children of Gad, to the children of Reuben, and to half the tribe of Manasseh the son of Joseph**: Numbers 32:33 introduces another tribe – actually, half the tribe of Manasseh – who were likewise content to settle on the lands east of the Jordan River. In total, two and one-half tribes received their possession of land east of the Jordan River.

> i. "It could be that the representatives of Manasseh took no part in the negotiations until Moses had approved in principle a settlement in Transjordan." (Wenham)

c. **The children of Machir the son of Manasseh went to Gilead and took it**: We don't have a detailed explanation of why the tribe of Manasseh divided into two parts, with one part living on the east side of the Jordan and the other part on the west side. It probably had to do with the **children of Machir** conquering significant and good land east of the Jordan and deciding it would live on that land.

Numbers 33 – Review of the Exodus, Preview of the Conquest

A. Introduction: Leaving Egypt.

1. (1-2) The account of Israel's journey, written by the command of the LORD.

These *are* the journeys of the children of Israel, who went out of the land of Egypt by their armies under the hand of Moses and Aaron. Now Moses wrote down the starting points of their journeys at the command of the LORD. And these *are* their journeys according to their starting points:

a. **These are the journeys of the children of Israel**: Numbers 33 is the remarkable record of the journey of Israel from Egypt to the threshold of the Promised Land. 42 place names are given, starting with Rameses of Egypt and ending with the plains of Moab.

i. As Israel prepared itself to cross the Jordan and conquer Canaan, it was good for this second generation from Egypt to remember the faithfulness of God over the last 40 years. Remembering God's goodness in the past was preparation for the challenges of the future.

ii. "From Rameses, the place of departure, to Abel-shittim, in the plains of Moab, forty-two stations in all are given at which the Israelites pitched. Of these about twenty-four are named either in Exodus, in other parts of the Book of Numbers, or in Deuteronomy. Some eighteen, therefore, are mentioned in this passage and nowhere else." (Watson)

iii. Allen describes the difficulty the following list gives to the geographer: "The chapter presents numerous difficulties, however, once one brings out the map. Most of the sites were desert encampments, not cities with lasting archaeological evidences. Many of the places in the listing are not recorded elsewhere in Exodus and Numbers (e.g., most of the places in vv.19–29)."

b. **Moses wrote down the starting points of their journeys at the command of the LORD**: Moses compiled his written record over the 40 years of Israel's journey in the wilderness and did so at God's command.

i. Both Wenham and Cole organize the list into six cycles of seven places each. This arrangement is presented below. "It appears as a bare and uninteresting list of names and yet it tells the story of a people guided by God through discipline." (Morgan)

ii. "The unknown places, like those men remembered only for their inclusion in a family tree, receive recognition as sites where God's eternal purposes were worked out. Though from a human point of view nothing memorable may have happened at Dophkah or Alush, these are recorded as places where the hosts of Israel, the Lord's army, marched through on their way to the promised land." (Wenham)

iii. Several commentators point out that this list is presented in the style that ancient kings in the Near East listed their conquests and triumphs. This was Yahweh's victory procession from Egypt to the edge of Canaan.

2. (3-4) The departure from Egypt.

They departed from Rameses in the first month, on the fifteenth day of the first month; on the day after the Passover the children of Israel went out with boldness in the sight of all the Egyptians. For the Egyptians were burying all *their* firstborn, whom the LORD had killed among them. Also on their gods the LORD had executed judgments.

a. **The children of Israel went out with boldness in the sight of all the Egyptians**: Though they were slaves for hundreds of years, they did not leave Egypt in shame. God gave them the boldness to leave as conquerors, not as escaping slaves.

b. **On their gods the LORD had executed judgments**: The plagues the LORD brought upon Egypt were not randomly chosen. They were specifically intended to humble the people and rebuke the people for their belief in the bizarre and demonic Egyptian deities.

B. Israel's Journey from Egypt to the Plains of Moab.

1. (5-10) Stage 1: From Egypt to the Red Sea (Exodus 12-16).

Then the children of Israel moved from Rameses and camped at Succoth. They departed from Succoth and camped at Etham, which *is* on the edge of the wilderness. They moved from Etham and turned

back to Pi Hahiroth, which *is* east of Baal Zephon; and they camped near Migdol. They departed from before Hahiroth and passed through the midst of the sea into the wilderness, went three days' journey in the Wilderness of Etham, and camped at Marah. They moved from Marah and came to Elim. At Elim *were* twelve springs of water and seventy palm trees; so they camped there.

They moved from Elim and camped by the Red Sea.

a. **Succoth...Etham...Pi Hahiroth....Marah...Elim...the Red Sea**: These six places (counting after the starting place of Rameses) mark Israel's journey in the first stage cf the exodus. According to some sources (Allen, Clarke, Trapp), the names of these places have the following associations.

- Succoth: *Booths.*
- Desert of Etham (unknown).
- Pi Hahiroth: *Mouth of Burning.*
- Marah: *Bitter Spring.*
- Elim: *Place of Trees.*
- The Red Sea: *Sea of Reeds.*

  i. As is often the case with the meanings of biblical names, one must be careful to not invest too much spiritual significance in what are sometimes speculative interpretations. "Mr. Bromley, in his *Way to the Sabbath of Rest*, considers each name and place as descriptive of the spiritual state through which a soul passes in its way to the kingdom of God. But in cases of this kind *fancy* has much more to do than *judgment*." (Clarke)

  ii. **The Red Sea**: "By the *Red Sea* we are not to understand a sea, the waters of which are *red*, or the *sand* red, or any thing else *about* or *in* it *red;* for nothing of this kind appears. It is called in Hebrew *yam suph*, which signifies the *weedy sea*." (Clarke)

b. **They moved from Marah and came to Elim**: With a wonderful touch, God made no mention of Israel's great sin at **Marah** but did note the refreshing springs at **Elim** (**twelve springs of water and seventy palm trees**).

  i. "In his enumeration of the halting places of Israel, Moses mentions Marah and Elim. In the case of the former, he does not dwell on the murmuring of the people over the bitter stream: but in the case of Elim, he loves to dilate on the twelve springs of water, and the three-score and ten palm trees, under which they pitched. Years of weary travel had not obliterated the memory of the refreshment afforded by those seventy palms." (Meyer)

ii. "There is no word of their murmurings, either at Marah or Rephidim. It is thus that God deals with us. 'I, even I, am He that blotteth out thy transgressions for mine own sake, and will not remember thy sins.' When God forgives, He forgets." (Meyer)

2. (11-17) Stage 2: From the Wilderness of Sin to Hazeroth (Exodus 16-19; Numbers 10-11).

They moved from the Red Sea and camped in the Wilderness of Sin. They journeyed from the Wilderness of Sin and camped at Dophkah. They departed from Dophkah and camped at Alush. They moved from Alush and camped at Rephidim, where there was no water for the people to drink.

They departed from Rephidim and camped in the Wilderness of Sinai. They moved from the Wilderness of Sinai and camped at Kibroth Hattaavah. They departed from Kibroth Hattaavah and camped at Hazeroth.

a. **Camped in the Wilderness of Sinai**: This portion of the journey took them about a year, but most of the time was not spent in traveling, but in receiving the law at Mount Sinai.

b. **Wilderness of Sin...Dophkah...Alush...Rephidim...Wilderness of Sinai...Kibroth Hattaavah...Hazeroth**: These seven places mark Israel's journey in the second stage of the exodus. According to some sources (Allen, Clarke, Trapp), the names of these places have the following associations.

- Wilderness of Sin (unknown).
- Dophkah: *Beaten.*
- Alush (unknown).
- Rephidim: *Spreading.*
- Wilderness of Sinai (unknown).
- Kibroth Hattaavah: *Graves of Desire.*
- Hazeroth: *Settlements.*

i. In this and the following stages are many places not previously recorded in Exodus, Leviticus, or Numbers. "Numbers 10:33–13:25 mentions only three stopping-places between the mountain of the Lord and Kadesh in the wilderness of Paran, Taberah, Kibroth-hattaavah and Hazeroth (11:3, 34–35), whereas Numbers 33:16–36 mentions twenty-two stages beginning with the wilderness of Sinai and ending 'with the wilderness of Zin (that is Kadesh)'." (Wenham)

3. (18-24) Stage 3: From Rithmah to Haradah.

They departed from Hazeroth and camped at Rithmah. They departed from Rithmah and camped at Rimmon Perez. They departed from Rimmon Perez and camped at Libnah. They moved from Libnah and camped at Rissah. They journeyed from Rissah and camped at Kehelathah. They went from Kehelathah and camped at Mount Shepher. They moved from Mount Shepher and camped at Haradah.

a. **Rithmah...Rimmon Perez...Libnah...Rissah...Kehelathah...Mount Shepher...Haradah:** These seven places mark Israel's journey in the third stage of the exodus. According to some sources (Allen, Clarke, Trapp), the names of these places have the following associations.

- Rithmah: *Binding.*
- Rimmon Perez: *Pomegranate Beach.*
- Libnah: *White.*
- Rissah (unknown).
- Kehalathah: *Assembly.*
- Mount Shepher: *Mount of Beauty.*
- Haradah: *Frightening.*

4. (25-31) Stage 4: From Makheloth to Bene Jaakan (Deuteronomy 10).

They moved from Haradah and camped at Makheloth. They moved from Makheloth and camped at Tahath. They departed from Tahath and camped at Terah. They moved from Terah and camped at Mithkah. They went from Mithkah and camped at Hashmonah. They departed from Hashmonah and camped at Moseroth. They departed from Moseroth and camped at Bene Jaakan.

a. **Makheloth...Tahath...Terah...Mithkah...Hashmonah...Moseroth... Bene Jaakan:** These seven places mark Israel's journey in the fourth stage of the exodus. According to some sources (Allen, Clarke, Trapp), the names of these places have the following associations.

- Makheloth: *Place of Assembly.*
- Tahath: *Lower.*
- Terah (unknown).
- Mithcah: *Sweetness.*
- Hashmonah: *Swiftness.*

- Moseroth: *Bands.*
- Bene Jaakan: *Sons of Yaaqan.*

5. (32-41) Stage 5: From Hor Hagidad to Zalmonah (Numbers 20-21).

They moved from Bene Jaakan and camped at Hor Hagidgad. They went from Hor Hagidgad and camped at Jotbathah. They moved from Jotbathah and camped at Abronah. They departed from Abronah and camped at Ezion Geber. They moved from Ezion Geber and camped in the Wilderness of Zin, which *is* Kadesh. They moved from Kadesh and camped at Mount Hor, on the boundary of the land of Edom.

Then Aaron the priest went up to Mount Hor at the command of the LORD, and died there in the fortieth year after the children of Israel had come out of the land of Egypt, on the first *day* of the fifth month. Aaron *was* one hundred and twenty-three years old when he died on Mount Hor.

Now the king of Arad, the Canaanite, who dwelt in the South in the land of Canaan, heard of the coming of the children of Israel.

So they departed from Mount Hor and camped at Zalmonah.

a. **Hor Haggidgad…Jotbathah…Abronah…Ezion Geber…Kadesh… Mount Hor…. Zalmonah**: These seven places mark Israel's journey in the fifth stage of the exodus. According to some sources (Allen, Clarke, Trapp), the names of these places have the following associations.

- Hor Haggidgad: *The Hollow of Gidgad.*
- Jotbathah: *Pleasantness.*
- Abronah: *Regions Beyond.*
- Ezion Geber: *Mighty Trees.*
- Kadesh: *Sanctuary.*
- Mount Hor (unknown).
- Zalmonah: *Resemblance* or *Image.*

b. **Aaron the priest went up to Mount Hor at the command of the LORD**: The camp at **Mount Hor** is given special mention, honoring the death and burial place of Aaron, the brother of Moses and first high priest of Israel.

6. (42-49) Stage 6: From Punon to the Plains of Moab (Numbers 21-22).

They departed from Zalmonah and camped at Punon. They departed from Punon and camped at Oboth. They departed from Oboth and camped at Ije Abarim, at the border of Moab. They departed from Ijim and camped at Dibon Gad. They moved from Dibon Gad and camped at

Almon Diblathaim. They moved from Almon Diblathaim and camped in the mountains of Abarim, before Nebo. They departed from the mountains of Abarim and camped in the plains of Moab by the Jordan, *across from* Jericho. They camped by the Jordan, from Beth Jesimoth as far as the Abel Acacia Grove in the plains of Moab.

a. **Punon…Oboth…Ije Abarim…. Dibon Gad…Almon Diblathaim… the mountains of Abarim**: These six places (up to the **plains of Moab**) mark Israel's journey in the sixth stage of the exodus. According to some sources (Allen, Clarke, Trapp), the names of these places have the following associations.

- Punon (unknown).

- Oboth: *Water Skins.*

- Ije Abarim: *The Heaps of Abarim.*

- Dibon Gad: *Built Up by Gad.*

- Almon Diblathaim: *Hidden Figs* (possibly).

- Mountains of Abarim: *The Mountains Beyond.*

b. **They camped by the Jordan, from Beth Jesimoth as far as the Abel Acacia Grove in the plains of Moab**: This was Israel's current position, on the threshold of Canaan. In a few months, they would go from the **plains of Moab** across the Jordan, into the Promised Land.

i. "The encampments of the thousands of Israel stretched from Beth Jeshimoth…to Abel Shittim…in the lowlands of Moab. The distance from these two sites, north to south, was over five miles—a suitable spread for the thousands of the tribes of Israel." (Allen)

C. Looking ahead: The conquest of Canaan.

1. (50-53) The command to conquer the inhabitants of Canaan.

Now the LORD spoke to Moses in the plains of Moab by the Jordan, *across from* Jericho, saying, "Speak to the children of Israel, and say to them: 'When you have crossed the Jordan into the land of Canaan, then you shall drive out all the inhabitants of the land from before you, destroy all their engraved stones, destroy all their molded images, and demolish all their high places; you shall dispossess *the inhabitants of* the land and dwell in it, for I have given you the land to possess.

a. **You shall drive out all the inhabitants of the land from before you**: God had a special role for the nation of Israel regarding the people of Canaan. He used them as a unique instrument of judgment against the Canaanites.

i. This challenge or command looks forward to the *seventh* stage of Israel's journey from Egypt. Led by Joshua, Israel would conquer the land of Canaan and **drive out** the Canaanites.

b. **Drive out all the inhabitants of the land...destroy all their engraved stones...destroy their molded images...demolish their high places**: This strong language, expressed in four different Hebrew verbs (translated **drive out**, **destroy**, **destroy**, and **demolish**), explained God's command to leave nothing of Canaanite culture to encourage idolatry and immorality.

i. Israel was not to tolerate a co-existence with the depraved idolatry and immorality of the Canaanites, which included even human sacrifice. "No false pity or selfish motive was to operate in such fashion as to leave any corrupting influence behind. The unequivocal command to drive out all, was based on the tenderest regard of God for the well-being of the chosen people, and through them, the whole [human] race." (Morgan)

ii. "Shall we suffer those vipers to lodge in our bosoms till they eat out our hearts?" (Trapp)

iii. "Pluralism in the form of peaceful coexistence with idolatry would be impossible, both for the well-being of the people and the sanctity of the land Yahweh had given as a gift to his people." (Cole)

iv. **Demolish their high places**: "We know from the Book of Judges and subsequent history, the law, especially in regard to the demolition of high places, became practically a dead letter." (Watson)

2. (54) The command to possess the land of Canaan.

And you shall divide the land by lot as an inheritance among your families; to the larger you shall give a larger inheritance, and to the smaller you shall give a smaller inheritance; there everyone's *inheritance* shall be whatever falls to him by lot. You shall inherit according to the tribes of your fathers.

a. **You shall divide the land by lot as an inheritance among your families**: God's intent was not only to bring judgment on the corrupt culture of the Canaanites but also to give the land to Israel to possess.

b. **To the larger you shall give a larger inheritance, and to the smaller you shall give a smaller inheritance**: God commanded that the land be distributed fairly, generally according to the size of the tribe.

3. (55-56) Israel is warned of the consequences of not driving out the Canaanites and their influence.

But if you do not drive out the inhabitants of the land from before you, then it shall be that those whom you let remain *shall be* irritants in your eyes and thorns in your sides, and they shall harass you in the land where you dwell. Moreover it shall be *that* I will do to you as I thought to do to them.'"

a. **If you do not drive out the inhabitants of the land from before you, then it shall be that those whom you let remain shall be irritants in your eyes and thorns in your sides**: If Israel failed to drive the Canaanites out of the land, they could still occupy the Promised Land. However, the idolatry and immorality of the Canaanites would find a place among Israel and be a source of constant trouble and irritation.

i. "The description of trouble is, of course, sadly prophetic. The remaining Canaanites were to be barbs in the eye and pricks in the side (images that Joshua uses in his farewell address; see Joshua 23:13)." (Allen)

b. **It shall be that I will do to you as I thought to do to them**: This warning was eventually fulfilled in Israel's history. Though they possessed the land, they did not fully drive out the Canaanites or destroy their influence. By following the Canaanite idolatry and immorality, eventually God drove Israel out of the land in exile.

i. The abiding spiritual principle teaches us that it is of no use for the church to succeed in the eyes of man – as Israel had succeeded when they occupied the land and became a legitimate nation, instead of an enslaved people – if it merely allows the corrupt practices and attitudes of the Canaanites to take root among God's people. If, spiritually speaking, a similar thing happens among God's people today, they should expect to be eventually driven from their place of apparent success or influence.

Numbers 34 – The Boundaries of the Land, Men Chosen to Portion the Land

This chapter is a celebration of God's gifting, a liturgy of geography. It presents a trust deed, a legal document from God to his people. (Ronald Allen)

A. The boundaries of the land of Canaan.

1. (1-2) Introduction.

Then the LORD spoke to Moses, saying, "Command the children of Israel, and say to them: 'When you come into the land of Canaan, this *is* the land that shall fall to you as an inheritance; the land of Canaan to its boundaries.

a. **This is the land that shall fall to you**: Numbers 34 describes to Moses and the children of Israel the borders of **the land of Canaan**. Though the lands on the eastern side of the Jordan River belonged to Israel, those lands were not considered to be Canaan.

i. **The land of Canaan**: "Canaan was a recognized geographical entity from the 15th century BC onwards and is mentioned frequently in texts from Egypt of the following centuries, a period it was under nominal Egyptian control. These extra-biblical texts do not spell out the boundaries of Canaan as this chapter does, but they evidently presuppose much the same limits to Canaan as the Bible." (Wenham)

ii. It will be helpful for the reader to consult a good Bible map. "All description here is useless. The situation and boundaries of the land of Canaan can only be known by actual survey, or by consulting a good map." (Clarke)

b. **As an inheritance**: Israel had to take control of the **land of Canaan** by conquest. They would have to drive out the inhabitants to take possession and never believe that the land was given to them because they *earned* it. It was given to them by God **as an inheritance**. Inheritances are freely given, not earned.

i. Matthew Poole gave three reasons why God detailed the boundaries of Canaan for Israel: "1. To direct and bound them in their wars and conquests, that they might not seek the enlargement of their empire, after the manner of other nations, but be contented with their own portion. 2. To encourage them in their attempt upon Canaan, and assure them of their success. 3. To guide them in the approaching distribution of the land."

ii. "It is God that assigns us our quarters, and cuts us out our several conditions, 'appointing the bounds of our habitation.' (Acts 17:26) This should make us rest contented with our lot, and, having God our portion, say howsoever, as David did, 'The lines are fallen to me in pleasant places.' (Psalm 16:6) It is what our Father sees fit for us." (Trapp)

2. (3-5) The southern border of the land of Canaan.

Your southern border shall be from the Wilderness of Zin along the border of Edom; then your southern border shall extend eastward to the end of the Salt Sea; your border shall turn from the southern side of the Ascent of Akrabbim, continue to Zin, and be on the south of Kadesh Barnea; then it shall go on to Hazar Addar, and continue to Azmon; the border shall turn from Azmon to the Brook of Egypt, and it shall end at the Sea.

a. **The Ascent of Akrabbim**: This place, "Scorpion Pass," is also mentioned in Joshua 15:3 and Judges 1:36. It was probably a well-known landmark of the desert.

i. "The southern border passed just south of the famous 'Scorpion Pass,' a winding road from the Nahal Zin basin into the Negeb south of Mampsis, that continued to be known by that name through the Roman period and is so even until today." (Cole)

b. **To the Brook of Egypt**: Some different small streams have been proposed as marking this portion of the southern boundary. A few commentators have suggested that this describes some branch of the Nile.

i. "*The river of Egypt* The eastern branch of the river Nile; or, according to others, a river which is south of the land of the Philistines, and falls into the gulf or bay near *Calieh*." (Clarke)

3. (6) The western border of the land of Canaan: The Mediterranean Sea.

'As for the western border, you shall have the Great Sea for a border; this shall be your western border.

4. (7-9) The northern border of the land of Canaan.

'And this shall be your northern border: From the Great Sea you shall mark out your *border* line to Mount Hor; from Mount Hor you shall mark out *your border* to the entrance of Hamath; then the direction of the border shall be toward Zedad; the border shall proceed to Ziphron, and it shall end at Hazar Enan. This shall be your northern border.

> a. **This shall be your northern border**: These landmarks fall well north of the northern border of modern Israel, north of the ancient cities of Tyre, Sidon, and Byblos.

> > i. "The only points on the northern border that can be positively identified are *Lebo-Hamath* [**the entrance of Hamath**] (13:21), probably modern Lebweh, and *Zedad* which can be equated with Sedad." (Wenham)

> > ii. "Lebo Hamath [**the entrance of Hamath**] is also the northern boundary of the Israelite kingdom during the monarchy of David and Solomon (1 Kgs 8:65), from which the people were summoned to celebrate the great feast during the dedication of the Temple to the Lord in Jerusalem." (Cole)

5. (10-12) The eastern border of the land of Canaan.

'You shall mark out your eastern border from Hazar Enan to Shepham; the border shall go down from Shepham to Riblah on the east side of Ain; the border shall go down and reach to the eastern side of the Sea of Chinnereth; the border shall go down along the Jordan, and it shall end at the Salt Sea. This shall be your land with its surrounding boundaries.'"

> a. **You shall mark out your eastern border**: The **eastern border** starts southward from the eastern point of the northern border, **Hazar Enan**. It then extends southward on an uncertain line until reaching **the Sea of Chinnereth** (also known as the Sea of Galilee), and the **Jordan** and **Salt Sea** afterward.

> > i. "The eastern border until it reaches the eastern slopes of the sea of Galilee…is quite problematic: Shepham, Riblah and Ain cannot be located." (Wenham)

6. (13-15) The land the nine and one-half tribes settling on the western side of the Jordan River would divide.

Then Moses commanded the children of Israel, saying: "This *is* the land which you shall inherit by lot, which the LORD has commanded to give to the nine tribes and to the half-tribe. For the tribe of the children of Reuben according to the house of their fathers, and the tribe of the children of Gad according to the house of their fathers, have received *their inheritance;* and the half-tribe of Manasseh has received its inheritance. The two tribes and the half-tribe have received their inheritance on this side of the Jordan, *across from* Jericho eastward, toward the sunrise."

a. **The land which you shall inherit:** This was the land God promised to Abraham (Genesis 15:18-21), Isaac (Genesis 26:4), Jacob (Genesis 28:13-14), and the children of Jacob. It was to be divided **by lot**, guided by God's providential hand according to the general principle that the larger tribes received a larger inheritance.

i. "Nevertheless Canaan as defined here is a much larger area than ever Israel settled. David controlled most of Canaan and much of Transjordan as well, but the land defined here does not correspond to Israel's actual boundaries at any time in her history." (Wenham)

ii. **By lot:** "Such was *the land,* and such were the advantages that this most favoured people were called to possess. They were called to possess it *by lot* that each might be satisfied with his possession, as considering it to be appointed to him by the especial providence of God; and its boundaries were ascertained on Divine authority, to prevent all covetousness after the territories of others." (Clarke)

iii. This was a wonderful and prosperous land, but in comparison with other places in the world, there was much it did *not* have, and God expected His people to be content with what He allotted to them. "As Canaan had neither gold nor silver, neither coal nor iron mines, as its seaboard was not well supplied with harbours, nor its rivers and lakes of great use for inland navigation, so we may say the life open to the Christian has its limitations and disabilities." (Watson)

b. **The two tribes and half tribe have received their inheritance on this side of the Jordan:** The land divided by lot described in this chapter was for the nine and a half tribes west of the Jordan River. The two and a half tribes east of the Jordan **have received their inheritance**, as described in Numbers 32.

i. **Have received:** "Thrice over the words are repeated in reference to them, they 'have received.' They had made their own choice and it was now ratified." (Morgan)

B. Leaders appointed to divide the land.

1. (16-17) Joshua and Eleazar appointed to divide the land.

And the LORD spoke to Moses, saying, "These *are* the names of the men who shall divide the land among you as an inheritance: Eleazar the priest and Joshua the son of Nun.

> a. **Eleazar the priest and Joshua the son of Nun**: The division of the land of Canaan was, in fact, a potentially divisive – even explosive – issue among the people of Israel. It was right to take the two most godly and prominent leaders of the nation to direct this essential and controversial duty.

> b. **Eleazar the priest**: The mention of the high priest reminds the modern believer that our inheritance is allotted and guaranteed by Jesus Christ, our High Priest.

> > i. "Pointing to the High Priest of the new covenant, by whom we have entrance into the promised inheritance, whither he is gone before to prepare a place for us, and hath told us, that in his 'Father's house are many mansions,' room enough." (Trapp)

2. (18-29) Leaders from each of the twelve tribes are appointed to help Joshua and Eleazar divide the land.

And you shall take one leader of every tribe to divide the land for the inheritance. These *are* the names of the men: from the tribe of Judah, Caleb the son of Jephunneh; from the tribe of the children of Simeon, Shemuel the son of Ammihud; from the tribe of Benjamin, Elidad the son of Chislon; a leader from the tribe of the children of Dan, Bukki the son of Jogli; from the sons of Joseph: a leader from the tribe of the children of Manasseh, Hanniel the son of Ephod, and a leader from the tribe of the children of Ephraim, Kemuel the son of Shiphtan; a leader from the tribe of the children of Zebulun, Elizaphan the son of Parnach; a leader from the tribe of the children of Issachar, Paltiel the son of Azzan; a leader from the tribe of the children of Asher, Ahihud the son of Shelomi; and a leader from the tribe of the children of Naphtali, Pedahel the son of Ammihud."

These *are* the ones the LORD commanded to divide the inheritance among the children of Israel in the land of Canaan.

> a. **You shall take one leader of every tribe**: As expected, this list includes only ten tribal leaders. Two of the tribes (Reuben and Gad) received all their inheritance on the eastern side of the Jordan River.

i. "The tribes are listed in rough order of their settlements, beginning with Judah and Simeon in the south and ending with Asher and Naphtali in the north (cf. Joshua 14–19)." (Wenham)

b. **These are the ones**: The description of a definite land with definite boundaries, to be divided under the leadership of definite men emphasizes the real nature of God's promises. There is a spiritual aspect of these promises and this inheritance, but for ancient Israel on the plains of Moab, these were plain and literal promises.

> i. F.B. Meyer reflected on the truth that the description of the boundaries of the land reminds us not only of our inheritance, but also of our borders, our limits. "We may expect to be blameless, but not faultless, till He present us to Himself: to be delivered from temptation, but not freed from its assaults: to be kept in perfect peace, but not secured from the pressure of adversity: to be dead to sin and self, but not daring to say that either is dead within us: to be delivered from this present evil world, as to spirit and temper, though still called to inhabit it as its salt and light. Take possession of every inch of God-given territory in Jesus, but beware of going beyond it."

Numbers 35 – Cities for Levites, Cities for Refuge

A. Appointment of the Levitical cities.

1. (1-3) The command to provide cities and common-lands for the Levites.

And the LORD spoke to Moses in the plains of Moab by the Jordan *across from* Jericho, saying: "Command the children of Israel that they give the Levites cities to dwell in from the inheritance of their possession, and you shall *also* give the Levites common-land around the cities. They shall have the cities to dwell in; and their common-land shall be for their cattle, for their herds, and for all their animals.

> a. **Command the children of Israel that they give the Levites cities to dwell in**: The tribe of Levi had no "state" or "province" within Israel. Their inheritance was to be the LORD alone: *Then the LORD said to Aaron: You shall have no inheritance in their land, nor shall you have any portion among them; I am your portion and your inheritance among the children of Israel.* (Numbers 18:20)

>> i. This provision of **cities** and associated **common-land** did not contradict the principle that the Levites had their inheritance in the LORD. "Even with the surrounding pasture-lands for the cattle, the total area assigned to the Levites came to 15 square miles (40 km²), about 0.1% of the land of Canaan. In a society where farm-land was wealth, this minute fraction of the land meant that the Levites would still be dependent on the generosity of the secular tribes among whom they lived." (Wenham)

> b. **They shall have cities to dwell in**: Yet, the Levites had to live somewhere. God commanded that each tribe give cities to the Levites so that the Levites would be sprinkled throughout the whole nation. These cities were formally appointed to the Levites in Joshua 21.

>> i. "We do know of priest-towns, however, in later Scripture. Anathoth is the most celebrated (Joshua 21:18; 1 Kings 2:26; Jeremiah 1:1;

32:7–8); yet Bethel (Judges 20:18; 1 Samuel 10:3; 2 Kings 17:28), Nob (1 Samuel 21:1; 22:19), and Shiloh (1 Samuel 1:3) also come to mind." (Allen)

2. (4-5) Measuring the common-land around each city.

The common-land of the cities which you will give the Levites *shall extend* **from the wall of the city outward a thousand cubits all around. And you shall measure outside the city on the east side two thousand cubits, on the south side two thousand cubits, on the west side two thousand cubits, and on the north side two thousand cubits. The city** *shall be* **in the middle. This shall belong to them as common-land for the cities.**

a. **Shall extend from the wall of the city outward a thousand cubits all around**: The actual mapping out of these dimensions can be a challenge. Wenham does the best job of explaining, including helpful diagrams.

i. "Later in Jewish history this passage was used as the basis for determining the 'Sabbath day's journey distance,' which was generally measured at two thousand cubits from the gate of the city. Thus the territory would expand with the city as it grew and enlarged the perimeter of its fortification walls." (Cole)

b. **As common-land for the cities**: The Levites were to be given more than just the cities; around each city, they were to be given **common-land** – land suitable for the grazing of their animals and small-scale farming.

3. (6-8) The number of Levitical cities and their distribution.

"Now among the cities which you will give to the Levites *you shall appoint* **six cities of refuge, to which a manslayer may flee. And to these you shall add forty-two cities. So all the cities you will give to the Levites** *shall be* **forty-eight; these** *you shall give* **with their common-land. And the cities which you will give** *shall be* **from the possession of the children of Israel; from the larger** *tribe* **you shall give many, from the smaller you shall give few. Each shall give some of its cities to the Levites, in proportion to the inheritance that each receives."**

a. **Among the cities which you will give to the Levites**: There were to be a total of 48 Levitical cities; six cities of refuge, and 42 additional cities. God wanted the Levites spread throughout all of Israel.

i. "Thus the Levites were dispersed throughout the land for instruction of the people; so ought ministers of the gospel, who are fitly called the salt of the earth, that being sprinkled up and down, may keep the rest (as flesh) from rotting and putrefying." (Trapp)

b. **From the larger tribe you shall give many, from the smaller you shall give few**: The cities were to be distributed proportionally throughout the nation, so that where there were larger populations and larger areas of land, there would be more Levitical cities, so that no one in Israel would be far from a city of refuge.

c. **In proportion to the inheritance that each receives**: This reflects God's desire to evenly distribute the Levites – who were to be the most spiritually focused Israelites – the full-time ministers, so to speak – evenly throughout Israel, so that their influence could be distributed throughout the whole nation.

i. This shows the wisdom of God in not making a Levitical state that others would have to go to. God intended that these ministers go out among the people, to influence them for the LORD.

ii. According to Leviticus 10:11, one responsibility of the priests (and by extension, the Levites) was to teach God's word to the people of Israel. Leviticus 10:11 says, *That you may teach the children of Israel all the statutes which the LORD has spoken.*

iii. This responsibility on the part of the priests (and their associates, the Levites) is often overlooked. We tend to look at them as only those who offered sacrifices. They did that, of course, but they also were called to be active Bible teachers. The "teaching priest" is seen in many Old Testament passages.

- Deuteronomy 33:10: *They shall teach Jacob Your judgments and Israel Your law.*

- 2 Chronicles 17:7: *Also in the third year of his reign he sent his leaders, Ben-Hail, Obadiah, Zechariah, Nethanel, and Michaiah, to teach in the cities of Judah.*

- 2 Chronicles 15:3: *For a long time Israel has been without the true God, without a teaching priest, and without law.*

- Nehemiah 8:7: *Also Jeshua, Bani, Sherebiah, Jamin, Akkub, Shabbethai, Hodijah, Maaseiah, Kelita, Azariah, Jozabad, Hanan, Pelaiah, and the Levites helped the people to understand the Law.*

- Micah 3:11: *Her heads judge for a bribe, her priests teach for pay, and her prophets divine for money.*

- Ezekiel 7:26: *Disaster will come upon disaster, and rumor will be upon rumor. Then they will seek a vision from a prophet; but the law will perish from the priest, and counsel from the elders.*

- Malachi 2:7: *For the lips of a priest should keep knowledge, and people should seek the law from his mouth; for he is the messenger of the LORD of hosts.*

- Ezra 7:25: *And you, Ezra* [a priest], *according to your God-given wisdom, set magistrates and judges who may judge all the people who are in the region beyond the River, all such as know the laws of your God; and teach those who do not know them.*

- Hosea 4:6: *My people are destroyed for lack of knowledge. Because you have rejected knowledge, I also will reject you from being priest for Me; because you have forgotten the law of your God, I also will forget your children.*

- Jeremiah 18:18: *Then they said, "Come and let us devise plans against Jeremiah; for the law shall not perish from the priest, nor counsel from the wise, nor the word from the prophet."*

iv. Therefore, spread evenly through the land as the Levites were, no one in Israel would be far from the ministry of God's word.

v. Today, God also wants to distribute His people broadly throughout the world. God does not intend that there be a Christian country or state where all the Christians live together in spiritual bliss, and simply say to the world, "come and join us if you want." Instead, God wants Christians to be sprinkled throughout the whole world, influencing people for Jesus Christ and being messengers of His word.

B. Cities of refuge.

1. (9-12) The purpose of the cities of refuge.

Then the LORD spoke to Moses, saying, "Speak to the children of Israel, and say to them: 'When you cross the Jordan into the land of Canaan, then you shall appoint cities to be cities of refuge for you, that the manslayer who kills any person accidentally may flee there. They shall be cities of refuge for you from the avenger, that the manslayer may not die until he stands before the congregation in judgment.

a. **Appoint cities to be cities of refuge**: This command to appoint **cities of refuge** would be fulfilled in Joshua 20. Deuteronomy 19:2-3 tells us that proper roads were to be built and maintained to these cities of refuge. The city was not much good to the slayer if he could not get to it quickly.

i. Though Joshua 20 describes the establishment of these cities, there is no case in the history of the Old Testament that shows the use or misuse of the **cities of refuge**.

b. **That the manslayer who kills any person accidentally may flee there**: The purpose of the cities of asylum was to protect **the manslayer who kills any person accidentally**. They were to protect someone in the case of *manslaughter* as opposed to *murder*.

> i. "The term translated 'accidental' (*bisgaga*) in the NIV is the same as the word translated 'unintentional' in Numbers 15:22–29, which addressed matters of atonement for inadvertent sins." (Cole)

c. **They shall be cities of refuge for you from the avenger**: The one who accidentally killed another person needed protection from the **avenger**. The Hebrew word for this phrase is *goel*, and in this context means the representative from the victim's family charged with making sure justice is carried out against the murderer of the family member.

> i. In the ancient culture of Israel, it was not left entirely up to the government to avenge a murder. Each extended family had a recognized **avenger** who would ensure that one who murdered a family member would likewise be killed. The institution of the family **avenger** was never commanded in Scripture; it was a broad cultural practice that was regulated by Scripture.

> ii. This practice was based upon a correct understanding of Genesis 9:6: *Whoever sheds man's blood, by man his blood shall be shed; for in the image of God He made man.* The state's right to use the sword of execution is also stated in the New Testament (Romans 13:3-4).

> iii. "The avenger of blood is a relative of the slain who will take it on himself to protect the family rights, to avenge his relatives of the loss suffered by the family. In fact, the term *goel* often translated 'redeemer,' has this basic idea; the *goel* is principally the 'protector of family rights' (see Leviticus 25:48; Ruth 3:13)." (Allen)

> iv. "The permission to carry out this act was not an unrestrained right. Howard notes that 'the "avenger of blood" was not free to take private vengeance: the Bible clearly reserves vengeance to God alone (Deuteronomy 32:35; Isaiah 34:8; Romans 12:19).'" (Cole)

d. **That the manslayer may not die until he stands before the congregation in judgment**: The use of the **avenger** had its purpose in a culture without sufficiently developed institutions of justice. Yet, it also had a critical weakness. What if the **avenger** hunted someone, who had accidentally killed another person but had not murdered them? What if a death was accidental, yet it was difficult to prove that it was accidental?

> i. We can picture the situation easily: Two men work together, chopping down trees, when one man swings an ax and the ax head flies

off, striking the other man in the head and instantly killing him. The surviving man had good reason to believe the avenger of blood from the dead man's family would track him down and kill him, believing the death was murder.

ii. "It is quite possible to do unjust things in the name of justice. It was against such a possibility that these cities were provided." (Morgan)

iii. Therefore, such a man could flee to a city of refuge – an appointed Levitical city, where he could stay, safe from the avenger of blood, until he could stand **before the congregation in judgment** and he could leave the city of refuge safely.

2. (13-14) The placement of the cities of refuge.

And of the cities which you give, you shall have six cities of refuge. You shall appoint three cities on this side of the Jordan, and three cities you shall appoint in the land of Canaan, *which* **will be cities of refuge.**

a. **You shall have six cities of refuge**: There were to be six cities of asylum, with three on each side of the Jordan River. Each of the three cities on either side would be positioned as north, central, and south.

i. Joshua 20:7-8 records the actual choice of the cities. They fulfilled the plan of being evenly distributed perfectly. Deuteronomy 19:3 also tells us that proper roads were to be built and maintained to these cities of refuge. A city of refuge was no good to the slayer if they could not get there quickly.

ii. "The cities that were later selected as the asylum cities are Bezer, Ramoth-Gilead, and Golan in Transjordan, and Hebron, Shechem, and Kedesh in cis-Jordan (see Deuteronomy 4:43; Joshua 20:7–8; 21:13, 21, 27, 32, 36, 38)." (Allen)

b. **Which will be cities of refuge**: This meant that the cities were close to everyone; no one was very far from a city of refuge. This was obviously important when the avenger of blood was in pursuit.

3. (15) The people eligible for protection in the cities of refuge.

These six cities shall be for refuge for the children of Israel, for the stranger, and for the sojourner among them, that anyone who kills a person accidentally may flee there.

a. **That anyone who kills a person accidentally may flee there**: Anyone – a **stranger** or a citizen of Israel – who needed to find protection in the cities of refuge could. Their protection was not limited to the children of Israel.

4. (16-21) How to judge if a death was truly murder.

'But if he strikes him with an iron implement, so that he dies, he *is* a murderer; the murderer shall surely be put to death. And if he strikes him with a stone in the hand, by which one could die, and he does die, he *is* a murderer; the murderer shall surely be put to death. Or *if* he strikes him with a wooden hand weapon, by which one could die, and he does die, he *is* a murderer; the murderer shall surely be put to death. The avenger of blood himself shall put the murderer to death; when he meets him, he shall put him to death. If he pushes him out of hatred or, while lying in wait, hurls something at him so that he dies, or in enmity he strikes him with his hand so that he dies, the one who struck *him* shall surely be put to death. He *is* a murderer. The avenger of blood shall put the murderer to death when he meets him.

a. **He is a murderer; the murderer shall surely be put to death**: Significantly, the Bible makes the clear distinction between *killing* and murder. All murder is killing, but not all killing is murder. Society needs laws to establish the principles that decide a death to be either an unfortunate killing or true murder.

b. **If he strikes him with an iron implement**: Murder could be judged depending on the weapon used; if it were an **iron implement** (likely to kill), or if it were a **stone** or a **wooden hand weapon, by which one could die**, then the killer could be found guilty of murder.

c. **If he pushes him out of hatred or, while lying in wait, hurls something at him so that he dies**: Murder could also be judged by discerning the state of heart and presence of premeditation in the killer. If the killing happens **while lying in wait** or if the killer strikes **in enmity**, murder can be judged.

d. **The avenger of blood shall put the murderer to death when he meets him**: If a killing could justly be understood to be murder, then **the murderer** was to be put **to death** – either by the judges of Israel or the **avenger of blood**.

i. "If a person committed the intentional 'sin of a high hand' and thus despised the word of the Lord, that person was to be cut off from his people. In like manner the intentional murderer was afforded no refuge or protection under the law." (Cole)

5. (22-24) How to judge if a death was truly manslaughter.

'However, if he pushes him suddenly without enmity, or throws anything at him without lying in wait, or uses a stone, by which a man could die, throwing *it* at him without seeing *him*, so that he dies, while he was not his enemy or seeking his harm, then the congregation shall judge

between the manslayer and the avenger of blood according to these judgments.

a. **If he pushes him suddenly without enmity**: If there was the absence of murderous intent, or the absence of premeditation, or if the death was clearly accidental, then the man was not guilty of murder and could not be turned over to **the avenger of blood**.

b. **Then the congregation shall judge between the manslayer and the avenger of blood according to these judgments**: Joshua 20:4 explains that this was done before the elders of the city of refuge. Both sides of the story were considered. Judgment was not to be made hearing only one side of the story.

i. "The fact that a man slayer reached one of those cities did not ensure him against inquiry and investigation. It rather made such inquiry necessary and thus gave him opportunity of explanation and ensured the certainty of just action." (Morgan)

6. (25-28) If the killer is declared to be innocent of murder.

So the congregation shall deliver the manslayer from the hand of the avenger of blood, and the congregation shall return him to the city of refuge where he had fled, and he shall remain there until the death of the high priest who was anointed with the holy oil. But if the manslayer at any time goes outside the limits of the city of refuge where he fled, and the avenger of blood finds him outside the limits of his city of refuge, and the avenger of blood kills the manslayer, he shall not be guilty of blood, because he should have remained in his city of refuge until the death of the high priest. But after the death of the high priest the manslayer may return to the land of his possession.

a. **So the congregation shall deliver the manslayer from the hand of the avenger of blood**: Having been judged innocent of murder, the manslayer could live in peace and safety – but only within the walls of the city of refuge.

i. Significantly, someone who killed another – but was innocent of murder – still had their life profoundly affected. They had to move from their city, and presumably their family as well, and had to live the rest of their lives in a city of refuge. The tragedy also affected their life.

ii. "He would have a fair trial; but even if he were found innocent, he must stay within the city, into which the avenger of blood could not by any possibility come. If he went out of the city, the avenger might kill him. He was therefore to suffer perpetual banishment, even for causing death accidentally, in order that it might be seen how much

God regarded the rights of blood, and how fearful a thing it is to put a man to death in any way." (Spurgeon)

iii. **Shall return him to the city of refuge where he had fled**: "The mention that the person convicted of manslaughter would be sent back to the city suggests that the trial would have taken place outside the city walls, whereby a person convicted of murder could be easily rendered to the blood kinsman for execution. One also assumes that the participation of the Levites whose lives were dedicated to the Lord would ensure fairness and justice in their decision making." (Cole)

b. **He shall remain there until the death of the high priest**: The only thing that could set the man free from the city of refuge was the death of the high priest; at the death of the high priest, the avenger of blood no longer had any claim over the man in the city of refuge.

i. "There was an atoning significance for the entire populace when the high priest (notice the phrasing: 'who was anointed with holy oil') would die. If the high priest died during the period of the slayer's exile in the asylum city, then he was not only free to leave the city, but he could resume his normal life again, including his stake in his ancestral land." (Allen)

ii. "Atonement for manslaughter came through the death of the high priest. This is shown by the ban on ransoming murderers and manslaughterers. Just as a murderer cannot buy his life for money (31), so a manslaughterer cannot purchase freedom (32). Both have caused the death of another man, and only the death of a man can atone for the killing." (Wenham)

iii. The very use of the phrase **death of the high priest** reminds us that our High Priest, Jesus Christ, ever lives. He is a *High Priest forever* (Hebrews 6:20), and Jesus is the High Priest *according to the power of an endless life* (Hebrews 7:16) and *because He continues forever*, Jesus *has an unchanging priesthood* (Hebrews 7:24).

c. **But if the manslayer at any time goes outside the limits of the city of refuge where he fled**: Until the time of the high priest's death, if the man who sought protection in the city of refuge wandered outside the walls of the city, he was fair game for the avenger of blood – only within his place of refuge was he safe.

7. The cities of refuge as a picture of Jesus.

a. The Bible applies this picture of the city of refuge to the believer finding refuge in God on more than one occasion.

i. Psalm 46:1: *God is our refuge and strength, a very present help in trouble.* More than 15 other times, the psalms speak of God as our refuge.

ii. Hebrews 6:18 also explains, *That by two immutable things, in which it is impossible for God to lie, we might have strong consolation, who have fled for refuge to lay hold of the hope set before us.*

b. There are many points of similarity between the cities of refuge and our refuge in Jesus.

• Both Jesus and the cities of refuge are *within easy reach* of the needy person; they are of no use unless someone can get to the place of refuge.

• Both Jesus and the cities of refuge are *open to all,* not just the Israelite; no one needs to fear that they will be turned away from their place of refuge in their time of need.

• Both Jesus and the cities of refuge become a place where the one in need can *live*; you don't come to a city of refuge in time of need just to look around.

• Both Jesus and the cities of refuge are the *only alternative* for the one in need; without this specific protection, they will be destroyed.

• Both Jesus and the cities of refuge provide protection *only within their boundaries*; to go outside means death.

• Both Jesus and the cities of refuge provide full freedom upon (or because of) the death of the High Priest.

c. There is a crucial distinction between the cities of refuge and our refuge in Jesus.

• The cities of refuge only helped the *innocent,* but the *guilty* can come to Jesus and find refuge.

i. We must take advantage of the refuge, the asylum offered to us in Jesus Christ. "The law of God is the blood-avenger that is on your track! You have wilfully transgressed, you have, as it were, killed God's commandments, you have trampled them under your foot; the law is the avenger of blood, it is after you, and it will have you in its grasp ere long; condemnation is hanging over your head now, and it shall surely overtake you." (Spurgeon)

ii. "Take heed that it is to Christ you flee; for, if the man who had slain his neighbour had fled to another city, it would have been of no avail; had he fled to a place that was not an ordained city of refuge." (Spurgeon)

C. Laws regarding murder.

1. (29-30) Two witnesses are required before the punishment for murder.

'And these *things* shall be a statute of judgment to you throughout your generations in all your dwellings. Whoever kills a person, the murderer shall be put to death on the testimony of witnesses; but one witness is not *sufficient* testimony against a person for the death *penalty*.

a. **Whoever kills a person, the murderer shall be put to death**: When a person was justly found to be a **murderer**, God commanded that their life be taken. This principle goes back at least as far as the covenant God made with Noah (Genesis 9:5-6).

i. Adam Clarke gave two reasons why God's law against murder was so strong: "No wonder God is so particularly strict in his laws against murderers, 1. Because he is the author of life, and none have any right to dispose of it but himself. 2. Because life is the time to prepare for the eternal world, and on it the salvation of the soul accordingly depends; therefore it is of infinite consequence to the man that his life be lengthened out to the utmost limits assigned by Divine Providence."

b. **One witness is not sufficient testimony against a person for the death penalty**: One witness was never enough to condemn a murderer to death. Furthermore, the witnesses had to be so certain that one of them must be willing to initiate the actual execution – to "cast the first stone" (Deuteronomy 17:6-7).

i. This puts the words of Jesus regarding the woman taken in adultery in John 8 in perspective: *He who is without sin among you, let him throw a stone at her first* (John 8:7). Jesus asked for the official witness to step forward and go on record as having witnessed this act of adultery. Whoever did so would show himself to be a hypocrite – one who would condemn the woman but excuse the man guilty of adultery.

ii. The principle that **one witness is not sufficient testimony** extends beyond the physical act of murder. It is possible to "murder" someone's reputation without adequate testimony of even one witness.

iii. God is concerned about the murder of reputation, as well as physical murder, and commands *Do not receive an accusation against an elder except from two or three witnesses* (1 Timothy 5:19) – the same standard as for proving murder.

iv. "As we know, even the provision of multiple witnesses will not automatically preclude collusion; witness the shocking perversion of Israel's justice system by the foreign priestess Jezebel in the incident of Naboth (1 Kings 21)." (Allen)

2. (31-32) A murderer's life cannot be ransomed.

Moreover you shall take no ransom for the life of a murderer who *is* guilty of death, but he shall surely be put to death. And you shall take no ransom for him who has fled to his city of refuge, that he may return to dwell in the land before the death of the priest.

a. **You shall take no ransom for the life of a murderer**: If someone was guilty of murder, they could not make monetary restitution in the place of their life. The principle of Genesis 9:6 stands: *Whoever sheds man's blood, by man his blood shall be shed; for in the image of God He made man.*

i. "Other ancient Near Eastern law permitted composition, that is payment of a ransom in place of the death penalty. However, this law insists that no monetary composition is possible." (Wenham)

b. **You shall take no ransom for him who has fled to his city of refuge**: This reflects an important principle; namely, that money cannot replace justice. Sometimes a monetary reward satisfies justice (as in Exodus 22:4, for example); but other times it does not and should not be used as a replacement for justice.

3. (33-34) The urgency to bring murderers to justice.

So you shall not pollute the land where you *are;* for blood defiles the land, and no atonement can be made for the land, for the blood that is shed on it, except by the blood of him who shed it. Therefore do not defile the land which you inhabit, in the midst of which I dwell; for I the LORD dwell among the children of Israel.'"

a. **For blood defiles the land, and no atonement can be made for the land**: Unjudged murders *defile* a nation. When murderers are not brought to justice, there is a blot on a nation that only the severe judgment of God can cleanse.

i. "It is paradoxical that in the right place blood is the most effective purifier, the only means of atonement between God and man, but in the wrong context it has precisely the opposite effect: *for blood pollutes the land* (33; cf. Deuteronomy 19:10; 21:9, 23)." (Wenham)

ii. "With all the attention we (rightly) give to issues of ecology and pollution in our own day, there is an act of pollution that far transcends the trashing of rivers, the killing of lakes, the denuding of forests, and the spilling of oils to mar even the seas; this is the abuse of persons. The worst abuse of all is wrongful death. God will not draw near a land where blood is the polluting agent." (Allen)

b. **Except by the blood of him who shed it**: The way to avoid this defilement is to judge and execute murderers – *no atonement can be made for the land, for the blood that is shed on it, except by the blood of him who shed it* (Numbers 35:33).

i. One may say that because of the stain of so many unpunished murders, the United States of America is a defiled land. Across the country, many are murdered and few are brought to justice. The blood of the slain cries out before God, the **blood defiles the land**.

ii. "Be not cruel to your own land by making it a den of murderers." (Poole)

Numbers 36 – Laws Concerning Women Heirs

A. The problem of female and tribal inheritance.

1. (1-2) The background.

Now the chief fathers of the families of the children of Gilead the son of Machir, the son of Manasseh, of the families of the sons of Joseph, came near and spoke before Moses and before the leaders, the chief fathers of the children of Israel. And they said: "The LORD commanded my lord *Moses* **to give the land as an inheritance by lot to the children of Israel, and my lord was commanded by the LORD to give the inheritance of our brother Zelophehad to his daughters.**

> a. **The LORD commanded my lord Moses to give the land as an inheritance**: This passage is a reference back to Numbers 27:1-11, where the daughters of Zelophehad were concerned that their father's inheritance would vanish because there were no sons in their family.

> b. **Was commanded by the LORD to give the inheritance of our brother Zelophehad to his daughters**: God, through Moses, declared that if a father had no sons, the inheritance should then go to the daughters.

2. (3-4) The problem raised by the solution regarding Zelophehad's daughters.

Now if they are married to any of the sons of the *other* **tribes of the children of Israel, then their inheritance will be taken from the inheritance of our fathers, and it will be added to the inheritance of the tribe into which they marry; so it will be taken from the lot of our inheritance. And when the Jubilee of the children of Israel comes, then their inheritance will be added to the inheritance of the tribe into which they marry; so their inheritance will be taken away from the inheritance of the tribe of our fathers."**

> a. **If they are married to any of the sons of the other tribes of the children of Israel, then their inheritance will be taken**: If the land was given to the daughters, then when the daughters married, the land would

then go to their husband's tribe – and eventually, the original tribe's lands would become depleted.

i. "At issue is not a complaint or a grievance against women per se so much as a concern for the continuity of the lines of inheritance within the tribes." (Allen)

b. **So their inheritance will be taken away from the inheritance of the tribe of our fathers**: Solving the problem of Zelophehad's daughters had created another problem – how to keep the property in a tribe through the generations.

i. This illustrates an important principle – that there are rarely perfect solutions to problems; there are usually answers that are trade-offs in other areas. Maturity can make and accept the right decisions even when they aren't perfect, "cost-free" solutions.

ii. Cole observes that the land in question would not return to the original tribes in the Jubilee year (Leviticus 25:13-55): "The Jubilee statutes applied only to purchased property and not to property that had been inherited, such as that which accrued to the daughters of Zelophehad."

B. God's answer to the issue of daughter's and tribal inheritance.

1. (5-9) How to keep the land within the tribes.

Then Moses commanded the children of Israel according to the word of the LORD, saying: "What the tribe of the sons of Joseph speaks is right. This *is* what the LORD commands concerning the daughters of Zelophehad, saying, 'Let them marry whom they think best, but they may marry only within the family of their father's tribe.' So the inheritance of the children of Israel shall not change hands from tribe to tribe, for every one of the children of Israel shall keep the inheritance of the tribe of his fathers. And every daughter who possesses an inheritance in any tribe of the children of Israel shall be the wife of one of the family of her father's tribe, so that the children of Israel each may possess the inheritance of his fathers. Thus no inheritance shall change hands from *one* tribe to another, but every tribe of the children of Israel shall keep its own inheritance."

a. **But they may marry only within the family of their father's tribe**: The solution was simple – if a daughter in a family received an inheritance of land, she must marry within the tribe. Since the tribes were large enough, this was not understood to be a significant burden.

i. "The women are permitted to marry whomever they choose—a surprising turn, as we usually think of women being chosen in biblical times! Perhaps the fact that they inherited land made them active rather than passive agents in marriage. But they must choose their husbands from within their own clans." (Allen)

ii. The interests of the individual woman were not always given more regard than the interests of the tribe; the larger community. This principle has many applications in the present day when the rights and interests of individuals seem to be regarded as far more important than the rights of the larger community.

b. **Every tribe of the children of Israel shall keep its own inheritance**: The repetition of this phrase in both verses 7 and 9 is for emphasis. If a daughter married outside the tribe, she had to forfeit the inheritance. This was because the **tribe** had **inheritance** rights, not only the individual. A daughter's individual right of inheritance was not the only nor the greatest consideration.

i. "And the principal reason why God was solicitous to preserve tribes and families unmixed was, that the tribe and family too out of which the Messiah was to come, and by which he should be known, might be evident and unquestionable." (Poole)

ii. Clarke quotes Ainsworth for a point of application: "By this example, and the law of inheritances in the Holy Land, the people of God are taught to hold fast their inheritance in his promises, and their right in Christ, which they hold by faith; that as the Father hath made them meet to be partakers of the inheritance among the saints in light, Colossians 1:12, so they may keep the faith and grace which they have received to the end."

2. (10-12) The application of the principle to the daughters of Zelophehad.

Just as the LORD commanded Moses, so did the daughters of Zelophehad; for Mahlah, Tirzah, Hoglah, Milcah, and Noah, the daughters of Zelophehad, were married to the sons of their father's brothers. They were married into the families of the children of Manasseh the son of Joseph, and their inheritance remained in the tribe of their father's family.

a. **Their inheritance remained in the tribe of their father's family**: In their case, not only did they marry within the tribe, but they **were married to the sons of their father's brothers** – their cousins. This obviously kept the land inheritance within the tribe, and even within the larger family unit.

3. (13) Conclusion to the book: **In the plains of Moab, by the Jordan**.

These *are* the commandments and the judgments which the LORD commanded the children of Israel by the hand of Moses in the plains of Moab by the Jordan, *across from* Jericho.

a. **By the hand of Moses in the plains of Moab by the Jordan**: The book of Numbers began *in the wilderness* (Numbers 1:1). It now finished on the threshold of the land of Canaan.

i. "Throughout there is manifest the forward movement of God along the highway of His own purpose. This forward movement is not of man but of Jehovah. The book is a revelation of the sure procedure of God toward the final working out into human history of the regeneration of humanity, the first movements of which were recorded in the close of the Book of Genesis, the central forces of which came in the Incarnation of the Son of God, and the final victories of which are not yet." (Morgan)

b. **Across from Jericho**: As the children of Israel stood across from the city of **Jericho**, we should consider what it took to take them from Egypt to this place **across from Jericho**.

i. From their encampment at Mount Sinai, God gave Israel the opportunity to grow from being a slave people to becoming a people suited for God's Promised Land. He taught them how to be ordered, organized, cleansed, separated, how to give, and how to receive the tools to advance into the Promised Land. He blessed them, reminded them of His deliverance, and gave them His own presence.

ii. Then, as the nation set out from Mount Sinai to the land of Canaan, they found themselves struggling with the flesh – they murmured, complained, and rebelled; most of all, they failed to enter by faith into what God had set before them – and a generation of unbelief was condemned to perish in the wilderness.

iii. After that, God led the nation for some 38 years in the wilderness, with much motion but no progress – enduring more episodes of rebellion and murmuring, but essentially waiting until the generation of unbelief had died and a generation willing to trust God for big things had come to maturity.

iv. So they set out towards the land of Canaan again and faced the same challenges of the flesh – but dealt with them better this time until they made their way to the threshold of the Promised Land.

v. By spiritual analogy, many Christians die in the wilderness because they will not trust God and will not enter into what He has promised them. Sadly, many Christians live more in the wilderness than on the threshold of the Promised Land.

vi. It would take courageous faith to move the children of Israel from **across from Jericho** to the Promised Land. Staying on the shores of the Jordan River was better than being in the middle of the wilderness but it wasn't the land of Canaan yet. They came this far by faith and would need faith to take them the rest of the way, under the leadership of Joshua.

Bibliography

Allen, Ronald B. "Numbers" *The Expositor's Bible Commentary Volume 2* (Grand Rapids, Michigan: Zondervan, 1990)

Clarke, Adam *The Holy Bible, Containing the Old and New Testaments, with A Commentary and Critical Notes* (New York: Eaton and Mains, 1826)

Cole, R. Dennis Numbers *The New American Commentary – Numbers* (Nashville, Tennessee: Broadman & Holman Publishers, 2000)

Courson, Jon *Jon Courson's Application Commentary, Old Testament Volume 1* (Nashville, Tennessee: Thomas Nelson, 2006)

Ginzberg, Louis *The Legends of the Jews, Volumes 1-7* (Philadelphia: The Jewish Publication Society of America, 1968)

Keil, C.F. and Delitszch, F. *Commentary on the Old Testament, Volume I – The Pentateuch* (Grand Rapids, Michigan: Eerdmans, 1983)

Maclaren, Alexander *Expositions of Holy Scripture, Volume 1* (Grand Rapids, Michigan: Baker Book House, 1984)

Meyer, F.B. *Our Daily Homily* (Westwood, New Jersey: Revell, 1966)

Morgan, G. Campbell *An Exposition of the Whole Bible* (Old Tappan, New Jersey: Revell, 1959)

Morgan, G. Campbell *Searchlights from the Word* (New York, Revell: 1936)

Poole, Matthew *A Commentary on the Holy Bible, Volume 1* (London, Banner of Truth Trust, 1968)

Spurgeon, Charles Haddon *The New Park Street Pulpit, Volumes 1-6* and *The Metropolitan Tabernacle Pulpit, Volumes 7-63* (Pasadena, Texas: Pilgrim Publications, 1990)

Trapp, John *A Commentary on the Old and New Testaments, Volume 1 – Genesis to Second Chronicles* (Eureka, California: Tanski Publications, 1997)

Watson, Rev. Robert A. *The Book of Numbers* (New York: Hodder & Stoughton, 1894)

Wenham, Gordon J. *Numbers – An Introduction and Commentary* (Leicester, England, Inter-Varsity Press, 1980)

Winterbotham, R. "Numbers" *The Pulpit Commentary, Volume 2 – Leviticus, Numbers* (McLean, Virginia: MacDonald Publishing, ?)

Authors Remarks

As the years pass I love the work of studying, learning, and teaching the Bible more than ever. I'm so grateful that God is faithful to meet me in His Word.

Once again I am tremendously grateful to Alison Turner for her proofreading and editorial suggestions, especially with a challenging manuscript. Alison, thank you so much!

Thanks to Brian Procedo for the cover design and the graphics work.

Most especially, thanks to my wife Inga-Lill. She is my loved and valued partner in life and in service to God and His people.

David Guzik

David Guzik's Bible commentary is regularly used and trusted by many thousands who want to know the Bible better. Pastors, teachers, class leaders, and everyday Christians find his commentary helpful for their own understanding and explanation of the Bible. David and his wife Inga-Lill live in Santa Barbara, California.

You can email David at
david@enduringword.com

For more resources by David Guzik,
go to www.enduringword.com